Accession no.
01007798

D1615014
Library
WITHDRAWN

Why was the art of landscape painting invented in the fifth century BC, abandoned with the collapse of Rome, and revived again in the High Middle Ages? Did the Greeks, or the ancient Christians, perceive the natural world differently from the way we do now? In *Poetry, space, landscape* Chris Fitter traces the history of nature-sensibility from the ancient world to the English Renaissance, setting poems and paintings in the widely differing cultural contexts that created them. He suggests a new social and historical theory of the conceptualization of space, explaining the rise and fall of the idea of 'landscape'. And he argues the dialectical case that enduring basic categories of perception create different readings of natural reality determined by our social and material relations with nature. A chapter on seventeenth-century English poetry concludes with fresh and substantial re-readings of Milton, Marvell, and many of their contemporaries in the light of this long tradition of landscape art.

Literature, Culture, Theory 13

Poetry, space, landscape
Toward a new theory

Literature, Culture, Theory

General editors

RICHARD MACKSEY, *The Johns Hopkins University*

and MICHAEL SPRINKER, *State University of New York at Stony Brook*

The Cambridge *Literature, Culture, Theory* series is dedicated to theoretical studies in the human sciences that have literature and culture as their object of enquiry. Acknowledging the contemporary expansion of cultural studies and the redefinitions of literature that this has entailed, the series includes not only original works of literary theory but also monographs and essay collections on topics and seminal figures from the long history of theoretical speculation on the arts and human communication generally. The concept of theory embraced in the series is broad, including not only the classical disciplines of poetics and rhetoric, but also those of aesthetics, linguistics, psychoanalysis, semiotics, and other cognate sciences that have inflected the systematic study of literature during the past half century.

Titles published

Return to Freud: Jacques Lacan's dislocation of psychoanalysis
SAMUEL WEBER
(*translated from the German by Michael Levine*)

The subject of modernity
ANTHONY J. CASCARDI

Parody: ancient, modern, and post-modern
MARGARET A. ROSE

The poetics of personification
JAMES PAXSON

Possible worlds in literary theory
RUTH RONEN

Critical conditions:
postmodernity and the question of foundations
HORACE L. FAIRLAMB

Introduction to literary hermeneutics
PETER SZONDI
(*translated from the German by Martha Woodmansee*)

Anti-mimesis: from Plato to Hitchcock
TOM COHEN

Mikhail Bakhrtin: between phenomenology and marxism
MICHAEL F. BERNARD-DONALS

Theories of mimesis
ARNE MELBERG

Poetry, space, landscape

Toward a new theory

CHRIS FITTER

Rutgers University

Published by the Press Syndicate of the University of Cambridge
The Pitt Building, Trumpington Street, Cambridge, CB2 1RP
40 West 20th Street, New York, NY 10011-4211, USA
10 Stamford Road, Oakleigh, Melbourne 3166, Australia

© Cambridge University Press 1995

First published 1995

Printed in Great Britain at the University Press, Cambridge

A catalogue record for this book is available from the British Library

Library of Congress cataloguing in publication data

Fitter, Chris.
Poetry, space, landscape: toward a new theory/Chris Fitter.
p. cm. – (Literature, culture, theory: 13)
Includes bibliographical references and index.
ISBN 0 521 46301 7 (hardback)
1. Poetry – History and criticism. 2. Landscape in literature.
3. Nature in literature. I. Title. II. Series.
PN1064.F57 1995
809.1′936 – dc20 94-7606 CIP

ISBN 0 521 46301 7 hardback

TAG

For my Mother and my Father
With the dearest of my love

'Reality can only be penetrated and understood as a totality ... The specialisation of skills leads to the destruction of every image of the whole. Despite this, the need to grasp the whole – at least cognitively – cannot die out.'

(Lukács, *History and Class Consciousness*)

'Am I
To see in the Lake District, then,
Another bourgeois invention like the piano?'

(Auden, *Bucolics*)

Contents

Illustrations

Between pages 146 and 147

Acknowledgements

In researching this book I have incurred many debts of gratitude, which it is my pleasure to acknowledge here. Scholars in a range of disciplines have generously shared with me their time and specialist knowledge. In particular Drs Glenn Black, John Bramble, John Carey, Helen Cooper, John Farquhar, Nicholas Gendle, and E. W. Nicholson have helped me negotiate a far warier passage across wide landscapes of academic maze and minefield than I first attempted. If, nonetheless, there still recurs the brash tug of clumsy feet against sensitive scholarly tripwires, without these scholars' expertise there would have been endless detonation.

A Vaughn-Cornish bequest enabled me to visit a number of Renaissance Country Houses and gardens, and for this I should like to thank its Trustees. To Ms Joan Dawson of Nun Appleton House I am grateful too, for her kindness in allowing a visit to certain well-known acres. I am obliged to the editors of *Essays in Criticism* for gracious permission to reproduce certain pages of my article on the verse of Henry Vaughan. And I should like to thank the College of Liberal Arts in the University of Mississippi for a grant towards the completion of the book. To Ms Sara Selby and Ms Kathy Williams of the University of Mississippi goes my heartfelt gratitude for sheer, cool miracles at the keyboard.

My gratitude, finally, to Michael and Margaret Fitter is of a depth I cannot word.

Abbreviations

CHLGEMP	*The Cambridge History of Later Greek and Early Medieval Philosophy*, ed. A. H. Armstrong (Cambridge: 1967)
Curtius	E. R. Curtius, *European Literature and the Latin Middle Ages* (1953; rpt. London: 1979)
Gilson	Etienne Gilson, *History of Christian Philosophy in the Middle Ages* (1955; rpt. London: 1980)
Glacken	Clarence J. Glacken, *Traces on the Rhodian Shore* (Berkeley and Los Angeles: 1967)
PG	*Patrologiae cursus completus ... series Graeca* (Paris: 1857–99), ed. Jacques Paul Migne
PL	*Patrologiae cursus completus ... series Latina* (Paris: 1844–1902), ed. Jacques Paul Migne
P&S	Derek Pearsall and Elizabeth Salter, *Landscapes and Seasons of the Medieval World* (London: 1973)

I

Toward a theory of 'landscape' and landscape perception

The need for an historicist aesthetics

The contours of landscape in poetry perhaps cannot be satisfactorily mapped. The subject tends alarmingly to enormity and amorphousness, veering simultaneously towards trackless continents of cultural immensity and into the finest tissues of subjective inwardness. Poetic approaches to natural description indeed easily assume the aspect of an incommensurable difference. Within what framework of common analysis may we seek to meditate not only lines such as those of the Hellenistic poet, Anyte –

I, Hermes, have been set up
Where three roads cross, by the windy
Orchard above the grey beach.
Here tired men may rest from travel,
By my cold, clean, whispering spring

but those also of a Hebrew prophet's exultant affirmation:

ye shall go out with joy, and be led forth with peace: the mountains and the hills shall break forth before you into singing, and all the trees of the field shall clap their hands.

And what relation, if any, may be established between these passages, these singular forms of discrepant sensibility, and a phenomenon, for example, such as the popular hyperbole of English Cavalier poets of the seventeenth century?

We all Pearles scorne,
Save what the dewy morne
Congeals upon each little spire of grass;
Which careless shepeards beat down as they pass;

And gold ne're here appears,
Save what the yellow Ceres beares.[1]

How, moreover, may we connect these with the canvasses of the great European landscape painters? An historicist approach to the subject has seemed to me the only answer, on three important counts.

First, in order to reconstruct as fully as possible the landscape-consciousness of an earlier poet, we must outstep the limits of the text, and endeavour to reconstruct its enabling cognitive world. For, given the problematic plenitude of the external world, the infinite of the visible in any landscape, presenting 'nature' is a task analogous to confronting the irreducibility of the Godhead: metonymy is inescapable. God and world alike must be consigned to formulae. Reductive encoding of landscape in verse will be governed by the decorum of genre: landscape is amplified, for instance, in secondary Epic but spare in the classical Ode. Paradoxically, while aesthetic conventions banish entire dimensions of contemporary landscape perception and response, they retain full intelligibility only in balance with the tacit social complex of relations with nature. Vincent Scully, for example, insists of Greek art that 'the very absence of landscape background in most ... vase paintings and reliefs may be better taken as indicative of the fact that archaic and classic Greeks experienced the landscape only as it was, at full scale ... all Greek art, with its usual sculptural concentration upon active life and geometry, may be properly understood and adequately valued only when the Greek's counter-experience of his earth is kept in mind'.[2] Intellectual 'comprehension', as the word suggests, entails a comprehensive whole: to comprehend representational form, we must try to grasp the assumed whole which assigns determinate meaning to the figurative part.

Second, the landscape-consciousness of every culture is historically distinct and subjective, a fact often belied by superficial continuities of landscape presentation: the traditions of tree and flower catalogue, the propagation by medieval rhetoricians of the Greco-Roman *locus amoenus*, the deference of Renaissance painters to the authority of inventories of landscape content found in Vitruvius and Pliny.

1 Anyte, trans. Kenneth Roxroth in *The Greek Anthology* ed. Peter Jay (Harmondsworth: 1981), poem 113 (9.314 in the original anthology); *Isaiah* 55.12; Henry Wotton, *Reliquiae Wottoniae* (London: 1651), pp. '232'–'333', i.e. 532–33.

2 Vincent Scully, *The Earth, the Temple and the Gods* (New Haven and London: 1962), p. 2.

Third, fundamentals of aesthetic development in landscape-consciousness can be seen to correspond, in fact, to broad stages of historical development. In the light of this, we can begin to grasp why it is that the idea of 'landscape' itself arises in world history only with classical Greece, not to recur within the cycle of European civilization until the fifteenth century in Flanders and Italy. If, as Ruskin suggested, there is 'a science to the aspects of things, as well as of their nature',[3] it is by an historicist aesthetics that we must seek it.

Most recent approaches to the question of landscape aesthetics overlook this. On the one hand we find a reckless atavism, reducing man's topographic imagination to that of a beast; and on the other, studies of poetic landscape that package the forms and features of the literary surface – topoi, motif, catalogue, archetype – in disconnection from the mental climate that generated them. *Fin-de-siècle* studies, such as Geikie's *The Love of Nature among the Romans*, subscribe to timeless topologies, but more recent studies, such as those of Curtius, Hansen and Piehler are similarly deplete through a methodological disinclination to acknowledge the implications of an 'essential "historicity" of the eye in regard to perspective, volume, distortion and codes of chromatic or gestural meaning'.[4] The works of Kenneth Clark and Pearsall and Salter[5] are in this respect outstanding, bedding ways of seeing and centuries of landscape art in the sensibilities of their historical moments.

The 'habitat theory' of Jay Appleton, however, is a controversial recent version of the essentialist approach. It offers 'the proposition that aesthetic satisfaction, experienced in the contemplation of landscape, stems from the spontaneous perception of landscape features which, in their shapes, colours, spatial arrangements and other visible attributes, act as sign-stimuli indicative of environmental conditions favourable to survival..."Habitat theory" thus asserts that the relation between the human observer and the perceived en-

3 John Ruskin, *Modern Painters*, ed. E. T. Cook and A. Wedderburn (London: 1904), vol. 5, p. 387.

4 Archibald Geikie, *The Love of Nature among the Romans* (London: 1912); E. R. Curtius, *European Literature and the Latin Middle Ages*, trans. Willard R. Trask (1948; rpt. London: 1979); Niels Bugge Hansen, *That Pleasant Place* (Copenhagen: 1973); Paul Piehler, *The Visionary Landscape* (London: 1971). Quotation from George Steiner, *On Difficulty* (Oxford: 1978), p. 2.

5 Kenneth Clark, *Landscape into Art* (1949; 2nd edn London: 1976); Derek Pearsall and Elizabeth Salter, *Landscapes and Seasons of the Medieval World* (London: 1973).

vironment is basically the same as the relation of a creature to its habitat'.[6] From this principle Appleton deduces that the landscape beautiful is that which facilitates survival in the world of predation: a 'balanced landscape' equally strong in 'prospect' (to detect prey) and 'refuge' (for stalking or flight). Loveliness, one deduces, conciliates seclusion and clean visibility, preserves alike from exposure and claustrophobia. 'Open glades and close woodland' thus 'will be found to be a common feature of much poetry'.[7] Occasionally, as with the eighteenth-century 'sublime' movement, 'hazard' values will be emphasized – these consisting in 'all kinds of potentially dangerous phenomena'.[8] Moreover, an unconscious symbolism extends such values. We respond positively to 'indirect prospect symbols' which 'symbolically invite the speculation that they command a further field of vision'. Such phenomena include high places, 'pointed objects', mountains, trees, clouds and spires. Light itself is 'the ultimate prospect symbol'.[9]

The theory is exciting, promising the firm granite strata of scientific certitudes beneath the lush emotionalism and flowering rhetorics of our nature-feeling. Beyond agreement, however, that a pleasant landscape will usually contain (among much else, and surely almost unavoidably) a certain degree both of visibility and 'cover', I can find little with which to concur. Indeed even here there are marked exceptions. The fresco of the Garden of Livia from Prima Porta, a masterpiece of classical Roman landscape painting, presents an unbroken wall of trees and foliage, gemmed with birds and fruit, fresh, exact, delicate, yet without even the most shallow prospect (plate 4). This is an 'unbalanced' extreme of 'refuge-dominant' landscape, yet has drawn enchanted comment now just as presumably it did then.

Appleton's postulated 'atavistic' consciousness is elusively general (is it Mesolithic? Neolithic? or perhaps still that of tree-bound Ramapithecus?) and his identifications appear wild: that of pleasure in clouds, for example, with the unconscious conviction that they would prove a fine coign of vantage. Moreover this 'unicausal' scheme is perceptibly 'underdetermined': what possible ecological advantage is conferred on man by the flower?

6 Jay Appleton, *The Experience of Landscape* (London: 1975), pp. 69–70.
7 Jay Appleton, *The Poetry of Habitat* (Hull: 1978), p. 7.
8 *Poetry of Habitat*, p. 18; *Experience of Landscape*, pp. 95–101.
9 *Experience of Landscape*, pp. 85–109; *Poetry of Habitat*, pp. 13, 33, 37.

> Thy mercy, O Lord, is in the heavens;
> And thy faithfulness reacheth unto the clouds.
> Thy righteousness is like the great mountains.
>
> I will lift up mine eyes unto the hills
> From whence cometh my help.[10]

Clouds here are not utilitarian vantage-points, and the mountain symbolism is surely mediated from secondary, tactile qualities: permanence, superhuman inviolability, and by association, fortitude. Flowers incarnate gentleness, innocence or delicacy, sources of human well-being far subtler than the imperatives of nutrition and slaughter.

Moreover it is a commonplace of anthropology today that the concerns even of earliest man, given his richness of psychic integration in the welfare of the total natural community of his environment, were far from exclusively instrumental. 'Untamed' thinking pays more attention for its world-view to what animals eat than to which animals can be eaten.[11] Eliade recalls that Australian aboriginals continued visiting and worshipping in their sacred landscapes even after they had come to depend for their food and whole economy upon white men. 'What they sought from these places was to remain in mystical union with the land and with the ancestors who founded the civilization of the tribe.'[12]

But the cardinal criticism of 'habitat theory' must be that it misconceives the character of human cultural development, assuming 'atavistic mechanisms' to be simply overlain, lying dormant but intact[13] in a more technologically advanced environment, activated sporadically by such activities as fox-hunting and rock-climbing.[14] To take the transcendental Neanderthal as the universal human subject-position is to ape, in fact, the discredited essentialist and positivist assumptions of much nineteenth-century thought: to miss the dialectical construction of environmental 'reality' through the interplay of the physical with the psychical universe. Man's landscape values are not predative but *occupational* and *ideological*; and 'habitat theory' ignores the historical reformations of nature-sensibility as man modifies and extends his habitat through the developments of pasturage, agriculture, commerce and the metropolis.

10 *Psalms*, 36.5–6; 121.1–2.
11 Claude Lévi-Strauss, *The Savage Mind* (London and Chicago: 1966.)
12 Mircea Eliade, *Patterns in Comparative Religion* (London: 1979), pp. 368–69.
13 *Experience of Landscape*, pp. 67, 70.
14 Ibid., pp. 184, 187.

Another version of essentialist aesthetics, this one rooted in mythicist–religious rather than 'scientific' impulses, is argued by Mircea Eliade. For Eliade, the mind of man has always grouped the infinite plurality of natural phenomena into a 'canon' of seven paramount features, whose sacramentality and essential identity of meaning endures across all cultural frontiers, being compatible even with the abstract metaphysical systems of the higher religions.[15] 'The inaccessibility, infinity, eternity and creative power (rain)' of the sky, its shining and its soaring height reveal a transcendent creator-deity ('Our Father who art in heaven ...'), and some scholars have argued for a primitive sky-monotheism.[16] The primeval pair of earth and sky are virtually universal in mythology, the earth signifying the foundation of the universe, repository of sacred forces, the eternal *Tellus Mater*.[17] The sun has not inspired universal worship, but had often been amalgamated with the sky-god as a supreme being, before 'slipping' downwards into a magico-religious fertility role, solar heroes 'rescuing' fertility from 'death' in night and winter.[18] The moon's essence is her cyclical mystique, her mode of being rhythmic and imperishable, 'inexhaustible in her own regeneration'[19] as she governs and unifies all the natural spheres that are of 'eternal returning': water and rain, plant-life, fertility and the menstrual cycle. 'That is why the symbolism and mythology of the moon have an element of *pathos* and at the same time of consolation, for the moon governs both death and fertility, both drama and initiation.'[20] Water stands for the formlessness of primal substance, and the myths of the Deluge and cataclysm, as well as the rituals of immersion, show 'a temporary reintegration into the formless', a dissolving of all form, that may purify. But the 'water of life' is also latent, containing in its babbling, flowing life 'the seeds of things': and hence belief in the curative properties of magic wells, and the mythological identity of sperm, rain and rejuvenation.[21] Rock, on the other hand, incompressible, invulnerable, has a reality, force and permanence beyond the precariousness and renewals of the life-flow. 'Its reality is coupled with perenniality',[22] and it shows man as 'an absolute mode of being'.[23]

15 *Patterns in Comparative Religion*, pp. 6–7, 268, 384, 463.
16 Ibid., pp. 38–40. 17 Ibid., pp. 239–64. 18 Ibid., pp. 124–53.
19 Ibid., p. 158. 20 Ibid., pp. 154–87; quotation p. 184.
21 Ibid., pp. 188–215; quotation p. 212.
22 Eliade, *The Myth of the Eternal Return*, trans. Willard R. Trask (1954; rpt. Princeton: 1971), p. 4. 23 *Patterns*, pp. 216–38; quotation p. 216.

Rock and mountain are the dwellings of spirits, the monuments of the dead, the markers of sacred places, and centres of energy at the heart of magico-religious activity as incorruptible instruments.[24] Vegetation, finally, is the yield of 'the living cosmos', the 'bio-cosmic sacredness' of energy that flows through all. 'Trees and plants in general always embody inexhaustible life – which, in primitive ontology, corresponds to absolute reality ... The forces of plant life are an epiphany of the life of the whole universe.'[25] The apparent pluralism of vegetation cults is 'merely an illusion of modern vision; basically they flow from one primitive ontological intuition (that the *real* is not only what *is* indefinitely the same, but also what *becomes* in organic but cyclic forms)'.[26]

Eliade's erudition is superhuman, his style sorcerously lovely and his thesis romantically entrancing. His professed contempt, however, for the empty temporality of the realm of history[27] blinds him to the concrete fortunes of his timeless canon. The 'myth of the eternal return' is a myth indeed, for the symbols returned to in each case possess unique determinate meaning. The Tree of Life in Eden, Yggdrasil in Nordic mythology and the Lotus in Indian may all symbolize 'inexhaustible life', but 'mean' to their believers perhaps incommunicably more than this abstraction. Moreover, with secular cultures and their advanced, pictorial art, natural features are increasingly apprehended within a new epistemological framework: beheld primarily in visual rather than mythological terms, as objects in space rather than vocabulary of the cosmic narrative. Rock and moon assume new modes of prominence as leading images in pictorial compositions. We shall see how the values behind 'landscape', their rationalizing 'entzauberung' (or 'dis-enchantment'),[28] banish the light of mythological seeing.

A further important counter-example is the *locus amoenus*. We may remark here what the compartmentalization of disciplines has I think kept hitherto unseen, the continuity of anthropology's 'sacred microcosm' with literary criticism's *locus amoenus*. Eliade, following Przyluski and Mus, has noted that 'the most primitive of the "sacred places" we know of constituted a microcosm ... a landscape of stones,

24 Ibid., pp. 216–38.

25 Ibid., pp. 265–330; quotations from pp. 309, 325.

26 Ibid., p. 315.

27 *Myth of the Eternal Return*, pp. 156–62.

28 Max Weber, *General Economic History* (New York: 1961), p. 265; *Economy and Society* (New York: 1968), vol. 3, p. 975.

water and trees', and he cites many examples from primitive cultures of this miniature landscape as a sacred '*imago mundi*', a place of absolute reality as converging the everlastingness of stone, the endless cycle of vegetative life, and the 'latencies, seeds and purification' of water.[29] It is precisely this miniature landscape that Curtius has documented as the *locus amoenus* of Greco-Roman poetry: appearing as the haunts of the nymphs and Calypso's grotto, as gracing perfect harbours, and, in later verse reappearing in the Theocritean harvest-home, in Virgil's eclogues and his Carthaginian harbour, and Ovidian forest grottoes.[30] *Pace* Curtius, it does *not* however recur in the Middle Ages, which customarily abstracts the element of rock, preferring flower-carpets, breeze and birdsong.[31] 'Archetypal' imagination is thus once again demonstrably subject to transforming cultural specificity: it is surely the Christian conviction of earthly impermanence that finally deletes the imperishable element from amongst 'the charms of landscape'.

An alternative approach: innate drives within historical transformation

Against the reductive tendencies of such theories as those outlined, dehistoricizing, depoliticized, offering to unlock a universal natural aesthetics by a single interpretive key, this book will foreground scrutiny of historical change as the condition for comprehension of human landscape perception.

We can usefully emphasize the historical subjectivity of landscape perception by momentarily borrowing, I suggest, the terms of 'reader-response' literary theory, and saying that a landscape, no less than a text, is 'read' by mutable 'interpretive communities', each with its distinct 'horizons of expectation'. Historical communities and individuals, intimately conditioned by social, economic and ideological

29 *Patterns*, pp. 269–71.

30 *European Literature and the Latin Middle Ages*, pp. 185–86; Homer, *Odyssey* 12.102; 5.57–76; 6.124; 17.205; 9.140–41; 13.96–105; Theocritus, *Idylls* 7.135–46; Virgil, *Eclogues* 1.51–58 and 9.40–43.; *Aeneid*, 1.158–69; Ovid, *Metamorphoses* 1.568–76; 3.155–62.

31 E.g. Matthew of Vendôme's *descriptio loci* in his *Ars Versificatoria* in *Les Arts Poétiques du XIIe et du XIIIe siècle*, ed. E. Faral (Paris: 1923), p. 149; discussed by P&S, pp. 47–49.

forces, will project varied structures of attention onto external nature, thereby actualizing different configurations of feature and meaning. No landscape can ever thus be 'autotelic' – bearing a perennial and 'objective' appearance and significance independent of its 'reader': cultural projection by a landscape's beholder will complete its necessarily partial 'self-formulation'. No poet, we shall see, remarked a sunset before the Italian painters of the Quattrocento 'discovered' them; autumn tints are a leap in perception as rare in Renaissance verse as they are inescapable in the eighteenth century. Again, the viewer of an eighteenth-century 'picturesque' prospect perceives a particular code of appearances invisible to an eye uninitiated in this taste, and one whose enabling structure of occlusions renders its 'reality' historically relative.

This book will accordingly seek to map certain historical varieties of landscape perception and poetry in three ways. First, mindful of the primacy of cultural horizons, we shall seek to demonstrate that 'landscape-consciousness' with its apparent 'immediacies' of perception always in fact subsists within broader, historically local structures of 'nature-sensibility' that condition, direct and limit it. Within our historical survey we shall accordingly seek to characterize each period's nature-sensibility, which is always a product of its particular economic structure and its working relations with the earth, its social conditions and formal thought; and then suggest the mediated, peculiar forms of landscape-consciousness, reconditioning our perceptual drives, and crystallizing fresh descriptive figures in poetry.

Second, we shall structure our survey further by seeking to document the answer to a question of childlike simplicity, which, in the proverbial fashion of a child's questions, turns out to raise issues of a daunting magnitude: why was it the Greeks, apparently, who invented landscape painting in the fifth century BC? Why didn't earlier civilizations produce painted and poetic landscapes, and why did these again disappear with the fall of Rome not to reappear for around a millennium? To transpose this into more formal terms: why is it that the very concept of 'landscape' – the concern for an organized visual field, for localized and circumstantial description, replete with exact optical effects – transpires to be but an historically contingent form for the representation of 'nature', and not a universal of human art?

In answering this, it will be necessary hereafter to distinguish between 'landscape' and 'landskip': the latter term (popular in the seventeenth century) will designate the narrower, technical concern, in painting or poetry, for naturalistic, pictorial effects and the composed 'view'. Landskip derives, we shall argue, from the particular complex of values by which a highly advanced commercial civilization, of secular and materialist tendencies, engages and construes the natural world. Indeed we can, as it were, 'unearth' from landskip five constitutive cultural elements, five forms of interest in space, which have come gradually into being and accumulated over the centuries. In effect we shall thus be arguing the case for an economic and social determination of the taste for landskip, the more so since we shall try to suggest that each of the five structural elements, emerging at a certain stage of historical development, is itself an economically conditioned development. These elements we shall analyse as managerial, comparative, quotidian, possessive and rational space: terms we shall explain in our following chapter. Chapter two will accordingly expound and chart the successive stages of emergence of these architectonic conditions of landskip in the ancient world, characterizing nature-sensibility in its evolutions from that correlative to the hunter-gathering livelihood to that of the Roman empire. Our medieval chapter (chapter five) will locate the incremental reappearance of these categories of interest in space, a millennium later, as pictorial landscape is gradually reborn. Chapter six will then examine the poetry of seventeenth-century England, illustrating the birth of landskip in English verse, and noting the revival of that increasingly metropolitan, secular and materialist relation to nature that encourages a personalized, empirical and affective engagement of landscape. Close readings of Milton, Marvell and Vaughan in particular will demonstrate this return to an affective individualism in landscape response, a subjective 'liberation of the image', such as had characterized the descriptive approach of the poetry of Theocritus, Apollonius Rhodios and Virgil in the epoch of ancient metropolitan greatness. Earlier chapters – on nature-sensibility in the Bible and in late antiquity – will serve both to establish a continuity of survey of its western development, and to demonstrate through contrast the extent to which landskip is but one, historically contingent form of conceptualizing and perceiving natural space, dominant though it has become since the seventeenth century.

Our analysis of landscape in poetry will incorporate a third and final analytical principle. Whilst surveying historical change, in the form of varied structures of nature-sensibility and the development of the conditions for landskip, we shall also suggest the existence of certain rooted perceptual drives in human beings. Drawing from Freud the recognition that just below our conscious mind teem the pressures of the unconscious, with its desires, fears and associations, and taking too the principle from Existential Psychoanalysis that consciousness is constituted by intentionality (that consciousness is not a separated subject that intends an object: it *is* the intention), I wish to argue that perception of a landscape can never be 'disinterested': that it is always 'libidinal': has always a structuring, desiring agenda of needs and hopes and warinesses, conscious or otherwise. Human needs in and from landscape are many: we may seek material security or provision, the psychological reassurance of environmental integration or dominance, the cognitive pleasures of recognition, verification and understanding, or aesthetic gratification from the comely and perennial. Consequently, in contrast to unicausal theories of landscape perception such as those of Appleton and Eliade, I suggest that landscape-consciousness is always generated from multiple bases of awareness, and propose that we may recognize, in ourselves and in poetry, the enduring formative pressure of what we may term four matrices of perception. 'Ecological' perception scans nature as the field of potential satisfaction of requirements for subsistence and security; 'cosmographic' perception is alert in landscape to the forces and processes of the world-order, as current cosmology conceives it; 'analogical' perception gratifies the understanding in apprehending phenomena in terms of analogy, polarity, symbol and type; while 'technoptic' perception is pleasured and replenished by recognizing among the myriad forms and configurations of nature those it has learned from art.

Before I explain further and attempt to justify such a grossly arithmetic methodology, a word on the character of these categories. They do not, of course, form a complete theory of landscape perception, since this process is wider, richer and less stable (as we all know as readers of the stream-of-consciousness novel) than the elementary schema to which they analytically constrain it. Rather, these categories constitute certain originative directive forces in landscape-consciousness and writing, drives that weave together unconsciously to abstract and distinguish certain forms and configurations in the environment, which then serve as paradigms and hierarchies of attention and remembrance. But if they suggest cardinal values in vision, significantly pluralistic codings for the eye, it must be admitted that these categories no more than partially element the manifold of consciousness. A host of lesser, personal, and conjunctural factors will further condition sight.

These matrices of perception I believe to exist trans-historically, as deep-seated functions of our material and social being: but the objects or fields of attention which these intentional categories light up, we will demonstrate to be in constant historical change.

I have bracketed off fuller discussion of these matrices for the final section of this chapter. That section will seek to demonstrate the dyad of variable historical contents to enduring trans-historical categories, in a separate miniature survey. I have decided upon a separate sub-chapter, in order that the reader unhappy with extensive theory may skip a densely theoretical section, moving directly on to the concrete empirical survey; he or she will already have gained by this point a sufficient, explanatory outline of my analytical framework and terms. But I have also bracketed this section for methodological and historiographical reasons. I wish them not to impede the clarity of the central organizing and analytic principle of this book: the rise and fall of landskip. Moreover, although these matrices exert, I feel, a determinative force upon our landscape-consciousness considerable enough to merit extended demonstration and meditation, during the years of researching this study I have come strongly to feel that history is the record of more than that limited transformation which is permutation within old, perennial categories; that it is most profitably grasped as a true dynamic, a trajectory of emancipations, from confining economic and intellectual shells, of emergence into widening possibility and genuine historical novelty. It is in order to make salient this historiography of momentum and invention, operating within broad laws of development, that I set the birth and rebirth of landskip in art and poetry at the centre of this study, and will draw on our rooted matrices of perception as a continuing but subordinate frame of analysis.

One further important element for the thorough analysis of literary landscape, a discussion of the differential development of landscape perception within the existing ensemble of artistic forms – within distinct literary genres and varied pictorial media (tapestry, fresco, canvas) each with their own history and separate tempo of development, influenced by institutional relations of theory and practice between 'the sister arts' – this dimension of the study of landscape aesthetics cannot here find space. A further entire volume would have been necessary to accommodate such issues. Simplified, but large-scale, an historical overview of the fundamentals of nature-feeling and poetic crafting of landscape, and above all of the progressive rise of landskip, is our objective.

Such a programme is vulnerable to criticism from each of the opposing camps in the sensibility of contemporary literary studies: the traditionalist, empirically oriented critics may dislike the many classifications of the theoretic structure, whilst conversely, those more versed in philosophic and sociological approaches to literature may miss a closer working alignment with existing models of cultural analysis, and regret 'looser' sections of empirical detail. Further, specialists in any one of the several historical fields that this work traverses may feel hostility toward my 'trespass' on their territory, and toward the very principle of large-scale analysis by anyone who is not an expert in each and every of the periods examined. (One scholar whom I consulted, having discretely signalled his antipathy to the scope of the study, coughed, and explained 'You see, I'm mainly a 430s to 420s BC man.') My defence of this kind of project is thus partly philosophic: aptly, if acidly, it has been said that 'To ask larger questions is to risk getting things wrong. Not to ask them at all is to constrain the life of understanding to fragments of reciprocal irony or isolation.'[32] And certainly, whilst studies, say, in landscape in the relief sculpture of one period, of flower catalogues in another, or of garden design in a third, are admirable for rigour and specialist authority, and thus indispensable to reliable scholarship, there is no reason why their virtues should preclude our appreciation of those which derive from synthesizing the larger picture: from making possible, that is, address of entirely fundamental questions. (Are there, for example, basic laws of history conditioning the fortunes of aesthetic perception? Are there commonalities of landscape response demonstrable in every culture?)

My reasoning is in part also practical: there exists, to the best of my knowledge, no other English-language study of landscape in poetry of this scope, let alone of an interdisciplinary character.[33] Doubtless I shall be chastised by specialists for all manner of shortcomings, and

32 George Steiner, *On Difficulty* (Oxford: 1978), p. xi.

33 Kenneth Clark's inspiring and brilliant *Landscape into Art* (1949; rev. 1976) is probably the closest alternative; but it is, of course, substantially a study of painting, containing little poetry, no theology, and scant social history. Nor, of course, does it seek to address pre-classical feeling for landscape, or even much in the way of classical.

doubtless I shall deserve it; but I have written the kind of book that I would myself dearly have liked to have come across a decade ago when I turned to the subject, haunted both by my own love of landscape, and by W. H. Auden's provocative question in his *Bucolics*: 'Am I / To see in the Lake District, then, / Another bourgeois invention like the piano?'[34] This book offers a broad historical outline of western nature-sensibility, unified by a thesis as to the reason for landskip's emergence, and making available to the non-specialist, within a single exegetical narrative, materials from formal thought, painting and social history, as well of course as from poetry. There is need of such a study: a need which this work can but begin to approach.

Four matrices of perception

Thus far we have emphasized the ineluctable historicity of our seeing. Large-scale revolutions of production in society create transformations of 'nature-sensibility': they engender altered relations of power with nature, fresh priorities of need and desire, and attendant 'new fronts' of visual acuity and familiarity in the manifold of landscape. We shall see for example how late medieval poetry and graphic art, absorbing the crusading energies of agricultural expansion and new population mobility, sally often beyond the inherited high walls of a fixed symbolic vocabulary to exercise a new empiricising, documentative eye, observing closely the energetic terrains of seasonal agricultural labour (plate 8), and studying plant species with scientific accuracy in painted *millefiore* settings and decorative cathedral carvings. As a civilization of wood embarking on large-scale deforestation, its arts renew a curiosity for penetrated wilderness and invaded forest depths, as poetry notes ragged moss trailing from tangled trees and painted *sous-bois* record sudden surprises amid exact complexities of dimness. Among the poets, on the other hand, of seventeenth-century England, conditioned by the economic centrality and social autonomy of its teeming London metropolis, the rural world has ceased to signify a realm of hazard and labour for much literate culture, and the calendar eye gives way to the urban appetite for an innocent, recreative and idyllic 'countryside'. 'Straight mine eye hath caught new pleasures / While the landscape round it measures' writes Milton, as poets learn to conjure grand prospects, genteel citizens armed with emblem books

34 Auden, 'Mountains', lines 23–25, in *Bucolics*.

escape into refreshing solitudes for edifying scrutiny of symbolic natural harmonies, and a new sentimental eye for human depredation and cruelty sets in.

The very concept of 'landskip' – that is, of representing natural reality in terms of empirical material appearances and the illusion of spatial depth on a flat two-dimensional surface – was itself an historical novelty, produced by classical Greece. 'Naturalism' as such cannot be said to be natural. Yet 'nature' is a concept that I think we should nonetheless not abandon entirely. A human species-nature perceptibly persists, in transformation and deformation, and at a very fundamental level, throughout the historical process, and constitutes a category to be constructed on the far side of the record of cultural variation. Not only for conservative literary critical and religious forms of 'essentialist' thought, but for Marx, too, humanity has a core nature: the category is structurally integral to his dialectic, insofar as the concept of alienation itself implies a residual and recoverable human authenticity.[35] In application to landscape, I wish to argue for the existence of enduring perceptual drives, rooted in human material and cognitive needs, but constantly subject to changing cultural pressures. It is the plasticity of these trans-historical drives within diverse historical climates that this section seeks to sketch.

Four primary drives, or matrices of perception, we have identified as perennial are the ecological (the eye to subsistence and security), the cosmographic (apprehending a conceived world-order, its operative agency and structure), the analogical (perceiving structures of similarity and symbolicity), and the technoptic (identifying in visual experience those codes of appearance it has learned in art).

Ecological perception and aesthetics register the 'Nature' that serves our material and productive needs. Crucial to ecological perception is the dimension of territorial feeling. The primitive conceives nature as an indissociable whole, and his calendar rituals sustain this 'topocosm': 'the entire complex of any given locality is not merely the human community of any given area ... but the total corporate unit of all elements, animate and inanimate alike, which together constitute its distinctive character and atmosphere'.[36] Subscription to an idea of universal consonance is a pervasive (though

35 See Norman Geras, *Marx and Human Nature: Refutation of a Legend* (London: 1983). 36 Theodor H. Gaster, *Thespis* (New York: 1961), pp. 17, 24.

not unanimous) tradition of Greco-Roman thought, which often saw the world in a harmony patterned on music, resembling Apollo's flute: a belief running from Pythagoras through Plato's World-Soul to Horace's *concordia discors*.[37] The ancient world, from Stonehenge to Hellenistic Athens, provides many examples of buildings or whole cities oriented on world-axes or astronomical schemes, observing the harmonies of earth and sky. The Greek temple, for example, customarily faced East. This cognitive world of 'archaeastronomy', opening up spectacularly within contemporary Maya scholarship, represents perhaps one of the major intellectual traditions of humanity, active across the ancient world. Such conviction of cosmological solidarity extended to a shared moral condition – Homer and Hesiod sing of the prospering of crops and flocks that attend the well-governed kingdom[38] – or, in the secular Lucretius, to an intuited universal vitality in whose rhythms man, beast and fields quicken and rejoice.

> ... life-giving Venus, it is your doing that under the wheeling constellations of the sky all nature teems with life, both the sea that buoys up our ships and the earth that yields our food. Through you all living creatures are conceived and come forth to look upon the sunlight. Before you the winds flee, and at your coming the clouds forsake the sky. For you the inventive earth flings up sweet flowers. For you the ocean levels laugh, the sky is calmed and glows with diffused radiance.[39]

This sense of the oneness of the world in health and time – Spitzer applies the term 'stimmung', signifying that quality of feeling 'which extends over, and unites, a landscape and a man'[40] – produces in poetic natural description a 'world-sense': from Sappho's lyric evocation of silent nature under night and moonlight, and Euripides' marvellous depiction of dawn around Parnassus at the opening of *Ion*,[41] to the medieval topos of seasonal change. Nonetheless, against such unitive forms of feeling, historical development will increasingly promote a differential sense of the world, probing it primarily as an

37 Cf. Leo Spitzer, *Classical and Christian Ideas of World-Harmony* (Baltimore: 1963), pp. 1–13. Horace's *concordia discors* (*Epistles* 1.12.19) is somewhat ironic in context.

38 For the reorientation of the Athenian agora see John Onians, *Art and Thought in the Hellenistic Age* (London: 1979), pp. 169–79. Homer, *Odyssey* 19.109–14; Hesiod, *Works and Days* 225–39.

39 *On the Nature of the Universe*, 1.2–9, trans. Ronald Latham (Harmondsworth: 1951), p. 27.

40 *Classical and Christian Ideas*, p. 7.

41 Sappho, fragment 96; Euripides, *Ion*, 80–89.

unfolding of places, profiling localities. With the agricultural revolution, the subsequent settling of cultures within defended frontiers, and the concomitant genesis of myths of lost or inaccessible paradise, territorial feeling gains new primacy and demarcates the earth into the contrasting 'domains' of cultural space, wilderness or chaos, and mythic space (heaven, hell, the home of the blessed). These powerful ontological classifications have long dominated landscape-consciousness, and we shall trace hereafter their modulations under the impact of commercial and metropolitan habits of thought and appetite.

At the most primitive level ecological aesthetics include the 'habitat values' of Appleton's theory, but as we move from the atavistic to the historic, criteria of serviceability multiply, to include agricultural fertility, territorial defensibility, and possibilities for civil order. The anguished Homeric excitement over the unworked lush arable of the goat-isle near the Cyclopes' land is one instance of ecological perception directly manifest in poetry.

> ... craftsmen would have turned the island into a fine colony for the Cyclopes. For it is by no means a poor country, but capable of yielding any crop in due season. Along the shore of the grey sea there are soft water-meadows where the vine would never wither; and there is plenty of land level enough for the plough, where they could count on cutting a deep crop at every harvest-time, for the soil below the surface is exceedingly rich.[42]

Hesiod's *Works and Days,* Virgil's *Georgics,* are simultaneously 'literature' and viable manuals of agricultural lore. For Theocritus and Hesiod the highpoint of natural pleasure is at harvest time: in sprawling languour amid the fattened landscape of summer plenty.

> Many an aspen, many an elm bowed and rustled overhead, and hard by, the hallowed water welled purling forth of a cave of the Nymphs ... All nature smelt of the opulent summer-time, smelt of the season of fruit. Pears lay at our feet, apples on either side, rolling abundantly, and the young branches lay splayed upon the ground because of the weight of their damsons.[43]

Another joy of 'competent space' is the serviceable harbour, sheltered, shelving, from the beginning and throughout antiquity a set-piece in its own right.[44] A fabulous exploitation of the world is boasted both

42 Homer, *Odyssey,* 9.130–35, trans. E. V. Rieu (Harmondsworth: 1946), p. 142.

43 Theocritus, *Idylls* 7.135–37, 143–46: Loeb trans. (J. M. Edmonds, Cambridge, Mass.: 1928). Compare Hesiod, *Works and Days* 589–97.

44 With Homer they form already a digressive topos: cf. Gordon Williams, *Tradition and Originality in Roman Poetry* (Oxford: 1968), p. 640: e.g. *Odyssey* 9.136–41; 10.87–94; 13.96–105. Later treated by Virgil, *Aeneid* 1.158–69; Ovid, *Metamor-*

in Roman frescoes (the vast commercial harbours of Pompeian painting, for instance, with their wharves and warehouses, shipping and monuments) and in Roman verse: one thinks of Statius on the technological triumphalism of the country villa:

> Thence a colonnade climbs slantwise up the cliff, vast as a city, and its long line of roof gains mastery over the rugged rocks ... Here, where you now see level ground, was a hill; the halls you enter were wild country; where now tall groves appear, there was once not even soil: its owner has tamed the place.[45]

With the division of labour and stratification of society, ecological perception necessarily multiplies into a class-consciousness of landscape. The farmer and field worker survey a realm of named boundary landmarks, experience the 'close-to' perception of worked growth, are alert to signals of changing weather in cloud, sky, wind and animal behaviour, all of which contrasts the aesthetic concern with anonymous topographic form, the painterly eye for landscape as vista, enjoyed by urban traveller and privileged possessing classes. If this is particularly evident with the eighteenth and nineteenth centuries, when those who could afford the books and paintings which furnished the taste jockeyed like William Gilpin to and fro on propitious hillsides until convenient plane trees secured prospects authentically picturesque, and when Wordsworth could oppose the proposed Kendal-Windermere railway on the ground that the urban lower classes were incapable of appreciating barren rocks and mountains without preparatory courses in aesthetic education, it is true for antiquity also. Horace jokes in his *Epistles* about his improper relation to nature, grubbing about in the rocks and soil of his estate like a slave. And Telemachus, with the aesthetic emancipation of taste conferred by noble rank, declares the steeply sloping wilds of Ithaca where only goats can run and crops may not be grown to be more *attractive* (ἐπή

phoses, 11.228, and cited by Vitruvius as a standard feature of landscape frescoes (*On Architecture* 7.5.2). For the classical and Christian metaphor of joy in 'haven' after the 'storm', see C. Bonner, 'Desired Haven' in *Harvard Theological Review*, 34 (1941), 49–67. The harbour-landscape can be found in painting as early as 1700 BC in the Miniature Frieze of the West House at Thera: see *The Wall-Paintings of Thera* by Christos Doumas (Athens: 1992), pp. 27, 47–49.

45 *Silvae* 2.2.30–31, 54–56 (Loeb, trans. J. H. Mozley: Cambridge, Mass.: 1928). Compare *Silvae* 3.1.97–101; 3.1.167–70, and Pliny, *Epistles* 2.17; 5.6; Martial, *Epigrams* 8.68; 6.42. Cf. Zoja Pavlovskis, *Man in an Artificial Environment: The Marvels of Civilization in Imperial Roman Literature* (Mnemosyne: Lugduni Batavorum: 1973), Suppl. 25, pp. 1–53.

ρατος) than the broad and fertile arable of Menelaus' kingdom. The preference may make of Telemachus the first of the Romantics; but the eye that can favour such sterile terrain enjoys a 'landlord's view'.[46]

Cosmographic perception and description respond to what in landscape illustrates religious or philosophic beliefs and instincts about the structural order of the universe and the forces or laws governing it. We know, for example, that belief in Hell lent a new dimension to contemplation of fire in the Middle Ages;[47] that antique Greece 'beheld' sexual passion in the breaking of waves, the ecstasy of Aphrodite in the surging *ἀφρός* or hot white foam that rode toward the seashores.[48] The Christian tradition indeed long advocated conscious scrutiny of the 'Book of Nature' as an exercise in piety. We can perhaps simplify developments in this category into the succession of three broadly defined conceptions of world-order: mythological and animistic (lasting into classical antiquity); the rational-geometric (classical, Hellenistic and Roman, with a reprise in Renaissance Europe); and the Christian anagogic. These cosmological frameworks, I suggest, affect sensory sensibility and its artistic expression on several counts.

They determine the degree of sensory immediacy of the art-work: the Homeric immersion in sensuous reality, its continuous physical 'foregrounding' of action, is to develop with the confidence of a secular rationalism under which the old volatile, incompletely figurable landscape of divine immanence can be logically organized, coolly contracted into intellectually determined units: whether the delicate tonal experiments of Theocritus' bucolic scenes, or the Hellenistic painter's composed and computed frames, informed by the same 'geometric imagination' that introduced gridded town-planning. With Christian dualistic philosophy, standardized, non-empirical rhetorical schemes occlude direct landscape experience, while allegorical gardens and *paysage moralisé* point upwards beyond the order of appearances. Thus from Homeric epic develop, in one climate, the organized visual

46 For Gilpin, see John Barrell, *The Idea of Landscape and the Sense of Place* (Cambridge: 1979), p. 5, quoting a fragment of Gilpin published in C. P. Barbier, *William Gilpin* (Oxford: 1963), p. 77. *Wordsworth's Guide to the Lakes* (5th edn, 1835) ed. Ernest de Selincourt (London: 1977), pp. 150–55. Horace, *Epistolae* 1.14.39. Telemachus' words are in Homer, *Odyssey*, 4.605–08. On the concept of 'the landlord's view' see Raymond Williams, *The Country and the City* (St Albans: 1975), pp. 62, 160; John Barrell, pp. 5, 59, 63; and Margaret Drabble, *A Writer's Britain* (London: 1979), p. 55.

47 John Berger, *Ways of Seeing* (Harmondsworth: 1972), p. 8.

48 Peter Brown, *The Body and Society* (New York: 1988), pp. 17–18.

field (Virgil's Carthaginian harbour,[49]) and in another, the (pseudo-) *locus amoenus* and tree catalogue.

Affected too, will be basic susceptibilities towards spatial mood and colour. An animistic universe elicits special sensitivity to motion (rustlings of leaves and flights of birds as omen and augury); to contrasts of brightness and darkness, or mistiness; to silence (all nature ceases sound before the presence of a god, as in Euripides' *Bacchae*[50]). Virgil is highly sensitive to such atmospherics in the *Aeneid*'s recreation of primaeval, animistic apprehension: the Trojans' boat slipping round the long river bends as the dense forests wave on the water's surface; the sinister awe of the rocks and trees of the glade that will become the Capitol.[51] The '*Odyssey* landscapes' (plate 5), Roman frescoes based on Hellenistic originals, are built on startling contrasts of sun and shadow, and recede into mysteriously misty skies. Apollonius Rhodios makes considerable capital from filling his revisited epic world with sophisticated obscurities of shadow, mist and sudden theophany.

Likewise influenced by changing 'taste in universes'[52] is the level of 'system-consciousness' in nature that will prevail. The Hellenic conviction of an intelligible order operating in all things, leads Homer in his description of Calypso's grotto casually to adduce a rationale of ornithological habitat ('a verdant copse ... was the roosting-place of feathered creatures, horned owls and falcons and garrulous choughs, birds of the coast, whose daily business takes them down to the sea'[53]), whereas Hebraic sensibility, untouched by the comparativist, rationalistic habits of a voyaging culture, avoids the presumption of natural history and beholds nature submissively, registering with pious awe and wonder the whirlwind and the uncontrollable sea.

A final cosmographic variant, we shall see, is the favoured scale or 'dimension' of natural focus. The ancient topocosmic 'world-sense' evolves with late antique pessimism into a 'vertical imagination' that acclaims the mighty spaces above our heads in contrast with humanity's puny pinfold, whilst Stoic–Christian monism reveres the dignity of the miniature. The 'prospect' is a pleasure of the rational, secular, measuring mind, foreign to the artistic impulses of both mythological and anagogic ways of seeing.

49 Homer, *Odyssey*, 10.87–94 and 13.96–105; Virgil, *Aeneid* 1.158–69.

50 *Bacchae*, 1084–85.

51 *Aeneid*, 8.95–96; 8.348–50.

52 Phrase from C. S. Lewis, *The Discarded Image* (Cambridge: 1964), p. 222.

53 *Odyssey*, 5.63, 65–67, trans. E. V. Rieu (Harmondsworth: 1946), p. 89.

Analogical perception receives and redacts the external world through the faculty of similitude. Man's symbolic and typological workings derive at one level from the automatic sorting activity common to all organisms. Organisms automatically classify stimuli to reduce their diversity for cognitive economy, so that anterior to their presentation in the conscious mind, phenomena have already been framed within a system of correlations. As Cognitive Psychology puts it, 'the perceived world is not an unstructured total set of equiprobable co-occurring attributes. Rather, the material objects of the world are perceived to possess...high correlational structure. That is, given a knower who perceives the complex attributes of feather, fur and wings, it is an empirical fact provided by the perceived world that wings co-occur with feathers more than fur.'[54] The earth and its forms, sounds and impressions exist for consciousness from the outset as a great web of correspondences, types and oppositions. The intuition of likeness informs the classification of the environment in the ethnobiological taxonomies of primitive peoples[55]; the belief that correspondences between objects were supernaturally ordained, pointing with occult force at one another, inspired the practices of augury and faith in homeopathic magic. Literature as early as *The Epic of Gilgamesh* and *The Odyssey* invests its major protagonists with symbolically appropriate locales, whilst Vincent Scully has argued that archaic Greeks pursued the profound instinct for the symbolic import of scenery both in myth and settlement practice, founding cities on sites auspiciously marked by the crescent moon of twin peaks.[56]

While the category of analogical perception inevitably overlaps with that of cosmographic vision (the establishment of a system of identities and oppositions is the structural heart of all cosmology), instances and orders of analogy of a non-religious or philosophic kind will also often present themselves. Sexual and corporeal analogies, conscious or otherwise, are virtually ubiquitous. Long before Freud[57] set literati about exposing phallic symbols in myth or art, poets were conscious that we derive from landscape's uncoverings, fertility and stirrings intimations of love and limb. Far more ancient than the delicate erotic botany of the *Pervigilium Veneris* –

54 Eleanor Rosch and Barbara B. Lloyd, *Cognition and Categorization* (Hillsdale, New Jersey: 1978), p. 29.

55 See Ibid., ch. 1.

56 Scully, *The Earth*, passim.

57 Paul Shepard, *Man in the Landscape* (New York: 1967), pp. 99–116 is lively on 'Freudian' landscape consciousness.

Behold: the purple flowers have revealed their blush
and a blaze of roses has burst from the warm buds;
the goddess herself has made the roses unveil
themselves like new brides naked in the light of day[58] –

is the *Song of Songs*, where we read of the beloved as a private garden of rich spice-beds and living waters, a sealed orchard of pleasant fruits. She is associated with secret places and the cleft of a rock (2.14), and her lover feeds on her breasts as roes among lilies (4.5; 6.3).

Thy stature is like to a palm tree,
And thy breasts to clusters of grapes.
I said, I will go up to the palm tree,
I will take hold of the boughs thereof.
Now also thy breasts shall be as clusters of the vine ...[59]

Similitude, of course, is far more central to literary landscape than is scrupulous visual impression. If it takes a Turner and a canvas to capture the aerial swirl and mystery of Victorian fog and mist, Dickens can summon at a stroke its phantasmagoric ambiguity by suggesting an emerging Megalosaurus waddling up Holborn Hill.[60] Literary landscape overtly beds the optical in the ideological; working by metaphor or wit, fancy or piety, it is permanently closer than art to ideation, to the world of relations, to explicit networks of thought. Historical change in this category of perception will switch, however, between faculties of symbolization: from mythopoeic and sensory to conceptual and schematic. *The Song of Songs*, for example, which sings of sexual joy through metaphors that derive from a sensory order of association, drawing voluptuously on taste, colour and smell, is radically reconstructed when Jerome renders it an allegory of the love between Christ and his church by re-encoding the imagery within a developing lexicon of theological symbolism. Analogical variation as to literality and externality will also interpose: the topocosmic sincerities of Homer will become the sentimental correspondence of

58 *Pervigilium Veneris*, anonymous, trans. as *The Night Watch of Venus* by Harold Isbell in his anthology *The Last Poets of Imperial Rome* (Harmondsworth: 1971), p. 40, lines 31–5.

59 *Song of Songs*, 7.7–8.

60 *Bleak House*, opening paragraph. The instance is taken from J. R. Watson, 'Literature and Landscape: Some Relationships and Problems' in *The Aesthetics of Landscape*, the proceedings of a symposium at the University of Hull (Didcot: 1980), p. 28.

the 'pathetic fallacy' with Hellenistic poets; the terse topographic objectivism of *The Iliad*'s similes yield to the delicately inward 'phenomenological' poetics of Theocritus.

Our final category of perception is the 'technoptic'. Since so much of our perceptual activity is, unconsciously, a desiring, monitoring process working through the selection and classification of stimuli, much that we 'perceive' in landscape will in fact be the gratifying recognition within the natural manifold of certain elements identified according to codes of beauty learned in our experience of art. Topographical description in graphic art is thus better defined as a proceeding of 'Art into Landscape' than 'Landscape into Art', since painters repaint the painted: a recognition, as Gombrich points out, dating back at least to Richard Payne Knight.[61] Early views of nominally North American scenery, for example, are often so deeply conditioned by the soft Italian prospects of the Masters that one almost suspects the painter not actually to have set foot outside the Uffizi. The alleged *View from Apple Hill* of Samuel B. Morse (1829) for instance, is so obediently structured as a cleanly ordered landscape of central perspective receding in measured parallel planes of sombre tones under cold light *à la Poussin*, that the primitive American lakeside hills emerge as no baccy-chewing frontiersman was likely ever to recognize them. The experience of art however, may affect even the layman's perception of the phenomenal world in ways fundamental or minute: whether highlighting the optical peculiarities of spatial recession, newly perceived and imitated by seventeenth-century English poets from contemporary perspective painters, or, more locally, conditioning a preference for certain shades of blue over another. A certain 'sophistication about blues', for instance, resulted in fifteenth-century Italy from large differences in the cost of blue pigments: as such, a natural sky of ultramarine, a hue reserved for principal figures in painting, might appear to an Italian far lovelier or holier a manifestation of the heavens than one of 'German blue', whose contemporary cheapness consigned it to secondary figures and works.[62]

For the Hebrews, in deep contrast, the interdiction of graven images precluded pictorial consciousness from developing at all; and their

61 E. H. Gombrich, *Norm and Form* (1966; 3rd edn Oxford: 1978), p. 117.

62 Michael Baxandall, *Painting and Experience in Fifteenth Century Italy* (1972; rpt. Oxford: 1974), pp. 6, 11.

natural description accordingly projected onto landscape a form of legitimate artistic expression, which to us appears extraordinary. The mountains and stars of the Old Testament clap their hands, dance and sing, in a festive exhilaration more exuberant than any Brueghel, in whirling epiphanies scarce dreamt by Attic maenads. The degree to which this tropology conditioned a Hebrew individual's empirical landscape consciousness is impossible to judge; but the dance imagery precisely figures that miraculous plasticity of man and creation alike before the prodigious impact of the Creator's will, which was a formidable religious literality for the Hebrews. Pictures could never express the creation that Miriam and Moses sensed limitlessly volatile about them, as they sang to the timbrels beside the Red Sea which had just, so murderously, snapped-to; or as Moses in the wilderness trembled before the bush that had abruptly burst all flame.

The historical variations of our landscape consciousness may indeed seem limitless; and it is to a pattern behind them that we now turn.

2

The values of landskip: an historical outline in the ancient world

For the argument of this book we must distinguish between 'landscape' and 'landskip': the latter term, popular in the seventeenth century, signifying the concern in painting or poetry specifically for the technique of pictorial naturalism, with its careful commitment to the empiric authenticities of perspectival recession, chiaroscuro and localizing detail. This concern with external nature as a carefully composed naturalistic 'view' is far from a universal of western art and verse; and it will be my argument that the aesthetic values which nurture landskip derive from an engagement of the natural world distinctive to an advanced commercial civilization. We can discern, I will argue, five key components of that relation – in effect, five socio-historical determinants of the aesthetic taste for landskip – which emerge gradually through the centuries. These determinants constitute what we will term 'managerial', 'comparative', 'quotidian', 'possessive' and 'rational' forms of interest in space. Major revolutions of economic and productive life lie at their heart, which we may trace in very simplified terms through the following general typology.

The nomadic topocosm.

The world for primitive nomadic man was, as we have said, above all unitary. In Lévi-Bruhl's words, 'To these natives, a sacred spot never presents itself to the mind in isolation. It is always part of a complexus of things which includes the plant or animal species which flourishes there at various seasons, as well as the mythical heroes who lived, roamed or created something there and who are often embodied in the very soil, the ceremonies that take place there from time to time, and all the emotions aroused by the whole.'[1] This holistic vision did not

1 Lévy-Bruhl, *L'Expérience Mystique et les Symboles chez les Primitifs* (Paris: 1938), p. 183; quoted and Englished by Eliade, *Patterns*, p. 367.

mean that hunter gathering man was unconscious of the land as heterogenous extension: Leenhardt notes that for the Kanakas of New Caledonia 'an innumerable number of rocks and stones with holes in them in the bush have some special meaning. One crevice is helpful if you want rain, another is the dwelling of a totem, one place is haunted by the vengeful spirit of a murdered man. In this way the whole landscape is alive and its smallest details all mean something; nature is rich with human history.'[2] However, this did mean that the primitive's understanding of the earth was not reducible, not quantifiable in purely spatial terms, in the way a landscape painting takes for granted. 'The first realization of the religious significance of the earth was "indistinct": in other words, it did not localize sacredness in the earth as such, but jumbled together as a whole all the hierophanies in nature as it lay around – earth, stones, trees, water, shadows, everything.'[3] The primitive, moreover, construes reality in the vocative case. 'For modern, scientific man the phenomenal world is primarily an "it"; for ancient – and also for primitive – man it is a "Thou".'[4]

Colin Turnbull, who has lived among hunter-gatherers of our own day, the Pygmies of the Congo, notes how, typically of the primitive, they address their expressivity to an indissociable whole of natural reality. The 'molimo' – the ritual in which they praise the divinity of the forest – involves the reproduction, through a wooden trumpet, of all the sounds of the forest: the cries of leopard, elephant and buffalo, mixed with human song. Late one night, when the moon was full, Turnbull heard a 'curious noise' from near the camp, and went to investigate:

> There in the tiny clearing, splashed with silver, was the sophisticated Kenge, clad in black cloth, adorned with leaves, with a flower stuck in his hair. He was all alone, dancing around and singing softly to himself as he gazed up at the treetops.
>
> Now Kenge was the biggest flirt for miles, so, after watching a while, I came into the clearing and asked, jokingly, why he was dancing alone. He stopped, turned slowly around and looked at me as though I was the biggest fool he had ever seen; and he was plainly surprised by my stupidity.

2 *Notes d'Archéologie Néocalédonienne* (Paris: 1930), pp. 23–24; trans. Eliade, *Patterns*, p. 367.

3 Eliade, *Patterns*, p. 242.

4 H. and H. A. Frankfort, et al. *The Intellectual Adventure of Ancient Man* (Chicago: 1946), p. 4.

'But I'm *not* dancing alone', he said. 'I'm dancing with the forest, dancing with the moon.' Then, with the utmost unconcern, he ignored me and continued his dance of love and life.[5]

Agrarian territorialism.

The 'Neolithic revolution', with its transition to agriculture, growth of settled societies and division of labour, inevitably revolutionized such nature-sensibility. Although there had been no clean break between hunter-gathering culture and the development of agriculture, since the former would often burn and clear forest cover to encourage favoured food plants, tend wild plants, and even irrigate on a small scale,[6] the development of large, class-stratified cities from 3000 BC in the Near East completed a permanent alteration of ecological consciousness. Ironically, from both psychological and ecological perspectives, we can now see that lost hunter-gathering lifestyle as representing (thus far) history's optimal level of social and natural integration: for agriculture inaugurated progressive degradation of the environment, entailed longer, harder hours in food production, and subjected the majority of people in the world, as field labourers, to drudge in surplus extraction for local elites whilst enduring chronic undernourishment, low life-expectancy and the constant threat of famine.[7] Further, material competition among growing cities and their rulers bequeathed humanity the lasting curse of militarism. The city walls of Uruk by the third millennium were built twelve to fifteen feet thick and ran six miles in circumference, strengthened by defensive towers.

The nature-sensibility of such sedentary cultures, settling in permanence upon their bounded zones of cultivation, evolved into a fearful 'world-dualism', pitting 'civilization' against profane, anarchic space. In Mesopotamian mythologies, the world 'in which the presence and the work of man are felt – the mountains that he climbs, populated and cultivated regions, navigable rivers, cities, sanctuaries – all these have an extraterrestrial archetype, be it conceived as a plan, as a form, or purely and simply as a "double" existing on a higher cosmic level'. Unknown seas, deserts and uncultivated lands lack a prototype of this kind. They 'do not share with the city of Babylon, or the Egyptian Nome, the privilege of a differentiated prototype.

5 Colin Turnbull, *The Forest People* (New York: 1962), p. 272.
6 Clive Ponting, *A Green History of the World* (New York: 1991), pp. 33, 38.
7 Ibid., pp. 88, 109.

They correspond to a mythical model, but of another nature ... assimilated to chaos; they still participate in the undifferentiated, formless modality of pre-Creation. That is why, when possession is taken of a territory – that is, when its exploitation begins – rites are performed that symbolically repeat the act of Creation: the uncultivated zone is first "cosmicized", then inhabited.'[8] This stands in powerful contrast to the flexible territorial sense of hunter-gathering man, for whom 'subsistence space is bounded, but these boundaries are vague and not defended'. The Kalahari bushmen, for instance, are typical in sustaining a widespread agreement to maintain regular and free access to such resources as permanent water.[9] If for primitive peoples 'frontiers' are often marked by sacred stones, trees, rivers or lakes, upon whose crossing magico-religious taboos may be placed[10], for the stationary cultures of the neolithic world the 'outlands' beyond take on the character not merely of foreign territory but of diabolic terror. Myths arise of civilized heroes subjugating monster-haunted wilderness (as in the myths of Heracles, *The Epic of Gilgamesh* and *Beowulf*).[11] Panic in the wilds beyond the 'god-given' order within the cultural pale survives well into the ancient Egyptian empire. One scribe writes of the road to Meger: 'Shuddering seizes thee, (the hair of) thy head stands on end, and thy soul lies in thy hand. Thy path is filled with boulders and pebbles, and there is no passable track, for it is overgrown with reeds, thorns, brambles, and wolf's pad. The ravine is on one side of thee, while the mountain rises on the other.'[12] The Old Testament praises divinity for its rectilinear dispensation, which makes possible level furrows and straight ways in the wilderness.[13] 'Climb upon the wall of Uruk', urges the *Gilgamesh*-poet, 'walk along it, I say: regard the foundation terrace and examine the masonry: is it not burnt brick and good? The seven sages laid the foundations.'[14]

8 Eliade, *Myth of Eternal Return*, pp. 9–10.

9 Richard B. Lee and Irven De Vore, *Kalahari Hunter-Gatherers* (Boston: 1976), pp. 79, 86, 96.

10 Arnold van Gennep, *The Rites of Passage* trans. H. Vizedom (Chicago: 1960), pp. 15–18.

11 Cf. Paul Piehler, *The Visionary Landscape*, pp. 72–75; also Eliade, *Myth of Eternal Return*, p. 40, note 70.

12 *Anast*. 1.24.1–4; Frankfort, et al., *Intellectual Adventure* p. 39.

13 *Isaiah* 11.16; 35.8; 40.3–4. Cf. Northrop Frye on Isaiah's 'engineering imagination': *The Great Code* (1982; rpt. London: 1983), pp. 160–61.

14 *The Epic of Gilgamesh*, trans. N. K. Sandars (1960; 2nd edn Harmondsworth: 1972), p. 61.

The passage's pride in the towering walls, unshakeable foundations and exact lines of architecture running smooth, in these achieved ramparts against a dangerous and magical beyond, highlights the stark polarization of cosmos and chaos established with the advent of agriculture and the settled *οἰκουμένη*.[15] Further, the alienation from harmony with the wide unitary earth which the retreat into the walled world of city and guarded arable enacts, is to generate 'the most enchanting dream which has ever consoled mankind, the myth of a golden age in which man lived on the fruit of the earth, peacefully, piously, and with primitive simplicity'.[16] Increasingly, supreme sacred places are seen as remote, guarded, inaccessible (the Garden of the Hesperides, the Isles of the Blest), penetrable only by ordeal, attained only by the great.[17]

In art, the spacelessness of palaeolithic painting, with its ungrouped, single creatures jumbled on a void, is now predictably qualified: by the introduction on Sumerian vases and Egyptian vases from the Old Kingdom of ruled ground lines on which characters are placed. The exclusive concern is no longer with animals; the picture surface is controlled, 'oriented', with an up and down; and the groundline localizes kings and followers in their 'own', definite space. The Akkadian victory stele of Naramsin (c. 2300 BC), though non-perspectival, locates its triumphant monarch in mountainous country as indicated by conical hill, the climbing outlines of soldiers, and irregularly placed trees. The whole surface of the stele is treated not as the customary series of bands, but as a single spatial composition.

Agriculture introduced, too, the idea of *ownership* of nature. Where hunter-gatherers felt 'topocosmic' integration into a shared natural bounty, cultivation increasingly subordinated the ancient holistic 'world-sense' to an exploitative concern for 'place': to an appraising acquisitive eye for 'resource' annexation and potential 'land-value'. The Corn-Mother and property rights oust the Earth-Mother in the dawning age of dictatorship and Demeter.

The cardinal change as far as the story of landskip is concerned, the emergence of its first enabling condition, lies in the revolutionary

15 This term possessed six shades of meaning in antiquity, but essentially designated the area of the world inhabited by the 'civilized': see Clarence J. Glacken, *Traces on the Rhodian Shore* (Berkeley, Los Angeles and London: 1967), pp. 17–18; Arnold Toynbee, *Mankind and Mother Earth* (Oxford: 1976), p. 27.

16 Kenneth Clark, *Landscape into Art* (1949; 2nd edn London: 1976), p. 109.

17 See Eliade, *Patterns*, pp. 380–84.

development of this essentially dominative *managerial relation* of man to nature. Although in many cultures it seems long to have been felt a sin to 'wound' the Earth-Mother by the slicing of the plough[18] (a sentiment still poetically echoed in Virgil's fourth eclogue), subsistence now depended and civilizations advanced on the competence of the 'interrogative eye' so well exemplified in Hesiod. Organizing nature's forms and scrutinizing natural law, man gazed afresh at the land in a measuring contemplation, surveyed a more intelligible, classifiable, divisible world, in whose construing he was partner.

Corresponding to this came the abstract rationalism of geometric art: its schematizing impulse reflecting the intellectualism of the new planned economy and regulated social order. 'Art now tries to hold fast the idea, the concept, the inner substance of things – to create symbols rather than likenesses of the object ... it is no longer the imitator, but the antagonist of nature.'[19] Within this cognitive world, a landscape feature, when sacred or vital, may be construed less in terms of material particularity than as constituting a recurring archetype, existing simultaneously as one and several places. Thus the world's oldest spot, for Egyptian religion, is the 'primeval hill' located in the Holy of Holies of the temple at Heliopolis – and, simultaneously, in temples of different dates throughout the land.[20] Nothing could be more distant from the absorption in contingent appearances on which landskip will thrive than this denaturalizing conceptualism. Similarly, Egyptian tomb painting[21], such as that of Ti at Saqqara, dating from the Old Kingdom (c. 2450 BC) is highly stylized, depicting scenes of seasonal work – cattle fording a river, slaves driving a flock of sheep – in pictographs. The canon of formalized 'typifications' will endure throughout ancient Egyptian art. Moreover, the aim in tomb painting is to furnish 'the eternal mansion' of the deceased, and record the status he had enjoyed in life: non-narrative and undramatic, the images represent a kind of eschatological accountancy, a business-like abstract of workers' productive labour, rather than self-validating delight in natural scenes. Likewise, in Hesiod's *Works and Days*, a somewhat wearied manual of dogged toil,

18 Ibid., p. 246.

19 Arnold Hauser, *The Social History of Art* (1951; rpt., in 4 vols., London: 1962), vol. 1, pp. 8, 12.

20 Frankfort et al., *Intellectual Adventure*, pp. 20–23.

21 H. A. Groenewegen-Frankfort, *Arrest and Movement* (1951; rpt. Cambridge, Mass.: 1987), pp. 28–62.

nature is apprehended and drawn purely as seasonal scheme and calendar task. The year's glad highpoint, the summer meal among ripened crops, is consumed in a minimally defined spot of respite and breeze.

> But when the thistle blooms and on the tree
> The loud cicada sits and pours his song…
> Exhausting summertime has come. The goats
> Are very fat, and wine is very good.
> Women are full of lust, but men are weak,
> Their heads and limbs drained dry by Sirius,
> Their skin parched from the heat. But at this time,
> I love a shady rock, and Bibline wine,
> A cake of cheese, and goat's milk, and some meat
> Of heifers pastured in the woods, uncalved,
> Or first-born kids. Then may I sit in shade
> And drink the shining wine, and eat my fill
> And turn my face to meet the fresh west Wind,
> And pour three times an offering from the spring.[22]

Aesthetic appreciation along visual lines doesn't enter Hesiod's head: he eyes the land as a serial code, as recurring signals to prescribed interventions, not as an outspread view.

Neither Hesiod nor Egyptian tomb painting are purely the product of the stationary cultures of 'agrarian territorialism', of course; each (and Hesiod's art more markedly) belong to later economies where commerce and travel have alleviated the hieratic anxiety and siege mentality of the world *Gilgamesh* recollects, and whose art, no longer narrowly geometricist, allows a measure of flexibility and empiricism into conventions of representation. Nonetheless they do retain much of that rigorously functional and schematizing perception of nature, little concerned for sensuous values, which characterizes the new mentality of '*managerial space*'.

The world of commercial geography.

Nature-sensibility is again dramatically transformed by the growth of international trade, and the impact of invasive *Völkerwanderungen* circa the eighteenth and thirteenth centuries, which together break the

22 Hesiod, *Works and Days* lines 581–97, trans. Dorothea Wender (Harmondsworth: 1973), pp. 77–78.

stranglehold of cultural insularity and the fear of 'wild' hinterlands, as regional civilizations in the Near and Middle East enter into ecumenical relations.[23] Gradually, therefore, through the later second millennium a countervailing curiosity develops for the variousness of the natural world and the variety of civilized economies. Homer's Odysseus will be perhaps inevitably 'that resourceful man who roamed the wide world after he had sacked the holy citadel of Troy. He saw the cities of many peoples and he learnt their ways.'[24] We have moved, as one may term it, from a world of agrarian territorialism toward the demystifying mentality of commercial geography.

Imperial Egypt had been exhilarated by the new cultural diversity opened up to her by her conquests – one Eighteenth Dynasty depiction of kneeling captives paints Nordic blondes alternating with African blacks[25] – but the period's art, controlled by the tradition of a reinforced Pharaonic and military autocracy, never saw the development of such interests into artistic concern for contrastive topography. The 'polycentric' culture of first millennium Greece, however, with its loose federation of trading city-states, lacked such absolutist curb. It is thus with the voyaging, coastal culture of archaic Greece, with its easily navigable waters and the natural south-easterly run of its sea-lanes, led by island-chains, towards the rich civilizations of Asia and Egypt, that '*comparative space*' – the second indispensable condition of landskip values – makes deep impact on art. The interest in comparing and contrasting places and nations, soils and climes, is very evident in the extended natural description of *The Odyssey* (which developed in Ionia, centre of world trade at the time, and a melting pot of Aegean and Oriental cultures), as in the Homeric formulaic epithets: 'rocky Calydon', 'Ithome with its terraced hills', 'deep-soiled Larissa', 'Pteleus deep in grass'.[26] Auerbach notes the objectifying qualities of Homeric narrative, pointing to 'externalized, uniformly illuminated phenomena, at a definite time and in a definite place, connected together without lacunae in a perpetual foreground', a mode which 'sends down strong roots into social usages, landscape, and daily life'.[27] *The Iliad*, though subordinating landscape by keeping it

23 Toynbee, *Mankind*, chapters 13–14.
24 *Odyssey*, 1.3, trans. E. V. Rieu (Harmondsworth: 1946), p. 25.
25 Donald B. Redford, *Akhenaten The Heretic King* (Princeton: 1984), p. 23.
26 *Iliad*, 2.640, 729, 841, 697: Penguin edn, trans. E. V. Rieu (Harmondsworth: 1950), pp. 56–62.
27 Erich Auerbach, *Mimesis* (1946; rpt. Princeton: 1968), pp. 11, 13.

encapsulated within simile, frequently 'sites' characters: Sarpedon rests under a beech near the Scaean gates, which serves also as meeting place for Apollo and Athene, and by which Hector later stands. There is also a wild fig-tree, and a beautiful plane above Aulis' altar.[28] This device of 'epic adumbration', referred to by Curtius, was termed by the Greeks *τοπογραφία*, and by the Romans 'positus locorum' or 'situs terrarum'.[29]

The Odyssey, in contrast, frequently unfolds landscape into the narrative body. Circe, Calypso, Alcinous and Eumaeus have each their 'own' landscape. The epic's digressive formulae that exist 'to turn the reader's or listener's attention deliberately for a short time, away from the narrative to enjoy a type of digression that invites poetic treatment on its own account'[30] include expansions of landscape description such as the passage on the Ithacan cove where Odysseus is put ashore. (Comparable is the elaboration of the nocturnal simile, at the close of Book 8 of *The Iliad*, beyond the point of comparison, for its own pleasure.[31]) Moreover the verb *θεάομαι* is frequently used in *The Odyssey*, never in *The Iliad*, of gazing upon objects; both Hermes and Odysseus (respectively beholding Calypso's grotto and the garden of Alcinous) are said to stand, transfixed by scenic beauty, to gaze their full.[32] The taste for what will be termed *περιήγησις*, the 'sketch' or itinerary of travelled lands (Pausanius' work of this title being the most celebrated example), is very clear, and conversely Homer's account of the Cyclopes (*Od.* 9.126–28) as a backward people incapable of ship-building and seafaring is of lordly derision. Travel and landscape-consciousness are everywhere knit: topographic epigrams are inscribed in the Hellenistic period on wayside shrines: 'I, Hermes, have been set up / Where three roads cross, by the windy / Orchard above the grey beach. / Here tired men may rest from travel, / By my cold, clean, whispering spring.'[33] The first defined 'prospect' in Greek poetry occurs when Jason, in the *Argonautika* (1.1112 ff.)

28 *Iliad*, 6.237; 7.22; 11.70; 6.432; 2.307. Point taken from Curtius, p. 186.

29 Curtius, p. 200. Cf. also Theodore M. Andersson, *Early Epic Scenery* (Ithaca and London: 1976) on Homer's 'latent space': pp. 15–52, contrasting Virgil's 'visible space': pp. 53–103.

30 Gordon Williams, *Tradition*, p. 640.

31 *Iliad*, 8.555–61. Point from L. P. Wilkinson, *The Georgics of Virgil* (Cambridge: 1969), p. 4.

32 *Odyssey*, 5.75–6; 7.133–34.

33 Epigram by Anyte in the Palatine *Greek Anthology*, 9.314; here translated by Kenneth Rexroth, in *The Greek Anthology*, Penguin selection edn, Peter Jay (Harmondsworth: 1981), p. 78, as no. 113. Cf. likewise no. 114.

sends his voyaging comrades to climb Mount Dindymon to scan the view: 'From the summit they could see the Macrian heights and the whole length of the opposite Thracian coast – it almost seemed that they could touch it. And far away on the one side they saw the misty entrance to the Bosporus and the Mysian hills, and on the other the flowing waters of Aesupus and the city and Nepeian plain of Adresteia.' Indeed, as early as Homer, 'reconnaissance' landscape is eagerly purveyed: 'When I climbed a crag to reconnoitre, I found that this was an island, and for the most part low-lying, as all round it in a ring I saw the sea stretching away to the horizon. What I did catch sight of, right in the middle, through dense oak-scrub and forest, was a wisp of smoke' (*Od.* 10.194–97). The Homeric eye is fine-tuned to the transformation of appearances through *movement*: the golden fallow turning black behind the driving plough, the Phaeacians' country looking from far out at sea like a shield laid on the misty sea (*Iliad* 18.548; *Od.* 5.281). The development of Greco-Roman pictorial perspective is arguably a culminating expression of this acuity, the elated sense of participation in a dynamic world of movement into a transmuting third dimension. Panofsky notes that classical perspective is conceived in terms of relations between *objects*, rather than as a stable homogenous system of space; and White, that perspectival foreshortening on Greek vases was long applied only to chariots, whirling shields and billowing sails, not to altars or furniture: seemingly because 'the emotional motivation' was 'excitement at ... rushing speed', the desire to effect the impression of motion.[34]

Homeric international scene-painting is thus greatly superior in wealth and particularity to *mise-en-scène* in *The Epic of Gilgamesh*, of which the following is the fullest among few examples:

> Together they went down into the forest and they came to the green mountain. There they stood still, they were struck dumb; they stood still and gazed at the forest. They saw the height of the cedar, they saw the way into the forest and the track where Humbaba was used to walk. The way was broad and the going was good. They gazed at the mountain of cedars, the dwelling place of the gods and the throne of Ishtar. The hugeness of the cedar rose in front of the mountain, its shade was beautiful, full of comfort; mountain and glade were green with brush wood.[35]

34 Erwin Panofsky, *Renaissance and Renascences in Western Art* (1960; rpt. New York: 1972), pp. 121–22. John White, *The Birth and Rebirth of Pictorial Space* (1956; 2nd edn Boston: 1967), pp. 240–41.

35 *Epic of Gilgamesh*, p. 77.

Contrast of this passage with the account of Calypso's grotto (*Od.* 5.57–74) at once highlights Homer's descriptive amplitude and scenic organization.

He found the lady of the lovely locks at home. A big fire was blazing on the hearth and the scent from burning logs of split juniper and cedar was wafted far across the island. Inside, Calypso was singing in a beautiful voice as she wove at the loom and moved her golden shuttle to and fro. The cave was sheltered by a verdant copse of alders, aspens and fragrant cypresses, which was the roosting-place of feathered creatures, horned owls and falcons and garrulous choughs, birds of the coast, whose daily business takes them down to the sea. Trailing round the very mouth of the cavern, a garden vine ran riot, with great bunches of ripe grapes; while from four separate but neighbouring springs four crystal rivulets were trained to run this way and that; and in soft meadows on either side the iris and the parsley flourished. It was indeed a spot where even an immortal visitor might pause to gaze in wonder and delight.[36]

We note the painstaking catalogue of trees and birds, the measuring approval of arrangements for shade and irrigation, the steady expansion of focus from cave to trees, fountains, rills, field and meadow-flowers. Nonetheless, each passage presents a 'synoptic' sensory whole of evocation: the first concerned with shade and headway, the other with 'soft' meadows and varied odours. Properly pictorial focus requires still further determinants.

Following 'managerial' and 'comparative' space, the next key condition for the development of landskip is the appetite for what we may term '*quotidian space*'. In the wake of a wealthy commercial order, where non-aristocrats enjoy social power and political identity, an art may emerge which favours routine activity and typical experience over images of the mythical, remote and awesome. Hauser notes, for instance, 'the connection between naturalism and progressive politics, on the one hand, and between formal rigorism and conservatism on the other',[37] a connection particularly clear with regard to Classical and Hellenistic Greece. In Pharaonic Egypt, artistic tradition had from 3000 BC with the Palette of Narmer deliberately banished landscape reference in order to present the Pharaoh's authority as outside space and time; yet even there,[38] the cosmopolitan conditions of the New

36 *Odyssey*, trans. E. V. Rieu, pp. 89–90. 37 Hauser, *Social History*, p. 75.
38 Groenewegen-Frankfort, *Arrest and Movement*, pp. 18–23.

Kingdom – 'a sophisticated age of predominant town life'[39] with its voluptuously enriching international trade and swelling of Thebes and Memphis into large imperialist cities – had introduced a new, sensuous quality and interest in actuality into the old canonic themes of tomb painting. Some localization entered with depictions of specific temples and buildings; while genre 'incidents' – in harvesting, a girl falls and is helped by a friend, at a banquet one guest is sick – imported the variability of the everyday. Following the Amarna period, tomb owners were shown as happily *participating* in the daily agricultural scenes that previously they had overlooked (plate 1); while gardens and a wealth of foliage became persistent features lovingly detailed.[40] Yet relish for the transitory and actual, which landscape always represents, comes fully to fruition only with Greece. Here, the anti-traditionalist spirit of the market, combined with the absence of an hereditary priesthood or autonomous church, fosters an unrestrained appetite for temporal content, for an art concerned not to glorify an absolute sovereign, aggrandize a ruling military caste, or purvey esoteric religious symbolism, but to savour the recreative and occupational scenes of everyday life. This secular, documentative aesthetics will eventually culminate, under the Romans, in the 'rhyparographos'[41] or 'painter of the commonplace' whose paintings of cobblers' stalls, asses and barbers' shops fetched higher prices than the largest works of more orthodox painters. Moreover, the seeds of what we shall later discuss as 'phenomenological' landscape can be found here: contingent appearances are contemplated with pleasure in their own right – Hauser writes of a new 'aesthetic culture' and a 'carefree play with forms'[42] – and the developing concern for a subtler, sensuously affective relation to reality perhaps compensates for the Weberian 'entzauberung', the draining of magical and religious meaning from the world with the advance of a rationalistic attitude of mind toward phenomena.

This quotidian focus is not, however, purely a compensatory or carefree affair. As comprising a materialist definition of the environment, housing human identity in observed locales, it arguably represents the same comparativist and demographic impulse as 'comparative space': it is domestic περιήγησις. The same commercial

39 Ibid., p. 80.
40 Ibid., 79–91; 111–12.
41 Mortimer Wheeler, *Roman Art and Architecture* (London: 1964), p. 205.
42 Hauser, *Social History*, pp. 69–70.

basis of pressure applies: the discontinuous world of the city, with its raw, proximate cultural pluralism, its figures, appearances and network of power constantly changing, is the new arena of economic survival, whose typicalities and detail its citizens must master.[43]

There are interesting affinities, I suggest, between this source of acumen for landscape, and that urban tendency towards social interrogation and reflexivity in the spheres of religion and language noted in the tradition of Durkheimian sociology. As advancing division of labour and the complex differentiation of a social formation cause any clear pattern of social control and authority to fade – a condition of which the great commercial city is the supreme example – religions tend to devolve onto an anti-ritualist, individualist basis, moving beyond traditional symbolism and fixed rules towards empirical private judgement and introspection. Likewise the functioning of language, among middle-class speakers in modern cities, has been observed to modulate from a 'Restricted Code', internalizing the hold of traditional authority in the minds of its speakers, into an 'Elaborated Code', a language whose lexical and syntactic enrichment facilitates a newly inquisitive order of perceptual activity: one which elucidates and reviews existing categories of thought, and makes explicit a sense of difference between the values and feelings of the self and others.[44] The impulse therefore of poetry and graphic art in the ancient metropolis toward quotidian landscape – as the objectification of daily scenery and the formulation of characterological space – is thus surely a cognate aspect of a recurring phenomenon: the empiric and interrogative reconditioning of human thought and perceptual patterns within the deracinating commercial cultures of great cities.

Reviewing in these terms the actual incidence of landscape painting in western history, we may better understand, I feel, the absence of

43 See Hauser, p. 240, on medieval bourgeois naturalism.

44 Mary Douglas extends Durkheim's distinction between societies governed by mechanical and organic forms of solidarity in her study in the sociology of symbolicity and ritualism, *Natural Symbols* (1970; rpt. Harmondsworth: 1973), where she contrasts the ritualism of medieval and 'Bog Irish' Catholicism with the reflexive, individualist sensibility of urban Protestantism. Basil Bernstein's work contrasts the Elaborated Code of geographically and socially mobile modern middle-class speakers with the Restricted Code of contemporary working-class speakers: members of smaller and more local communities of shared fundamental assumptions. See his paper 'A Socio-Linguistic Approach to Socialization' in *Directions in Socio-Linguistics*, eds. J. Gumperz and D. Hymes (New York: 1970).

pre-classical landskip. The murals of the reign of Akhenaten, of the Egyptian Eighteenth Dynasty (1350 BC) may seem to contradict this statement, since they betray a marked concern for nature, in Nilotics portraying fishing and fowling, swimming ducks and running stags, wild bulls leaping in the swamps. And this despite the new despotic absolutism of the Pharaohs of the period of the Empire, under which the powers of the commercial class were severely curtailed. This art, however, is but the promotion of an ancestral subordinate 'low-style', extrapolated from the tradition whereby rulers were stylized but animals and servants portrayed in a freer, more naturalistic mode.[45] Akhenaten has elevated an undeveloped 'demotic' stratum of tradition – 'modest asides in the Theban tomb paintings'[46] – to ruling idiom. Moreover, given the short ascendancy of this Pharaoh and his naturalism, this art never has the chance to develop its potential – a new inclusiveness of content, perspectival draughtsmanship, freed play of form. As Hauser remarks, it is the persistence of the old seigneurial form for the new content that is most striking. Given the continuing hold of the priest-caste on culture, Egypt was never fully to evolve a secularized, sensuously affective 'quotidian space', as both classical and Christian art were to do. However, we may observe that conditioning this Pharaonic landscape art are certain anti-traditionalist impulses shared with highly commercial cultures. Akhenaten was a revolutionary Pharaoh, disposed against conservative tradition by his bid to break the power of the priestly caste through the introduction of monotheism. In this sense his 'laicized' landscape is wilfully anti-hieratic, a climactic break with the past. The extended and eager natural iconography he fostered, deliberately displaced the anathematized mythological symbols of polytheist tradition: particularly those of chthonic deities and the Osirian afterworld – rivals to his 'terrestrial' monotheism. Insofar, however, as such exaltation of the visible world magnified his own exclusive status as reigning Son of the Sole Creator, Aten ('Akhenaten' means 'Effective for the Sun-disc'), these landscapes represent only a propagandist actualism: not nature for herself, but a politically instrumental cult of the glorified sunlit scene.

With Minoan Crete, whose architectural remains reveal a society in which people of all classes led lives of prosperity, and where equality

45 Cf. Hauser, *Social History*, pp. 40–42.

46 Ibid, p. 38; Cyril Aldred, *Akhenaten and Nefertiti* (New York: 1973), pp. 53–55.

was extended even to women (there was no public activity from which they were debarred; Crete had even its female bull fighters), the first instances of 'pure landscape' are found in the western world, at a period prior to 1500 BC. The subject-matter of Minoan art derived mainly from the natural world, including the sea. On the painted walls of affluent homes on the island of Thera, we find mountainous undulations with lilies in bloom and mating swallows (plate 3). In one frieze (plate 2), a colourful fleet progresses across dolphin-filled seas into a port whose topographic features leave it identifiable even today as Akrotiri, and make of the painting 'a primitive maritime chart or portolan, perhaps the oldest ... in the world'.[47] Framing its events at sea, pastoral scenes of herdsmen and shepherds evoke the peaceful life of the hinterland, and recall the *Iliad*'s rustic digressions from epic action. A riparian landscape features palms, other trees and bushes, where wild ducks swim and jackals prowl; elsewhere we have playful monkeys, and antelopes. Unmistakably this is 'quotidian space', an art of joy in the familiar world; and the familiar determinants are there. 'City life was probably nowhere so highly developed as in Crete';[48] religious worship seemingly played little role in public life (no large temples or monumental religious statues have been found); and trade was eagerly concentrated in the hands of the ruling class, its interests thus prevailing unhampered. Yet Minoan art arguably remained landscape rather than landskip; it never developed perspective, or thus the 'view'. Two further stimuli were needful, which were to emerge in Greece.

Quotidian space in Greece is very clearly an aspect of the classical period's urge to material and sociological self-definition. 'Scenery' was introduced within a popular drama in which 'high' myth was being rearticulated in pointed relation to contemporary social institutions. It was for Aeschylus' *Oresteia*, culminating in the celebration of the Areopagus and Athenian justice, that Agatharcus introduced, in 456 BC, the earliest Greco-Roman landskip, as background perspective scenes on the σκηνή (the wooden stage or scaffold on which the actors performed). This was probably simple perspective painting upon scattered panels or canvasses in wooden

47 Doumas, *Wall-Paintings of Thera*, p. 27.

48 Hauser, *Social History*, p. 45. Compare Doumas, *Wall-Paintings*, pp. 22–29, on Thera's remoteness from theocratic and centralized power as permitting artistic experiment and 'secular' freedom.

frames. Sophocles went further, and invented 'skenographia', and was 'thus the first to put behind actors a defined background... The figures of Sophocles must have appeared against the *skene* in sharply defined silhouettes, unlike the figures of Aeschylus, which were seen in the round.'[49] (We may compare Sophocles' patriotic binding of site into narrative in his specification of Oedipus' death-place.)[50] It is hard to infer much about early theatrical scenery from the plays – even Aeschylus' renowned spectacle and extravagance is now controversial[51] – but Ling suspects classical satyr-drama to have used large-scale work, probably of grottoes and arbours, and without staffage, and Webster likewise feels it to have been 'cave and vine' background.[52] Certainly the breakthrough revolutionized Greek painting, and 'skenographia' exerted considerable influence on Hellenistic and Roman poets. Virgil's celebrated landskip of the Carthaginian harbour he termed a 'scaena', and Vitruvius uses the term 'scaenographia' to designate any perspective view.[53]

The impulse to landskip as assigning 'a local habitation and a name' is quickened by developing individualism. Portraiture and biography each emerge with the fifth century BC. 'The high gods can be envisaged in an airy environment of nothingness; not so the butcher, the baker, the candlestick-maker... Landscape, in however subordinate a role, is an inevitable counterpart of the portrait and the historical narrative...Note how closely these developments tally in time: the emergence of portraiture and the new status of the individual; the New Comedy and idyllic poetry.'[54] Theocritus' idylls indeed offer 'milieu studies' (as Watt will call the same phenomenon in the eighteenth-century novel)[55]: his landscapes are always figure-related, always profiled habitat. Throughout antiquity landskip will never fully escape the condition of 'scaena', of elaborated backdrop, yet with Theocritus such specificity turns gain, as a 'poetry of place'

49 Margarete Bieber, *History of Greek and Roman Theater* (Princeton: 1961), p. 29.

50 *Oedipus at Colonus* 1590–96.

51 Cf. Oliver Taplin, *The Stagecraft of Aeschylus* (Oxford: 1977), p. 40; also appendix C, 'The Skene in Aeschylus', pp. 452–59.

52 Roger Ling, 'Studius and the Beginnings of Roman Landscape Painting' in *Journal of Roman Studies* 67 (1977), 15; T. B. L. Webster, *Hellenistic Poetry and Art* (London: 1964), p. 164.

53 Virgil, *Aeneid*, 1.164; Vitruvius, *De Architectura*, 1.2.2 and 7. praef. 11.

54 Wheeler, *Roman Art*, p. 182.

55 Ian Watt, *The Rise of the Novel* (1957; rpt. Harmondsworth: 1963), pp. 203–04, 210.

is born. The Harvest Home (Idyll 7) borrows the device of the bird-catalogue from Homer's Calypso, and the nightingale singing from the thicket is directly Homeric; but the assiduous naturalism – the accurately reported positioning of the landmarks along the eight kilometre walk to Phrasidamus' farm – and the correct natural history (the rare tomb-crested lark, and the other birds referred to, seem always to have been resident in Cos)[56] embed a paradisal tonality in the closely mapped familiar world.

Western landscape painting has been well defined as '*possessive space*', its perspective techniques 'a series of traps for the capture of objects'.[57] Yet long before illusionistic space was born, the first topographic references had been introduced into art by the impulse of ostentatious display: the astonishing Macehead of King Scorpion[58] (c. 3100 BC) set the pre-Dynastic Egyptian king among trees beside a river bank to commemorate the opening of his great canal. Though the innovation was soon after abolished by the hieratic spacelessness of Pharaonic tradition, the triumphal impulse behind empirical landscape remained historically clear: in Roman art, for instance, identifiable topography is introduced in the second century BC in celebratory paintings of victorious battles,[59] which perhaps were carried through the streets in triumphs. Proprietory vanity works a similar effect: both in the case of Europe, where patrons' castles help transform 'calendar art' into the earliest 'views', and in the ancient 'villa landscapes' of Roman painting, with companion panegyrics to civilized estate in Pliny and Statius. The new competitive climate of fabulous luxury, imperial pride and spectacularly acquisitive *parvenus* produces, from the reign of Augustus, the villa paintings pioneered by one Studius (or Ludius) which, while reproducing the broad vista with figures in the Hellenistic manner, exhibited wealthy Roman villas with colonnaded façades (often of several stories), looking out onto a garden or fronting a lake, and featured citizens strolling, sailing or riding in carriages.[60] If

56 Homer, *Odyssey*, 5.66–67; 19.518–20. On the verisimilitude of the Idyll see Geoffrey Arnott, 'The Mound of Brasilas in Theocritus' Seventh Idyll' in *Quaderni Urbinati di Cultura Classica*, New Series 3 (1979), 99–106.

57 Samuel Beckett, 'Three Dialogues by Samuel Beckett and Georges Duthuit' rpt. in *Samuel Beckett*, ed. Martin Esslin (Englewood Cliffs: 1965), pp. 17–18.

58 Groenewegen-Frankfort, *Arrest and Movement*, pp. 19, 22.

59 Eleanor Winsor Leach, *The Rhetoric of Space* (Princeton: 1988), pp. 79–81.

60 Described by Pliny, *Historia Naturalis*, 35.116–17; cf. Ling, 'Beginnings', passim.

these paintings appear flimsy impressions in comparison with the seigneurial towers and odes to filigree of *Les Très Riches Heures du Duc de Berri*, it is perhaps because the Roman nobility lived not at the centre of extensive estates, but close together in cities; as such, more prestigious than commissioning a 'view' of the villa was purchasing a villa with a view. This is precisely what we find both in Pliny, who recommends that a villa command a prospect over surrounding scenery, and in Statius, who praises a friend's villa for yielding a different vista from each chamber.[61] The illusionistic mock-view that came to stimulate the skill of the landscape painter in antiquity, thus arose in part perhaps as simulated possessive display, much as landskip was later to develop among medieval practitioners as flattering imagings of lordly estates. Vitruvius notes how prospect paintings on villa walls feature harbours and headlands, temples and groves, even hills, cattle and shepherds; and along the tall, dark corridors of Nero's 'Golden House' on the Esquiline, false windows displayed parklands and romantic scenery.[62]

In poetry too a competitive pride of place generates the most important landscaping. Virgil's *Georgics* is a topographic apotheosis of chauvinism, hymning the landscape that embodies temperate Roman superiority over the decadent East and the wilderness of the North. 'But neither Media's groves, land of wondrous wealth, nor beauteous Ganges ... may vie with Italy's glories ... she is the home of olives and of joyous herds ... Here is eternal spring, and summer in months not her own ...'[63]. Though we lack space to elaborate it here, the *Georgics* pictorialize a *patriotic* ruralism. Composed in the years immediately before and after Actium, it extols with a politic nostalgia, the peace and fertility of the scenes among which the *vetus colonus* nourished the traditional virtues that were to establish the greatest of world empires (see esp. 2.513–40). To consolidate the emergent national rather than the old city-patriotism, no particularity of locale is allowed to obtrude above the generalized picture of the whole 'Saturnian land': the *laus italiae* evokes the typicalities of ancient towns on steep crags above gliding streams, of rich soil and swelling fruits. Yet throughout, as Wilkinson demonstrates, Virgil strikingly translates Varro's abstractions into the form of pictures. The *Georgics* is 'the first poem in all literature in which description may be said to be the chief *raison d' être*

61 Pliny, *Epistolae*, 5.6; Statius, *Silvae*, 2.2.75–86.
62 Vitruvius, 7.5.2
63 *Georgics*, 2.136–38, 144, 149.

and source of pleasure ... if [it] has to be assigned to a genre, it is Descriptive Poetry'.[64]

The final condition for a highly developed art of landskip is the creation of what we shall term *rational space*: a demystifying, materialist definition of space, intellectual and epicurean. This developed in the cultural climate of an advanced commercial economy, amid large-scale cities autonomous of the daily agricultural grind. Gone is nature as the physico-moral power of Homer, and the treacherous seasonal realm of Hesiod with its threatful vicissitudes: from the fifth century on, *χώρα*, meaning vacant space, becomes the common word for the countryside in the teeming cities;[65] while *ἀγροικία* or 'rusticity' becomes in an urban/e culture a term of reproach, similar to the English 'boorishness'.[66] With the confident subjugation of nature as an order of utility and picturesque diversion, country picnics become an Alexandrian delight, while the rural cults of Pan, Hermes, Artemis and Asclepius grew in importance, tempting Athenians into their hinterlands and appearing on Hellenistic vases and marble reliefs.[67] Intrinsic to this idealizing relation is the dwindling of archaic topocosmic feeling into the sentimental poetic trope of the 'pathetic fallacy', beloved of Theocritus, Virgil and their successors. 'Here, for the first time in Greek literature, man establishes a "false" relation with nature, one that does not include the full truth of its power, the range of its manifestations.'[68] Hellenistic epideictic rhetoric developed a new line of eulogistic natural description, and orators had to be warned 'not to drag ecphrasis into forensic oratory: verdicts would not depend on a description of a storm'.[69] In like vein, Horace is to inveigh in the *Ars Poetica* against sewing 'purple patches' of rural

64 Wilkinson, *The Georgics*, p. 11, 4.

65 Onians, *Art and Thought*, pp. 51–52.

66 Cf. section entitled *ἀγροικία* in Theophrastus' *Characters*; also Menander, *Dyskolos*, 202, 956.

67 Onians, pp. 50–51.

68 C. P. Segal, 'Nature and the World of Man in Greek Literature' in *Arion*, 2 (1963), 46. For influential early 'pathetic fallacy' cf. *Idylls* 1.71–72; 7.74–77; *Eclogues* 1.38–9; 5.20–39; 7.55–56; 10.8; 10.13–16; for the analogous but earlier trope/belief of the magical efflorescence of landscape in the presence of gods or beloved mortals cf. Hesiod, *Theogony* 194–95; Homer, *Iliad*, 14.347–51; Theocritus, *Idylls*, 8.41–48; Lucretius, *De Rerum Natura*, 1.7–9; Virgil, *Eclogues*, 5.58–64. See also F. O. Copley, 'Pathetic Fallacy in Greek Poetry' in *American Journal of Philology* 58 (1937), 194–209.

69 Wilkinson, p. 7: Dionysus of Halicarnassus, *Rhetoric*, 10.17.

reverie – winding streams, beautiful valleys, rainbows – upon serious work.[70] Theocritus' introduction of a low-life ideality within a naturalistic frame in the new mode of pastoral is paralleled by the bowers, leafery and fruit-clustered grottos of contemporary vases;[71] while second century BC stone reliefs now forsake their shallow, 'surface art' to discover 'real, volumetric space', opening up large depths of penetrated space, and clothing trees with densely leafy boughs.[72]

The taste for an idealized countryside flourished perhaps inevitably among cultivated Romans, as a society of leisured urban affluence, consciously modelling itself upon Hellenic graces,[73] and often restricted by censorship to a depoliticized literature of rhetoric, antiquarianism and fancy. Brendel's perception of a distinctively Roman separation of public and private spheres in painting, the former limited in style and theme, the latter varied, experimental and prodigal in landscape, seems to consolidate such a view. Roman villas developed on their walls intricate and glamorous simulations of colonnaded vistas and landscaped gardens: 'fictions of luxury', whose extravagant and illusory private realms perhaps compensated for the restrictions of political actuality. The popular Roman genre of 'sacro-idyllic' landscape painting, with its misty images of rustic shrines, sacred tree or column, and streamside offerings, was born with the death of the Republic. The contemporary verse of Horace, Tibullus and Propertius is similarly rich in votive motifs and epigrams, so that poetry and painting alike appear to demonstrate both 'craving for withdrawal ... into a self-gratifying, private world of fantasy'; and the heavy impact of Augustus' propaganda for the renewal of ancient ritual.[74]

With the new high-urban, rationalistic age, wilderness, for most citizens, has been demystified and lost its inchoate menace. Under the Pax Romana and with radiating networks of paved Roman roads, tourists could take in not only Sicily, Athens, Delphi and Olympia but

70 *Ars Poetica* 17.

71 Webster, *Hellenistic Poetry*, pp. 162–64; also Onians, *Art and Thought*, pp. 50–51.

72 Maureen Carroll-Spillecke, *Landscape Depictions in Greek Relief Sculpture* (Frankfurt and New York: 1985), pp. 29–31, 177.

73 Cf. Jasper Griffin, 'Augustan Poetry and the Life of Luxury' in *Journal of Roman Studies*, 66 (1976), 87–105.

74 Otto Brendel, *Prolegomena to the Study of Roman Art* (Yale: 1979), pp. 155–56; Leach, *Rhetoric*, pp. 95–108, 212, 222–38, 245.

the Pyramids of Egypt and the temples of Karnak. Hadrian went out of his way to climb both Mt. Casius (in Syria) and Mt. Etna to enjoy the sunrise view from the summits[75]; indeed, the latter peak attracted so many visitors that the town at its base blossomed like an ancient Zermatt, and an inn for climbers was provided near the summit.

The citizen is now, I would argue, beckoned to a choice of pleasures between a 'primal' rugged world of Telemachan taste and the fat peace of cultivated landscape bespeaking benediction to the patriotic heart – a dualism inconceivable as options to the Gilgamesh-poet. Expressed in antiquity at their most beguiling in the respective sceneries of the *Aeneid* and the *Georgics*, in the late Middle Ages they re-emerge as Northern taste against Southern, the Danube school as against the Venetian; and later still become sublime landscape as against picturesque, romantic in opposition to classical. Telemachus against Menelaus, Altdorfer against Giorgione, Rosa against Claude, the Mower against Gardens, Wordsworth against Thomson: the opposition as formulated in reciprocally positive terms only becomes possible in general taste, I suggest, when the city has subjugated the country.

The correlation of popular aesthetic relish for landskip with a secular, rationalistic confidence in human and metropolitan hegemony is suggested by the enthusiasm's very demise. The early Christian centuries, with their sense of the progressive withdrawal of divinity from the world, will flee the wide-open Hellenistic and Campanian landskips, the 'open pleasance', for landscapes of retreat: for an anchoritic aesthetics of mountain bastions, unclimbed peaks,[76] foreshadowing the beauty of immunity and enclosure of the medieval *hortus conclusus*. Furthermore, earthly landscapes will become transcended by the brooding terrestrial pessimism of the late antique 'vertical imagination', in which the earth shrinks to a trivial pinpoint,[77] the Isles of the Blessed are located on the moon,[78] the starry heavens

CHESTER COLLEGE LIBRARY

75 J. P. V. D. Balsdon, *Life and Leisure in Ancient Rome* (London: 1969), p. 232.

76 E.g. Claudian, *Epithalamium de nuptiis Honorii Augusti*, 49–58 and *De Raptu Proserpinae*, 1.160–69; also Bacchus' inaccessibly lofty sacred grove in Statius' *Achilleid*, 1, lines 593–602, and the natural fortress of the bandits' mountain cave at the close of Book five of Apuleius' *Metamorphoses*.

77 E.g. Marcus Aurelius 6.36 and 4.3, parodied in Lucian of Samosata's *Icaromenippus* 18; also Cicero, *Somnium Scipionis*, 3.16; see E. R. Dodds, *Pagan and Christian in an Age of Anxiety* (Cambridge: 1965), pp. 7–8.

78 See Franz Cumont, *The Afterlife in Roman Paganism* (New Haven: 1922), pp. 94–96.

are an object of spiritual entrancement, water-nymphs adore star-gods,[79] astral determinism is a popular philosophical fashion, and moonlight scenery enters Roman painting.[80] 'The scene of your voyages, your wars, your allocation of empires, is a dot!' writes Seneca. 'The mighty spaces are above our heads; and into their freehold the human soul is admitted'.[81] The goatherd piping under the trees by the waterfall, the quiet labours of the *vetus colonus* among ancestral meadows, are displaced by the topos of the soul's flight through the universe, of the penetrating mind piercing the celestial spheres.[82]

Philosophic rationalism, however, the impulse carrying scenic values to the zenith of landskip art, had been evident from the fifth century in Greece. The 'nameless and sexless atoms of Democritus'[83] challenged mythological cosmology, just as Anaxagoras rendered bright Apollo a red-hot giant stone. *On the Sacred Diseases* rejected moral and divine causality behind human illness, which it ascribed instead to physiological imbalance; while Thucydides' historiography perceived man as an autonomous agent, creating his own destiny through negotiation of laws of human nature. In this secular rationalist climate nature shrinks and clarifies into φύσις: a finite body of regular laws subject to human discovery, and thus command. No longer source of order and ground of ethics – Herodotus and Protagoras establish φύσις as antonym of νόμος, differentiating 'environmental' laws from those of human 'culture' – no longer a manifold of unseen and arbitrary divine forces, the natural world is accurately representable as landskip. A strictly material seeing, the purely spatial statement, are becoming, within urban intellectual circles, ontologically authentic.[84] Ironizing this rupture, Plato bequeathes Hel-

79 Claudian, *De Raptu Proserpinae*, 3.16–17.

80 See F. Wickhoff, *Roman Art*, trans. S. A. Strong (London: 1900), p. 178.

81 *Naturales Quaestiones*, 1, praef. 8–11; trans. C. J. Herington, *Senecan Tragedy* in *Essays on Classical Literature*, ed. N. Rudd (Cambridge: 1972), p. 187.

82 E.g. Cicero's *Somnium Scipionis*; also *Corpus Hermeticum*, 11.20; and Plotinus, *Enneads*, 5.1.2.1; see Dodds, *Pagan and Christian*, pp. 82–84.

83 Segal, '*Nature and the World*', *p.* 28.

84 The concept of a classical secular rationalism is one unavoidably controversial. Some scholars insist that beyond a small circle of philosopher–intellectuals, traditional polytheism, with its epiphanies and mystery, continued among the Greek and Roman masses undiminished. (See for instance Robin Lane Fox, 'Seeing the Gods' in *Pagans and Christians* [1986; rpt. London: 1988], pp. 102–67, esp. pp. 117–23. 'Pagan religiousness ... was not the preserve of a few

lenism an influential scenery as he seats Socrates outside Athens' walls in a detailed *amoenus.* Delighted by the thick-grassed shade beneath a flowering plane tree and alongside a clear-flowing stream, Socrates comments appreciatively on the freshness of the air, on the breeze, the cicadas, the peace, and feels this to be a place holy to the nymphs: only to add, in satire of fashionable Sophistic ideas, that of course 'trees and open country won't teach me anything, whereas men in the town do'.[85] Quite logically it is therefore Democritus, anti-teleological philosopher of atomic materialism, and the secular rationalist Anaxagoras who develop 'post-mythic' space, extending Agatharcus' ideas on the problems of spatial projection in painting.[86] Plato had felt that imprecise sketches sufficed for landskip[87]: yet between the fifth and first centuries BC, antiquity developed focused perspective in both theory and practice.[88] Painters fathom, dismantle and outgo the sensible world in their exposure of optical fraudulences and creation of *trompe l'oeil* illusionism,[89] and in this aspect pictorial landscape, though less valued than portraiture, is bravura intellectual performativity: the *amoenus* is a *locus* of mimetic triumphalism.

The developing assumption that a civilized, rational man will be at home in the observation of space, that the trained and retentive landscape eye is an elementary intellectual credential, is evident from Roman rhetoric. Rhetorical schooling required composition of the vivid *enargeia,* the cogently lifelike scenic sketch; and its *ars memoria* counselled memorization of a speech's points through mapping their sequence onto the landmarks of a familiar journey.[90]

The supreme example, of course, of landscape art as the product of a 'rational', materialist orientation lies in the astonishing verse of Lucretius. Everywhere rendering and clarifying the abstract ideas and invisible forces of his Epicurean cosmology in terms of sight, of

antiquarians: it still animated whole cities' [p. 425].) The absence of a widely shared and deeply held materialist epistemology would be an important element in explaining why classical landskip never developed the level of technical elaboration and popular addictiveness that the Medieval was to do.

85 *Phaedrus,* 229–30 in *Plato: The Complete Dialogues,* ed. Edith Hamilton and Huntingdon Cairns (1961; 2nd edn Princeton: 1963), pp. 478–79. For its possible influence on the Theocritean pleasance and Hellenistic approaches to landscape see Adam Parry, 'Landscape in Greek Poetry' in *Yale Classical Studies* 15 (1957), 15 ff.

86 Vitruvius, 7 praef. 11.

87 *Critias,* 107c-d.

88 John White, *Birth and Rebirth,* pp. 257–58, 262.

89 Cf. Onians, *Art and Thought,* pp. 42–46.

90 Leach, *Rhetoric,* pp. 7–23 (*enargeia*), 75–79 (*ars memoria*).

panoramic *enargeia*, Lucretius employs landscape as the very 'embodiment of reality and the symbol of spatial extension'.[91]

Soft though it is by nature, the sudden shock of oncoming water is more than even stout bridges can withstand, so furious is the force with which the turbid, storm-flushed torrent surges against their piers. With a mighty roar it lays them low, rolling huge rocks under its waves and brushing aside every obstacle from its course. Such, therefore, must be the movement of blasts of wind also. When they have come surging along some course like a rushing river, they push obstacles before them and buffet them with repeated blows ... Here then is proof upon proof that winds have invisible bodies, since in their actions and behaviour they are found to rival great rivers, whose bodies are plain to see.[92]

As rationalism 'maps' land, in geography, optical treatises and oratory, landskip becomes a function of a 'geometrizing' imagination. 'The imaginary line became accepted as essential for the conceptualization of much of reality'.[93] The variegated sensuous world is submitted to the imposition of an abstract geometric system in Eratosthenes' invention of longitude and latitude, in the progress of solid geometry and the science of acoustics, and in the mathematical purity of Hippodamus'[94] grid-form reconstruction of the Piraeus. Intellectually probed, regimented and theorized, yet sensuously enjoyed perhaps more than ever, the natural world swings between symbolic and naturalist modes of representation throughout the history of Roman art. To its evolution there is limited chronological logic; and its bold perspective constructions were ever internally inconsistent. Characteristically hybrid, a Hellenistic tradition arises of 'chorography', which produces maps illustrated with views of characteristic places. Demetrios, the famous Alexandrian 'topographos' of the second century BC, was perhaps a map illustrator; and the tradition influenced the great Nilotic mosaics, ancestors of the celebrated Barberini Mosaic at Palestrina. An elaborate chart of the Nile, this mosaic offered simultaneously a gallery of inset exotic

91 Ibid., p. 129.

92 Lucretius, *De Rerum Natura*, 1.290–98, trans. Ronald Latham as *On the Nature of the Universe* (Harmondsworth: 1951), pp. 35–36.

93 Onians, *Art and Thought*, p. 164. Onian's concept of a 'geometric imagination' as an element within Hellenistic art is not, of course, to be confused with the widely used classification 'Geometric art', which refers to the artistic style of Archaic Greece.

94 Ibid., p. 119.

vignettes: the 'map' forms a compendium of pictorial information of North African landmarks, architecture and game.[95]

Hellenistic poetry likewise displays acumen for the subtleties of pictorialism, establishing itself in the vanguard of perception. No longer confined to formulaic brevity or mythological trope ('deep-soiled Larissa', 'rosy-fingered dawn'), nor to the economy of what we might term 'pragmatic space', whereby natural facts are meted out only as they exert influence on narrative action or possess a beauty derived from practical value (deep harbours, well-made huts, luxuriant orchards), landscape in poetry gains status as painterly craft. Apollonius Rhodios, as Webster notes, 'saw like a painter',[96] imitating *chiaroscuro* effects, such as made his contemporary Antipholus celebrated. Jason, for instance, rejoices in the fleece as a girl in her silken gown when full moonlight spills on it in her dark attic room. Medea's heart flutters like a patch of sunlight dancing on a wall when reflected from a pail of swirling water.[97] Apollonius' sensitivity to light-effects revolutionizes Homeric chronography, introducing into dawn formulae clear white light reflected from roads, shores and hills, sunshine across dewy plains and shores washed clean by the sea. At evening, anticipating Virgil's eclogue closes, his fields are new-shadowed beneath the peaks.[98] Virgil likewise purveys fine discrimination between luminescent tones, perceiving the shimmer of moonlight on the ripple of the sea, and, recalling Apollonius, conceiving Aeneas' heart as leaping in thought like the quivering light from water swaying in a basin.[99] His Carthaginian harbour (1.158–69), with its symmetrical cove, twin peaks, and high black grove overhanging quiet water, undeniably projects 'the ... amplitude of the finished painting ... the subordination of graphic fact to scenic harmony'.[100]

Epistemologically companion to this outward mimesis is the rarefied mood-music, the refined tonal space of experiential or 'phenomenological' landscape. As affective response to the natural world empties of traditional religious reverence and vigilance, it refills with an epicurean, delicately aestheticizing apperception that savours sensuous textures and suggestivity. In Apollonius' revisited epic, the

95 Leach, *Rhetoric*, pp. 91–95.
96 Webster, *Hellenistic Poetry*, p. 71.
97 *Argonautika*, 4.167; 3.755.
98 Ibid., 4.109; 3.122; 1.519; 1.1280; 2.164; 3.1223; 4.109; 4.1170. Evening peak-shadows: 1.450; Virgil, *Eclogues*, 1.83; 2.67; 10.75–77. Cf. Webster, *Hellenistic Poetry*, p. 70.
99 *Aeneid*, 7.10 and 8.22–25.
100 P&S, p. 6.

high level of scenic allusiveness, its impact on consciousness help form the distance, I think, between the simpler dynamism of the Homeric psyche and the troublous sensibility of the Hellenistic, between resourceful Odysseus and Jason *ἀμήχανος* (distressed, at a loss). Apollonius' Argonauts are civilized heroes in a world of primitive supernatural perils, and their susceptibility to the strange landscapes through which they are moved is one aspect of a debilitated state of impressionability. Particularly fine accordingly are the awesome and melancholy scenes – Apollo perceived in the exhausted dawn twilight in the lonely harbour of Thynias, the mists and reefs of Libya, Phaethon's laval lake and wailing winds, the overhung cave of Hades in the icy silent glen near the deserted seashore.[101] The sensibility much resembles that of the Vatican 'Odyssey Landscapes' (Roman paintings based on Hellenistic originals), where rocky coasts and sea-views dwarf sketchy human figures, and vivid light effects, 'misty skies and melting horizons' produce an 'unreal, almost spectral quality' (plate 5).[102] In Theocritus, scenery becomes a medium of delight, as topography is dispersed into flavours, into intangibles figuring fragility. 'For neither sleep, nor a sudden spring day, / Nor flowers to the bees, are as sweet as they.' The nymph Nycheia has 'springtime eyes'. Shepherd-songs luxuriate in the pleasured consciousness that drinks the mingled musics of whispering pine, falling water and the melody of flute, and they declare they would not give up for anything to sit on the rocks and watch the Sicilian sea or praise soft greenbeds by the cool brookside. The charms of these favoured beauty-spots are as ardently contested as those of paramours.[103] The recurrent descriptive frame here is what we may term the 'peritopos': local natural features are given as they relate to the person – phenomena lying underfoot, shading one overhead, resting the back – in a 'synoptic' tradition such as we found with Calypso, but that here is elaborated sensual luxury. The exquisite peritopos recurs as the substance of bucolic epigram, with Theocritus' contemporary, Anyte:

> Sit down in the shade of this fine-spreading laurel,
> draw a welcome drink from the sweet flowing stream,

101 *Argonautica*, 2.670; 4.1246; 4.605; 2.735.

102 P&S, p. 15, drawing on Erwin Panofsky, *Early Netherlandish Painters* (Cambridge, Mass.: 1953), p. 9.

103 *Idylls*, 9.33–35; 13.45; 5.31–34; 5.45–49; 8.53–56. Translated by J. M. Edmonds, *The Greek Bucolic Poets* (1912; rpt. Cambridge, Mass. and London: 1977).

> and rest your breathless limbs from the harvesting
> here, where the West wind blows over you.[104]

The under-the-tree tradition has ancestors in Hesiod's summer picnic ideal and in the *Phaedrus' amoenus*, it passes into Hellenistic and Byzantine art in the form of the 'stele', and perhaps explains that tradition in classical landscape painting of walling-in greenery close-ups without perspectival glimpses such as we find in the frescoes of several Pompeian houses (plate 4).

Prospect and peritopos, pictorial landscape and phenomenological space, landscape known through ideation and landscape at the sensate level: the two forms equally comprise 'rational space', products of a climate of secular materialism that consummates the art of landskip.

Summary

We have attempted to establish, within our construction of a very general and rudimentary historical typology of nature-sensibility (traced from the topocosmic sense of hunter-gathering man, through the defensive territorialism produced by agricultural settlement, to the stage of 'commercial geography', culminating with the great commercial civilizations of Greece and Rome) the gradual emergence of five forms of interest in space which determine the taste for that particular and contingent construction of natural reality which we know as pictorial landscape ('landskip').

The earliest is the evolution of a 'managerial' relation to nature with the development of agriculture, wherein humanity is no longer merely participant in but deliberative designer of landscape. Managerial space is evident in the schematizing rationalism of geometric art, the conceptual stylization of natural scenes in Egyptian tomb painting, and the calculating calendar eye of Hesiod's verse. 'Comparative space', born of the interpenetration of sedentary regional civilizations through extensive trading relations, records the taste of a voyaging, commercial culture for comparativist sketches of peoples and places, evident so early in Homer and continuing until late antiquity. 'Possessive space' is the concomitant impulse that celebrates a homeland and ownership: the patriotic and proprietorial pride producing Greco-Roman villa paintings, panegyrics in Pliny and

104 Anyte, trans. Sally Purcell, no. 112 in *The Greek Anthology*, p. 78 (no. 9.313 in the original collection).

Statius to the Country House, and that long pictorializing ode to the temperate Saturnian *patria* which is Virgil's *Georgics*. Finally, with Greece and Rome arise secular tendencies that stimulate the furthest development of landscape art and writing. We categorized here the impulses to 'Quotidian space' (illustrating routine activity and typical experience, occupational and recreative, rather than religious and panegyric motifs); and also to a post-mythological 'Rational space', in which a close material definition of nature is sought: both objectively, in 'scientific' pictorial mimesis, and subjectively, as 'phenomenological' poetry of heightened sensuous affectivity and nuance. In Apollonius Rhodios, Theocritus and Anyte we found developing a poetics of apperception of material sensation, which explores landscape as a field of finely discriminated physical stimuli.

The degree, however, to which these, the values of landskip, are historically local and aesthetically limited, may be gauged through a contrast with the traditions of presentation in the Bible: to which we now turn.

3

Landscape and the Bible

As the supreme text of the Christian West – 'the Great Code' in Northrop Frye's phrase – and as the source of innumerable rural motifs that are to receive reverent elaboration in the nature-writing of succeeding Christian cultures, the Bible is an indispensable component in the overview of western climates of nature-sensibility. Yet very little, I find, has ever been written in a systematic way on the subject of landscape in the Bible: not least because the forms of reference to natural reality there so little resemble our own concept of landscape. Exploration of Hebraic nature-sensibility is instructive, however, not only for the suggestive definition of very different values in nature-perception, a reminder of the historical artifice of our own habits of seeing. It also illustrates the persistence of our four 'matrices of perception', as outlined in chapter one, within all perceptual climates.

Hebrew nature-sensibility: environmental and intellectual bases

The epistemological sensibility of the Hebrews was the very contrary of materialist: it was disposed towards the numinous and inward, rather than the sensory and externalizing. The Hebrew writings nowhere suggest that rounded immanence of meaning to experience, or the sufficiency of sense-oriented aesthetics, whose expression we encounter in Hellenic culture.

The geographical setting of the Hebrews in ancient Palestine was crucial to the development of their religious vision, and hence of their nature-sensibility. Politically, the Hebrews were squeezed inexorably in a nutcracker of superpowers, in the semi-circle between the Egyptian and Mesopotamian empires. The narrow coastal belt on which they settled was the corridor between these, so that the Chosen People were to find themselves continually humiliated and dwarfed, their survival provisional, their lifestyle an endless campaigning through military and economic struggle. As such, they are an elite in toils, a people of flawed election, perennially in immediate consciousness of the delimitations of their power.

> Keep me as the apple of the eye,
> Hide me under the shadow of thy wings,
> From the wicked that oppress me,
> From my deadly enemies, who compass me about.[1]

Consequently, in the Hebrew religious temperament there strangely commingle strains both of exultant pride and nationalism –

> what one nation in the earth is like thy people?[2]

– and yet of self-abasement, prostration before humiliating omnipotence:

> But I am a worm, and no man;
> A reproach of men, and despised of the people.[3]

These ambiguities of status, of trounced sovereignty and hegemonic vassalage, are incorporated directly into nature-sensibility. Bultmann has declared that 'in the last analysis, the Old Testament doctrine of creation expresses a sense of the present situation of man. He is hedged in by the incomprehensible power of Almighty God'.[4] We might well, I suggest, substitute for 'man', 'the Israelites', and for 'God', 'imperial Asian superpowers'. Just as the Israelites were both conquerors – victors over the Canaanites, repellers of the Amalekites, Midianites, Edomites and Philistines – and a dwarfed subject state squeezed between empires, so man's position in nature is analogous: he is both overlord and overawed servant. Nature on occasion may be like the crocodile, 'a King over all the children of pride'; and Behemoth (the hippopotamus) is at home in the world with a majestic satisfaction and inviolability wholly eluding God's erring Chosen People:

> He lieth under the shady trees,
> In the covert of the reeds, and fens.
> The shady trees cover him with their shadows;
> The willows of the brook compass him about.

1 *Psalms*, 17.8–9. All scriptural quotation will be from the Authorized Version of 1611.
2 2 *Samuel*, 7.23.
3 *Psalms*, 22.6–7.
4 Rudolf Bultmann, *Primitive Christianity in its Contemporary Setting*, trans. R. H. Fuller (London: 1956), p. 18.

> Behold, he drinketh up a river, and hasteth not.
> He trusteth that he can draw up Jordan into his mouth.[5]

Man's hopeless vulnerability without the divine protection calls out tender imagery of buds opening in the parched ground, ostrich eggs warmed in the dust crushed underfoot and unfed young ravens wandering with desolate cries.[6] His dignity is as steward:

> When I consider thy heavens, the work of thy fingers,
> The moon and stars, which thou has ordained;
> What is man that thou art mindful of him?...
> [Yet] Thou madest him to have dominion over the works of thy hands;
> Thou hast put all things under his feet.[7]

He is Adam set to garden in Eden, caught between powers: a worried satrap, perhaps, ambiguously remote from central power. Exalted in lordship, he is nonetheless confronted by an abject dependence on powers above, and by recalcitrant orders below.

Moreover, the Hebrew's military vulnerability was matched by agricultural. It has been estimated that it took two centuries to transform the Israelites from a nation of 'shepherds in the desert' into one of competent agriculturalists.[8] Forced by the Amorites and others to forswear the valleys and remain in hill country, they struggled with terrace agriculture, easily swept away by rainwater, neglect or enemy sabotage, and attempted crop concealment in secret mountain sites to escape despoliation by annual invasions of Trans-Jordan nomadic tribes. Ezekiel in captivity in level Babylon was to long for 'the mountains of Israel', a phrase of his own which he uses sixteen times as a synonym of 'Israel':

> And I will feed them upon the mountains of Israel, by the streams and in all habitable places of the country. I will feed them in a good pasture, and upon the high mountains of Israel shall their fold be ...[9]

Yet on return to Palestine after the Babylonian captivity, the exiles found they had lost the art of a hill agriculture so different from that they had practised on the irrigated flats of Babylon. 'Ye have sown much, and brought in little', Haggai observes in woe.[10]

Fertility, further, is not secured *ex opere operato*, by outward ritual propitiation of appropriate gods: it is ethical in provenance,

5 *Job*, 41.34; 40.21–23.

6 *Job*, 38.26–7; 39.14–15; 38.41.

7 *Psalms*, 8.3–4, 6.

8 See Yehudi Feliks, *Nature and Man in the Bible* (London: 1981), pp. 36–37, 146.

9 *Ezekiel*, 34.13–14; cf. Feliks, pp. 144–47.

10 *Haggai*, 1.6.

precariously the just desert of continuing righteous fealty to the absolute omnipotence of a deity entirely transcendent. *Genesis' creatio ex nihilo* articulates a God ontologically removed in unspeakable power and splendour; a conception whose consequence for nature-sensibility is an attitude to the world very different from the Greek: not interrogation and manipulation – 'The world is never objectified as a natural order whose external laws are open to intellectual apprehension'[11] – but obedient custodial diligence, reverence for the Lord's estate, and submissive awe before the universe as prodigy. Hesiodic agricultural generalship and rapacious Homeric periegesis are neither to be expected nor found. In *Job* God answers from the whirlwind to annihilate man's presumptuousness in interrogating the scheme of things:

> Where wast thou when I laid the foundations of the earth?
> Declare, if thou hast understanding.

His mocking catalogue of rhetorical questions –

> Knowest thou the time when the wild goats of the rock bring forth?
> Or canst thou mark when the hinds do calve?
> Canst thou number the months that they fulfil?
> Or knowest thou the time when they bring forth?[12]

– sounds ironically like a borrowing from *The Works and Days* of facts that Hesiod *does* know and has painstakingly tabulated.

Genesis, it has been argued by Auerbach, exhibits priorities precisely contrary to those of Homer: its narrative is mystical, autocratic, elliptical, interior, as opposed to circumstantial, explicative and sense-oriented. Time and place are customarily undefined. The centre of the garden story of *Genesis* 2–3 is not the magic tree, which is enigmatically preserved in sensory indeterminacy, but the human guilt, fear and alienation from God following the disobedience of eating from it.[13] Abraham's journey to the mountain of sacrifice proceeds through a vacuum, 'a silent progress through the indeterminate and contingent ... a blank duration'.[14] Nonetheless, given the multiplicity of authors and periods of composition of the scriptures, with the attendant fluctuation between narrative modes – the mystical austerity of the Pentateuch, for instance, where the Yahwist's concern

11 Bultmann, *Primitive Christianity*, p. 17.
12 *Job*, 38.4; 39.1–2.
13 Joseph E. Duncan, *Milton's Earthly Paradise* (Minnesota: 1972), p. 12, drawing on *The Interpreter's Bible* (New York: 1952), vol. 1, pp. 501–04.
14 Erich Auerbach, *Mimesis*, pp. 9–10.

for place is limited to the naming of sanctuary sites of the fathers still in contemporary use,[15] is at odds with the jubilant empiricisms of much of the Hagiographa, particularly of the so-called 'Poetical Books' of *Psalms, Proverbs* and *Job* – sufficient presentation of creation is given for us to detect the operation of our matrices of perception within distinctively Hebraic narrative values.

Ecological perception

Hebrew sensibility, we have suggested, was theocratic and visionary rather than sense-explorative; 'ecological' perception is as such remote from their genius. The Hebrews made no single important scientific discovery in any field. In technology, their bridges and tunnels were of the most rudimentary kind, and they produced no architecture of their own worthy of mention: the celebrated temple of Solomon was built by Phoenician carpenters and stonemasons. The Hebrews themselves could muster for it no more than an unskilled labour force.[16] The Old Testament makes no direct reference to contemporary science, and its cosmology is of a very unscientific kind. As Frye points out, *Job's* 'He hangeth the earth upon nothing' is characteristic of its mystical priorities.[17] Old Testament cosmology is riddled by contradictions that would have infuriated Greek common sense: Cain is said to build a 'city' at a time when it appears there were only half a dozen people in existence;[18] the two creation sequences in *Genesis* contradict one another; and conflicting estimations are given in *Genesis* both of the duration of the Flood, and the number of pairs of animals Noah took aboard the Ark.[19] The earth and her forms cannot centre committed attention, scientific, technological or speculative, since the Lord in the height of his majesty is a transcendent God, and his kingdom on earth is yet to come.

There is, consequently, little in scriptural ecological perception that is specific to Canaanite topography. In later centuries the Crusaders, lacking the literary percipience of Auerbach, were heartbroken to find, as the climax to months of sweltering in armour through rocky

15 *Genesis,* 12.7–9; 13.4, 18; 26.25; 35.14. See Roland de Vaux, *Ancient Israel: its Life and Institutions,* trans. John McHugh (2nd edn, London: 1965), Book 4, sections 1–2, esp. pp. 289–94.

16 Roland de Vaux, *Ancient Israel,* pp. 312, 328.

17 *Job,* 26.7; Frye, p. 67.

18 *Genesis,* 4.17; Frye, p. 144.

19 G. W. Anderson, *A Critical Introduction to the Old Testament* (1959; rpt. London: 1979), p. 23.

desolations, that the 'land of milk and honey' was a baking mountainous landscape of semi-wilderness.[20] (*Deuteronomy*'s 'a land of brooks of water, of fountains and depths that spring out of valleys and hills' [8.7] was clearly due for allegorical interpretation.) Unsurprisingly in a literature evolving on a torrid land of much mountain and wilderness, the arboreal is sanctuary:

> Hope deferred maketh the heart sick:
> But when the desire cometh, it is a tree of life.

Wisdom is likewise 'a tree of life to them that lay hold upon her'.[21] Water, too, is a delight to meditate, converging almost sensuous frisson upon precept:

> The words of a man's mouth are as deep waters,
> And the wellspring of wisdom as a flowing brook.
>
> Counsel in the heart of a man is like deep water;
> But a man of understanding will draw it out.[22]

Similarly, the beloved oasis as a line of paradise imagery (the righteous man is 'like a tree planted by the rivers of water, / That bringeth forth his fruit in his season'),[23] and the sharp distinction between fresh water and dead, evoke general conditions common to all torrid zones.[24]

An agricultural eye is occasionally in evidence however, and of a characteristically ambivalent confidence. No other religion of the world has taught that even in the perfect state, the 'Golden Age', man ruled over his fellow-creatures.[25] Agricultural dominion, for the Hebrews, is kingly ('thou hast made him a little lower than the angels ... Thou hast put all things under his feet').[26] Claus Westermann has argued persuasively that despite the curse of the Fall at *Genesis* 3.17

20 Maurice Keen, *Pelican History of Medieval Europe* (Harmondsworth: 1969), p. 123. 'Milk and honey': *Deuteronomy*, 11.8–12; *Exodus*, 3.8.

21 *Proverbs*, 13.12; 3.18. Compare *Job*, 29.19, *Hosea*, 14.5–7. For botanical glosses on the species of trees referred to in the Old Testament, see Feliks, *Nature and Man*, chapters 17, 23, 31, 32, 40, 74, 75.

22 *Proverbs*, 18.4; 20.5. Compare, for liquid blisses, *Proverbs*, 11.25; 14.27; 19.12; 25.26; 27.15; *Job*, 29.22–23; *Micah*, 5.7; *Amos*, 5.24.

23 *Psalms*, 1.3.

24 E.g. *Psalms*, 1.3; *Canticles*, 4.12–16; *Job*, 40.21–23. Such imagery overlaps with that of the idealized pastoral life, e.g. *Psalm* 23. Waters: point taken from Northrop Frye, *The Great Code* (London: 1983), pp. 144–47, who refers to *Ezekiel*, 26.19; 47.1–17; *Zechariah*, 14.8; *Joel*, 4.18; *John*, 4.10; *Revelation*, 22.17. Compare Feliks, *Nature and Man*, ch. 43.

25 John Passmore, *Man's Responsibility for Nature* (1974; 2nd edn London: 1980), p. 7.

26 *Psalm* 8.5, 6.

– which is after all removed at *Genesis* 8.21 – labour possesses a kind of supernatural dignity, linked to the divine blessing at *Genesis* 1.28. The *Genesis* garden-story differs from its Sumerian-Babylonian sources insofar as the emphasis on man as 'carrying the yoke of the gods' in a life of drudgery has been excised: 'Man is created not to minister to the gods but to civilize the earth.'[27] The emergence and creativity of human civilization as sketched in *Genesis* 4 – agriculture, the foundation of a city, nomadism and cattle-rearing, metallurgy and the development of music – though it evolves under the shadow cast by Cain's guilt, is thus not regrettable at all. Toil is not the moisture of epigons but the unfolding of God-given fertility in humankind, propelling civilization on to ever wider achievements in its lofty libido. 'For thou shalt be in league with the stones of the field: And the beasts of the field shall be at peace with thee.'[28]

We accordingly recognize in certain parables and Psalms snatches of ecological description. *Isaiah* 5.1–7 describes the steps in construction of a vineyard. The Proverb:

> The King's heart is in the hand of the Lord, as the rivers of water:
> He turneth it whithersoever he will

derives from field irrigation.[29] *Proverbs* 20.4 refers to the need for ploughing fallow fields in winter; and the lines of *Psalms* 65.10

> Thou waterest the furrows thereof abundantly:
> Thou settlest the ridges thereof:
> Thou makest it soft with showers

evoke, argues Feliks, distinctively Palestinian agricultural practice: wherein Israelite farmers ploughed their fields with unusually wide furrows immediately before rain in order to trap rain-water, upon which the ridges would slowly ease back to produce level and well-irrigated fields.[30]

Feliks argues that the Hebrew peasant was actually 'far in advance' of neighbouring peasants in his complex threshing implements;[31] and the Gezer Inscription (a schoolboy's tablet listing annual agricultural occupations) suggests the teaching of agriculture in the time of the Judges.[32]

27 Claus Westermann, *Creation* (Philadelphia: 1974), pp. 50–55.

28 *Job*, 5.23. 29 *Proverbs*, 21.1. Cf. Feliks, *Nature and Man*, ch. 72.

30 Feliks. ch. 59. The Authorized Version appears to have crossed over 'ridges' and 'furrows' by error. Feliks' translation in exchanging them makes better sense.

31 Feliks, *Nature and Man*, p. 93. 32 Ibid., p. 36.

Hebrew attitudes toward the business of cultivation are nonetheless remote from the Hesiodic. Although 150 species of animals and 100 of plants are recorded in the Bible,[33] they are given in unsystematic and clipped fashion, mainly as the matter of similes (the Carob tree, for instance, widespread then as now through Israel, is nowhere recorded). Dependence on the omnipotence of a pre-existent and transcendent deity, as against local and immanent gods of the natural order, produced in the Hebrews a diffident externality to nature that precluded the mastering definition of creation as *φύσις* or system. 'The keeping of Jaweh's covenant meant ... sacrificing the greatest good ancient Near East religion could bestow – the harmonious integration of man's life with the life of nature ... Man remained outside nature, exploiting its first fruits as a sacrifice to Jaweh, using its imagery for the expression of his moods, but never sharing its mysterious life.'[34] Unlike the Egyptian hymns which are their counterpart, Old Testament Psalms are not descriptive but exhortative, calling the hearer to a praise he neglects at his peril. Agricultural prosperity is the highly revocable gift of the Lord, who 'turneth rivers into a wilderness' and 'a fruitful land into barrenness'. Consequently, behind the Psalms 'there is hidden anxiety, whether God will really be praised enough', and an 'unseen hands' attribution of productivity away from blistered human palms toward transcendent dependence: 'Thou visitest the earth, and waterest it: / ... Thou preparest them corn, when thou hast so provided for it.'[35] Fearful visions of dereliction, of cultivation choked and smashed by the invasions of bramble, briar and forest haunt the Prophets:

And I will lay waste her vines and her fig trees ...
and I will make them a forest and the beasts of the fields shall eat them.[36]

Likewise, sudden turbulent winds and crop-destroying rainstorms invade in *Proverbs* and elsewhere.[37] Ecological perception is for good reason secondary to the nervous hymns of the cosmographic.

33 Ibid., pp. x and 149.

34 Henri Frankfort, *Kingship and the Gods* (Chicago: 1948), pp. 342, 344.

35 *Psalms*, 107.33–34; Claus Westermann, *Praise and Lament in the Psalms*, trans. Keith R. Crim and Richard N. Soulen (Edinburgh: 1981), p. 161; *Psalms*, 65.9–10.

36 *Hosea*, 2.14; compare *Isaiah*, 17.9; Feliks, *Nature and Man*, ch. 8.

37 *Proverbs*, 27.15; 28.3; 25.23; *Jonah*, 4.8; *Ecclesiastes*, 11.4; 12.2.

The territorial imagination

Curiously coexistent with its worry over fertility, the Old Testament retains a nostalgia for the pious simplicities of the desert life as against the contaminations of luxurious sedentary civilization. The point introduces us to a brief consideration of Old Testamental landscape-consciousness in terms of its conceptions of the 'domains' of the world: the mapping of the earth into the territorial zones of cultural space, wilds or chaos, and the 'mythic' space of supernatural location.

The nomadic ideal of 'shepherds in the desert' honours the pre-settlement era of the Patriarchs, wanderers led by God. This stage of nature-sensibility lingers on in the imagery of the Promised Land as one of 'milk and honey' (produce of the nomadic life); in the Pentateuch's deity as 'El Shaddai (the wilderness god, of storm, mountain and open country); and the cult of the Rekabites, sworn to abstention from wine (produce of cultivation) and to dwelling only in tents, not houses.[38] The resultant ambivalence towards wilderness is clear in Jeremiah:

> Thus saith the Lord; I remember thee, the kindness of thy youth, the love of thine espousals, when thou wentest after me in the wilderness, in a land that was not sown ...
>
> Where is the Lord that brought us up out of the Land of Egypt, that led us through the wilderness, through a land of deserts and of pits, through a land of drought, and of the shadow of death, through a land that no man passed through, and where no man dwelt? And I brought you into a plentiful country, to eat the fruit thereof and the goodness thereof ...[39]

Life in the desert is the signifier of an existence hallowed by submission to Yahweh; yet fertility is a language of blessing. The wilderness may thus be represented as the haunt of outlaws, demons and wild beasts,[40] yet is also the locus of the blessed time, bridal chamber in Israel's youthful betrothal to Yahweh.[41] Hosea and Zephaniah both prophesied a blessed state of return to the

38 Milk and honey: *Deuteronomy*, 11.8–12; *Exodus*, 3.8; 'El Shaddai literally means 'One of the Mountain': see *Theological Dictionary of the Old Testament*, ed. G. J. Botterweck and H. Ringgren, trans. J. T. Willis (Michigan: 1977), vol. 1, pp. 242ff.; Rekabites: see De Vaux, *Ancient Israel*, pp. 14–15.

39 *Jeremiah*, 2.2–3, 6–7.

40 *Isaiah*, 13.21–22; 34.11–15; *Leviticus*, 16.10, 21–22; *Job*, 30.1–8.

41 *Jeremiah*, 2.2; *Hosea*, 13.5; 2.14.

wilderness;[42] yet Jeremiah, who as a native of Anatot, on the fringes of the Judean desert, had a close knowledge of its realities, imaged the downfall of the nation in terms of the incursion of the desert – which he could see to the east – into the lushness of the cultivated Judean hills – visible to the west. ('They have made my pleasant portion a desolate wilderness ...')[43]

Some explanation of these tensions lies in the fact that the Patriarchs' lifestyle had only ever been *semi*-nomadic: never the true nomads or Bedouin who are camel breeders and can traverse strictly desert regions (i.e. where annual rainfall is less than four inches), the first Patriarchs themselves grazed the borders of settled regions and began to settle: some living in houses, some tents. In consequence they were wary outsiders both to wilderness proper and to wholly sedentary cultivation.[44] Cain's story exemplifies this, for here the farmer finds less favour in God's eyes than the pastoralist (contrary to the versions of the settled Sumerians), yet his punishment for fratricide is the exile of the desert proper.[45]

No wonder, then, that in the course of centuries as the Hebrews dug, ditched and died across Canaan, imagery of the traditional pastoral life (of which *Psalm* 23 is a typically idealizing example) became integrated with the language of vintage and harvest, and the wilderness customarily reduced to propaedeutic to the Promised Land.[46] 'I will make the wilderness a pool of water, and the dry land springs of water. I will plant in the wilderness the cedar, the shittah tree, the myrtle, and the oil tree; I will set in the desert the fir tree, and the pine, and the box tree together.'[47] The crisis of the values of settlement – does cultivation bring decadence and apostasy? Is 'El Shaddai capable of conferring fertility in Canaan? – has been resolved by the time of Hosea (eighth century) at the latest. It is Yaweh, not Baal, who will confer corn, wine and oil;[48] 'The God of the whole earth shall he be called.'[49] The social ideal is now that every man should live 'under his vine and under his fig tree';[50] whilst Isaiah articulates what has been called 'an engineering imagination', with his

42 *Hosea*, 12.10; 2.16; *Zephania*, 2.6–7.

43 *Jeremiah*, 12.10–11; see Feliks, *Nature and Man*, ch. 33.

44 De Vaux, *Ancient Israel*, pp. 3–4.

45 *Genesis*, 4.2–5, 12–17; see De Vaux, ibid., pp. 13–14; compare the fate of Ishmael: *Genesis*, 16.12.

46 *Exodus*, 3.8; *Proverbs*, 8.31; *Psalms*, 107.33–40, 4–5.

47 *Isaiah*, 41.18.

48 *Hosea*, 2.8.

49 *Isaiah*, 44.5.

50 1 *Kings*, 5.5; *Micah*, 4.4; *Zechariah*, 3.10.

command to the Chosen People to 'make straight in the desert a highway for our God', and his anticipation of the time when 'every mountain and hill shall be made low: and the crooked shall be made straight, and the rough places plain'.[51] The life of cultivation and human regimentation has finally triumphed over the submissive wanderings of pastoralism.

Given this typological ambivalence towards wilderness, the topographic zone which establishes itself as the type of chaos, abomination beyond the frontiers of 'cultural space', is that turbulent mystery, the sea. No natural ports broke the unindented coastline of steep cliffs south of Carmel, and so the *mare infidum* remained yet more fearsome for the Israelites than for the seafaring Romans. The sea, like the wilderness, was a trackless chaos (tohu) full of demons and monsters, and it lay lurking just under the world of men and women. George Williams writes well of 'the ancient Semitic feeling for the interconnection of the desert, death and the deep'.[52] Moreover, the Israelites doubtless inherited from the Canaanites the myth of the battle of Ba'al/Yahweh with the sea-monster Yam: inspired by the awesome sight of recurrent electrical storms flashing low over the convulsing Mediterranean. To a nation of potential Jonahs, divine constraint of the sea, commanding it to keep within boundaries ('who shut up the sea with doors ... And said, Hitherto shalt thou come, but no further: / And here shall thy proud waves be stayed?'[53]), and stilling its storms, were a perennial frisson of omnipotence.

> He commandeth, and raiseth the stormy wind,
> Which lifteth up the waves thereof.
> They mount up to the heaven, they go down again to the depth:
> Their soul is melted because of trouble.
> They reel to and fro, and stagger like a drunken man,
> And are at their wit's end.[54]

In typological realization, Christ will still the waves.[55] Perhaps the nation's maritime stupefaction is most poignantly expressed in *Proverbs*:

> There are three things which are too wonderful for me ...
> The way of an eagle in the air;

51 *Isaiah*, 40.3; 40.4. The term is Frye's, p. 161.

52 George H. Williams, *Wilderness and Paradise in Christian Thought* (New York: 1962), pp. 12–29.

53 *Job*, 38.8, 11; See also *Psalms*, 107.29; 104.26; *Job*, 26.8–12; *Proverbs*, 8.29.

54 *Psalms*, 107.25–27.

55 *Matthew*, 8.23–27.

> The way of a serpent upon a rock;
> The way of a ship in the midst of the sea.[56]

Jonah however was rescued by God and Christ cancelled tempests: the most salient aspect of Hebrew territorial imagination is that with monotheism, territoriality is transcended by universalism. In the desert falls God's rain for his wilder creatures; while even on 'the face of the waters' moves the spirit of God.[57]

Hebraic 'myth-space', the landscapes of heaven and hell, as transmitted from the Bible are surprisingly scanty. Hell, of course, was an Iranian rather than Hebrew conception: in the Old Testament the dead live only a shadowy existence in Sheol. Jesus was to talk of an undying worm and unquenched fire, drawing on *Isaiah*,[58] but otherwise the hints[59] of the resurrection of the soul are rare, atypical, speculative and without topographic framework. Similarly heaven does not exist for the Old Testament, although models of the celestial paradise will later extrapolate from the terrestrial. Eden for the Yahwist was less a topographic and material paradise, a felicity whose cause is place, than a pristine state of grace, of 'energy without alienation' in Frye's apt phrase.[60] The Hebrew word 'Eden' meant 'flatland', and was perhaps associated with the Hebrew verb 'to delight'. *Genesis* has only an enclosed garden or park, but with the Septuagint in the third century BC Eden is translated as the Greek word for 'paradise', and thus clothed with connotations of a pleasure garden. (The Vulgate renders a 'paradisum voluptatis'.) It is thus largely from classical literature that heaven and hell acquire their forms and motifs: from Tartarus, Ampsanctus and *Aeneid VI* on the one hand, from the Blessed Isles and the Golden Age on the other.

But the *loci viles* of apocalyptic panorama are purely Biblical. The iconography of proud cities in haunted devastation, peopled by owls and beasts, their palaces overgrown by brambles,[61] may be matched by the melancholic vignettes of the Greek Anthology. The majestic scale of cosmic cataclysm however, may not. *Isaiah*, *Ezra* and *Daniel*, like II *Peter* and *Revelation*, bequeath a morbid titanism of atrocity: stars running out of course, fires breaking from the bowels of the earth, trees dripping blood, stones crying out, corpses of massacred armies

56 *Proverbs*, 30.18–19.
57 *Genesis*, 1.2; *Job*, 38.25–27; *Psalms*, 104.10–11.
58 *Isaiah*, 66.24; *Mark*, 9.43–44.
59 *Ecclesiastes*, 3.21; *Isaiah*, 53.12; 26.19.
60 Frye, p. 76.
61 *Isaiah*, 34.11–15; 13.21–22.

stinking across the earth, the sun turning black and the moon to blood, mountains heaving from their places; and the heavens departing 'as a scroll when it is rolled together'.[62]

The scale of fantasia is distinctively Hebrew: the inverse articulation, perhaps, of that exultant instinct for omnipotence and omnipresence which characterizes, as we shall see, the Bible's cosmographic perception.

Cosmographic perception

To the monotheistic mind locality is footling within the illimitable plenitude of the 'world-sense'. 'All places' are called on to praise the Lord (*Psalm* 103.22), while *Psalm* 104 soars and plummets within the euphoria of scale: '... Who stretchest out the heavens like a curtain: / Who layeth the beams of his chambers in the waters: / Who maketh the clouds his chariot: / Who walketh out upon the wings of the wind ... / Who laid the foundations of the earth,' and parades the teeming of creatures, from conies and birds to the lions and leviathan.[63] But to the exuberant plethora of works and the dazzle of magnitudes no *imago mundi* or definitive model of the world is given. Hebrew thought is not analytic or symbolic in such a way as to produce such a paradigm: concepts of cosmic symbolism did not emerge until long after the destruction of the Temple.[64] It is, I would suggest, precisely this lack of an intelligible frame, a constructional *gnosis*, that gives to the evocation of the Hebrew 'world-sense' its essential character. For the aim, in *Job*, in *Psalms*, is not to achieve that pleasuring comprehension, that diverted equanimity, of narrative action clarified through the details of space which Homeric epic supplies: and which can contribute to Odysseus' sensation that the truest pleasure is to listen after a meal to the ῥαψῳδός.[65] The goal of natural depiction in the Old Testament is not to delight the senses or underwrite intelligibility: far fiercer, it is ethical and religious: it aims to inculcate radical attitudes of fear, submission: pious exaltation of Creation's God of uttermost *terribilità* before whom mountains tremble. This authoritarian mode of presentation of the manifold is thus not one of mastering objectification, as with pictorialism, but is rather an autocratic successivity. Like grapeshot, phenomena are fired at us in

62 IV *Ezra*, 5.4–12; *Isaiah*, 34.2–4; *Daniel*, 7; *Matthew*, 24.15–22; II *Peter*, 3.10; *Revelation*, 6.12–17; 8, 9 passim.

63 *Psalms*, 104.2–3, 5, 24–25.

64 De Vaux, *Ancient Israel*, p. 329.

65 *Odyssey*, 9.1–12.

loose formations at high velocity with intent to subjugate. We buckle under a rapid-fire sequence of prodigies, of overmastering disclosures of divine omnipotence. Nature is registered as ecstatic assault. Tellingly, the abrupt sightings of *Psalm* 104, as hymn, prove closely parallel to *Job* 38 where the intent to chastise and overawe is explicit ('Where wast thou when I laid the foundations of the earth?... Who laid the cornerstone thereof?... Or who shut up the sea with doors?')[66] The world-sense is aggregate not paradigm, totalizing yet pluralized, a plenitude unitary only in dependence on the Creativity beyond human schema.

To even the most cursory reading of Old Testament landscape presentation, the overwhelming ascendency of cosmographic over other matrices of perception is immediately clear. The world focuses almost continuously as divine creation and manifestation.

The Hebrews indeed had no conception of matter as opposed to spirit, specialist scholars tell us.[67] Their relation to the world, we might say, is not the engagement of space but an accommodation to time: to the dialectics of divine favour, the rhythm of exile and deliverance in sacred history. God is a God who will come, the Hebrews are his Chosen People, and the world thus the medium of Revelation in time, an essentially teleological and epiphanic creation, rhythmically alight with the divine. This is hardly surprising, given the formation of Hebrew sensibility through a long history of exile and struggle: the emigration of Abraham from Ur, the Egyptian bondage and desert wanderings, the ensuing protracted warfare to gain security in Canaan, to be succeeded by the Babylonian captivity, and again release. ('Cast me not away from thy presence; / And take not thy holy spirit from me. / Restore me unto the joy of thy salvation.'[68]) The Old Testament 'dreams dreams' of restitution, longs beyond nature's condition of predation and effortfulness: to another nature where man essentially belongs.

> The wolf also shall dwell with the lamb, and the leopard shall lie down with the kid; and the calf and the young lion and the fatling together; and a little child shall lead them... They shall not hurt nor destroy in all my holy mountain: for the earth shall be full of the knowledge of the Lord as the waters cover the sea.[69]

66 *Job*, 38.4–5, 6, 8, 9. Compare *Psalms*, 95.4–6.
67 Bultmann, *Primitive Christianity*, pp. 46–48.
68 *Psalms*, 51.10–12.
69 *Isaiah*, 11.6, 9; cf. likewise *Job*, 40.21–23.

And in that day will I make a covenant for them with the beasts of the field, and with the fowls of heaven, and with the creeping things of the ground: and I will break the bow and the sword and the battle out of the earth, and will make them to lie down safely.[70]

In landscape reference nature is accordingly figured in her positive aspect at those points where she may be displaced upward into sacred history. Nature-feeling may yearn away from the postlapsarian world, into primaeval time –

> When the morning stars sang together,
> And all the sons of God shouted for joy

or end time –

For ye shall go out with joy, and be led forth with peace: the mountains and the hills shall break forth before you into singing, and all the trees of the field shall clap their hands.[71]

The sense of the physical world as natural history is eclipsed by the inspiration of it as sacred history: volatile with divine insurgences, the medium of miracles, deliverances, festivals, national glories and future blessings.

> O God of our salvation …
> Which stilleth the noise of the seas, the noise of their waves,
> And the tumult of the people.
>
> When Israel went out of Egypt …
> The sea saw it, and fled:
> Jordan was driven back.
> The mountains skipped like rams,
> And the little hills like lambs …
> Tremble, thou earth, at the presence of the Lord,
> At the presence of the God of Jacob;
> Which turned the rock into a standing water,
> The flint into a fountain of waters.[72]

Likewise the primacy of history over nature was reflected in the annual feasts, which were transformed from cyclical pastoral and agricultural festivals into historical commemorations.[73] Place means nothing

70 *Hosea*, 2.18. 71 *Job*, 38.7; *Isaiah*, 55.12. compare *Ezekiel*, 47.12; *Joel*, 4.18.

72 *Psalms*, 65.5, 7; 114.1, 3–4, 7–8. Cf. 18.6–19; 66.5–6; 105.27–45, 78.13–54; 97.3–5; *Nahum*, 1.3–6.

73 De Vaux, *Ancient Israel*, Book 4, sections 17–18.

without the impress of momentous occasion: hence the praise of sacred mountains such as Sion, and the abundant catalogue of sactuaries in the Pentateuch.[74] Hence, too, the delight in a topography of election: the parted Red Sea, the pillar of fire in the desert: the Lord of Creation most clearly disclosed as the Lord of History. Nature only valuably exists on the plane of Bethel, not as locale but as teleological trace. 'He looketh on the earth, and it trembleth: / He toucheth the hills, and they smoke ...'

Nature as sanctified and transfigured, updrawn from customary obliquity as postlapsarian contingence by the ecstatic moments of God's returns in time, is recurrent in harvest harmonies. 'Thou crownest the year with thy goodness; / And thy paths drop fatness ... / The pastures are clothed with flocks; / The valleys also are covered over with corn ...'[75] The *Psalms* well illustrate these Old Testament priorities, for in them 'descriptive' Psalms are rooted in 'declarative' ones.[76] A small body of Psalms evolve whose descriptive concern is marked:[77]

> He sendeth the springs into the valleys,
> Which run among the hills.
> They give drink to every beast of the field:
> The wild asses quench their thirst.
> By them shall the fowls of the heaven have their habitation,
> Which sing among the branches ...
> He causeth the grass to grow for the cattle,
> And herb for the service of man ...
> The high hills are a refuge for the wild goats;
> And the rocks for the conies.[78]

These Psalms, nonetheless, manifestly unfold description in the context of praise ('O Lord, how manifold are thy works! / In wisdom hast thou made them all'[79]), and, deriving from 'declarative' tradition wherein specific instances of God's saving action are commemorated, they simply constitute the expansion of one motif – God's majesty in creation – into independent Psalms.

Such 'descriptive' values, furthermore, are, as we shall see, far from pictorial.

74 Cf. ibid., sections 1–2, esp. pp. 289–94.

75 *Psalms*, 104.31–32; 65.12–13.

76 Cf. Westermann, *Creation*, pp. 32, 116–42, 152–55.

77 The 'Descriptive' Psalms are 8, 19, 29, 104, 139, 148; discussed by Westermann, p. 139.

78 *Psalms*, 104.10–12, 14, 18.

79 Ibid., verse 24.

Technoptic perception

Quite logically, the Old Testament shows comparatively little technoptic perception. The creation itself is not τέχνη, for the Hebrews did not share the Greek's supreme valuation of craftsmanship; and following the interdiction of graven images (*Exodus* 20.4), ancient Israel did not possess pictorial art. This is not to deny the pervasive influence of Near-Eastern habits of perception and art on Old Testament writings: *Canticles*, for example, has been linked with Theocritus' *Idylls*, as well as Syrian marriage songs and attenuations of the Adonis cult;[80] and *Psalm* 104 is ultimately descended from the Egyptian *Hymn to Aten*, of c. 1380 BC.[81] The *Psalms*, nonetheless, are not pictorial like their Egyptian counterparts, which are often 'quite clearly the descriptive praise of an onlooker.'[82]

Thou beautiful sun with glowing light ... thou splendid sun with white light ... Thou awakest in beauty ... thou child of flame with sparkling beams ... Thou makest green, thou makest green, O Nile, thou makest green ...[83]

However, 'our understanding [of the beautiful] is strongly coloured by the Greek understanding where the beautiful is primarily a being. In the Old Testament the beautiful is primarily an event; the proper approach to the beautiful is in this context not the beholding of something which is there, an image or perhaps a statue, but the encounter ... This is true both in regard to man and in regard to what has been created ... all art was realized in vocal art and in the art of speech.'[84] Man's vital relation to nature, and his vital relation of nature, is accordingly one of praise: a relation of song.

80 M. Rosler, *Commentationes de Antiquitate Classica*, 1 (1954), pp. 33–48 argues for the influence of the *Bucolics*; Moses Hadas, in *J.H.I.* 19 (1958), 5, retorts that it is more probable that Alexandrian lyric poetry is itself dependent on oriental models, such as Egyptian. For this debate, cf. Martin Hengel, *Judaism and Hellenism* (London: 1974), vol. 2, p. 74, note 16. For the tracing of motifs in common to *Canticles* and earlier literature, cf. T. H. Gaster, *Myth, Legend and Custom in the Old Testament* (New York: 1969), pp. 808 ff, section 331.

81 Printed in J. B. Pritchard, *Ancient Near Eastern Texts*, pp. 369 f. Cf. *Psalm* 104, cf. R. J. Williams, *The Hymn to Aten*, in D. Winton Thomas, ed. *Documents from Old Testament Times* (New York: 1961), pp. 142–50.

82 Claus Westermann, *Praise and Lament in the Psalms*, trans. Keith R. Crim and Richard N. Soulen (Edinburgh: 1981), p. 48.

83 From *Die Literatur der alten Agypter* (Leipzig: 1923) ed. A. Erman, pp. 374–75, 193; trans. by Westermann, *Praise and Lament in the Psalms*, p. 48.

84 Westermann, *Creation*, p. 63.

> Where wast thou when I laid the foundations of the earth?...
> When the morning stars sang together,
> And all the sons of God shouted for joy?...
>
> The voice of the Lord is upon the waters:
> The God of glory thundereth...
> The voice of the Lord is powerful;
> The voice of the Lord is full of majesty.
> The voice of the Lord breaketh the cedars.
>
> Praise him in the heights...
> Praise him ye sun and moon:
> Praise him all ye stars of light.
> Praise him ye heavens of heavens,
> And ye waters that be above the heavens.
>
> Make a joyful noise before the Lord, the King.
> Let the sea roar, and the fulness thereof;
> The world, and they that dwell therein.
> Let the floods clap their hands;
> Let the hills be joyful together... [85]

Creation is called into being by voice; Adam realized his power over the animals in giving them their names, as God calls the stars by theirs.[86] Again, the telling contrast is with the Greeks, for voice, rhythm and epiphany stand in for pictorialism and categorization. For the Hebrews, to 'freeze' nature into a pictorial composition as a 'landscape' would be to empty it of its essential significance as the platform of an ancient and continuing divine drama, as endlessly, preciously transfigurable. The concept of an 'intelligible', optically mimicked, fathomed landskip would have seemed to the Hebrews a blasphemous dehydration of creation, an unenlightened reductivism to mere 'latent' space. Rather, they evoke the dynamized, numinous realm into which God drives down: place as astoundingly immediate with deity, space overmastered by time, bonding God and his faithful together in history. We may compare Milton, where the sense of the liveness of God in creation, the dynamic landscapes of personification, strenuous verbs and mountains dancing is produced precisely by the primacy of historical time over mere space: the excitation of Milton's

85 *Job*, 38.4, 7; *Psalms*, 29.3–5; 148.1, 3–4; 98.6–8. Compare *Psalms*, 19.1–3; 104.7; 65.12–13; 66.1; 96.11–12; *Deuteronomy*, 32.2; *Isaiah*, 55.12; 44.23.

86 *Genesis*, 2.19–20; *Psalms*, 147.4.

landscape is *millenarian.* The external world is a medium of confrontation, a voice, and God is 'heard' not seen: to see God would be to die.[87] Instead the relation is audition, and epiphanies of song:

> Give ear, O ye heavens, and I will speak;
> And hear, O earth, the words of my mouth.
> My doctrine shall drop as the rain,
> My speech shall distil as the dew,
> As the small rain upon the tender herb,
> And as the showers upon the grass.
>
> The pastures are clothed with flocks;
> The valleys also are covered over with corn;
> They shout for joy, they also sing.
>
> And it shall come to pass in that day, I will hear, saith the Lord, I will hear the heavens, and they shall hear the earth; and the earth shall hear the corn, and the wine, and the oil; and they shall hear Jezreel.[88]

The jubilant energy of nature, like Wisdom, breaks into primal song, *ludens in orbe terrarum,*[89] as the Vulgate has it. God is not the divine geometer, but the transcendental Larynx, the Logos.

Analogical perception

Characteristically in the Old Testament, the comparative instinct in nature-consciousness polarizes experience, casts the world into a dualistic typology. Thus we often find idealized images with demonic counterparts: in Eden there is a Tree of Life, and a forbidden tree; the beauteous trees of God's garden are counterpointed by the short-lived giants of *Ezekiel* and *Daniel.*[90] Likewise the sea, symbol of chaos constrained at the creation, and drowner of Jonah, is agent of righteous destruction in the Deluge and in the drowning of the Egyptians crossing the Red Sea. Given the character of Judaism and Christianity as historically linear religions of prophecy and fulfilment, the New Testament regularly takes up the Old to match type with anti-type. The Deluge and the Red Sea crossing are thus taken as types of the baptism, where a symbolically new shore is reached by the

87 *Micah,* 6,8; *Judges,* 13.22; 6.22; *John,* 1.18.

88 *Deuteronomy,* 32.1–2; *Psalms,* 65.13; *Hosea,* 2.21–22.

89 *Proverbs,* 8.31.

90 *Ezekiel,* 31.1–18; *Daniel,* 4.10–27. Compare also the joy in 'the arboreal as sanctuary', discussed above, as against the fear of forest as encroaching on cultivated land in times of recession.

righteous.[91] Just as in the Old Testament the Promised Land became the type of the restored Israel, so in the New Testament Eden, the primitive home, becomes a type of the celestial paradise, and the imagery of a dramatically restored Israel the iconography of apocalypse.[92] Ezekiel's vision of a valley of dry bones springing into life is taken as a type of the resurrection.[93]

It is true that, foreshadowing Medieval pastoral poetry, landscape is occasionally drawn on for veiled political allegory, and sketched in some rhetorical fullness. Assyria is compared to a topmost cedar of Lebanon, prodigiously tall, washed about by rivers, rich in shadowy foliage, roost of all the fowls of heaven, even the envy of the trees of Eden. Naturally it is hacked down at the word of the Lord, and its boughs are shattered, washed away in rivers, outflung limbs inhabited now by the beasts of the field.[94]

But commoner far than such elaborated allegorizing, with its misleading hint of descriptive and sensuous inclinations, are the ubiquitous, clipped similes drawn from pasturage and cultivation. After *Psalms*, it is in *Proverbs* and *Job* that environment most often focuses, and it is disclosed with mnemonic brevity in didactic starkness. 'A continual dropping in a very rainy day / And a contentious woman are alike.' 'Whoso boasteth himself of a false gift / Is like clouds and wind without rain.'[95] Where any experience is defined by landscape simile it is rudimentary in emotional texture.

Superlatively anomalous is the 'Song of Songs'. Scholarship has hazed this brilliant poetic star into a constellation of foreign influences, to which Heisenberg's Uncertainty Principle clearly applies, and there is no question that its vocabulary is highly individual. In content too, it is something of a mystery as to how it achieved canonical status. The novelty as regards its landscape imagery resides in a relation to

91 Deluge: *Genesis* 7–8 and I *Peter*, 3.21; Red Sea crossing: *Exodus* 14 and I *Corinthians*, 10.2. Cf. also water as a blessing (*Genesis* 8.22; *Psalms* 1.3, 74.17; *Jeremiah* 17.8; *Isaiah* 58.11) as contrastive with the peril of flood: *Job* 6.15, 18; *Psalms* 69, 2–3, 16.

92 Common to *Eden* and the *Celestial Paradise* are: the running river (*Genesis* 2.10, *Ezekiel* 31.4 for Eden, and *Revelation* 7.17 and 22.1 for Heaven); fruitful tree (*Genesis* 2.9, *Ezekiel* 31.8 for Eden, and *Revelation* 22.2 for Heaven); and precious stones (*Genesis* 2.11–12, *Ezekiel* 28.13, *Revelation* 21.18–21). Matthew's Apocalypse at 24.15 echoes *Daniel* 9.27 explicitly, whilst *Revelation* 6.13–14 takes from *Isaiah* 34.4 the falling planets and the heavens rolling up as a scroll.

93 *Ezekiel*, 37.1–14. 94 *Ezekiel*, 31.2–18. Cf. the imitation in *Daniel*, 4.10–27.

95 *Proverbs*, 27.15; 25.14.

nature which is consistently sensuous, strikingly imaginative, and which approaches Theocritean habits of perception in the rendition of sense as 'mood-music'. Ascending levels of sensory excitation and imaginative receptivity operate within it. The lover as an apple-tree, sweet in shade and fruit, is of familiar agricultural provenance,[96] but the association of love with the awakening of spring and the blood's call to the pair to wander together abroad is redolent of pagan religious rites and a primordial nature mythology, usually absent from the ethically austere and inward Old Testament.

> Rise up, my love, my fair one, and come away.
> For lo, the winter is past,
> The rain is over and gone;
> The flowers appear on the earth;
> The time of the singing of birds is come,
> And the voice of the turtle is heard in our land;
> The fig-tree putteth forth her green figs,
> And the vines with the tender grape
> Give a good smell.
>
> Arise, my love, my fair one, and come away.[97]

With 'thine eyes [are] like the fishpools of Hebron' we enter onto a Theocritean ground of metaphoricity in delicate empiric atmospherics (compare the nymph in *Idyll* 13 with 'springtime eyes').[98] Similitudes of the exquisite, and rarefied correspondences, likewise include the cheeks like a bed of spices (5.13), breasts and lips like lilies (5.15, 4.5), and the belly like an heap of wheat (7.2). But the *tour de force* is the reverie of the *hortus conclusus*:

> A garden inclosed is my sister, my spouse;
> A spring shut up, a fountain sealed.
> Thy plants are an orchard of pomegranates, with pleasant fruits;
> Camphire, with spikenard,
> Spikenard and saffron;
> Calamus and cinnamon, with all trees of frankincense;
> Myrrh and aloes, with all the chief spices:
> A fountain of gardens,
> A well of living waters,
> And streams from Lebanon.
>
> Awake, O north wind; and come, thou south;
> Blow upon my garden, that the spices thereof may flow out.[99]

96 *Canticles*, 2.3; compare *Ezekiel*, 15.1–8. 97 *Canticles*, 2.10–13.
98 *Idylls*, 13.45. 99 *Canticles*, 4.12–16.

From here, landscape dissolves into fantasia, where we deliquesce upon mountains of myrrh and hills of spices (8.14, 4.6). Roes come leaping to feed among soft lilies all night, in a nectarine topography of rhapsodic sexual liquefaction. Locks are filled with dew (5.2), lilies drop myrrh (5.13), living fountains gush (4.15), spices flow out on the breeze (4.16), grape-clusters are seized (7.7–8) and many floods cannot quench love (8.7). Aromatic Hellenism now perfumes the Hebraic bosom, it appears. *Semel insanivimus omnes.*[100]

Composition of the poem is usually dated to the third or second century BC, but is seen as being rooted in older and foreign religious or erotic hymn or ritual. Greek and Persian loan-words, and frequent scholarly suggestions of Syrian or other Near-Eastern models, such as hymns in the cult of Ishtar, confirm that its poetics correspond to the sensibility of a society very different from that of rural Israel. The frame of perceptual subjectivity, the deployment of natural images as a notation of delicate interiority, an exquisite tonal vocabulary, belong with the nature-feeling of a sophisticated metropolitan culture, emancipated and distanced from 'ecological' and religious apprehension of nature: precisely the liberated metaphoricity of landscape, hypersensuous and poignant, that we found in the 'bucolic' poetry of Theocritus at the court of Alexandria.

The New Testament

The narrative values of the New Testament are further removed from sense-engagement than even those of the Old. The Parousia (Second Coming) is imminent, the heavens about to depart as a scroll when rolled together, and humanity must be snatched from its evils at this farthermost edge of time. Landscape description is clearly the last art to be commissioned by 'the Congregation at the end of days.'[101] The Gospels are urgent, concentrated kerygma; the epistles are deeply occasional in character, bulletins of arbitration or exhortation. Meditations on Creation, and Psalmist's effusions have no place in the stringent communiqués of the dying aeon. The imbecility of attending in these times to nature's appearances whilst not to the spiritual climate is made clear. 'When it is evening, ye say, It will be fair weather: for the sky is red. And in the morning, It will be foul weather

100 'We all have been crazed once.' (Roman proverb.)

101 Phrase from Rudolf Bultmann, *Theology of the New Testament* (London: 1954), 1, p. 37.

today: for the sky is red and lowering. O ye hypocrites, ye can discern the face of the sky; but can ye not discern the signs of the times?'[102] Moreover, 'There is not a single book in the New Testament which is the direct work of an eyewitness of the historical Jesus':[103] and, therefore, never the colours of personal memory to tempt to particularity and scene. The giddy panorama of Christ's mountain-top Temptation, where reach out 'all the kingdoms of the world, and the glory of them' will be lavishly pictorialized by Milton in *Paradise Regained*, but remain for the Synoptics in Stygian unillumination.[104] Likewise the Storm at Sea, a favourite theme of the Greco-Roman rhapsode (the *Aeneid* opens with Epic's great chords of maritime terror) is instantly rendered featurelessly placid by Christ and evangelist alike.[105]

Even such meagre circumstantiality as does dot the Gospels in the form of bare place-names and itineraries is misleading. As '*Formgeschichte*' (form-history) has revealed in our century, settings are actually invented, as 'typical', constructed out of the Church's 'generalized memory' and chosen as apposite to the 'saying' which they carry.[106] Settings and stories alike are subordinate to the passion narrative – the gospels have been well described as 'passion narratives with extended introductions'[107] – for the evangelists seek to differentiate Christ as thaumaturge from other Hellenistic wonder-workers by linking his miracles to the kerygma (missionary preaching) of passion and resurrection. Emphasis is, therefore, not on the winning human individuality of Jesus, favoured by nineteenth-century homiletics but upon his supernaturalism, affirmed by miracle and resurrection, which inaugurates the process that will end the world.[108] Narrative intention thus sets Christ down in a light terrestrial biography, cancels place beyond artificial itineraries, only to withdraw him again into the clouds of the other-worldly, and impress on its receivers the doom of this earth. The 'kerygma of the cross' is stringently vertical.

The effect of such values on the territorial imagination is emphatic.

102 *Matthew*, 16.3. Compare *Luke*, 12.54–56.
103 R. H. Fuller, *A Critical Introduction to the New Testament* (London: 1971), p. 197.
104 *Matthew*, 4.8; *Paradise Regained*, 3.251–345; cf. 4.541–61.
105 *Mark*, 4.37.
106 Fuller, pp. 108–11.
107 M. Kahler, *The So-Called Historical Jesus and the Historic Biblical Christ* (1892; rpt. London: 1964), p. 80.
108 Bultmann, *Primitive Christianity*, pp. 195–201; compare E. R. Dodds, *Pagan and Christian* (Cambridge: 1965), p. 119.

The Old Testamental tensions between patriarchal pasturage and sedentary culture, between the Promised Land and its gentile aggressors, have disappeared. Mark, it has been suggested, is more interested than the other synoptists in wilderness, hillside and lake, recounting two miraculous mass-feedings in the desert, and this emphasis perhaps reflects an antipathy to the cultus of the temple and synagogues, Mark favouring the assembly of prospective converts in remote outdoor retreats.[109] Yet even in *Mark*, the world is now seen essentially *sub specie aeternitatis*, and the significance of terrestrial boundaries abolished. In its place is the vaster, cosmic polarization of sublunar world and the New Kingdom, the lifestyle of sin and the regenerate life. The world is the realm of Satan, 'the god of this world',[110] and creation subject to vanity and corruption.[111] Demonic powers rule over the earth,[112] and Christ sees himself locked into cosmic warfare against myriad devils and their leader: 'I beheld Satan as lightning fall from heaven.'[113] All Creation is in travail and groaning for deliverance,[114] and Christians know that they are 'strangers and pilgrims' on this alien earth, their 'citizenship' being in heaven.[115] 'Lay up treasure in heaven'[116] exhorts Christ; for soon there will be a new heavens and a new earth.[117] Old Testament apocalyptic builds to a crescendo of reiteration,[118] as men, in Pauline adumbration of Greek dualism, are urged not to be 'carnally minded' but 'led by the Spirit'.[119] In this sense of 'the withdrawal of divinity from the material world', of paths as ambushed by demons and physicality as the soul's bondage, Christianity partakes of a 'crisis sensibility' common to Gnosticism and the mystery-religions.[120] But God's transcendence is not conceived ontologically for the Christian, as in Gnosticism:[121] divine grace frees the regenerate soul from mortal terrors, and the world then recovers its aspect of Creation. 'Every creature of God is good, and nothing to be refused, if it be received with thanksgiving: for it is sanctified by the word of God and

109 See George H. Williams, *Wilderness and Paradise*, p. 24.
110 2 *Corinthians*, 4.4; *John*, 12.27.
111 *Romans*, 8.19–22.
112 *Galatians*, 4.3, 4.9. Cf. also E. R. Dodds, *Pagan and Christian*, ch. 1 passim, esp. pp. 16–17.
113 *Luke*, 10.18.
114 *Romans*, 8.19, 8.22.
115 I *Peter*, 2.11; *Philippians*, 3.20.
116 *Luke*, 12.33; *Matthew*, 6.19–21.
117 2 *Peter*, 3.13; *Revelation*, 21.1.
118 *Matthew*, 24.3–43; *Luke*, 21.5–28; *Revelation*, passim; 2 *Peter*, 3.10.
119 *Romans*, 8.1, 8.6.
120 Cf. E. R. Dodds, *Pagan and Christian*, p. 37.
121 Bultmann, *Primitive Christianity*, pp. 189–95, 206–07.

prayer.'[122] The Christian accordingly inhabits the world in 'a dialectic of participation and inward detachment':[123] perhaps mildly ascetic[124] but appreciative, theoretically at least, that 'the earth is the Lord's, and the fullness thereof'.[125]

Commensurate with the Gospels' dissolution of the ancient territorial imagination – *oikoumene* and barbarism, cultivation and wilderness – is its evangelical internationalism. The concepts of 'citizenship of the world', of the irrelevance of geography in the face of cosmic conditions, of rain and sun falling on good and bad alike throughout the world, Christianity shares with Stoicism;[126] its proselytizing vehemence is its own. The Church acts on its universalist statements to throw out missions 'to the uttermost part of the earth'.[127] The New Testament takes the bulk of the Eastern Empire for its narrative setting, from Palestine to Rome, its founder and apostles conspicuously peripatetic. A religion of grace, it is for two centuries decentralized, the outward Temple at Jerusalem ambiguously snubbed by Christ[128] and its doom firmly prophesied. Christ himself conducted his mission in backward, poor and racially mixed Galilee far more than in Judea, and Paul broke decisively with the 're-Judaizing' Jerusalem Church, to found communities across the Greek-speaking world that were far more liberal in their attitudes to Jewish law and its sacred place.[129] Christianity is thus from very early on an urban religion, spreading through a cosmopolitan empire, its success ascribed sometimes in large degree to its appeal to the urban exiled through its unusually full community care.

In the light of this transportation of religion from the Old Testament rural world to an urban one, and the bursting of the boundaries of a nationalistic 'Promised Land', it is not hard, I think, to see why New Testament references to paradise are weaned off both the Restored Israel, and the traditional idealized pastoral of oasis and luxuriant tree-scape. Eschatology tends instead to the Celestial City,

122 I *Timothy*, 4.4; *Romans*, 14.14.

123 Bultmann, p. 207.

124 Cf. Dodds, pp. 29–36; cf. I *Corinthians*, 7; *Matthew*, 19.12.

125 I *Corinthians*, 10.26.

126 For an outline of these ideas and their *loci classici*, cf. C. Fitter, 'Native Soil', in *Milton Studies* xx, 1984. For links specifically between St Paul and Seneca, cf. J. N. Sevenster, *Paul and Seneca* (Leiden, 1961).

127 *Acts*, 1.8.

128 For a recent and thorough discussion of scholarly interpretation of Christ's attitudes toward the Temple, and thereby Judaism, cf. E. P. Sanders, *Jesus and Judaism* (London: 1985), chs. 1, 2.

129 Fuller, *New Testament*, pp. 26–30.

or reaches beyond this doomed globe altogether into the clouds. Great mystery prevails as to the character of 'the New Kingdom'[130] with its limited set of analogies to the social order (the imagery of banqueting, and the assignation of places)[131]. John, however, anticipates 'many mansions', and *Revelation* resumes the motif of fabulous architecture from *Ezekiel,* enlarging on the bejewelled brilliance, huge extent, great walls and many gates of the holy city.[132] Paul suggests a redemption 'in the air': 'For the Lord himself shall descend from heaven with a shout, with the voice of the archangel, and with the trump of God: and the dead in Christ shall rise first: then we which are alive and remain shall be caught up together with them in the clouds, to meet the Lord in the air: and so shall we ever be with the Lord.'[133] The Gospels likewise, suggest the gathering of the Elect on the four winds.[134] The hope for a completely new and higher kingdom rather than simply a 'corrected' social order surely derives not just from Christ's putative, but from the Apostolic Church's actual transportation far beyond the physical terrain of Judah. A multinational, multilingual and scattered Church, populous with exiles, hungers for a new plane entirely, an ecumenical heartland, on the far side of the clouds from disunity and diaspora. Paradise is no longer assimilable to terrestrial geography.

There does emerge, however, one interesting opposition in the presentation of the external world which suggests, I think, a persisting Hebraic inflection of territorial imagination in the New Testament: and that is the opposition, probably entirely unconscious, between the rural fertilities of the Gospel parables and the urban adversities of *Acts*.

Despite the aspiring and actualized universalism of the Church, the exalted 'world-sense' and celebration of plenitude recurrent through the Old Testament are conspicuously absent. Paul has declared that 'the invisible things of [God] from the creation of the world are clearly seen, being understood by the things that are made, even his eternal power and Godhead'. The infinity of the Creator manifest and living in nature is again asserted on the Areopagus. 'God that made the world and all things therein, seeing that he is Lord of heaven and earth, dwelleth not in temples made with hands ... seeing he giveth to all life,

130 *Acts,* 1.6–7; I *Corinthians,* 2.9; 2 *Corinthians,* 12.3–4; cf. Sanders, *Jesus and Judaism,* ch. 8.

131 *Matthew,* 8.11, 20.21; *Luke,* 13.28 f; *Mark,* 10.37, 14.25.

132 *John,* 14.2; *Revelation,* 21 passim, 22.1–3.

133 1 *Thessalonians,* 4.15–17.

134 *Matthew,* 24.31; *Mark,* 13.27.

and breath, and all things; and hath made of one blood every one of us: for in him we live, and move, and have our being; as certain also of your own poets have said.'[135] Yet these brusque rudiments are designated rather as a rebuttal of polytheism than as praise or evocation of nature and her great scale. More typical is the uncolouring perspective of the devaluative Parousia: 'For the earnest expectation of the creature waiteth for the manifestation of the Son of God ... For we know that the whole creation groaneth and travaileth in pain together until now.'[136] Sublunar thraldom effaces deiform grandeur.

Dispatching his disciples, Christ had warned 'beware of men: for they will deliver you up to the councils, and they will scourge you in their synagogues; and ye shall be brought before governors and kings for my sake, for a testimony against them and the Gentiles'. Paul's 'glories' confirm the prediction:

> Thrice was I beaten with rods, once was I stoned, thrice I suffered shipwreck, a night and a day I have been in the deep; in journeyings often, in perils of waters, in perils of robbers, in perils by mine own countrymen, in perils by the heathen, in perils in the city, in perils in the wilderness, in perils in the sea, in perils among false brethren; in weariness and painfulness, in watching often, in hunger and thirst, in fastings often, in cold and nakedness.'[137]

The general impression drawn from *Acts* is one of the grimness of a race set against geography, perilous and vast, rather than of harmony with God's nature or elation in the magnitude of his handiwork. Its record is a kind of 'anti-Odyssey': its proud itinerary of cities and countries void of sensory or documentary interests, its *frisson* unflagging purposiveness as against the self-validating explorativeness of Homer, its battlings through the 'uttermost part of the earth' revealing in angular invincibility only that the mission is 'everywhere spoken against' and converts won hardly.[138]

The urban experience of *Acts*, I would argue, is thus a framework of adversity: angry mobs in temple and forum, stonings, lashings, imprisonments, escape by basket down outer walls. It is a world imaged in terms of hostility and recalcitrance—where authority is unsympathetic and the Christian swallowed up by the throng. All this contrasts markedly with the rural experiences of the Gospels, where Christ himself is thaumaturgic authority, crowds mainly adulatory or eager to hear (the significant exception is again urban: the Jerusalem

135 *Romans*, 1.20; *Acts*, 17.24–28. 136 *Romans*, 8.19, 22.
137 *Matthew*, 10.17–18; *II Corinthians*, 11.25–27. 138 *Acts*, 1.8, 28.22.

mob spurning Christ for Barabbas), and the imagery of agricultural labour connotes blessed rhythms of fruition, environmental command. Scant though natural references are in the New Testament, and wholly devoid of the explicitly enunciated contrast between country and city so familiar in contemporary Greco-Roman writing, the adumbrations are heavily weighted against the world of the city. We may contrast too the grief or disturbance of nature at Christ's death: the earth quaking, rocks rent, sun losing light and darkness covering the land.[139]

To cultivate the land in the countryside, however, is to enact the essentials of the holy life: to labour in acknowledgement of divine dependence, and to receive from nature God's favour. 'So is the kingdom of God, as if a man should cast seed into the ground; and should sleep, and rise night and day, and the seed should spring and grow up, he knoweth not how ... But when the corn is brought forth, immediately he putteth in the sickle, because the harvest is come.'[140] The Gospels compact a plethora of images, drawn from country life as a world of work, to figure the regenerate life. Nonetheless, a sharp contrast exists with the idealizing tone, the sacro-idyllic delicacies of much contemporary Greco-Roman poetry, which derive, I suggest, at least in part from the fact that for the latter culture rural labour was normally stigmatized by association with the slave labour that preponderated in the countryside.[141] In Palestine this stigma is absent, since slavery there remained across the centuries both smaller in scale and less abject in condition.[142]

Now he that planteth and he that watereth are one: and every man shall receive his own reward according to his own labour. For we are labourers together with God: ye are God's husbandry, ye are God's building.[143]

The labourers in the harvest, the fishermen, the good shepherd, the fortunes of the sower and the vineyard owner, grafting and axing fruit

139 *Matthew*, 27.51; *Mark*, 15.33; *Luke*, 23.45. 140 *Mark*, 4.27–29.

141 Cf. Perry Anderson, *Passages from Antiquity to Feudalism* (London: 1978), part one, p. 24.

142 The census of the Israelite community on its return from the Exile (sixth century) records 7,337 slaves as compared with 42,360 free persons; in contrast the slave labour-force in fifth century Athens has been situated in the region of 80–100,000 as against 45,000 citizens. (De Vaux, *Ancient Israel*, p. 84; Anderson, *Passages*, p. 22.) Moreover the slave in Palestine, far from being degraded to an *instrumentum genus vocale* tended to form part of the family, sharing sacrificial meals, resting on the sabbath, and being submitted to circumcision. He could even succeed to his master's inheritance in the absence of heirs. (De Vaux, pp. 80–90.) 143 I *Corinthians*, 3.7–9.

trees, the yoke and the net, and less commonly, the figure of the ploughman,[144] become the enduring typology of Christian writings.

Countryside in the Gospels is far from comprising idyllic fields of rewarded righteousness however. I would argue that precisely because they *are* deployed as the circumstances of graphic parable in the age of apocalypse—the vocabulary of reversed fortune and final things—the procedures of rural experience are sharply ambiguous. The country world, with its grazing flocks and caring pastor, its chicks secure under maternal wings[145] is simultaneously a terrain of violence, perversity and precarious fertility, of remorseless terminal divisions undoubtably reflecting Christ's own fierce moral dualism. At times Christ's version of the countryside has an almost Marvellian instinct for polarized possibilities. Thus the sower's seeds may fall on stony and thorny ground equally with soil, trees may bring forth corrupt fruit or sound, labourers in the vineyard may labour well for their master or kill his messenger.[146] Sudden irresistible segregation or destruction is dealt out to phenomena by man, as by God to men in judgement: 'And now also the axe is laid unto the root of the trees: therefore every tree which bringeth not forth good fruit is hewn down, and cast into the fire.'[147] The offending fig-tree is decisively cursed.[148] Wheat is gathered into the garner but the chaff is burned 'with fire unquenchable'; the sheep are divided off from the goats; for 'Is it not lawful for me to do what I will with mine own?'[149] This is the realm of sudden interventionism: 'Then shall two be in the field; the one shall be taken, and the other left. Two women shall be grinding at the mill; the one shall be taken, and the other left.'[150] The grass of the field, 'clothed' by God 'today is, and tomorrow is cast in the oven'. Suddenly possessed whilst grazing, the Gadarene swine 'ran violently down a steep place into the sea ... and were choked in the sea'.[151] Yet nature is also a scheme of well-appointed harmonies, man's relation to

144 *Luke*, 9.62. Cf. also Old Testament heritage: e.g. 'good shepherd' of *Psalm* 80.2 and 23.1; and *Isaiah*, 40.11. Cf. A. Low, *The Georgic Revolution* (Princeton: 1985), pp. 157–67; also Barbara Lewalski, *Protestant Poetics and the Seventeenth Century Religious Lyric* (Princeton: 1979), pp. 96–99, for the legacy of Biblical imagery of shepherding and husbandry in its importance for later poets.

145 *Matthew*, 15.24, 18.12, 25.33; *Mark*, 23.38.

146 *Mark*, 4.14–20; *Matthew*, 7.17–18, 20.1–16, 21.33–42.

147 *Matthew*, 3.10. Cf. likewise the Old Testament agriculture of judgement and wrath: *Jeremiah*, 1.10; *Job*, 19.10.

148 *Matthew*, 21.18–20.

149 *Matthew*, 3.10, 7.17; *Luke*, 3.9, 3.17–18; *Matthew*, 25.33, 20.15.

150 *Matthew*, 24.40–41.

151 *Matthew*, 6.30, 8.32; *Mark*, 5.13.

which is highly ironic: 'Behold the fowls of the air: for they sow not, neither do they reap, nor gather into barns; yet your heavenly Father feedeth them ...' The lilies, not a spinner amongst them, outdazzle Solomon in all his glory. Similarly, 'the foxes have holes, and the birds of the air have nests; but the Son of man hath not where to lay his head'.[152]

In contrast to the tendency toward aureate landscapes of his contemporary Virgil, Christ's awareness of the life of the fields is thus sharply ironic, and morally propelled toward dramas of life and death. If kerygma and apocalypse largely expel landscape from the New Testament, they likewise structure what rurality does enter. 'For these be the days of vengeance, that all things which are written may be fulfilled.'[153]

Summary

We have argued that Hebraic nature-sensibility, in its ambiguous strains—of domination and abasement, of Fall and civilizing dynamic, of ambivalence towards desert and agriculture alike—is mediated from the ambiguities both of the Hebrews' location, as petty conquerors in the corridor between imperialist superpowers, and of their evolution from semi-nomadic wanderers on the fringes of the desert to a settled nation committed to cultivation. We have seen too that this sensibility is in general 'visionary and theocratic rather than sense-explorative', its narrative priorities consequently precluding scenic interest in its own right. Nonetheless, in even so unpromisingly unempirical a sensibility, the four matrices of perception or perceptual drives that we argued to be universal are clearly identifiable.

We found, in the ecological category, a cautious 'unseen hands' version of productivity, where fertility is ethical reward and divine fiat; in the cosmographic category, far more substantial, a world-sense definitively without paradigm, uplifting and subduing alike, and a 'declarative' landscape of sacred history, the landscape of transfiguration, miracle and epiphany. In the technoptic category, we found a 'vitalist' landscape of song, rhythm and dance-energies rather than of pictorialism; and in the analogical category, the tendency toward dualistic typology and simple didactic metaphor. In the exception here, *Canticles*, a delicate order of hypersensuous subjective association clearly betrays a poetics imported from a far more advanced

152 *Matthew*, 6.26–30, 8.20.

153 *Luke*, 21.22.

commercial and metropolitan culture: a phenomenological mood-music that links it with the courtly verse of Theocritus and Virgil in the classical world, but that will not again be produced in western poetry until the conditions re-emerge that ripen St-Amant, John Milton and Andrew Marvell.

4

Late antiquity and the Church Fathers

Introduction

While traditional appraisals of Christian ideas of nature often emphasize a 'Satan-ridden earth' of the Fathers, establishing a sharp chiaroscuro contrast between 'medieval' gloom and 'renaissance' dawning, such a characterization of early Christian nature-sensibility looks drastically distortive today. The labours of scholars such as E. R. Dodds, Peter Brown and Robin Lane Fox have immeasurably deepened our understanding of late antiquity and patristic Christian thought; and it will accordingly be the argument of this chapter that the Christian and patristic valuation of nature was far more celebrative, as well as necessarily more complex, than such traditional sketches have allowed. It is true that Christian writings largely effect an epistemological revolt from classical materialism and science into an idealist registration of nature as an ontological and mystic ladder; and that thereby they emphatically derogate sense-experience, frequently substituting the discourses of symbolism and allegory. But the doctrines of the Incarnation and the Redemption, in rebutting Gnostic and Manichaean extremes of *contemptus mundi*, rehabilitate the physical order within a continuity of the sensible and intelligible worlds, whose essential character and final end is the creative miracle of divine love. Moreover, the Church Fathers appropriate from classical culture a wealth of elevated cosmological ideas and descriptive poetic rhetoric; they formulate a theological foundation for 'nature-mystical' experience; and, particularly in the period of the earlier Dominate, they articulate a sensibility of extraordinary dynamism and enterprise, rather than resignation, melancholia or mere anxiety. Indeed, we shall see that in certain respects the feeling for the physical world of early Christian poets bears striking resemblance to that of Milton.

In the following analysis we shall attempt first to characterize the climate of nature-sensibility in the late antique period (for our purposes, from the Apologists to Boethius and Maximus the Confessor); and proceed subsequently to discussion of the mediated landscape-consciousness in terms of its territorial imagination, its sense of natural dimensions, and the characteristic percepts and tropes it yields in exercise of our four basic matrices of perception.

Christian nature-sensibility: the status of the material world

The traditional 'Satan-ridden earth' of late antiquity is undeniably in evidence. Derogation of the sublunar world abounds in many forms.

'My heart sickens', writes St Jerome in 396, 'when I go over the catastrophes that have happened in our time. For more than twenty years, not a day has gone past between Constantinople and the Julian Alps without the shedding of Roman blood. How many matrons, how many virgins dedicated to God, how many free-born women of noble blood, have fallen into the hands of those wild beasts ... bishops imprisoned, priests slaughtered, churches defiled, horses tethered to the altars ... the world of Rome is falling to pieces. It is the fruit of our sins that the barbarians are strong, the fruit of our vices that the Roman army is defeated.'[1] The anarchic third century had been smitten by famines, epidemics and barbarian invasions. Between 245 and 270 every frontier collapsed; the Roman armies threw up twenty-five Emperors in forty-seven years, only one of whom died in his bed.[2] As for Jerome's period, the empire was finally sundered between two emperors in 395; the Vandals ravaged Gaul in 407, the Suevi invaded Spain and the Huns Thrace in 408; in 410 Rome was sacked, and by 439 the Vandals had taken Carthage. St Ambrose, in an oration on the death of his brother in 379, is comforted that he had at least been spared 'falling into the hands of the barbarians, being present at the massacre of all humanity, the end of the world'.[3]

Moreover, 'the historical sources of this period show us a despotic

1 *Letters*, 60, in *PL*, vol. 22, p. 600. Quoted by Lidia Storoni Mazzolani, *The Idea of the City in Roman Thought*, trans. S. O'Donnell (London: 1970), p. 235.

2 From Peter Brown, *The World of Late Antiquity* (London: 1971), pp. 22–24.

3 *De Excessu Sartyri*, 30, in *PL*, vol. 16, p. 1356; ref. Mazzolani, *City*, p. 234.

regime, a greedy and inhumane bureaucracy, a mental climate of espionage, cruelty and superstition. Such is the society depicted by Ammianus Marcellinus'.[4] So great were the abuses of officialdom and the crushing extortions of taxation that Roman citizens sometimes longed for and even aided the invasions of barbarians as relative liberators.[5] Zosimus, describing the fourth century, wrote that 'every town was filled with tears and complaints, all calling out for the barbarians, and imploring their assistance'.[6]

The spirit of embittered fatalism, engendered by the supersedure of civic and personal liberty in the stranglehold of empire, could reach to the emperor himself, and as early as the second century Marcus Aurelius regards human activities as 'smoke and nothingness', and the cherishing of objects as 'empty and rotten and trifling, like little dogs biting one another'.[7] Gregory of Nyssa eyes mens' works as but childrens' sandcastles, promptly washed away. 'His entire work is penetrated by a deep feeling of the unreality of the sensible world, which he calls *γοητεία*, a magical illusion.'[8] In one aspect, the countryside under Imperial Rome has come less to represent *χώρα*, the deeps of spacious escape, than the private agricultural factories of a tiny minority, where tens of thousands of slaves – and later, the new 'serfs' of the colonate – toil on the ruthlessly centuriated lands of vast Latifundia.[9] Cultivated landscape is now an unparalleled panorama of servitude, of dreary 'captive agriculture', fitting emblem of the bondage of the flesh and the loss of oneness with earth and fellow-men.

In the religious sphere, demonological terrors of the kind we have examined in relation to the New Testament continued unabated; whilst the expectation of the Parousia now popularized conviction of

4 Cf. Mazzolani, pp. 206–07.

5 Ibid., pp. 205–06, 214.

6 *Historia Ecclesiastica*, 4, 32.

7 *Meditations*, trans. Walter J. Black (New York: 1945), 10.31 and 5.33.

8 Gregory of Nyssa, in *PG*, vol. 44, 628c, 428c. References from E. R. Dodds, *Pagan and Christian*, pp. 10–11.

9 Prominent nobles of the first century BC could own over 200,000 acres; yet 'the aggregate possessions of rural magnates – often dispersed over many provinces – reached their peak [only] by the 5th century'. Brunt has estimated that by the end of the Republic some 3,000,000 slaves were at work in Italy alone. The empire thus viewed 'the emergence of slave-worked agrarian properties of a hitherto unknown immensity'. Perry Anderson, *Passages from Antiquity to Feudalism*, pp. 59–62, 93–96; P. A. Brunt, *Italian Manpower 225 BC–AD 14* (Oxford: 1971), pp. 121–25.

nature's senescence. 'Senuisse iam mundum' declares Cyprian. ('The world has now grown aged'.) The fertility of the fields and the fruit trees has decreased, the ore in mines and marble in quarries is declining, disasters multiply and the wrath of God sends plague after plague.[10] In this climate of pervading other-worldliness, the topos of the soul's flight upward from this terrestrial pinpoint is shared by pagan and Christian;[11] and happiness is not secure against fortune even on mountain-top fastnesses.

The careful man will wish
To build a lasting home
Unshakeable by winds
That thunder from the East.
He'll shun the open sea
That threatens with its waves,
And choose no mountain peaks
Which all the strength of winds
Buffet and beat from the South;
He'll choose no thirsty sands
That sink and melt away
Beneath the building's weight ...[12]

Only in the transcendent Kingdom will men find surety of peace. 'A Christian', wrote Augustine, 'is a man who feels himself a stranger even in his own house, in his own city; for our fatherland is on high. There we shall not be aliens; but here below everyone feels himself a foreigner, even in his own house.'[13] Extramundane values, it would seem, could be no more thoroughgoing. 'Nothing visible', said Ignatius, 'is good'.[14]

This account, however, is a landscape painted in one colour.

10 St Cyprian, *Ad Demetrianum*, 4 and 5, in *PL*, vol. 4, pp. 564–66. On the senescence of nature, cf. also Lucretius, *De Rerum Natura*, 2.1146 and 5.95.

11 Cf. Lucian's parody of the theme in his *Icaromenippus*; and its origins in Plato's 'wings of the soul' allegory of the chariot in the *Phaedrus*; given Christian echo in Gregory of Nyssa *De Virginitate*, *PG*, vol. 46, p. 365.

12 Boethius, *The Consolation of Philosophy*, trans. V. E. Watts (Harmondsworth: 1969), Book 4, metrum, p. 64.

13 St Augustine, *Sermons*, 111, in *PL*, vol. 38, p. 642.

14 *Ad Romanos*, 3: *όυδεν ψαινόμενον καλόν*. For exemplification of a climate of despondence and *contemptus mundi*, see Mazzolani, *City*, ch. 13: 'Spiritual Factors in the Crisis'; and Dodds, *Pagan and Christian*, ch. 1: 'Man and the Material World.'

Contemporary Christianity delighted in mosaic. 'Whatever is', counter-asserts Augustine, 'is good'.[15] Political corruption, barbarian crises, the spirit of fatalism and religious *contemptus mundi* all notwithstanding, sublunar reality was intensely ambiguous in value, beauty and spiritual significance. The view of a demoralized late antiquity indurated in anxiety, superstition and mortification not only overlooks certain reinvigorating social developments: it crucially omits the concept, and psychology, of salvation. Consequently, to mistake for static or passive gloom the climate of the period is to miss both the range and, in particular, the surpassing intensity of its spiritual encounters: struck as they are from the radical cosmologies of a crisis sensibility, whose options figure universes of the most satanic, as of also the most enrapturing, aspects. The extremes, moreover, can converge – perhaps did converge, for many besides Augustine – in the pattern of Christian conversion. The Christian lives out a spiritual dialectic of anguish and transfiguration, and must eschew sensual submersion and physical indifference alike, in the higher and spiritualized interaction with the natural world, which is the synthesis of the regenerate life. Hence, the sense of violent combat between ultimate forces of the universe, the awe of magnitude, yet also the blessedness of the *Pantocrator*'s nurture of creation, haunt through amazement and relief the Christian sensibility. Basil seeks for his audience that 'defamiliarization' of the routine world in the wonder of the *vestigia dei in mundo* which he has himself undergone. 'I want creation to penetrate you with so much admiration that everywhere, wherever you may be, the least plant may bring to you the clear remembrance of the Creator.'[16]

The polyvalence of Christian nature-writing results in part from the varieties of temperament and knowledge of the Christian writers. The contrasting purposes of individual texts also lend a potentially contradictory diversity: the poetic emphases of mystical theology sharply differ from those of homiletic and apologetic works, or of monastic instruction with its drive towards agricultural practice. Again, the internal character of hexaemeral literature is highly subjective and associative. 'Like most of these writings, the nine

15 *The Confessions*, 7.12, trans. R. S. Pine-Coffin (Harmondsworth: 1961), p. 148. Cf. his enthusiastic list of natural blessings: *City of God*, 22.24.

16 *On the Hexaemeron*, trans. Sister Agnes C. Way (Fathers of the Church Series, Washington, DC: 1963), vol. 46, 3.2.

"Homilies" of Basil contain less the systematic exposition of a philosophy than a medley of notions related to the problems which the text of scripture happened to suggest to his mind.'[17]

Presentation of 'the Christian view of nature in the late antique period', where it falls within a narrow compass, is therefore apt to distortion: a stricture to which my own brief survey is no doubt liable. Even confining our scrutiny within the parameters of the strictly theological, we find ambiguity borne into its master concepts by Judaic and Platonic traditions alike. Neoplatonism views sensibles as displacing attention from the intelligible world, yet accords them anagogic dimension. For the Old Testament, nature lies in post-lapsarian derangement, yet retains the wondrous plenitude we saw celebrated in *Psalms.* Deiform and deformed, the proportioning of the two is variable according to taste and purpose. Moreover, the availability within the Christian syncretism of terms from both traditions itself ensures fluctuations of value. The idea of nature as God's 'creation', particularly as produced *ex nihilo,* carries the contextual implications of her essentially exalted character. Designated as the realm of 'Becoming', however, nature recalls the insufficiency and contingency of mere shadow and flux.[18] Patristic writings thus present 'not a settled system, but a series of interrelated problematic themes'.[19] And Augustine was in recoil less from the natural world than from an epistemology, a particular mode of knowing creation. Wallace-Hadrill's observation on the Greek Fathers that 'it is seldom that we find them enjoying themselves sensuously, as though they were cats in the sun' is entirely to the point. As Augustine puts it – and his words could be those of any Greek or Latin Father – 'If we were mere beasts, we should love the life of sensuality and all that relates to it; this would be our sufficient good, and when this was satisfied, we should seek nothing further.' As rational beings, however, we endow 'dumb' beasts with 'voices of praise'; and ourselves ascend from 'corporeal' through 'intellectual' to 'spiritual' vision, elevating the gaze from sense to conception in contemplation of the divine ideas.[20]

17 Gilson, p. 55. On the infusion of classical ideas into a Christian teleology, see Glacken, ch. 5, pp. 176–253.

18 Norris, pp. 136–37.

19 Ibid., p. 139.

20 Wallace-Hadrill, *The Greek Patristic View of Nature* (Manchester: 1968), p. 80; Augustine, *City of God,* trans. Henry Bettenson (Harmondsworth: 1972), Book 11, ch. 28, p. 462; *Sermons, PL,* vol. 38, p. 1134.

The very real tension between ascetic and aesthetic extremes of response to nature – the 'disturbing oscillation between world acceptance and world renunciation', as Wallace-Hadrill expresses it – finds here its potential resolution. Steering its course between the reductive polarities of pagan nature-worship and Gnosticism's absolute contempt of matter, patristic Christianity can nowhere endorse contempt for nature *in toto*. 'It was impossible to reconcile with Christianity a radical pessimism about the created order. For this further involved a rejection of the Old Testament and the consequent disintegration of the central Christian pattern of creation and revelation within history.'[21] At most there can be depreciation of sense-perception. The natural order is accordingly to be regarded in the two-fold spirit of detachment (as against love of nature in herself) and contemplation (as against sensuous immersion). 'The man who is freed from the demands of nature is free to enjoy it fearlessly' and is detached sufficiently to unriddle its status.

Let us not seek in this [earthly] beauty that which it has not received, for because it has not received that which we seek it is on that account in the lowest place. But for that which it has received let us praise God, since even to this that is lowest He has given also the great good of outward fairness.[22]

Here is the very epitome of the paradoxical status of earth and countryside in early Christian thought. Whilst, in itself, nature is fundamentally good, it is merely a *means*: a provision-house for material provender, moral testing, and above all, religious knowledge of an absolute beyond itself. Provided that he continue to observe the imperative of detachment, the Christian may correctly enjoy the physical resources given to us in nature by Providence:

Our God has given all things to man and made him master of all the earth. All that the sky, the earth or sea produces in air, or field or flood: all these are mine just as I am his.[23]

21 *The Cambridge History of Later Greek and Early Medieval Philosophy*, ed. A. H. Armstrong (Cambridge: 1967), p. 167.

22 Wallace-Hadrill, *Nature*, p. 130; Augustine, *Contra Epistolam Manichaei quam vocant Fundamenti liber unus*, ch. 41, par. 48, in *Oeuvres Complètes de St. Augustin* [French and Latin texts], trans. into French and annotated by Péronne, Vincent, Ecalle, Charpentier and Barreau (Paris: 1872–78), vol. 25, p. 476; Glacken, p. 199.

23 Prudentius, *Cathemerinon* (*Hymns for the Various Hours and Days*), Hymn 3, in *The Last Poets of Imperial Rome*, trans. Harold Isbell (Harmondsworth: 1971), p. 162. Compare *Psalm* 8.5–8.

After all, it is the human interiority of motivation and judgement, rather than the material externality that he instrumentalizes, that is the true locus of virtue and vice in the world. Nature groans under malediction due only to human disobedience (*Genesis* 3.17).

The world is evil, yes, it is evil, and yet it is loved as though it were good. But what is this evil world? For the sky and the earth and the waters and the things that are in them, the fishes and the birds and the trees are not evil. All these are good; it is evil men who make this evil world.[24]

We sanctify our relation with nature through endeavour, through traversing it, as a pathway, a corridor of light, to the Being beyond; and for this we need always resort to intelligence, to interrogation:

But what is my God? I put my question to the earth. It answered, 'I am not God', and all things on earth declared the same. I asked the sea and the chasms of the deep and the living things that creep in them, but they answered, 'We are not your God. Seek what is above us.' I spoke to the winds that blow, and the whole air and all that lives in it replied, 'Anaximenes is wrong. I am not God.' I asked the sky, the sun, the moon, and the stars, but they told me, 'Neither are we the God whom you seek.' I spoke to all the things that are about me, all that can be admitted by the door of the senses, and I said, 'Since you are not my God, tell me about him. Tell me something of my God.' Clear and loud they answered, 'God is he who made us.' I asked these questions simply by gazing at these things, and their beauty was all the answer they gave.

Man, on the other hand, can question nature. He is able to catch sight of God's invisible nature through his creatures ... [although the world will not] supply an answer to those who question it, unless they also have the faculty to judge it.[25]

It is, I suggest, precisely in accordance with these values of endeavour and inquisition that Basil comes, very specifically, to slight the easy, outward appreciation of landscape *qua* prospect, urging alternatively meditation upon it as the work of divine τέχνη.

For, the Creator of all creation does not look at beauty with eyes, but He contemplates in His ineffable wisdom the things made. A pleasant sight, indeed, is a whitened sea, when settled calm possesses it; and pleasant also

24 Augustine, *Sermones ad Populum*, First Sermon, 80, 8, in *Oeuvres Completes de St. Augustin*, vol. 16, p. 573; also in Erich Przywara's *An Augustine Synthesis* (New York: 1958), p. 434; Glacken, p. 197. Compare the Pauline insistence on the primacy of conscience over cultic externals, there being 'nothing unclean of itself': *Romans*, esp. 1.18–26 and 14.14–23.

25 Augustine, *The Confessions*, pp. 212–13.

when, ruffled on the surface by gentle breezes, it reflects a purple or bluish colour to the spectators, when it does not beat violently upon the neighbouring land, but, as it were, kisses it with peaceful embraces. Surely, we must not think that the meaning of the Scripture [*Genesis*: 1.10] is that the sea appeared good and pleasant to God in this way, but here the goodness is determined by the purpose of the creative activity ... Consequently the sea is good in God's sight because of the permeation of its moisture into the depths of the earth; and it is good because, being the receptacle of rivers, it receives the streams from all sides into itself but remains within its own limits.[26]

Human restoration to harmony with nature in the regenerate life may extend, however, beyond enlightened contemplation. Through man's co-operation with grace, the complete and miraculous restoration of the natural world itself to pristine unity and goodness may be achieved. God's re-creative intervention in Christ is the start of the process: for Christ's Incarnation reorders, *in potentia*, the universal immanence in man. For Maximus, Christ reintegrates the divided domains of paradise and the inhabited earth (οἰκουμένη) as the incarnation of their common λόγος. For Augustine, man worships on behalf of voiceless creation, whilst for Gregory of Nyssa 'it is man's duty and destiny to be the agent by which the whole universe, in himself, is restored to its pristine nature, and to present it in him as a unity to the One'.[27] Man is thus, through providence, the agent both of nature's fall and her restoration, and in him may be effected 'the ultimate reunification ... of the whole creature, sensible and intelligible, with the Being in which it participates and from which it sprang'.[28] Exemplifying this, monastic hagiography abounds with the friendships of hermit and beast: Mark and Gerasimos with their lions, Paul fed by a raven, Antony assisted in burial duties by bounding lions.[29] As Montalembert writes, 'this supernatural empire of the old monks over the animal creation is explained by the primitive innocence which these heroes of penance and purity had won back, and which

26 Basil, *On the Hexaemeron*, trans. Sister Agnes C. Way, pp. 63–64, sect. 4.6.

27 Augustine, *Sermons, PL*, vol. 38, p. 1134. For Gregory of Nyssa, cf. *De Hominis Opificio*, 8, in *PG*, 44.144D-148C, and *The Catechetical Oration*, 6, in *PG*, 45.25B-28A; ref. in *The Cambridge History of Later Greek and Early Medieval Philosophy*, pp. 449, 504.

28 *CHLGEMP*, p. 456.

29 Cf. Helen Waddell, trans. *Beasts and Saints* (London: 1934), passim.; also her *Desert Fathers* (1936; rpt. London: 1974), esp. 'The Life of St. Paul the First Hermit', pp. 33–53.

placed them once more on a level with Adam and Eve in the terrestrial Paradise'.[30] This personal reintegration into harmony with brute life realizes *Job* 5.23: 'For you shall be in league with the stones of the field, and the beasts of the field shall be at peace with you.' As the bridge between nature and its creator, man may thus, in reordering his passions and reintegrating the fragmented human person, uplift creation to its former perfection as a resplendent vehicle of spirit. It is by precisely this continuation of the reintegrative work of the Incarnational Logos that the desert saints restore the wilderness to the peaceable Kingdom of Paradise.

In conclusion, Christian perspectives on nature in late antiquity, far from being entirely dominated by a bleakness of *contemptus mundi* enlivened by Satanic terrors, encompass a range of ambiguous and diverse positions. The world is created very good by God, and recreated by the Incarnation, yet must also be seen eschatologically as a fallen and finite testing-ground to prepare us for the eternal Kingdom, and as a visible reflection of a greater, unchanging and incorruptible spiritual and intelligential reality. Conceived thus, nature can emerge as the dazzling projection of the divine creative mind; and the wide earth itself may be restored, before time burns, to the garden-perfection of Paradise.

Christian Nature-Sensibility: the Character of the Material World

Nature as sacramental system: transcendence, mystification, symbolicity

From its beginnings, Christianity had accepted the peace-keeping Roman government, but vociferously opposed pagan cult and myth. Towards pagan philosophy, consensus attitudes were to change decisively from the time of Justin Martyr in favour of an increasingly triumphal policy of appropriation, transformation and preservation. With Clement of Alexandria and Origen, Christianity has advanced from being a caucus to a syllabus: from 'kerygma' to 'paideia'. The third and fourth centuries construct an elaborate Christian paideia, a

30 Count de Montalembert, *The Monks of the West, from St. Benedict to St. Bernard*, trans. John C. Nimmo (London: 1896), vol. 2, p. 212.

thorough intellectual and educational programme, equipped with its own corpus and scholarly apparatus, on the full Hellenic model.[31] This is of the utmost importance for the writing of nature-poetry, as for so much else in Christian culture, since it secured, under the auspices of the Church, the preservation and transmission of much of the finest in a thousand years of Greco-Roman verse, speculation and philosophy, to the civilization of Romanised medieval Europe.

This momentous stage in the assimilation of Hellenism took place within what one can only call a Late Antique Renaissance, which moulded nature-sensibility, both pagan and Christian, into a new rapport with the external world: 'a true Renaissance that has given Greco-Roman literature some of its greatest personalities, figures who have exercised a lasting influence on the history and culture of later centuries down to the present day'.[32] The new acumen developed from the comparatively meritocratic reconstruction of the empire during the effort to throw back the successive waves of barbarian invasions, between 240 and the close of the century. The army was doubled in size, made open to talent, and the senatorial aristocracy excluded from military command in 260. A new, creative and revitalizing government of the able came to power in a 'success-culture', both secular and ecclesiastic. 'In the late empire, indeed, one feels a sudden release of talent and creativity such as often follows the shaking of an *ancien régime*. A rising current of able men, less burdened by the prejudices of an aristocracy and eager to learn, maintained a tone of vigour and disquietude that distinguishes the intellectual climate of Late Antiquity from any other period of ancient history. Of the Fathers of the Church, for instance, only one – Ambrose – came from a senatorial family. The men who were able to leave their mark on the highest society of the empire had all of them made their own way from obscure towns.'[33] Against this background of riches and resilience sprang a soaring, dynamic individualism; and the imagination of glamorous promise, now injected into the sclerotic veins of antique fatalism, pulsed into the spiritual sphere, and altered the general tenor of relations with the material world. The revival of a rapt Neoplatonism routed melancholy Gnosticism, even as Christianity, prosperous in the Christianized empire of Constantine, developed optimism worldly and metaphysical. For Eusebius, Christianity was a

31 Cf. Jaeger, chapters 5–7.
32 Ibid., p. 75.
33 Peter Brown, *World*, pp. 30, 33.

'success-philosophy', rewarded by abundant blessings.[34] In this climate of ardour and individualism, 'the new mood appealed straight to the centre and away from the subordinate gods of popular belief – to the One himself, as a figure of latent, unexpressed power'. The resultant 'sense of imminent breakthrough of divine energy in the inner world of the individual' produced the phenomenon of 'conversion', and an array of great figures believing themselves to be the agents of vast forces, of an urgently personal God.[35] This spiritualisation of ambition and upward social mobility is supremely expressed by the mystical aspiration to the *visio dei*.[36] Neoplatonist and Christian hoped 'through rational contemplation to seize the intimate connection between every level of the visible world and its source in the One God. It was possible, therefore, to "touch" by thought the concentrated centre that had been sensed through the unrolled beauty of all visible things.' Contemporary religious and philosophic response to the sensuous life of flesh and field is thus, crucially, not 'otherworldly' but 'innerworldly'.[37] Not from scorn of nature, but from the enrapturing prospect of inward contemplative ascent through her hierarchies to the ultimate vision of the One came the impulse to the flight of mind beyond matter.[38] It is, as we shall see, this 'Church Militant' of driving ambition and spiritual oppugnancy[39] that introduced the savage landscapes of the anchorites' 'Ascetic Sublime'.

The Abbot Arsenius said, 'It sufficeth a monk if he sleep for one hour: that is, if he be a fighter.'[40]

34 Charles Norris Cochrane, *Christianity and Classical Culture* (1940; rpt. Oxford: 1980), p. 184.

35 Brown, *World*, pp. 52–53.

36 Cf. K. E. Kirk, *The Vision of God* (London: 1931), esp. p. 54.

37 Brown, *World*, pp. 74–78.

38 Compare Augustine on the euphoria of interior rangings within the universe of Memory: *Confessions*, Book 10, chapters 6–27.

39 It is now – the early fourth century – that the term 'pagan' ('paganus') to describe a non-Christian first appears: denoting, thinks Chadwick, unbelievers as 'civilians', in distinction from 'soldiers of Christ': Henry Chadwick, *The Early Church* (Harmondsworth: 1967), p. 152. Augustine conceives the sacraments as being similar to the tattoos branded on the back of the hands of imperial soldiers: signifying the right of the Church to command its 'ranks': *Sermones* 317.5; *de Bapt.* 1.4.5 and 3.19.25; ref. Peter Brown, *Augustine of Hippo*, p. 224.

40 *The Sayings of the Fathers*, trans. from the Greek by Pelagius the Deacon, Book 4, 3, in *Vitae Patrum*, ed. Rosweyde (Antwerp: 1628); trans. into English by Helen Waddell, *The Desert Fathers*, p. 99.

But if the new inbreaking of infinite appetite, and appetite for the infinite, made the charms of a merely terrestrial countryside seem trivial, it nevertheless left nature transfigured by the power of its hunger. As never before, she tantalized. Like the clothing of Salome, the veils[41] of nature impassioned the eye. Revealing yet concealing the object of all longing, these veils, ardently scrutinized, could grow suddenly diaphanous, baring the inner glory that gave them their form and their allure. Many passages on Creation in the Fathers express an almost erotic state of ecstasy and anticipation.

I have learnt to love you late, Beauty at once so ancient and so new! ... I searched for you outside myself and, disfigured as I was, I fell upon the lovely things of your creation. You were with me, but I was not with you. The beautiful things of this world kept me far from you and yet, if they had not been in you, they would have had no being at all. You called me; you cried aloud to me; you broke my barrier of deafness. You shone upon me; your radiance enveloped me; you put my blindness to flight. You shed your fragrance about me; I drew breath and now I gasp for your sweet odour. I tasted you, and now I hunger and thirst for you. You touched me, and I am enflamed with love of your peace.

If the court of the sanctuary is so beautiful, and the vestibule of the temple is so august and magnificent, dazzling the eyes of our soul with its surpassing beauty, what must be the holy of holies? And who is fit to venture within the innermost shrine? Or who can look into its secrets?[42]

In these centuries, Christianity appropriates the essential Hellenic conception of nature as an orderly system, rational and unitary, whose laws are open to human understanding; but it crucially qualifies this, desacralizing nature, derogating the scope of human understanding and redirecting analysis toward her symbolicity. Thus, much of classical science and empirical impulse are retained, but in deep subordination within an otherworldy framework.

Where classical Greek natural science presents the universe as a multiform and replete physical organism pervaded by Mind or Soul,[43] Christianity refers us in its primary move to that incorporeal mind

41 Sensible objects as 'veiling' the divine luminosity is a common metaphor. See, for example, Pseudo-Dionysius, *Ecclesiastical Hierarchy*, 5,2.

42 Augustine, *Confessions*, 10, 27, pp. 231–32; Basil, *Hexaemeron*, 2, 1, p. 21.

43 R. G. Collingwood, *The Idea of Nature* (1945; rpt. Oxford: 1960), part one.

itself, pre-existent, transcendent yet supremely desired, for which the material order furnishes only the lowest rungs of an ontological and epistemological ladder. The tireless Christian injunction to worship the creator beyond the creature[44] doubtless draws support from Plato as well as the Hebrew tradition;[45] and the late antique yearning for a supernal homeland beyond the spectacle of ruin and peril in the terrestrial world points constantly to 'our homeland in heaven', 'that blessed country which is meant to be no mere vision but our home'.[46] With the sack of Rome in 410, any remaining Eusebian confidence as to the prospering of the righteous within this world burns in the flames around the Capitol; the ensuing millennium is to be dominated by Augustine's explicit opposition of earthly city and heavenly. Natural theology buttresses such an opposition. It preserves the Old Testament's piously radical distinction between creature and creator by adhering, after early vicissitudes, to the non-Hellenic doctrine of the *creatio ex nihilo*. Like the Greeks, Justin Martyr and Athenagoras speak of the fashioning of the world from formless material or ὕλη, and Clement of Alexandria stands uncertain; but as early as the second century Theophilus had reinstated Philo's declaration that God created all things from nothing, and in the fourth century the Cappadocians bestowed the clarity of precise philosophic terminology to this position of future orthodoxy.[47] This *productio ex nihilo* secures the freedom of the divine creative activity from all compulsion or limitation, whilst the rejection of a pre-existing primordial substratum of more or less recalcitrant 'matter' safeguards against a universe doomed to an irremediable element of baseness or imperfection. Further, the eschewal of the Neoplatonic *creatio ex deo* preserves the distinction between divine substance and creation as absolute. Utter transcendence and unlimited causal omnipotence are thus accorded God, in a maximal exaltation of him as beyond any detraction in the realm of nature, as also beyond her full powers of representation.

44 *Acts*: 17.24–30; *Romans*: 1.25.

45 Athenagoras writes, for example, 'I will not pass God by to worship the elements, which can do no more than they are bidden,' and continues by quoting Plato, *Politics*, 269D. Cf. *A Plea Regarding Christians*, in *The Library of Christian Classics* (London: 1953), vol. 1, ch. 16; Glacken, p. 182.

46 *Letter to Diognetus*, recalling *Philippians*: 3.20; Augustine, *Confessions*, 7, 20, p. 154.

47 Justin Martyr, *Apology*, 1: 10, 20, 59, 67; Athenagoras, *Apology for Christ*, 15; Theophilus of Antioch, *To Autolycus*, 1.6, 7, 10; 2.4, 6, 10; Clement of Alexandria, *Stromateis*, 5.89, 92; Origen, *De Principiis*, 2.1.4: cf. Gilson, p. 39; and *CHLGEMP*, p. 189.

In a second move redirecting natural focus to the transcendent principle beyond her, natural theology centralises the act of creation for the understanding of the physical world. For Aristotle, nature is *φύσις* or self-moving matter, whose laws of cause and effect can be studied in effectual autonomy. But Christianity executes a causal displacement, referring all back to the primal divine creation. Not Aristotle's *Physics* nor Pliny's *Natural History* but the narrative of *Genesis* holds the key to science. The primary Christian meditations on the physical world thus consist in the hexaemeral literature, which comprise attempts at a classical 'scientising' of the Hebraic text. For Gregory of Nyssa and for Augustine, the creation contained all phenomena, together with their individual development and principle of generation according to natural law throughout time, as 'invisible germinal principles' within its originating activity.[48] 'Like mothers heavy with their offspring, the world is heavy with the causes of things still to be.'[49] This doctrine of 'seminal reasons' sharply subordinates understanding of material processes to theistic and metaphysical concerns; thereby distinguishing the 'nexus of creaturely, natural causality' from 'the creative causality of the "first cause"', in anticipation of the later scholastic distinction between the 'first cause' and a whole order of 'second causes'.[50]

Thus the doctrine of *creatio ex nihilo* affirms for God the transcendence of absolute pre-existence; and the doctrine of seminal reasons telescopes empirical natural law and process back into the supernatural creativity of that divine transcendent Being. It points that fundamental, astounding passage from void into replete material being: the primaeval *δύναμις* or propulsion of life from increate power into the concrete beasts and landscapes of our visible world. Nature now can only be fully understood in terms of this unseen primordial flash across the depthless ontological gulf. It is that outer edge of time in eternity, the drastic cliff-drop beyond nature's palpable *terra firma* into the plenum-void of God, unutterably beyond being, whose meditation permanently transforms the pagan analysis of the natural frame.

The two doctrines also assure deepest awe in the face of the

48 Augustine, *De Genesi ad Litteram*, 5.7.20; 9.17.32: *CHLGEMP*, pp. 398–400. Gregory of Nyssa, *Apologia in Hexaemeron*, 72; 77D; 113B; 121D: *CHLGEMP*, p. 447.

49 Augustine, *De Trinitate*, 3.9.16; *CHLGEMP*, p. 400.

50 *CHLGEMP*, pp. 399–400.

absolute divine omnipotence, and this is the second major qualification of Greek natural science. Classical Greece could proclaim man to be the measure of all things; but with the Roman Empire, it is as if his astronomical calculators, his *Chronographiae* and *Geographica*[51] are despairingly thrown away. God and nature both recede from man's rational grasp, enveloped in fear, mystery and awe. 'Felix, qui potuit rerum cognoscere causas' Virgil had sighed, yielding up natural questions in despair.[52] Lucan is content to leave cosmological problems such as the movement of tides in the decent mystery intended by the Gods.[53] Seneca 'quotes with approval the view that we should not trouble to investigate things that it is neither possible nor useful to know ... such as the principle of perspective'.[54] To this 'general change in the intellectual climate of the Mediterranean world' the 'nearest historical analogue may be the romantic reaction against rationalist "natural theology" which set in at the beginning of the nineteenth century',[55] for this late antique natural theology distinctively erodes the confidence and sureties of rationalism. Christianity's God is a stupendous and subduing deity of overawing omnipotence. The *terribilità* of the *Pantocrator's* resistless final Judgement produces a haunting trepidation to all things spiritual: even his great glory may damage men's 'eyesight' by its 'brilliance' unless careful preparation is made for it.[56] In the later fourth century, as the hysteria for anachoresis reaches its decadence and desert saints hurl themselves into redemptive spiritual warfare in the craggy solitudes of the margins of the empire, Christian art displaces its former idyllic imagings of paradise, where the blessed repose under serene stars or in bright arbours, by those of the Last Judgement.[57] 'An old man saw one laughing, and said to him, "In presence of Heaven and earth we are to give account of our whole life to God; and thou dost laugh?"'[58] Chrysostom taught that Christ never laughed, and Basil and Benedict

51 On Greek computation of space cf. John Onians, *Art and Thought*, ch. 5; A. G. Drachman, *The Mechanical Technology of Greek and Roman Antiquity* (Copenhagen: 1963); and G. E. R. Lloyd, *Greek Science after Aristotle* (London: 1973).

52 *Georgics*: 2.490–94. 'Happy who has been able to fathom the causes of things.'

53 *Pharsalia*: 1.414–19.

54 Seneca, *De Beneficiis*, 7.1.5: following Demetrius Cynicus, ref. E. R. Dodds, *The Greeks and the Irrational* (London: 1951), p. 249.

55 Dodds, Ibid., p. 248.

56 Gregory of Nazianzus, *Orations* 27.3, in *PG* 36.13D-16A; pseudo-Dionysius, *Ecclesiastical Hierarchy*, 501C.

57 Brown, *World*, p. 107.

58 *Vitae Patrum*, trans. Waddell, *Desert Fathers*, p. 97.

forbade it in their monastic regulations.[59] Theology insists that God exceeds intelligibility: 'how unsearchable are his judgements, and his ways past finding out!' 'What makes God comprehensible', argues Tertullian, 'is the fact that he cannot be comprehended, so that the very power of his greatness presents him to men as at once known and unknown'.[60] God is nameless, *τό θεῖον ακατονόμαστον*,[61] all human language about him relative and symbolic. His essence we cannot know.

Co-ordinate with this brow-beaten accent on man's intelligential dwarfishness is that on his deficiency of natural knowledge. Nature, too, is seen through a glass darkly. We are ignorant of the Nile's sources, the tides, the causes of lightning, rain and snow, cries Irenaeus; we do not know the reason for the phases of the moon, formation of metals, nor the homing places of migratory birds.[62] Wonder and awe supplant the bravado of classical *savoir faire* that had made landscape painting possible. Above all, natural law is reduced to *contingent* structure, its supposed autonomy and calculability denounced as pagan impieties. This expulsion of nature from man's secure computations into a darker, stranger, unprobed order of experience takes three forms. First, the *creatio continua*, hinted at in the New Testament,[63] insists upon her perennial dependence on God for very preservation and the maintaining of due processes. Augustine and Boethius alike firmly repudiate nature's self-subsistence.[64] Second, for the Christian, the One is in continual intercourse with his creation, and providence is not merely the pristine ordering of the world, but a continuing surveillance and 'pastoral' care.[65] As such, nature is irreducible to a purely determinate system, since it is always open to divine intervention, the unfolding of miracles, deliverances, 'particular providences'. 'Natural law' is a structure liable to melting, for the divine is a perennial 'excess' over such laws, biologically antinomian,

59 Chrysostom, *PG*, 57.69; Basil, ref. to in C. Butler's edition of Benedict's Rule (Freiburg: 1935), ch. 4; Benedict's Rule, ibid., chs. 4 and 6; ref. also E. R. Curtius, *European Literature and the Latin Middle Ages*, Excursus 4.2, pp. 420–22.

60 *Romans*: 11.33; Tertullian, *Apology*, 17.2; *Adversus Marcionem*, 1.4.2; ref. Richard A. Norris, *God and World in Early Christian Theology* (London: 1966), pp. 91–92.

61 Gregory of Nazianzus, *Orations*, 30.17.

62 *Against Heresies*, 2.25.3–4.

63 *Colossians*: 1.17; I *Corinthians*: 12.6.

64 *City of God*, 22.24, p. 1071; *Consolation*, 4.6: verse, 40–43.

65 See, for example, *Matthew*: 10.29, for the celebrated divine concern for a sparrow's fall from the sky.

just as Faith delivers men from Mosaic Law, without wholly cancelling it. Protagorean man is unmanned, disabled before a realm of hazards and wonders, his mathematizing mocked by miracles. Miracles for Augustine are 'not against nature, but against nature as known'. Thereby 'We are left with a conception of "nature" as compatible with any possible happening.'[66] The truth of Christianity is attested indeed not through normal experience but through the miraculous: Origen argues against Celsus for the clinching manifestations of divine power;[67] and so acerbic a scholar as Jerome appears avidly credulous in his life of St Paul, with his testifying Faun, talking beasts and leonine morticians.[68]

The third form of the 'mystification' of the natural in the reworking of classical ideas is the return to a semi-animistic physical nature, through the preservation of polytheism in demonized inversion. The debased Olympian pantheon and myriad lesser 'devils' infest the elements, pervade the fair fields. 'Millions of spiritual creatures walk the earth / Unseen' applies to more than angelic presences, and is laid down in Justin and Origen, among others.[69]

In summary, nature has been decisively desacralized through the insistence upon a God who utterly transcends it; and natural law has been qualified in such a way as to encompass any miracle or mythological grotesque, thereby depreciating and eroding humanity's rational command of nature, and his confidence in inhabiting the earth. Into the crystal-clear cosmos of Hellenism's 'geometrical imagination' come billowing the eerie mists of total possibility; credulousness finds theological sanction, even motivation, in the Christian interpretation of divine omnipotence. Tertullian's '*credo quia ineptum*' ('I believe it because it is absurd') is still echoing in Sir Thomas Browne's 'wingy divinities' and 'oh altitudo!' at the close of a millennium of the fideistic fabulous.[70] The lucid cosmology expounded by Basil, the Boethian praise of regularity and order, coexist with the speaking animals of hagiography, the agency of spirits in landscape, and a 'whole creation'

66 *City of God*, 21.8, p. 980; and 22.8–10, pp. 1033–49. *CHLGEMP*, p. 401.

67 *Contra Celsum*, 1.2.

68 *Vita Sancti Pauli*, trans. Helen Waddell, *Desert Fathers*, pp. 33–53.

69 Milton, *Paradise Lost*, 4.677; Justin Martyr, *First Apology*, 5; *Second Apology*, 5; Origen, *Contra Celsum*, 8.55; cf. *CHLGEMP*, p. 165; and M. D. Madden, *The Pagan Divinities and their Worship as Depicted in the Works of Saint Augustine* (Washington: 1930).

70 Tertullian, *On the Flesh of Christ*, 5; Browne, *Religio Medici*, 1.9.

in 'groaning and travailing' for liberation.[71] The poetic topoi of the Invocation of Nature, and of reflorescence in the coming of the divine maintain in Christianized adaptation a semi-animistic earth and fertility. In England Rogation ceremonies were to continue throughout the Middle Ages into the Civil War period, where seventeenth-century Protestants were to argue, correctly, that they were the Church's appropriation of pagan *ambarvalia*.[72]

Much has been conjectured about the consequences of the Christian 'de-animization' of nature:[73] but this is, as I have tried to suggest, an overstatement. Although the actual forms of nature were divested of supernatural agency, demonological infestation returned them in apotropaic practice to a supernatural association which could blend easily into outright animism. The medieval practice of reading scripture to springs or giving blessing to corn in order to preserve their wholesomeness – theologically by protecting them from corruption by spirits – could easily be misinterpreted by the rustic and unlettered. It came down only to a nicety of distinction between, in today's terminology, 'animism' and a mode of 'polytheism'. I suspect that the devaluation of the earth which Christianity undoubtedly helped establish was due more to its insistence upon a transcendent creator and homeland than its supposed cancellation of active 'pagan' vitalities in landscape.

A final major transformation of the Hellenic view of nature figures a cosmos (in Hopkins' phrase) 'adazzle, dim'.[74] The Christian redirects, in Platonic fashion, his perception of nature towards the bright perfection of its divine ground. 'The underlying reality of things is their likeness to God and their participation in him.'[75] Accordingly, in the sublime vision of mystical theology, reality is conceived as a shining sacramental ladder: the illumined soul surveys an ontology of pilgrimage. It is a world built up from Light.[76] Material creation may be cherished by all for its immanence: its complex forms, the jewelled

71 *Romans*: 8.19–22.

72 Keith Thomas, *Religion and the Decline of Magic* (1971; rpt. Harmondsworth: 1978), pp. 71–75, esp. p. 75, footnote 52.

73 See, for example, Lynn White, 'What Accelerated Technological Progress in the Western Middle Ages?,' in A. C. Crombie (ed.), *Scientific Change* (London: 1963), pp. 272–91.

74 *Pied Beauty*, line 9, in *Poems of G. M. Hopkins* ed. W. H. Gardner and N. H. Mackenzie (Oxford: 1967), p. 70.

75 *CHLGEMP*, p. 453.

76 For light as the true being of created being, cf. pseudo-Dionysius, *De Divinis Nominibus*, 4, 2.

necklace of the Eternal Being; while the mystagogue beholds a model of brightening tiers of light, interlaced and ever more luminous, ascending finally into the dark brilliance of the divine substance.[77] Of this 'illuminative cascade' and universal circulation of the Good, to be rhapsodically echoed, among others, by Henry Vaughan, Gilson summarises: 'The world of Denis can best be described as a circulation of the good, from the Good and toward the Good.'[78]

The celebrated scriptural foundation for a revelatory Creation is found in *Romans* 1.20: 'the invisible things of him from the creation of the world are clearly seen, being understood by the things that are made, even his eternal power and Godhead'.[79] Wedding this to Plato's Idealism, the Fathers proceed to a synthesis which dignifies and ennobles the cosmos, both visible and incorporeal, to a degree undreamt of by Plato – and perhaps by Paul, for whom nature resembled himself as groaning and travailing in eagerness for the Parousia. Material nature for the Christian is a given cosmos of real, concrete and individual substances, not mere Platonic shadows. Further, Christianity elevates the ideal world instantiated in the actual through that departure[80] from Plato by which the Ideas or Forms are exalted into the Divine Mind or Attributes. Still the perfect and eternal exemplars to which the demiurge looked as patterns on which to model the world, these are now also the thoughts of God, and associated with the second person of the Trinity as the *ideator mundi*. Bonaventura is to entitle this conception 'Exemplarism', but Christ as Logos is of course Johannine,[81] and the identification of the Ideas with God's self-contemplation dates at least from Clement of Alexandria.[82] Exalted in Exemplarism, the whole of creation takes on a sacramental character, and nature becomes 'the mirror of God', reflecting his perfection in varying degrees.

Ask the loveliness of the earth, ask the loveliness of the sea, ask the loveliness of the wide airy spaces, ask the loveliness of the sky, ask the order of the stars, ask the sun making the day light with its beams, ask the moon tempering the

77 For the Divine Dark, cf. Gregory of Nyssa, *Life of Moses* in *PG*, 44.377A; pseudo-Dionysius, *Ecclesiastical Hierarchy*, 5.2, and *Mystical Theology*, 1.3.

78 Gilson, p. 82. Cf. *De Divinis Nominibus*, 4.4; and *De Caelesti Hierarchica*, 1.1.

79 Cf. also *Acts*: 14.15–17.

80 Jaeger, pp. 45, 125, speculates that the Platonic Ideas as the thoughts of God may have derived from the Platonic school itself.

81 *John*: 1.1–5, 9–18. Cf. also Justin Martyr, *Second Apology*, 10 and 13.

82 *Stromateis*, 5, 3.16. Compare also Plotinus, *Ennead*, 3.9.1; and Philo, *De Opificio Mundi*, 4.

darkness of the night that follows ... ask all these things, and they will all answer thee, Lo, see we are lovely. Their loveliness is their confession. And these lovely but mutable things, who has made them, save Beauty immutable?[83]

As if such sublimation of both sensible and intelligible realms endangered the immaculate transcendence of the Father, or over-exalted the phenomenal world, Augustine insists that while God creates the visible world to show him forth, 'he remains always above and beyond it as well as hidden in its mysterious innermost being'.[84] The pseudo-Dionysius attempts to keep God aloft in 'super-being' (ὑπερούσιος): revealed in the symbolic theology but rescued from anthropomorphism in its negation (Apophatic theology), and preserved inaccessible in Divine Darkness.[85]

Nevertheless, in its symbolic resplendence as exalted by the Fathers, the *liber creaturarum* reveals a hierarchy of creatures each perfect in their kind.[86] Moreover, each creature as a 'participation' in God is a 'theophany',[87] whose divinely derived perfection may become visible to the illumined mind as the effulgence of its interior luminosity.[88] The intelligible forms of this world's composite sensible objects are 'rays' from the 'Father of Lights', the shining ενέργειαι which draw the creature back to its creator.[89] It was just this conception which Herbert is to draw on in 'The Elixir':

> A man that looks on glasse,
> On it may stay his eye;
> Or if he pleaseth through it passe,
> And so the heav'n espie.[90]

Thus the alienation of man from nature is overcome, despite the Fall, at the level of contemplation. On this view, the Christian relation to nature obviously cannot be said to be more denigratory or distressed

83 *Sermones ad populum*, second series, no. 241, ch. 2, in *Oeuvres Complètes de Saint Augustin*, vol. 18, p. 238.
84 *CHLGEMP*, p. 397: based on *De Trinitate*, 3.4.10.
85 *CHLGEMP*, pp. 457–62.
86 Origen, *Commentary on Saint John*, 13.37; Augustine, *De Moribus Manichaeorum*, 2.6.8; *De Vera Religione*, 32.60. Gilson, pp. 40, 74.
87 Gregory of Nyssa, *De Hominis Opificio*, 2.132–33; *In Canticum Canticorum*, 11. Pseudo-Dionysius, *De Caelesti Hierarchia*, 4.3. *CHLGEMP*, pp. 450, 463.
88 Gregory of Nyssa, *Apology*, 72D, 76C.
89 Ibid. *CHLGEMP*, pp. 448, 453.
90 George Herbert, 'The Elixir', lines 9–12, in *The English Poems of George Herbert* ed. C. A. Patrides (London: 1974), p. 188.

than the Hellenic, although, as we have seen, it does dethrone man from sovereign command and agency in nature. For if the Christian doctrine of *συμπάθεια* or harmony as the primary substance of the whole creation[91] is itself derived from Plato and Posidonius,[92] the Greco-Roman aspiration toward scientific suzerainty had later seemed to enthrone man over an apparently alien realm, had ruptured the sense of symbiosis in dissolving the anthropomorphic imagination. As early as the fourth century BC, Socrates could ironically indicate the 'humanist' estrangement from nature's ways of fashionable Athenian intellectuals in the opening of the *Phaedrus*: 'the people in the city have something to teach me, but the fields and trees won't teach me anything'.[93] In the Lyceum, Theophrastus was to query, and later the Epicurean school wholly repudiate, the teleologically ordered earth of Plato and Aristotle. Scepticism allowed no faith in the harmony of man and nature; and Celsus had argued that 'everything was made just as much for the irrational animals as for man'.[94] But the integrity of man and nature problematic in natural science is assured in natural theology. Though man's status in nature is to the Christian equivocal, the concept of nature herself is profoundly and unquestionably anthropocentric. 'Providence cares for the rational beings', Origen rounds on Celsus: 'while the fact that irrational animals also share in what is made for men has been a subsidiary result'.[95] The alienated triumphalism of patrician Rome, expressed in its 'picnic' relation to rurality and its dominative physical technology, cedes to the awesome supernal harmonics of Christianity, expressed in a humbler theology of dependent stewardship and remitted sin. 'Culture' no longer builds against 'nature', but, as the Church directed by Christ, seeks to propagate a culture restitutive of the pristine universal nature. For the Fathers, human consciousness and nature's energies dwell in communion, integrated in the emanation and reflection of the One. 'All things find in you their origin, their impulse, the centre of their being.'[96]

91 Basil, *Hexaemeron*, 2.2.33.

92 Plato, *Timaeus*, 32A; L. Edelstein, 'The Physical System of Posidonius' in *American Journal of Philology*, 57 (1936). Cf. also Leo Spitzer, *Classical and Christian Ideas*, ch. 1.

93 *Phaedrus*, 230E.

94 Origen, *Contra Celsum*, 4.75; trans. H. Chadwick (Cambridge: 1953), p. 243.

95 Ibid., pp. 243–44.

96 Augustine, *Confessions*, 1.2; cf. *Romans*, 11.36.

Agricultural activism

The Christian restoration of man and nature to unity on the planes of teleology and natural contemplation extends also into the realm of manual relations in the theory and practice of agriculture.

'All places are now accessible, all are well known, all open to commerce', remarks Tertullian with satisfaction; 'most pleasant farms have obliterated all traces of what were once dreary and dangerous wastes; cultivated fields have subdued forests; flocks and herds have expelled wild beasts; sandy deserts are sown; rocks are planted; marshes are drained; and where once were hardly solitary cottages, there are now large cities'.[97]

As in Epicureanism and Virgil[98], natural problems stimulate development of the arts, and man is exalted for his intellect which overcomes the hazards of nature. Mind imposes form on the substrate of raw matter. What, however, contradicts such classical triumphalism, and returns us to the novel Christian 'loving bond' with creation is, in part, the insistence that the significant agency in fertility is divine, not human skill: 'While man plants and waters, God Himself giveth the increase.'[99] More importantly, it is the basic reconception of cultivation as not coercion, but completion. Against the alienating interventionism of man the imperial animal, slicing the earth-mother with callous plough, we have farmer as man-midwife, bringing to the fulfilment of harvest acres and laden orchards an earth tangled and incomplete at creation. For Origen and Lactantius,[100] there is 'a continuity from the creative act of God to the art of man': nature is improved with divine approbation and intention, human technology and transformations being extensions of God's foresight.[101] Man now is not an estranged despot, but the Christian steward, partner of providence,[102] satisfying nature by satisfying himself. Monastic

97 Tertullian, *A Treatise on the Soul*, trans. Peter Holmes, ch. 30.3, in *The Ante-Nicene Fathers: Translations of the Writings of the Fathers Down to A.D. 325*, ed. Alexander Roberts and James Donaldson (rpt. ed. A. C. Coxe, Buffalo: 1885–1907), vol. 3, p. 210. 98 Virgil, *Georgics*, 1.118,esp. 'labor omnia vincit' at 1.145–46.

99 Augustine, *De Trinitate*, 3.5, 11; compare *Psalms*: 65.9–10; 107.33–39; *Job*: 1.21; *Deuteronomy*: 11.13–17; *Matthew*: 6.38; *Mark*: 4.27–28; I *Corinthians*: 3.7.

100 Lactantius: *The Epitome of the Divine Institutes*, chs. 68–69; *A Treatise on the Anger of God*, ch. 13; Origen: *Contra Celsus*, 4.75–80. Henry Chadwick's edition of this last work (Cambridge: 1953), p. 245, underlines pagan sources.

101 Glacken, p. 181.

102 Ambrose, *Letters*, trans. Sister Mary Melchior Beyenka (New York: 1954), Letter 8, p. 47; Theodoret of Cyrrhus, *Providence*; Augustine, *City of God*, 22.24.

penetration, clearance and planting of wilderness on this view may be not merely a propaedeutic to paradise regained, but itself the paradisal state anticipated. Thus, in some degree, it may be said that nature exists *in potentia*, and that man not only inhabits the universe, but as God's agent co-creates it. Man and nature are mother and nurse each to the other; and to God is the glory. The poet Mark, monk or pilgrim at Monte Cassino in the fifth or eighth century, articulates transformation of the natural:

> Lest men should tire who seek thy high abode
> Winds round its sides a gently-sloping road.
> Yet justly does the mountain honour thee,
> For thou hast made it rich and fair to see.
> Its barren sides by thee are gardens made,
> Its naked rocks with fruitful vineyards laid,
> The crags admire a crop and fruit not theirs,
> The wild wood now a bounteous harvest bears.
> E'en so our barren deeds to fruit thou trainest,
> Upon our arid hearts pure waters rainest.
> Turn now to fruit the evil thorns, I pray,
> That vex the stupid breast of Mark alway.[103]

What distinguishes this from the otherwise remarkably similar panegyrics we have found in Pliny and Statius, is the displacement of cause from man to God in the teleological faith of its humble vocative. Bound to man in a unity of purpose and mutuality of benefit, the things of nature can 'admire' a crop 'not theirs'. The Faith has forged 'a chain from theology to manuring'.[104]

The enthusiasm for agriculture as midwifery rather than matricide had determinants others than the metaphysical. Christian apologetics had often defended the new religion against charges of irresponsible negligence in renouncing the world – 'We sail with you, and fight with you, and till the ground with you'[105] Tertullian had protested – but with the fourth century a number of factors promoted a determined new productivist ethos. The Church is by now diffusing a culture to the labouring masses, beyond the 'welfare circles' of its urban bases, and is in effect educating the empire's producers. As such, its emphasis

103 Quoted in Justin McCann, *Saint Benedict* (New York: 1958), pp. 203–4; Latin text in Migne, *PL*, vol. 80, 183–86; I am indebted for this poem to Glacken, p. 304.

104 Phrase from Glacken, p. 351.

105 Tertullian, *Apology*, ch. 42.

on the privilege and importance of agricultural activity, and on a philosophy of service, subordinate partnership and honorific labour, can be seen as an aspect of this inculcation of a new 'dominant ideology' subsequent to the Edict of Milan. To the Church leaders, on the other hand, increasingly drawn from the ranks of the Roman hereditary aristocracy, the traditional patrician derogation of commerce consolidated the position, particularly since with the Church now a landed proprietor, bishops all over the West ran large estates. In *De Officiis* Ambrose declares an honest trade a contradiction in terms: a shipwrecked merchant deserves his ill fortune through his avarice, whereas the farming of inherited land was the only form of making money which gave no offence.[106] Furthermore, from the third century, in the Northern Provinces, a shrinkage of the rural population, and the abandonment of once cultivated lands set in, so that by 395 large areas of Campania were exempted from taxation as abandoned and uninhabited, and by 440 rural depopulation was such that the government actually lightened general taxation.[107] Lactantius, writing of the *agri deserti* in the early fourth century, records that 'Fields never repay the cost of cultivation ... the farmers are crippled by debts and cannot provide for the drainage of the soil, or the clearance of the land from brambles; and so the fertile countryside is converted to a barren swamp ... Everywhere we see abandoned farmland, full of weeds, bleak, deserted fields ... even the military roads are impassable.' Vineyards go unplanted, he complains, and fields unirrigated.[108] Moreover, marauding bands of *Bacaudae*, often swollen by the rural poor, waged guerilla wars against increasing numbers of soldiers in guard-posts established to police the countryside from the late second and early third century onwards.[109] Edicts of the late fourth century suggest that many citizens had begun to enlist private armies of men trained in the gladiator schools for their protection.[110] The Church itself was costly: 'a flock of sheep was needed to provide the parchment for copying a book by Seneca or Cicero';[111] and Perry Anderson argues that it was not its 'demoralizing doctrines or extramundane values' but the 'parasitic overweight' of the Church's

106 Paul Johnson, *A History of Christianity* (Harmondsworth: 1978), p. 107.
107 Mazzolani, *City*, p. 211.
108 Lactantius, *Panegyrics*, 8.6 and 7, trans., Mazzolani, p. 205.
109 F. Millar, *The Roman Empire and its Neighbours* (London: 1967), p. 6.
110 Mazzolani, p. 210.
111 Leclercq, p. 123.

'vast clerical apparatus ... which exhausted Roman economy and society'.[112] A gospel of work was clearly imperative.

Its foundation lay already to hand, however, in the Judaic tradition. Judaism alone of all the world's major religions had suggested that even in paradise man worked in governance of his fellow-creatures;[113] and we have seen that human labour as described in Genesis could be understood as the prosperous unfolding of divine blessing. Christ declares the labourer to be worthy of his hire, and several Epistles extol the self-sufficiency of labour.[114] The Judaic and primitive Christian legacies of meritorious perspiration are appropriated with a vengeance in the fourth century, as Augustine explodes the 'untoiling lily' reading of Christian lifestyle[115] in the *Retractiones*, and Pachomius and Basil likewise insist on idleness as corrosion of the soul, linking for the first time asceticism to manual labour. The Benedictine Rule put an end to the competitive self-torture often disfiguring anachoresis, establishing a cenobion of active *agape* which included manual work as a basic ingredient.[116] Acquiring the stature of holy worship, agricultural toil was undertaken by literate monks: *laborare est orare.*

Monastic cultivation was an innovation of the first significance not only as a solvent of the slave-mode of production, which had held agricultural technology in paralysis at virtually the Alexandrine level for centuries.[117] The reunion of mental and manual work with its de-stigmatization of axe, hoe and ox, its emancipation of rural labourer from the slave status of *instrumentum vocale,*[118] helped make possible, as we shall see, the close empirical involvement with landscape as a field of labour from which medieval calendar art was to emerge.

112 Perry Anderson, *Passages*, p. 132.
113 Passmore, *Man's Responsibility*, p. 7.
114 *Luke*: 10.7; *Ephesians*: 4.28; 2 *Thessalonians*: 3.10.
115 *Matthew*: 6.25–34; 1 *Corinthians*: 3.5–10; *Retractiones*: Book 2, ch. 21.
116 D. J. Chitty, *The Desert a City* (Oxford: 1966), pp. 20–21, 27; Herbert B. Workman, *The Evolution of the Monastic Ideal* (1913; rpt. Boston: 1962); A. H. M. Jones, *The Later Roman Empire* (Oxford: 1964), vol. 2, pp. 930–33.
117 Perry Anderson, *Passages*, pp. 24–28, 79–80, 135.
118 Ibid., pp. 24–25. Cf. Aristotle, *Politics*, 1.4.1253.

Landscape-consciousness

Topoi in Latin Christian verse

The civilization of classical Antiquity was defined by the development of superstructures of unexampled sophistication and complexity, over material infrastructures of comparatively invariant crudity and simplicity: there was always a dramatic disproportion in the Graeco-Roman world between the vaulting intellectual and political sky and the cramped economic earth beneath it. When its final collapse came, nothing was less obvious than that its superstructural heritage – now impossibly distant from immediate social realities – should survive it, in however compromised a form. A specific vessel was necessary for this, sufficiently apart from the classical institutions of Antiquity and yet moulded within them, and so capable of escaping the general wreckage to transmit the mysterious messages of the past to the less advanced future. The Church objectively performed this role ... No other dynamic transition from one mode of production to another reveals the same splay in superstructural development: equally, none other contains a comparable spanning institution.[119]

In terms of landscape in poetry, the 'superstructural heritage' of Hellenized Christianity, transmitted to Romanized Europe and to the succeeding romance-language cultures, displayed a remarkable continuity within radically altered socio-economic circumstances. The transposition of Christian scriptures into classical forms takes place on a significant scale from the fourth century. Prudentius is to become 'the Virgil and Horace of the Christians', and Lactantius 'the Christian Cicero'. In prose, the essentially Judaic form of the 'Hexaemeron' (the contemplation of the six days of the Creation) finds the Christian masters in Basil, Ambrose and Jerome, but as many as eighty specimens survive from the fourth to seventh centuries: 'almost all of them comparatively formless masses of erudite and discursive prose'.[120] In poetry, 'Apollinaris the Elder of Syria, and his son, confronted by an edict of Julian the Apostate forbidding Christians to teach the classics, proceeded to turn the narrative portions of the Old Testament into Greek epic verse, the Psalms into Pindaric odes, and the New Testament into Platonic dialogues. Virtually none of their work has survived to our own day.'[121] Aiming to seduce educated

119 Ibid., pp. 136–37.
120 Watson Kirkconnell, *The Celestial Cycle* (Toronto: 1952) p. xiv.
121 Ibid., p. xiii.

readership from the pagan classics to a higher Christian Muse, epics are composed by Juvencus, Sedulius, Avitus, and Dracontius, drawing on the gospel story, or in the last case, the whole of the Bible. Other Christian poets include Paulinus, Orientius, Venantius Fortunatus, and Ambrose as hymnodist.[122]

Within the corpus of Latin–Christian verse, I have found six 'landscape topoi', all of which are classical in descent, and all of which survive the collapse of Rome to grow peacefully within the hallowed gardens of Christian verse through after ages. These descriptive or didactic topoi of natural sight and meaning will be individually discussed in pages following according to how they embody particular categories of landscape consciousness. For the moment, their mere enumeration will serve to indicate the magnitude of the bequest of the late antique Christian poets to the nature-writers of posterity, from Dante to Milton. The legacy comprises, at the least: the topos of Ideal landscape as a determinate format; the sensuously embellished Eden, transformed from enclosure into luxurious pleasance; the Invocation of Nature; the efflorescence of nature in the presence of the divine; the description of Spring; and the Goddess Natura. Undoubtedly, further motifs remain to be traced, given the great quantity of early Christian verse.

The territorial imagination

We turn now to the apprehension of landscape in terms of the typical features of one or other of the primary 'domains' of the universe. In this respect, perception of landscape by the citizens of the Dominate[123] is something very different from what it had been for those of the Hellenistic world and the Principate. There have been two primary developments. First, the importance of the religious opposition between earth and afterworld, whose emergence we noted in the New Testament, becomes elaborated within Christian writings, and with the universalization of the faith, it dominates educated understanding of the terrestrial world. We shall therefore examine presentations of

122 For literary appraisals of these poets, cf. F. J. E. Raby, *A History of Christian-Latin Poetry from the Beginnings to the Close of the Middle Ages* (2nd edn, Oxford: 1953); and Pierre de Labriolle, trans. Herbert Wilson, *History and Literature of Christianity from Tertullian to Boethius* (London: 1924).

123 The period from Aurelian onward, when full-length prostration before the emperor, introduced in 274, prevails; the emperor being 'Dominus et Deus'.

Eden, Heaven and Hell, as 'mythic space' which conditions perception of the daily world. Second, in socio-economic reality, the slow decay of trade and the splintering of the universal state of Rome into the small, autonomous rural units that became the archipelago of the 'manorial' system, effect a relapse, in our terms of chapter two, from a world of 'commercial geography' into one of 'agrarian territorialism'. The seige-mentality of isolated economic localism and endemic fighting bisects space into the primal divisions of home-territory and Chaos: the worlds of a Beowulf, who dares the monsters of the fenlands, and of Hilarion, the hermit-saint daring the fiery heartland of the Syrian desert, are very close. The condition of the heroic world is an awesome topographic dualism.

We have glanced already at the progressive barbarization of the empire, and the darkening misery of the countryside from the later fourth century, with its weird archaic cults, its *Bacaudae*, invasions, guard-posts and depopulation, its bleak *agri deserti* traversed by cohorts of unstable semi-barbarian legionaries or foraging dogs and pack-animals relapsing into their wild state. Urban prosperity in the West had never recovered from the third-century crises, and the centralized bureaucracy of the empire is finally battered into political amorphism with the subsidence of the towns into a ruralized economy. Even in the late third century, only ten per cent of the population remained in the towns,[124] and cities were subsequently to degenerate into ghettoes of poverty, riot and famine, abandoned to delapidation by magnates retiring to fortified country estates, towards whose security the artisan class slowly drifted as the gap between rich and poor, the *secessio plebis*, became unbridgeable.[125]

To this increasingly 'castellar' rurality, no longer a unified expanse of imperial provinces centred upon towns, but increasingly a world of isolated giant estates dominated by powerful magnate strongholds or local monasteries, corresponds a new landscape aesthetic: the landscape of retreat. The Hellenistic ideal had featured the 'open pleasance' of tranquil Campanian landscape paintings, and the *otium* of a languid, free transhumance fluted in pastoral verse. We have quoted Tertullian above on the safe, open arable of the empire. The *Colonate* of the third century, however, tied thousands of peasants in the West permanently to their landlord's estates, and under the later patrocinium of Italy, Gaul and Spain peasants surrendered their lands to patrons

124 Brown, *World*, p. 84. 125 Perry Anderson, *Passages*, pp. 92–100.

who returned them only as temporary tenancies.[126] Paintings of the country villas of these powerful magnates or Roman 'barons' show them no longer to be single-storeyed but constructed with a closed lower storey and towers, to serve as a castle in times of invasion.[127] Venantius Fortunatus 'celebrates the castle of Bishop Nicetius [in Gaul] towering as a ward of defence above the river':

> Here we see the vast frowning fortress, with the river below; the mighty towers contrasting with the peace of field and vineyard; the threatening ballista and the fruitful orchards.[128]

As, in the battlemented West, geographical mobility – sightseeing, private travel, maritime traffic and commercial journeying – slows to a standstill, so appetite for περιήγησια or scenic itineraries and descriptive writings sickens, and falls into a kind of delirium. Forsaking factual topography – the 'Baedeker' literature of authors like Pausanias – human fears feed on the phantasmagoric conditions of hagiography, and yearn for inviolable seclusion. In communities increasingly isolated, stationary and beleaguered, swallowed up in a ubiquitous countryside, encircled by demons, marauders and dereliction, monks and poets pen an ideal landscape of seclusion, as sanctuary or sortie.

'The Abbot Nilenus said, "Invulnerable from the enemy is he who loves quiet: but he who mixeth with the crowd hath often wounds."'[129] Monastic penetration of those deep solitudes for which they have so many words – *vastinae, solitudines,* the *mansi, eremi loca invia, alsi, non vestiti*[130] – is only in part the affirmative aim to fulfil Isaiah and make glad the wilderness and the solitary place, the desert to blossom as the rose (*Isaiah*: 35.1, 7). Helen Waddell writes brilliantly of men

> Hungry for a quiet that could not be shaken even by the rustling of reeds [of which an Abbot complains] or the voice of a bird ... *Portus impassibilitatis, mansionem quietorum praeparare,* the haven of invulnerable living, to build a

126 Perry Anderson, *Passages,* pp. 94–100.

127 Brown, *World,* p. 39, fig. 29.

128 Trans. by F. J. E. Raby, *Secular Latin Poetry in the Middle Ages* (1934: rpt. 2 vols., Oxford: 1957), vol. 1, p. 130; P&S, pp. 23–24.

129 *Vitae Patrum,* trans. from the Greek by Pelagius the Deacon and John the Subdeacon, and trans. into English by Helen Waddell, *The Desert Fathers,* 2.11, p. 94. On the earlier Epicurean appreciation of serene 'sanctuaries of philosophy', cf. Lucretius, *De Rerum Natura,* 2.1–14.

130 Prosper M. Boissonade, *Life and Work in Medieval Europe,* trans. from the French by Eileen Power (New York: 1927), pp. 31–32; ref. Glacken, p. 291.

house in the land of quiet men, phrases such as these do but make articulate the sighing of the prisoners of a clattering world, the last delusion of the human heart that solitude is peace. Sentence after sentence from the Desert, the 'trackless place' of Antony's desire, fall on the ear with a dangerous enchantment: the remoteness of death is in the lovely rhythms of the old hermit's questioning. 'Tell me, I pray thee, how fares the human race: if new roofs be risen in the ancient cities: whose empire is it now that sways the world?'[131]

We noted in chapter two the predilection for mountain-top paradises in the verse of secular poets such as Claudian and Statius; Christian poets like St Ephrem Syrus, Lactantius and Avitus now locate Eden as a peak[132] and Basilian monasteries such as those on Mount Latomos or Mount Sinai are built in almost inaccessible places on lofty crags or steep mountain sides. Sometimes access is only by the climbing of long rope ladders or being hauled upwards in a cordial basket. Solitary anchorites abide 'one by one in their cells, a mighty silence and a great quiet among them',[133] records the Greek author of a history of the monks of Egypt; and Jerome's *Vita Sancti Pauli,* by an author with five 'epic years of desert sanctity behind him', takes pleasure, I find, in imaginatively detailing St Paul the Hermit's discovery of a perfect retreat, inaccessible yet self-sufficient, in a remote mountainside of the Lower Thebaid.

At length he came upon a rocky mountain, and at its foot, at no great distance, a huge cave, its mouth closed by a stone. There is a thirst in men to pry into the unknown: he moved the stone, and eagerly exploring came within on a spacious courtyard open to the sky, roofed by the wide-spreading branches of an ancient palm, and with a spring of clear shining water: a stream ran hasting from it and was soon drunk again, through a narrow opening, by the same earth that had given its waters birth ... Egyptian records declare that the place was a mint for coining false money, at the time that Antony was joined to Cleopatra.[134]

131 Waddell, *Desert Fathers,* p. 18, quoting her own translation, ibid. p. 48, of Jerome's *Vita Sancti Pauli.*

132 St Ephrem Syrus, *Des Heiligen Ephraem des Syers Hymnen de Paradiso und Contra Julianum,* ed. Edmund Beck (Louvain: 1957), pp. 5–60; ref. Duncan, *Milton's Earthly Paradise,* p. 60; Lactantius, *De Ave Phoenice,* 1–28, in *Anthologia Latina,* part one, ed. A. Rieses (Leipzig: 1869), pp. 188–89; ref. Giammati, *Earthly Paradise,* pp. 70–71; Avitus, *The Earthly Paradise,* trans. Frederick Brittain, *Penguin Book of Latin Verse,* p. 106.

133 *History of the Monks of Egypt,* trans. from the Greek by Rufinus of Aquileia, 22, trans. into modern English by Helen Waddell, *Desert Fathers,* p. 75.

134 Waddell, Ibid., p. 35; Jerome, *Vita Sancti Pauli,* trans. Waddell, ibid, p. 43.

Christian enthusiasm for the spell of the cave had in fact emerged early – by the early second century a 'grotto of the Nativity' was being shown off in the Holy Land[135] – and perhaps is in part another Christian appropriation of a pagan cultus. Caverns holy to the nymphs or gods abounded in Homer and Virgil, Horace and Ovid, and Fox records pagans as late as the fourth century AD still given to 'persistent potholing' to honour chthonic deities.[136] A 'speluncar theology' of the sacred cave develops in the Eastern Church's iconography of the desert, while in the West, by the time of Eusebius, caves all over the Holy Land become identified with Biblical figures. Caverns of the annunciation at Nazareth, of Lazarus' resurrection in Bethany and of Elijah on Mount Carmel are hallowed with shrines; while Constantine builds basilicas over the cave of the Nativity in Bethlehem, the sepulchre wherein Christ was buried, and the cavern on the top of the Mount of Olives whence he supposedly ascended.[137] The deepening fascination, however, surely owes much also to the taste for retreat in an age of anxiety, becoming coloured by outbreaks of Christian persecution, and climaxing in waves of monastic warfare against diabolic forces.

Jerome's axiom that there exists 'a thirst in men to pry into the unknown' points to the adventurist 'heroic' face of the landscape of retreat. 'We are not ignorant that in our land there are fair and secret places, where there be fruit trees in plenty and the graciousness of gardens, and the richness of the land would give us our daily bread with very little bodily toil ... But we have despised all these and with them all the luxurious pleasure of the world' boasts the soundly mortified Abbot Abraham: 'we have joy in this desolation, and to all this delight do we prefer the dread vastness of this solitude, nor do we weigh the riches of your glebe against these bitter sands'.[138] Monks, as Brown phrases it, earn their reputation 'as "prize-fighters" against the devil ... In villages dedicated for millennia to holding their own against nature, the holy man had deliberately chosen "anti-culture" – the neighbouring desert, the nearest mountain crags. In a civilization identified exclusively with town life, the monks had committed the absurd – they had "made a city in the desert."'[139] Infertile or barren

135 Robin Lane Fox, *Pagans and Christians*, p. 476. 136 Ibid., p. 673.
137 George H. Williams, *Wilderness and Paradise*, pp. 36–38.
138 *Of Mortification*, Cassian of Marseilles, trans. Waddell, *Desert Fathers*, p. 233.
139 Brown, *World*, p. 101.

landscape had never been lost to view even in the classical period: the *incomposita terra* (unserviceable land) theme found in Lucretius is re-echoed in Boethius and Ambrose.[140] But the 'inhospitality of the earth' in wasteland, abyss and massif is now sought out by the crack-troops of the *Pantocrator*; for anachoresis specializes in challenging the heart of terror in climactic landscapes of inhuman savagery and solitude, seeking to win, *solus ad solum*, the supreme achievement of the *visio dei*. 'I would set out solitary to explore the desert,' recalls Jerome, 'and wherever I would spy the depth of a valley or a mountainside or a precipitous rock, there was my place of prayer, there the torture-house of my unhappy flesh: and, the Lord Himself is witness, after many tears, and eyes that clung to heaven, I would sometimes seem to myself to be one with the angelic hosts'.[141] As Waddell puts it, 'he must have something craggy to break his mind upon';[142] but the motivation, I would argue, is generic to contemporary holiness, and is in some degree shared by the layman, who savours a hagiography not of Franciscan succour and ministry, but of daring a Conradian 'heart of darkness'. 'The fascination of abomination'[143] entails experiencing a powerful *frisson* from the stupendous in landscape, evinced in Augustine's derisive reference to misplaced marvellings: 'Men go out and gaze in astonishment at high mountains, the huge waves of the sea, the broad reaches of rivers, the ocean that encircles, or the stars in their courses. But they pay no attention to themselves.'[144] The longing we have seen of desperate and fearful men for the barbarians to sweep in, for climactic resolution in a climate of seige and dread, finds similar expression in the hermit saints' counter-offensive against the demons' homelands, an heroic 'advance front' beyond the enemies' own lines. Hermitage in furthermost wilderness[145] is as the ultimate terror, the ultimate victory: tranquillity is the palm of a maniacal courage that outfaces Lucifer's landscapes.

The venerable old man set out, supporting his feeble limbs on his staff, to go he knew not whither. And now came burning noon, the scorching sun

140 *De Rerum Natura*, 5.200–17; *De Consolatione Philosophiae*, 2.7 (Harmondsworth: 1969), p. 73; Ambrose, *Hexaemeron*, 1.28.

141 'Ad Eustochium', *Epistles*, 22.7, trans. Waddell, *Desert Fathers*, p. 37.

142 *Desert Fathers*, p. 37.

143 Joseph Conrad, *Heart of Darkness* (Harmondsworth: 1973), p. 9.

144 *Confessions*, 10.8, p. 216.

145 Compare again the Conradian truth or victory, met in 'the lost, forgotten, unknown places of the earth': *Lord Jim* (Harmondsworth: 1949), p. 243.

overhead, yet would he not flinch from the journey begun ... Antony continued to travel through the regions he had entered upon, now gazing at the tracks of wild beasts, and now at the vastness of the broad desert: what he should do, whither he should turn, he knew not ... Yet perfect love, as the Scripture saith, casteth out fear ... [146]

Almost legendary was Scete (Wadi 'n Natrun), fifty miles into the Nitrian desert south-west of Damanhur:

They said that he [Macarius of Alexandria] was a lover beyond all other men of the desert, and had explored its ultimate and inaccessible wastes ... The place in which the holy Macarius lived was called Scete. It is set in a vast desert, a day and night's journey from the monasteries on Nitria, and the way to it is to be found or shown by no track and no landmarks of earth, but one journeys by the signs and courses of the stars. Water is hard to find, and when it is found it is of a dire odour and as it might be bituminous, yet inoffensive in taste. Here therefore are men made perfect in holiness (for so terrible a spot could be endured by none save those of austere resolve and supreme constancy).[147]

Inhuman and demon-haunted desert landscape may of course fascinate many different cultures. Marco Polo records of the Gobi desert that travellers who lag behind caravans there will be called to by demons, using their names and assuming familiar voices, but who will lead them out to perish lost to human sight. Milton is perhaps echoing this in those:

> ... airy tongues that syllable mens' names
> On sands and shores and desert wildernesses.[148]

But Milton writes within an expanding culture of driving exploration, and his tone suggests the far away entrancements, that sweetness to the marvellous, which are the siren-music likewise of Ariel and the world of the *Tempest*. That very different sensibility which not only thrilled to 'antres vast and deserts idle / Rough quarries, rocks and hills whose heads touch heaven',[149] but actually created and inhabited Scete, searching out for ultimate ordeal wild heat and silence, we will christen and define as 'the Ascetic Sublime'. Like the eighteenth-

146 Jerome, *Vita Sancti Pauli*, trans. Waddell, *Desert Fathers*, pp. 44–47.
147 *History of the Monks of Egypt*, Rufinus of Aquileia, in *Desert Fathers*, pp. 79–80.
148 Marco Polo, *Travels*, 1.36; Milton, *Comus*, lines 208–09; ref. C. S. Lewis, *The Discarded Image*, pp. 145–46.
149 *Othello*, in *Complete Works of Shakespeare*, ed. Peter Alexander (London: 1951), 1.3.140–41. All references to and quotation from Shakespeare will be from this edition.

century Sublime, natural magnitude, remoteness and savagery are its focus of pleasing horror; but unlike the Sublime of Burke and Kant it is a terminal and agonistic field. Its terrain does not offer 'aesthetic' gratification, and it exerts not beneficent, healing influence, but rather trial by maximal personal pain. Under its awful shadow, man recognizes less his infinite faculties than his exquisite vulnerabilities and his abject need of God. Moreover, the landscape itself is but one variety of willed torment interchangeable with other forms, such as ingeniously filling one's cell with a stench of stagnant water whose brewed foulness astounds fellow monks.[150] The stupendous in landscape is sought only for contemptuous eclipse by the pure *virtus* of an indomitable mental transcendence: a topography of oppugnancy, landscape as a literal *arduus furor*. A narrative by Sulpicius Severus concerning an aged hermit twelve miles from the Nile converges both polarities of the anchoretic tradition: the 'paradisal' reconditioning of nature, and near-fabulous ferocity of chosen conditions:

He had a garden ... full of many sorts of vegetables: a thing against nature in the desert, where everything is so parched and burnt by the rays of the sun that it seldom gives root or seed, and then but scant. But the labour that the saint shared with his ox, and his own industry, were to profit ... I saw then what you men of Gaul will hardly believe, the pot of vegetables that he was preparing for our meal boiling without any fire under it: so great is the heat of the sun.[151]

The Ascetic Sublime is a phenomenon the more striking for attracting not only misfits, runaways and poor men hardened to privation, but also the most sophisticated intellectuals and committed scholars of the age: Arsenius, Evagrius, Jerome, Basil and Rufinus, all 'men of letters, cursed with a feeling for prose'.[152] To these sensitive lovers of Greek and Roman culture too, the rocks and precipices are a sweeter meditation than orchards, winepress and wheat-plains; and the contrast, the schizophrenia, involved in such dualism is to them a literary deliciousness. Even Basil, the reformer of fanaticism, exults in the aesthetic insanity of rigorist retreat in an ebullient correspondence with Gregory of Nazianzus. Describing his hermitage overlooking the

150 *Saying of the Fathers*, Pelagius the Deacon and John the Subdeacon, 4.5, trans. Waddell, *Desert Fathers*, p. 99.

151 *Dialogues*, in *Corpus Scriptorum Ecclesiasticorum Latinorum* (Vienna: 1866), 1.c13; trans. Helen Waddell, *Beast and Saint* (London: 1934), p. 3.

152 Waddell, *Desert Fathers*, p. 83.

river Iris, Basil produces what I think deserves to be known as a *locus classicus* of the new deviance, and the importance of the passage merits substantial reproduction here.

There is a high mountain covered with a thick forest, watered on its northerly side by cool and transparent streams. At its base is outstretched an evenly sloping plain, ever enriched by moisture from the mountain. A forest of many-coloured and multifarious trees, a spontaneous growth surrounding the place, acts almost as a hedge to enclose it, so that even Calypso's isle, which Homer seems to have admired above all others for itself, is insignificant in comparison with this. For it is, in fact, not far from being an island, since it is shut in on all sides by barriers. Two deep ravines break off abruptly on two sides, and on a third side, at the bottom of a cliff, the river which glides gently by forms a wall, being itself a continuous and impassable barrier; and since the mountain stretches along the fourth side, and is joined to the ravines, through bending sides which take the form of a crescent, the passes at the base are blocked off. However, there is one entrance here, and we are in control of it. Adjoining my dwelling is another neck of land, as it were, which supports at its summit a lofty ridge, so that from the former the plain below lies outspread before the eyes, and from the elevation we may gaze on the encircling river, which in my mind at least furnishes no less pleasure than they who receive their first impression of the Strymon from Amphibolis. For the latter, as it spreads out with somewhat sluggish current to form the lake, almost ceases to be a river by reason of the stillness of its waters; whereas the former, as it flows more swiftly than any other river I know, for a short space is roughened by the rock which borders upon it. As the river recoils from the rock it coils itself into a deep whirlpool, furnishing me and every spectator with a most pleasant sight, and providing the natives of the region with complete independence in regard to food, since it nourishes in its eddies an innumerable multitude of fish. Why need I mention the exhalations from the land, or the breezes from the river? Someone else might well marvel at the multitudes of flowers or at the song of birds; but I have not leisure to turn my thoughts to these. The highest praise, however, which I can give to the place is that, although it is well adapted by its admirable situation to producing fruits of every kind, for me the most pleasing fruit it nourishes is tranquillity, not only because it is far removed from the disturbances of the city, but also because it attracts not even a wayfarer, except the guests who join me in hunting.[153]

This account is fascinating, above all for being not, as Wallace-Hadrill interprets it, 'a breach of good taste'[154] but as a highly self-conscious celebration of the new by an expert versed in the old. Mingling his

153 Basil, *Epistolae*, 14, trans. Roy J. Deferrari, *St. Basil: the Letters* (London: 1926), vol. 1, pp. 106–10. The passage is reprinted with minor alterations by Wallace-Hadrill, *Nature*, pp. 87–89.

154 Ibid, p. 91.

tones between irony and sincerity, Basil represents his crag retreat both humorously as surpassing Greco-Roman beauty-spots by their own criteria, and seriously as an ideal sanctuary. The classical tradition is evoked in the 'mixed grove' and vegetative luxuriance associated with Calypso's grotto, in the hint of Alcinous' orchards in the reference to 'fruits of every kind', in the exaltation of Prospect (Amphibolis), and in the allusion to the standard features of the *locus amoenus*: breezes, flowers and birdsong. These are not only fulfilled to perfection in this mountain-top 'paradise', but supplemented by the virtues of the ideal retreat: invulnerability ('hedge' of forests, 'walls' of cliff, the single guarded entry), and productive self-sufficiency. Finally, in outright perversity, the Sublime is asserted, as the 'sluggishness' of calm Strymon is slighted for a hurtling mountain torrent, 'roughened' over rocks and plunging into a whirlpool: 'a most pleasant sight'.

To this, Gregory retorts of Basil's 'mousehole' that 'All that has escaped the rocks is full of gullies, and whatever is not a gully is a thicket of thorns; and whatever is above the thorns is precipice; and the road above that is precipitous and slopes both ways, exercising the mind of travellers and calling for gymnastic exercise for safety. And the river rushes roaring down, which to you is a Strymon of Amphibolis for quietness, and there are not so many fishes in it as stones, nor does it flow into a lake but dashes into abysses, O my grandiloquent friend and inventor of new names!'[155]

This last phrase is of the essence, showing Gregory not to be 'covering the breach' of landscape etiquette made by his friend,[156] but recognizing its conscious transformation and colluding in that teasing and erudite combat of topographic ideals proferred him by Basil. Taking up the zest for paradox and for ironic relations with the classical past, he elsewhere writes: 'O that I could go back to those early days, when I luxuriated with you in hard living!... O for the gatherings of wood and the cuttings of stone! O for the golden plane tree under which we sat, which I planted, and Apollos – I mean your worthy self – watered!'[157]

Turning now to the treatment of Paradise and Hell in early Christian literature we find the classical heritage making a series of triumphal entries, most frequently into the fair fields of Eden.

155 Gregory of Nazianzus, *Epistolae*, 4, Wallace-Hadrill, *Nature*, p. 89.
156 Wallace-Hadrill, p. 91. 157 *Epistolae*, 6, Wallace-Hadrill, *Nature*, p. 89.

The tradition which was to dominate the Middle Ages and Renaissance derives from the late fourth and earlier fifth centuries. Origen, seeking for a refined and spiritual vision of Eden, had, while not entirely rejecting a literal reading of *Genesis*, stressed figurative interpretation of it as a moral and spiritual allegory. Rejecting a primarily allegoric Eden, but motivated by a similar desire to sequester pristine perfection from the grossness of the contemporary world, Basil, Gregory of Nyssa and Augustine insist on a maximal conception of the Fall, incurring hereditary original sin.[158] A material garden, thus securely distanced from the world by the age addicted to the landscape of retreat, is then transformed from the spare park of *Genesis* into verdant richness by the infusions of classical rhetoric. This drenching of the Hebraic 'flatland' in Greek unguents has been recorded with delight and thoroughness by Giammati, Kirkconnell, Duncan and others,[159] and as such I do not propose to revisit at length the classical *parfumerie*. 'The weather is fair, springtime is perpetual, there is no suffering or disease, trees bear fruit, the grass is green.'[160] The Greco-Roman motifs are those of perpetual spring, the mixed forest, carpet of flowers and the miniature landscape of tree, spring and grass, whose derivations are examined by Curtius[161] and in our first chapter above. The Scriptural legacy of trees and four rivers (*Genesis*: 2.8–10) is often supplemented by the 'bejewelled' tradition deriving from *Ezekiel* 28.13–14, hinted in *Genesis* 2.11–12, and ultimately of Babylonian descent. The influence of Virgil is everywhere inhaled, in particular the sweet repetitions of the *amoena virecta* phrasing and the *Est locus* openings, found in Prudentius, Sedulius, Lactantius, Avitus and others, and well documented by Giammati.[162] Diederich has

158 *Origen on First Principles*, trans. G. W. Butterworth (London 1936), 4.3.288. On Basil, Gregory and Augustine, cf. Duncan, pp. 41, 53–56, and J. M. Evans, *'Paradise Lost' and the Genesis Tradition* (Oxford: 1968), pp. 93–95; cf. esp. Augustine, *City of God*, 14.10.

159 Joseph E. Duncan, *Milton's Earthly Paradise*; Watson Kirkconnell, *The Celestial Cycle* (Toronto: 1952); A. Bartlett Giammati, *The Earthly Paradise and the Renaissance Epic* (Princeton: 1966); J. M. Evans, *'Paradise Lost' and the Genesis Tradition*; Frank E. Robbins, *The Hexaemeral Literature* (Chicago: 1912).

160 Giammati, *Earthly Paradise*, p. 70.

161 *European Literature and the Latin Middle Ages*, ch. 10, pp. 183–202.

162 *Aeneid*: 6.638–39, echoed by Prudentius, *Cathemerinon*, 3.101, and Caelius Sedulius, *Carmen Paschale*, 1.53: Giammatti, pp. 68–75. For Lactantius, Avitus and the *Est locus* openings, cf. ibid., p. 77; also Gordon Williams, *Tradition and Originality in Roman Poetry* (Oxford: 1968), p. 640.

found in Ambrose's *Hexaemeron* over one hundred repetitions of the master's cadences 'when a kind of spiritual exaltation raises the allegory above the common level of thought ... At times it seems impossible for St Ambrose to dispel Virgil's poetic diction from his mind.'[163] Gilded classical rhetoric for Eden, in the last and darkest century of the western empire, seems indeed a logical necessity, estranging from an actuality circumscribed and penetrated by barbarism a locus of perfection lapped in Latinity. 'It is an injury', wrote the pseudo-Basil, 'to compare paradise to anything in this life, since any similarity is so far from the original truth'.[164] To this extent, the reliance by early Christian writers on Virgil and the classical bank of images may be seen less as imaginative weakness than a consequence of the Church's 'negative identification' with the pagan past as against the more threatening pagan present. Innovation is certainly rare, and where empiricism occurs it confirms an expulsion of Eden as far as is possible from the immediate physical world. Avitus, Bishop of Vienne, adds a poignantly Nordic note in adding to the relentless 'negative formula' ('in Eden there were no winds, no pains ...') the deliverance from rain, and imagines the light of Eden as sparkling on spring water more brilliantly than upon ice.[165] The major advance on the Elysian Fields and the Garden of the Hesperides is the new addiction to the *parfumerie* – 'one of the main paradisal hierophanies' as Duncan rightly notes[166] – but the compulsive cinnamon-sniffing and fragrance-fancying[167] itself surely corresponds to an inclination to dematerialize nature, to refine away sense into transcendence, which we will come to examine as an 'aesthetics of insubstantiality'. Prudentius, for example, conceives heaven thus:

> He calls them to enter the land of the just
> which is covered and sweetened by roses and

163 Sister Mary Dorothea Diederich, *Vergil in the Works of St. Ambrose* (Washington: 1931), pp. 25, 26, 13.

164 Pseudo-Basil, *De Paradiso*, in *Patrologiae Graecae*, ed. Migne, 30, cols. 63–70; ref. Duncan, p. 48.

165 *De Mosaicae Historiae Gestis*, 1.227–29, 257–60. Book 1.210–57 is translated by Giammati, *Earthly Paradise*, pp. 1–19.

166 Ibid, p. 60.

167 Cf. in particular Lactantius' *De Ave Phoenice*, trans. Frederick Brittain in *Penguin Book of Latin Verse*, pp. 62–65, which, enrapturing Phoenix and Christian alike by its rich distillation of exquisite perfumes, Assyrian and Arab, Pygmy and Indian, originates the cinnamon and Phoenix motifs in Christian paradisal writing, to be echoed by Avitus, lines 254–56, and by Sidonius Apollinaris, *Panegyric on Anthemius*, in *PL*, 58.654.

watered by many running streams that freshen
the marigolds, the violets and crocuses.

Rich balsam flows from its slender twigs, precious
cinnamon pours its scent and the leafy nard,
a most exotic scent, is carried along
the river which has seen the place of its source.[168]

The Eden of *Genesis* had been devoid alike of fragrance and flowers, and only rarely is fragrance specified in the Greco-Roman *locus amoenus*. It is absent from *loci amoeni* that we have examined in our classical section such as the Virgilian Elysian Fields, the bucolic beauty-spots of Theocritus and the vignettes of the fertile Goat-isle and the Groves of Alcinous in Homer. The delights of exquisitely perfumed air (as opposed to the topos of the flower-catalogue) are to be found in classical landscape – to my best knowledge – only in Calypso's grotto[169] and Theocritus' 'Harvest Home'[170] , and here, in each context, the scent is part of a highly *corporeal* textural and sensuously lush scenery. The split logs of juniper and cedar burning in Calypso's cave, and the squashy opulent repletion of midsummer indulgence in the sweet ripeness of Theocritean Cos, are profanely sybaritic to the chaste Christian nostril. The Eden of the Church dispenses a fragrance as elevated as that of the priestly censers, or of the ointments of the baptismal ceremony: perfume is the trace of the disembodied, a sensory medium of the refined spirit, the companion to light itself as a higher and supersensible suggestion.

Duncan's dogged poet-by-poet catalogue of motifs[171] otherwise suggests an almost undifferentiated monotony of classical flower-carpets, perpetual springs, natural abundance and negative formulae. Although the framework appears to have satisfied contemporary poets, a level of 'overkill' is perhaps suggested in that the rhetorical distancing of Eden from the familiar world appears eventually to have made that rhetoric so familiar as to return the *locus amoenus* to the empirical world as a geographical category: the phrase appears, as Curtius records, in Isidore of Seville's encyclopaedia not as a term of rhetorical ecphrasis but as a 'geomorphological concept', listed among other and factual geographic terms such as island, mountain, grove and desert.[172]

168 Prudentius, *Cathemerinon*, Fifth Hymn, in *Last Poets of Imperial Rome*, p. 175.
169 *Odyssey*: 5.70.
170 *Idylls*: 7.143–46.
171 Duncan, *Milton*, pp. 38–66.
172 Curtius, *European Literature*, p. 192.

The same polarizing tendency can be seen at work in the relation of the world to heaven. A millennial anticipation of post-apocalyptic paradise on *earth*, inherited from Judaism, and prominent in Apostolic times, has practically disappeared in Augustine, who routs it in the *City of God* (20.6–10).[173] Declining confidence in the imminence of the Parousia meant that 'the broad development within Christianity consisted in a shift of scene from earth to heaven (and hell); with divine judgement coming forward to the moment of each individual's death; and with a corresponding change of emphasis from body to soul'.[174]

Unsurprisingly, little concrete is added to the Biblical pictures, now systematized by the Fathers,[175] assimilations of heaven both to Edenic rurality[176] and to the City of *Revelations* 21 being made. Commodian's addition to the latter topos – 'there shall be no seiges, such as we see now, and no plundering'[177] – typifies the climate of otherworldly craving; indeed the decisive development in the conception of heaven produced by the Fathers is to effect once more a dematerialization of its object. The 'spiritual' character of Christianity figures heaven, albeit uncertainly, in mystic terms of transfiguration and beatitude, as the ecstatic apprehension of the One. As Kirk puts it, 'Christianity came into a world tantalized with the belief that some men at least had seen God, and had found in the vision the sum of human happiness; a world acting with the hope that the same vision was attainable by all.'[178] Augustine feels that, although 'it is difficult, if not impossible, to support this suggestion by any evidence of passages in holy Scripture', the condition of beatitude will consist in the endowment of a transformed physical eye for the immaterial medium. 'We shall then see the physical bodies of the new heaven and the new earth in such a fashion as to observe God in utter clarity and distinctness, seeing him

173 John Hicks, *Death and Eternal Life* (London: 1976), pp. 187, 190. On earlier Christian eschatology, cf. also E. C. Dewick, *Primitive Christian Eschatology* (Cambridge: 1912) and Ulrich Simon, *Heaven in the Christian Tradition* (London: 1958). There is also interesting material, particularly as regards pre-Christian mystical speculation, in K. E. Kirk, *Vision*.

174 Hicks, p. 198.

175 Dewick, *Primitive*, p. 371.

176 Cf. Prudentius, *Cathemerinon*, Fifth Hymn, stanzas 29–31, trans. Isbell, *Last Poets of Imperial Rome*, pp. 175–76; and the majority of Hexaemeral writers' extrapolations from *Genesis*: 2.8–10.

177 *Instructiones*, 2.3.12–13, trans. Mazzolani, *City*, p. 255.

178 Kirk, *Vision*, p. 54. For the New Testament *visio dei*, cf. I *Cor.* 13.12; *Matthew*: 5.8; *Rev.* 22.4.

present everywhere and governing the whole material scheme of things.'[179] His profoundly beautiful formula, 'There we shall be still and see; we shall see and we shall love; we shall love and we shall praise'[180] sums up a period in which topography has grown increasingly insubstantial and insignificant: refined into ecphrasis, rendered discarnate as allegory, and abandoned even as such for the supreme light of the *visio dei*.

Matter is, indeed, damnable: the topography of Hell is preserved in full scriptural literalism. Old and New Testaments furnish an abyss or underworld, cloaked in a mist of darkness, replete with fire, fire and worm, or a lake of fire and brimstone.[181] The Fathers seem as reluctant as do, curiously, our contemporary historians of Christian eschatological thought to dwell on this pit of furnaces, but Augustine and Irenaeus confirm the reality of flames.[182] The expansive Virgilian topography of rivers, sludge and reeds, silent forest and natural decay, shadowlands and iron tower,[183] appears not to have been adopted by poets and preachers as had been classicism's paradisal repertoire. For the contemporaries of the Vandals, Huns and Suevi, Hell as a landscape of despairing humans confronting endless burning inflicted by implacable power, appears to have been an amply concrete proposition.

The dimensions of the natural world

Late Stoicism, we noted in chapter one, was dazzled into melancholia in meditations on cosmic magnitude. The 'vertical imagination' of Marcus Aurelius and Seneca, the sense of man as 'lost in space', punily sublunar beneath the silent immensities, still find echoes in Christian stellar awe; but the incarnational unity of man and nature recentres the earth: stadium of the supramundane powers, with whose creation the very passage of time begins.[184] The celestial but confirms the providential glory:

179 Augustine, *City of God*, 22.29, trans. Bettenson, pp. 1086–87.
180 Ibid., 22.30, p. 1091.
181 Hell: as abyss: *Numbers* 16.31, *Psalms* 104.16, *Isaiah* 5.14, *Ezra* 26.20, *Philippians* 2.10; as darkness: *Matthew* 8.12, 22.13, 25.30, *Jude* 13, II *Peter* 2.17; as fire: *Ezekiel* 54.12, *Jude* 7, *Matthew* 13.42, 13.50, 25.41; as fire and worm: *Isaiah* 66.24, *Mark* 9.43–44; as fire and brimstone: *Isaiah* 30.33, *Revelations* 19, 20.10.
182 Augustine, *City of God*, 21.2–8, 23; Irenaeus, *Adversus Haereses*, 4.27.4.
183 *Aeneid*, Book 6.
184 Basil, *Hexaemeron*, 1.5.

Whoever tries to find Christ
should look in the high places:
it is there that one can see
the signs of lasting glory.[185]

Henceforth the astounding vastnesses are friend to man, wondering and unworthy in the tradition of *Psalm* 8.

O Maker of the starry world
Who, resting on thy everlasting throne,
Turnst heaven like a spindle
And hast the stars brought under law ...
Thou guidest all things to their certain goal.[186]

A novel form of wonder now derives, I think, from the marvel of omnipresence. Formless infinity stuns the mind with a conceptual vertigo, which Chrysostom finds may become literal. Standing alone by the sea, he is gripped, he says, not only by astonishment and admiration but by fear, stupor – and vertigo. This is, he feels, a religious experience, of 'sober intoxication', and he thinks that Paul's mystical seizures must also have seemed to him as a gazing upon some limitless ocean, awed in the presence of the *mysterium tremendum*.[187] Augustine records that simply learning from Ambrose that God's substance is spiritual, not material, and that the likeness to God of man's image is but analogical, was enough in itself to prise the Manichaean falsehoods from his mind. It is difficult today to re-experience the exhilarating revolutionary impact that the doctrine of an immaterial world of spirit had upon Augustine and other Christian converts. Almost all thinkers of the ancient world, indeed the main tradition of Greek thought from Homer through Stoicism to the Manichaeans, were materialists, conceiving the divine as rarefied matter, or 'pneuma': to this tradition, only Plato, Aristotle and

185 Prudentius, *Cathemerinon, The Twelfth Hymn*, in *Last Poets of Imperial Rome*, p. 208. Cf. also Boethius, *Consolation*, 4.6, metrum, lines 1–4, p. 141.

186 Boethius, *Consolation*, 1.5; trans. Waddell, *More Latin Lyrics*, p. 97.

187 Chrysostom, *De Incomprehensionis Dei*, 1, in *PG*, 48.705b; cf. also his *Homiliae in Johannem*, 1.30; ref. Wallace-Hadrill, *Nature*, p. 94. The sea is, of course, a recurrent symbol in mystical writings of all ages for the infinite: cf. R. C. Zaehner, *Mysticism Sacred and Profane* (Oxford: 1957), pp. 38–40, 103, 145; and Freud on the 'oceanic feeling' in *Civilization and its Discontents*, sect. 1, in *Civilization, Society and Religion*, vol. 12 of the Pelican Freud Library (Harmondsworth: 1985), p. 260.

Plotinus dissented.[188] The Christian notion of the divine as infinite was a contradiction in terms to the Greek mind, to which an infinite was an ἄπειρον – something without determining limit, merely indeterminate. Augustine's *Confessions* open with the exultant 'wonder-logic' of a God filling heaven and earth, saturating and overflowing in the world, immanent yet infinite and autonomous of matter.[189] This rapture of ethereal intimation in the world of sense is widely shared by early Christian poets, and Augustine's ardour for evocative formlessness is recurrent.

> But what do I love when I love my God? Not material beauty or beauty of a temporal ardour; not the brilliance of earthly light, so welcome to our eyes; not the sweet melody of harmony and song; not the fragrance of flowers, perfumes and spices; not manna or honey; not limbs such as the body delights to embrace. It is not these that I love when I love my God. And yet, when I love him, it is true that I love a light of a certain kind, a voice, a perfume ... but they are of the kind that I love in my inner self, when my soul is bathed in light that is not bound by space; when it listens to sound that never dies away; when it breathes fragrance that is not borne away on the wind ...[190]

Elsewhere we have seen how Greek and Roman verse and drama registered numinous presence in nature in terms of preternatural vegetative luxuriation, a sudden spellbound silence,[191] or a surging vitality animating all growing and moving things. In the Old Testament we found the 'divine returns' figured in the tropes of dance and song, or the agricultural blessing of lush pastures and fields thick with corn. In the world of Christian Platonism, where immateriality is conceived as the hightest stratum of reality, and spirit co-inheres in matter, the 'presencing' of the divine within creation is now sought and portrayed, I suggest, in a new aesthetics of insubstantiality. For the first time, an emphatic vocabulary of light, taste, fragrance and infinity pervade natural description, in a rhapsodic dematerialization and an exultation in vast aerial spaces that we are to re-encounter in

188 *Confessions*, 5.11, 5.14, 6.3, pp. 106, 108, 114. Peter Brown, *Augustine of Hippo* (1967; rpt. New York: 1986), p. 85.

189 *Confessions*, 1.2–4, pp. 22–23. Cf. 7.1, 7.5, pp. 133–34, 138.

190 Ibid., 10.6, pp. 211–12.

191 The earliest example being perhaps Euripides' *Bacchae* lines 1084–85: see G. S. Kirk's note on these lines in his edition of *The Bacchae* (Cambridge University Press: 1979), p. 114.

Milton. In a phrase of Peter Brown's, the mystical character of Christianity is 'innerworldly not otherworldly'.[192]

The paeans to Edenic fragrance at which we have glanced earlier belong to this tonality, and Dracontius invents their incorporation into the hexaemeral sequence. On the third day, 'the flowering countryside is redolent with perfumes of every kind. Earth, the sole mother, does not pour forth one sole gift, but mingles together as many odours as there are plants'.[193]

A remarkable diversity is consequently to be found in the presentations of the sensible world in the prose and verse of the fourth to sixth centuries. In Prudentius, for example, while the *Psychomachia* is regularly occupied with symbolic and allegorical narrative, there remain nonetheless in the *Cathemerinon* moments of the old classical sensuality, lucid vignettes from the observed world:

> Buckets brimming high with foamy milk
> that has just come from a full udder
> are emptied and a liquid is mixed
> with the milk to make it solid. Then
> the curd is pressed in a wicker frame.
>
> The new wax comb oozes with honey
> as fine as that found in Greece. The bee
> who has no time for marriage gathers
> this essence from the crystalline air
> and the dew which collects on the thyme.[194]

Yet a material form is also a shell, to be anagogically decoded in the stripping away of sensory qualities from its symbolic core, or to be 'looked through' to the interior brilliance, prized for its irradiant participation in the source of life. Substance may emerge – as from udder or soil – as nutritiously gross, plumped by providence for the digestive tract of man; or it may refine into the fragrances of a higher appetite, the summoning beams and balminess of an adumbrated immanence.

> O Father, give the spirit power to climb
> To the fountain of all light, and be purified.

192 Brown, *World*, p. 74.

193 Dracontius, *Carmen de Laudibus Dei*, trans. Brittain, *Penguin Book of Latin Verse*, p. 108.

194 *Cathemerinon* (*Hymns for the Various Hours and Days*), in *The Last Poets of Imperial Rome*, trans. Harold Isbell (Harmondsworth: 1971), p. 163.

> Break through the mists of earth, the weight of the clod,
> Shine forth in splendour.[195]

For the superlative sweetness of the immaterial exquisite is Light:

Splendor paternae gloriae,	O Brightness of the Father's glory,
De luce lucem proferens,	Bringing light from light,
Lux lucis et fons luminis,	O light of light and source of light,
Dies dierum illuminans.	O day illuminating all days.[196]

The relation of light and heat or of sun and ray, distinct yet utterly co-inherent, is held to represent that of divine Father and Son;[197] whilst the Biblical references to the Godhead as manifest in light and fire are myriad.[198] Dodd's suggestion of the influence also of the Platonic allegory of the Fire and the Sun (*Republic*, 506D–517A) is doubtless correct.[199] The divine rays from the Father of Lights are everywhere refracted in patristic writings; Augustine's suggestion, regarding proper knowledge of natural phenomena, that 'there is the light as of morning sunshine in the minds of those who contemplate them'[200] is more sensitive and original than most by far.

Whilst the cosmic sense celebrates an infinite omnipresence, 'bodiless sweet',[201] at the opposite end of the scale mens' focus on individual phenomena pays tribute not only to the particular but to the minute. The Christian hymn is also, as it were, to *Gloria in Parvulis*. It may initially seem an eccentric religious ardour that inculcates not an Assyrian equation of greatness with scale, nor a Hindu losing of the mind in inconceivable depths of time, but rather a stirring of admiration for the infinitesimal. We have seen already Basil's Wordsworthian assertion that the least plant should penetrate one with wonder, a perspective he returns to in the *Hexaemeron* when instructing us to

195 Boethius, *Consolation*, 3.9.22–26, trans. Helen Waddell, *More Latin Lyrics* (New York: 1976), p. 113.
196 Ambrose, *Hymn at Dawn*, trans. Brittain, p. 90.
197 For instance, Gregory of Nyssa, *Adversus Eunomium*, 1.36; Origen, *De Principiis*, 1.2.4; for further references cf. Wallace-Hadrill, *Nature*, p. 127, note 3.
198 Cf., for instance, *Isaiah*, 30.26, 40.5; *Exodus*, 24.17, 33.21; *Psalms*, 27.1, 4.6; *John*, 1.5; I *John*, 1.5; I *Timothy*, 6.16.
199 C. H. Dodd, *The Interpretation of the 4th Gospel*, p. 139.
200 *City of God*, 11.29, p. 465.
201 Phrase pirated from Edward Thomas, 'The Unknown Bird', line 21, in *Collected Poems* ed. R. George Thomas (Oxford: 1978), p. 87.

'recognize grandeur in the tiniest thing'.[202] Tertullian likewise directs our deference to 'a single tiny flower from any hedgerow ... a single shellfish from any sea ... a single stray wing of a moorfowl'. Augustine remarks that amongst 'living creatures of all shapes and sizes, ... it is the smallest in bulk that moves our greatest wonder – for we are more astonished at the activities of the tiny ants and bees than at the immense bulk of whales'.[203] We have, then, in early Christian nature-writing, a piety of miniaturist reverence. *Multa in parvis* is also, however, a contemporary secular theme: 'minimal' art was highly regarded, Apelles and Protogenes competing as to who could draw the finer line across a panel, other artists producing tiny cupids or ivory ants, triumphs of miniaturist craftsmanship.[204] The divine craftsman, it follows, is all the more to be praised for producing the living models of such artefacts on a scale so lavish as to risk neglect altogether. 'In all the varied movements of the creature what work of God's is not wonderful?' asks Augustine. 'And yet these daily wonders have by familiarity become small in our esteem. Nay, how many common objects are trodden underfoot which, if carefully examined, amaze us!'[205]

The Fathers' religious veneration for the small and humble things of creation, so much at odds with the Aristotelian association of beauty with size and greatness[206], and with the classical spirit of the fifth century epyllion the *Batrachomyomachia* (Battle of the Frogs and Mice) whose mock-heroic comedy implied the triviality of small creatures, derived impetus from Stoicism, expressed for instance in Virgil:

Some have taught that the bees have received a share of the divine intelligence, and a draught of heavenly ether; for God, they say, pervades all things, earth's and sea's expanse and heaven's depth; from Him the flocks and herds, men and beasts of every sort draw, each at birth, the slender stream of life; yea, unto Him all beings thereafter return, and, when unmade, are restored.[207]

Multa in parvis as a theme in the Fathers likewise seeks to transvaluate the comical and fanciful unexpectedness of classical 'paradoxical

202 *Hexaemeron*, 5.9.

203 *Adversus Marcionem*, 1.13; cit. Wallace-Hadrill, *Nature*, p. 84; Augustine, *City of God*, 22.24.909.

204 Cf. John Onians, *Art and Thought*, pp. 126–32.

205 Augustine, *Epistolae*, 137.3.10; ref. Glacken, p. 199.

206 Onians, *Art and Thought*, p. 121.

207 *Georgics*, 4.219–26, trans. H. R. Fairclough (1916; revised London: 1935), pp. 211–13; compare *Aeneid*, 6.723–29.

encomium', and docks with a familiar rhapsodic sincerity in a wider Christian doxography of Creation.[208]

In late antiquity 'landskip' dies: conspicuously displaced by *natura naturans*, by nature as the motion of a cosmic system, and as seasonal landscape.

The disappearance of the poetry of place into a verse that celebrates nature in non-differential terms, a unitary and universal nature, derives from many factors. Greek philosophy had held to a tradition of oneness underlying or unifying nature, from the single material principle of Thales, Anaximenes and Heraclitus, through Plato's world as a single, intelligent animal (*Timaeus*, 32a) to Stoicism's universal πνεῦμα. Justin Martyr had published a list of Greek poetic texts asserting monotheism.[209] The very conditions which encouraged monotheism likewise favoured focus on the regular and unitary aspects of the world. From the Hellenistic period, widespread deportations, exile, trade and travel sundered many men and women from symbiosis with place, uprooted them from local deities and disposed them to divinities and philosophies of wider scope. Secular unification under a Roman emperor consolidated this tendency in religion and thought, particularly pronounced in Christianity as a 'middlebrow' faith of 'immigrants at heart, ideological déracinés'[210] opposing pagan patrician localism. The Fathers indeed emphatically declaim the divinely ordained accord and blending of all things – Clement's 'synkrasis', Basil's 'sympatheia' – and the universal participation in the Logos.[211] Theology as a discourse, inheriting the Hellenic conception of nature as κόσμος, tends to the depiction of the visible and sensible world in totalizing terms as the principals of a system, in contrast to the Greek literary tradition with its experiential mimesis of place and landscape. Augustine's 'we now see the sun,

208 Compare the statement made on this theme by Marcus Cornelius Fronto, the Christian poet: 'The topic must everywhere be treated as if it were an important and splendid one ... the highest merit in this kind of discourse is an attitude of seriousness': Letter to Aurelius, c. 139, in *The Correspondence of Marcus Cornelius Fronto*, trans. C. R. Haines (London: 1920), vol. 1, 41; H. K. Miller, 'The Paradoxical Encomium with Special Reference to its Vogue in England 1600–1800', in *Modern Philology*, 53, no. 3 (1956), 149. For 'Much in Little' in Renaissance Literature, see Kitty Scoular, *Natural Magic* (Oxford: 1965).

209 *On Monarchy*, *PG*, 6, 311–25.

210 Brown, *World*, pp. 60–66.

211 Clement, *First Epistle to the Corinthians*, ch. 20; Jaeger, pp. 14, 18, 20–23; Basil, *Hexaemeron*, 2.2.33a; *CHLGEMP*, pp. 432, 437–38.

moon, stars, sea and earth and all things on the earth' serves a different appetite from Homer's 'everything in Ithaca, the long hill-paths, the quiet bays, the beetling rocks, and the green trees, seemed unfamiliar to its King'.[212] The influence of the *Psalms*, too, dissolves locality and landscape into universals:

> Let the flowing waters of the rivers, the shores of the oceans, rain, drought, snow, frost, timber and wind unite by day and night to praise you forever.[213]

But this Christian construction of a unitary or monolithic world becomes extraordinarily ironic when we consider that the Fathers' exalted accent upon spiritual bonding and oneness coincided, in the West, with the shattering of the empire into a thousand warring fragments. In the fourth century, Basil's Christian expansiveness had presented a 'wondrous picture of the whole prelapsarian world as an earthly paradise': but his grasp of postlapsarian geography had been perceptibly deficient.[214] By the later sixth and seventh centuries the irony has massively increased, as Maximus teaches that the Incarnation has abolished the difference between Paradise and the rest of the earth, in the period when the western Roman emperor has been violently deposed, Italy is the scene of fierce warfare between Lombards, Byzantines and Saracens, and the remainder of the western empire has been carved up among barbarian clans.

There is perhaps more than irony, however, to the disparity between the unitary earth of the ecclesiarchs and the reality of endemic disorder and economic localism. From the time of the establishment of the colonate, the agricultural workforce has been territorially imprisoned. 'The social function of the labouring man became confined to the business of sustaining his masters, his mental horizons to the bounds of the estate on which he lived.'[215] As such,

212 Augustine, *City of God*, 22.29, p. 1082; Homer, *Odyssey*, 13.194–96, trans. E. V. Rieu (Harmondsworth: 1946), p. 207.

213 Prudentius, *Cathemerinon*, Ninth Hymn, stanza 38, in *Last Poets*, p. 197. Compare the enumerative generic nature of such Psalms as numbers 95, 96, 98, 104, 139, 148.

214 *Hexaemeron*, homilies 5 and 6; the quotation is of Duncan, *Milton*, p. 47; Sister Agnes C. Way in her introduction to his *Hexaemeron* (*Fathers of the Church* series, Catholic University of America Press, no. 46 (1963)), p. x, notes the deficiency of his European geography, for which he is entirely reliant on Aristotle – by now dead for nearly 700 years!

215 Maurice Keen, *The Pelican History of Medieval Europe*, p. 52.

the propagation of a uniform world, an overwhelmingly homogenous nature, may well have a pacifying and consolatory effect to which a Church struggling to maintain order and clerical hegemony will not be blind. Against this unitary ideology, 'periegesis' and pictorial verse landscapes would figure as highly subversive. It is perhaps no accident that in an increasingly stationary, indurated economic system Gregory of Nazianzus and others direct polemics against pilgrimage: salvation is by interior routes, they insist, and merely geographic mobility a dangerous distraction.[216] Under the Benedictine Rule, a monk took a fourth lifelong vow, of *stabilitas loci*, or permanent attachment to his Abbey. We may compare the fourth century poet, Claudian, who writes a neo-Virgilian encomium of 'the stay-at-home' man, ageing in nature's quiet on paternal acres:

> Happy, the man who has lived his life in his own fields.
> The house that saw him as a little lad
> Sees him an old man: leaning on his staff,
> On the same earth he crawled on ...
> Fate has not dragged him through the brawling crowds,
> Nor ever, as a restless traveller
> Has he drunk at unknown springs ...
> That massive oak he remembers a sapling once,
> Yon grove of trees grew old along with him.
> Verona further seems than India,
> Lake Garda is remote as the Red Sea.
> Yet strength indomitable and sinews firm,
> The old man stands, a rock amid his grandsons.[217]

Monotheism's assertion of the derivation of all things from the Good[218] quietistically displaces grumbling attention from mere particulars – 'we must not, in the rashness of human folly, allow ourselves to find fault, in any particular, with the work of that great Artificer who created all things' – towards the greatness of 'the whole design, in which these small parts, which are to us so disagreeable, put together to make a scheme of ordered beauty'.[219] Basil's intent in his *Hexaemeron* is to show the creator's wisdom in the harmonious adaptation of all life to earthly conditions. The sun itself changes position in the heavens during the year so that there is no excessive

216 Compare Augustine, *Confessions*, 10.8, p. 216.
217 Claudian, trans. Helen Waddell, *More Latin Lyrics*, p. 77.
218 *Genesis*, 1.31; *Acts*, 17.26–28; Augustine, *City of God*, 8.10.
219 Augustine, *City of God*, 12.4, p. 475.

heat to one place but a ubiquitous temperate climate.[220] (Basil's precarious geography is clearly of assistance here!) Accordingly, the Fathers 'baptise' the traditionally pernicious: the sea, for Basil and Ambrose, is not the capricious *mare infidum* but is the source of rain, bulwark against barbarians, source of taxation and highroad between mainlands.[221] Minucius Felix, endearingly, describes the pleasure of the calm sea playing across his bare feet as he walks on the shore, the gentle waves sucking playfully at his toes and reabsorbing his footsteps; Augustine hymns 'the mighty spectacle of the sea itself, putting on its changing colours like different garments, now green, with all the many varied shades, now purple, now blue', and reiterates the Lucretian delight in observing its storms from the safety of land.[222] Similarly, God made poisonous plants along with nutritive ones, yet 'there is not one plant without worth, not one without use'. Starlings eat hemlock, and quails hellebore; mandrakes induce sleep.[223]

To this usefully anodyne unitary imagination corresponds 'one of the last religious experiences of the late-pagan world. She possesses inexhaustible vitality': the Goddess Natura.[224] Her birth in this period is, indeed, natural, for she incarnates the homogeneity of 'cosmic power', mother of all, nurse, sustainer and regulator, presiding over marriage and generation, standing between Zeus and the gods. As such her presence in Claudian and Statius as an allegorical figure[225] and in Cicero and Chalcidius as a mere personification[226] ranks her as one among numerous late antique 'unitary' divinities: Curtius compares the Venus of Lucretius, the Orphic hymns to 'Physis' and Pan, and Antonine inscriptions to Priapus as a universal god.[227] Lewis is quite right to insist that it was 'impossible that such a figure could ever arise in a genuinely mythopoeic age,' for she condenses the 'mythopoeia' of discrete and particular sensuous processes – marriage, sexuality,

220 *Hexaemeron*, 3.7.

221 Basil, *Hexaemeron*, 4.6; Ambrose, *Hexaemeron*, 3.5.22.

222 Minucius Felix, *Octavius*, 2.4–3.3; Augustine, *City of God*, 22.24, p. 1075; compare Lucretius, *De Rerum Natura*, 2.1–4.

223 Basil, *Hexaemeron*, 5.4, trans. Sister Agnes C. Way, pp. 71–72. The harm done by poisonous snakes and animals is always imputed to human sin: cf. F. E. Robbins, *The Hexaemeral Literature* (Chicago: 1912), p. 5 note 4.

224 Curtius, *European Literature*, p. 107.

225 Claudian, *De Raptu Proserpinae*, 1.249; *De Consulatu Stilichonis*, 2.424; *De quarto Consulatu Honorii*, 198 ff; Statius, *Thebaid*, 11.465 ff, 12.645 ff.

226 I take this point from C. S. Lewis, *The Discarded Image*, p. 36, which he does not reference.

227 Curtius, pp. 106–07.

birth, decay – into an abstract unity, an intellectual concept. Yet to shrink from her as 'unnatural', to deride this as 'a jejeune and inactive deity,' capable of poetic vitality only in opposition to something else (God, the individual, the unnatural)[228] is to miss her theological and political value precisely as a systemic, delocalizing entity, weaning men from the snares both of merely sensuous, empirical knowing, and of regard for the temporal distractions of worldly variousness. Topographia must not divert from the unitary telos of the one Creator, the one Logos, the one Redeemer, the one supernal homeland. Subordinated to God as his handmaiden, sustainer rather than begetter of men, the Goddess Natura is enrolled in the Christian faith by Lactantius, Prudentius and Dracontius.[229]

Likewise conditioned by monistic religion and economic localism, landscape in verse may no longer comprise a poetry of place, pagan in particularity, but must 'ascend' into generic landscape: *par excellence*, the landscapes of the seasons. Descriptive poetry of seasonal change had existed as an ancient and powerful tradition of embellished calendar writing, descending from Hesiod through Varro and Virgil's *Georgics*; but it is with late antiquity that it becomes an eclipsing passion, the supreme form for the poetic presentation of nature's expanses:

> ... when the spring grows warm
> The flower-bearing year will breathe sweet scent,
> In summer torrid days will dry the corn,
> Ripe autumn will return with fruit endowed,
> And falling rains will moisten wintry days.
> This mixture brings to birth and nourishes
> All things which breathe the breath of life on earth;
> This mixture seizes, hides, and bears away
> All things submerged in death's finality.[230]

The New Sophistic, developing the rhetoric of description (ἔκφρασις) enjoined the ἔκφρασις χρόνων (or depiction of time), as termed by the technographer Hermogenes and applied by Nonnus, Corippus, and in the *Anthologia Latina*.[231] The ecphrasis of spring sometimes burgeoned alone, and enjoyed Byzantine popularity among orators in their

228 Lewis, *The Discarded Image*, pp. 37–38.

229 Lactantius, *Divine Institutes*, 2.8.21–25, 3.28.4; Prudentius, *Contra Symmachum*, 1.12 and 327, 2.796; Dracontius, *De Laudibus Dei*, 1.23, 1.329, 3.3, 549.

230 Boethius, *Consolation*, 4.metrum 6, 25–35, p. 142.

231 Curtius, *European Literature*, p. 194, note 18.

exercises, correspondents in their letters and preachers in their sermons, often justified only as a virtuoso display with tenuous relation to the principal subject.[232] Christian homilies were particularly indebted to Libanius' celebrated ecphrasis, of the fourth century:

The spring ... frees the [sun's] rays from the clouds. Then the sun is bright and gentle and delightful ... The earth brings forth its products, and then green fields gladden the farmers with hope. And the trees also regain their foliage, and everything promises fruits ... Then the sea lies open to sailors. Then the waves are not high, nor are they like mountains, but the surface of the sea is smooth ... the perennial rivers are clear, the winter streams are more moderate ... Men seem to have returned to life ... taking delight in the songs of the birds and the scents of the flowers. The swallow sings in the spring, as does the nightingale ... The meadows are very sweet with the voices of lambs and, as I have said already, with flowers, with roses, with violets, with lilies, with all the other flowers that they are not only sweet to see, but also sweet to take in one's hands.[233]

Gregory of Nazianzus drew on this and gave it Christian respectability in his famous sermon on New Sunday, afterwards printed with his choicest sermons for regular 'liturgical' use during the course of the year.[234] Christian sermons might proceed by formal rhetorical ecphrasis, drawing on the sequences in pagan literature, or, more commonly, accumulate individual items, many from the Bible, in particular the Song of Songs.[235] In western and eastern Christianity alike, homiletic writings drew on springtime rhapsodies for the celebration not only of Easter but of the feast of the Annunciation, on 25 March: a divine logic being discerned which connected the expectation of the universal redeemer with the renewal of nature.[236]

Seasonal rotation indeed was not viewed by the Fathers as principally a testingly adversarial penalty of the Fall, a condition of grief: there was to be a world of difference, I shall argue, between patristic and medieval experience of the seasons. For imperial Christianity, an awesome power of consolation was to be derived from the spectacle.

The curse upon nature in the postlapsarian world was ambiguous as to its scope, in Christian thought. Jerome in the Vulgate had incorrectly

232 Henry Maguire, *Art and Eloquence in Byzantium* (Princeton: 1981), p. 42.
233 *Libanii opera*, ed. R. Forster (Leipzig: 1915), 8.479 ff; cit. and trans. Maguire, pp. 42–43.
234 *In novam Dominicam*, in *PG*, 36, cols. 617C-620B; and trans. Maguire, p. 43.
235 Ibid., p. 45.
236 Ibid., p. 44.

translated the Hebrew formulation of *Genesis* 3.17 as 'maledicta terra in opere tuo' instead of 'maledicta humus propter te'.[237] Consequent questions arose first, as to whether the entire earth was cursed and topographically disfigured or whether the soil alone had forfeited pristine fertility; and second, whether the curse now obtained intrinsically in nature, or in her relations with man alone. It is notable that, notwithstanding the contrast most usually projected in nature-studies between an anguished *contemptus mundi* in the age of Augustine and a buoyant humanist *rapprochement* in the Middle Ages, patristic estimates of nature's postlapsarian transformation actually prove generally more sanguine than those of subsequent theology. Augustine, although accepting Jerome's word 'terra', indicates in his commentary on the passage that the soil rather than the whole earth bears the curse, discussing thistles, thorns and hardships of tilling;[238] and Ambrose declares: 'Nec terra in se maledicta est; sed *Maledicta*, inquit, *in operibus tuis*, quod ad Adam dictum est. Tunc terra maledicta est, si habeas opera terrena, id est opera saecularia.' ('The world is not accursed in itself but is accursed, as God said to Adam, "because of your actions." Hence the world is accursed if you engage in worldly, that is non-spiritual, activities.')[239] Augustine's Pelagian foe, Julian of Eclanum, went further. The *maledicta* was but the subjective projection of the sinner's consciousness of affliction and sterility: with salvation and baptism such clouds would disperse. Adam's sin could not injure the earth herself.[240] Consequently, where medieval verse portrayed[241] a sense, wonderfully characteristic in the icy seas and desolate hail-storms of Anglo-Saxon verse, of the seasons as penal mutation –

> Eall is earfoðlic eorþan rice,
> onwendeð wyrda gesceaft weoruld under heofonum
>
> All is hardship in the earthly kingdom:
> Fate decrees change in this sublunary world[242]

– late antiquity contrariwise celebrated the seasonal cycle as the operation of an indefeasible providential rationality.

237 Marjorie Hope Nicolson, *Mountain Gloom and Mountain Glory* (Cornell: 1959), pp. 84–86; P&S, pp. 127–28.

238 *De Genesi contra Manichaeos*, 20, in *PL*, 34, 211–12; *De Genesi ad Litteram*, 38, in *PL*, 34.450.

239 *De Paradiso*, in *PL*, 14, col. 314; my translation.

240 Elaine Pagels, *Adam, Eve and the Serpent* (New York: 1988), pp. 137–38.

241 P&S, ch. 5.

242 *The Wanderer*, lines 106–07; trans. P&S, p. 122.

Thy power rules the changing year:
The tender leaves the North wind stole
The Spring West wind makes reappear;
The seeds that Winter saw new sown
The Summer burns as crops full-grown.
All things obey their ancient law
And all perform their proper tasks.[243]

As providence rather than penalty, the yearly cycle articulated the balancing cosmic equilibrium, or even, as a triumph of divine foresight, a *felix culpa* in external nature. Trees, beasts 'and other mutable and mortal things', writes Augustine, 'have received their mode of being by the will of their Creator, whose purpose is that they should bring to perfection the beauty of the lower parts of the universe by their alternation and succession in the passage of the seasons; and this is a beauty in its own kind, finding its place among the constituent parts of this world'.[244] It is folly to suppose that mere human action, vicious or virtuous, could thwart the divinely ordained magnificence of this complex world: 'For God would never have created a man, let alone an angel, in the foreknowledge of his future evil state, if he had not known at the same time how he would put such creatures to good use, and thus enrich the course of the world history by the kind of antithesis which gives beauty to a poem ... a kind of eloquence in events, instead of words.'[245] This perspective yields a 'self-moving' nature, a vast and awesome macrocosmic engineering whose grandeur of autonomy contrasts markedly with the seasonal landscapes that will emerge in the medieval period: there, initiative and fertility pass to the labouring, coercing agency of man, ploughing and sowing, ditching, gathering and hunting upon an earth recalcitrant or passive. But with early Christianity, beleaguered by violence, nature is joyously contemplated in her immense and inexorable self-renewals as a structure which, like the colossal Roman Pont du Gard at Nimes in the words of Kenneth Clark, was 'materially beyond the destructive powers of the barbarians'.[246] In the midst of human anarchy and political apocalypse, of crumbling cities and burning villas, under the smoking ashes of *Romanitas*, moved the steadfast rhythms of nature whose composure could not be disturbed. Scythian and Barbarian,

243 Boethius, *Consolation*, 1, metrum 5, 18–24; p. 47.
244 *City of God*, 12.4; p. 475.
245 Ibid., 11.18; p. 449.
246 *Civilisation* (London: 1969), p. 3.

says Chrysostom, Indian, Egyptian and all may read of God in the Book of Nature, contemplating the order of the seasons which 'like some virgins dancing in a circle succeed one another with the happiest harmony'.[247] It is the old Judaic theme – 'the earth bringeth forth fruit of herself'[248] – now put to inspiriting compensatory purpose, swallowing linear time in cyclical. Rome, perhaps, was too catastrophically fallen for nature's fall to be allowed severe. Man's faculties had been eroded but divine purpose drove on. 'The earth, flowering at His bidding in due seasons, brings forth abundant food for men and beasts and all the living things on its surface, without reluctance and without altering any of His arrangements.'[249] The condition of such 'determinist' cheer is the absence of 'voluntarist' credit to human agency: in contrast to the human competencies catalogued in the *Georgics* and medieval Calendar art, Lady Philosophia in late antiquity censures such hubris:

> Perhaps ... you find pleasure in the beauty of the countryside. Creation is indeed very beautiful, and the countryside a beautiful part of creation. In the same way we are sometimes delighted by the appearance of the sea when it's very calm and look up in wonder at the sky, the stars, the moon and the sun. However, not one of these has anything to do with you, and you daren't take credit for the splendour of any of them. The fact that flowers blossom in spring confers no distinction on you, and the swelling fullness of the autumn harvest is no work of yours.[250]

Seasonal 'landscapes', in summary, displaced classical landscapes of pictorialism and spatial localization, as presenting a politically opportune generic and uniform nature, and as comprising, poignantly, a heartening spectacle of providential security underanged by the falls of man and of Rome.

The matrices of perception

'Ecological' perception of landscape – that is, the utilitarian category of nature-perception, the eye to thriving – is abundantly evident in early Christian writings, asceticism and pious meditation of the

247 John Chrysostom, 'The Homilies on the Statues, or to the People of Antioch', in *A Library of the Fathers of the Holy Catholic Church*, trans. J. H. Parker (Oxford: 1842), vol. 9, pp. 162–70.

248 *Mark* 4.28.

249 *The Letter of St. Clement to the Corinthians*, trans. Francis X. Glimm, in *The Fathers of the Church. The Apostolic Fathers* (New York: 1947), p. 26.

250 Boethius, *Consolation*, 3, prose 5, 32–36, p. 66.

afterlife notwithstanding. Providence has provisioned the earth for use, as well as for contemplation. Even monks, seeking remote sites far from the comforts of civilization, were guided, after the reforms of Basil and Benedict, by the criteria both of beauty and utility. St Sturm, founder of Fulda monastery, was told by St Boniface: 'Go to the solitude which is called Bochonia and see if the place is fit for the servants of God to dwell in, for even in the desert God is able to prepare a place for His followers'; and, finding a place with a healthful soil and supply of water, was 'so charmed', according to Eigil, his biographer, 'with the beauty of the spot that he spent practically a whole day wandering over it, exploring its possibilities'.[251]

In early Christianity, the urban and commercial 'ecological' values of Roman civilization are still detectable. We have seen above that Hexaemeral writings can look upon the sea and observe not the wind-tossed abomination registered by Hebrew eyes, but the pathways of trade linking the continents. Similarly, Augustine can write of an early despair: 'My soul was a burden, bruised and bleeding ... but I found no place to set it down to rest. Neither the charm of the countryside nor the sweet scents of a garden could soothe it.'[252] Here the natural world is still of utility as a recreative respite from the urban, an affair of parks and gardens. Augustine, indeed, as a schoolmaster and bishop, was one of a small class of men who, even in late fourth-century North Africa, lacked direct contact with agricultural backbreak, and was easily able, therefore, to profess an 'urban' idealization of Adam and Eve's good fortune in working in a garden. 'When all is said and done, is there any more marvelous sight, any occasion when human reason is nearer to some sort of converse with the nature of things, than the sowing of seeds, the planting of cuttings, the transplanting of shrubs, the grafting of slips? It is as though you could question the vital force in each root and bud on what it can do, and what it cannot, and why.'[253]

Increasingly, the divinely ordained serviceability of nature is viewed in agricultural forms. This is hardly surprising in a culture which is committed to the scriptures of an agrarian economy and is

251 Eigil's *The Life of St. Sturm*, in *The Anglo-Saxon Missionaries in Germany*, trans. and ed. C. H. Talbot (New York: 1954), pp. 183, 188. Glacken, pp. 306–07.

252 *Confessions*, 4.7, p. 78.

253 Augustine, *de Gen. ad Litt.*, 8.8.16, quoted by Peter Brown, *Augustine of Hippo*, pp. 143, 21.

itself relapsing into one. Early Christianity regularly descries and describes with an agricultural eye, and is profoundly impressed with natural renewal. While this may suggest a nature deeply civilized, even elegant, in its graceful self-proffering

> The orchard's ripeness comes from the soil.
> The tree is shaken and its burden
> falls like a sudden shower of rain
> so that all of the ground is covered
> by a precious carpet of red fruit[254]

Clement of Alexandria, noting keenly the tremendous growth of greenery after rain, spies life springing even from dunghills, trees sprouting from sepulchres.[255] 'Surely', cries Basil to his audience of urban artisans and commoners, 'the perfect condition of the earth consists in its state of abundance: the budding out of all sorts of plants, the putting forth of the lofty trees both fruitful and barren, the freshness and fragrance of flowers, and whatever things appeared on earth ... by the command of God to adorn their mother'. 'The finishing of the earth is the adornment proper to it and according to its nature – cornfields waving in the hollows, meadows verdant and abounding with varied flowers, woodland vales in bloom, and mountain peaks shaded over with forest trees.'[256]

Turning to 'cosmographic' perception – that is, perception of the field of visible nature as directed by a particular conception of the world-order, of the cosmological structure – we have seen that natural phenomena for early Christianity are viewed as unified and systemic on the Greek model as *φύσις*. In contrast to the frequent Old Testament acclaim of the divine in creation as prodigy and Kratophany, and notwithstanding the fideist strain prominent in Tertullian, for the Fathers the perceptible world declares the divine technology, the astounding design, intricate of order. Wallace-Hadrill remarks that whilst 'pagan' literary natural description may, as in Lucian's 'Fly', comprise but a rhetorical showpiece, glancing, brilliant and shallow, the Fathers, like Marcus Aurelius, find significance in all they see.[257] Augustine directs our attention to *vestigia*, the archi-

254 *Cathemerinon, Third Hymn: Before Food,* stanzas 11 and 16, in *Last Poets of Imperial Rome,* pp. 162–63.

255 *Stromateis,* 1.7.37.1; ref. Wallace-Hadrill, *Nature,* p. 83.

256 *The Hexaemeron,* 2.1 and 2.3, pp. 22, 26.

257 Wallace-Hadrill, p. 102.

tectonic 'traces' of God, enduring 'in such wonderful stability' in the created frame about us, and pointing us to their Creator beyond.[258] The cosmology, astronomy and natural history of Basil's *Hexaemeron* present 'the general structure of the world ... [as] it will remain up to the end of the 14th century'.[259] Boethius' majestic verse summarizes the fused classical–Christian marvelling at creation as an immense scheme of cosmic rotational engineering, a superlative unity of ordered alternations:

> This concord tempers then the elements
> In equal measure, so that warring waters
> Yield in their turn to drought,
> And frosts make league with flame;
> The pendulum of fire swings to high heaven,
> The heavy clod settles with its weight.
> By self same cause the flowering year
> Breathes fragrance in the growing warmth of spring.
> Hot summer ripens grain: and autumn
> Comes laden home with apples: and the rain falls on the winter fields.
> This tempering of things gives food and brings to life
> Whatever breathes:
> And merges all that's born in final death.
> And in the midst the Maker sits on high.
> The reins are in his hands,
> Master and King, the well-spring and the source,
> The Law and arbiter of equity.[260]

Nature, though a structural, hierarchic framework of law, is not psychically estranged from man, nor 'closed' in insentient mechanism. Basil's cosmology, like that of Boethius, is influenced by the *Timaeus*, in which the world of nature is a vast living organism with its own soul: its plants and animals representing 'a specialized local organization of this all-pervading vitality and rationality,' and sharing psychical kinship with humanity.[261] Though drawn into postlapsarian conflict with man, and doomed to final conflagration, nature is an organism synergetically interlocked with man in origin, fortunes and purpose, given over to his command and 'named' by him, its

258 *City of God*, 11.28, p. 463; also *De Trinitate*, 12.5.5, 11.1.1.
259 Gilson, p. 55.
260 Boethius, *Consolation*, 4.6: Waddell's graceful translation in *More Latin Lyrics*, p. 119.
261 Collingwood, *The Idea of Nature*, pp. 3–4, 73. *Hexaemeron*, 2.2.33.

equilibrium disordered by human evil. In one aspect, 'semi-animate' nature is a chorus, a sentient multitude, and the things of the countryside may be seen as a participating, antiphonal host. The scientific monographs and formal analysis of the *Hexaemera* coexist extraordinarily with the mythopoeia of the poets, in those figurings of the natural seized from the melting pot of Aristotle and the Psalms, scholarship and apocalypse, reason and mysticism, that feeds early Christian writings. A number of poetic topoi or motifs present this echoic landscape intercommuning with man.

In Greek polytheism, nature is transfigured at the approach of a god in 'the pastoral hyperbole' of Hesiod, Homer and Euripides, bursting into sweetness and flowers. The motif passes into Lucretius, and into the pastoral mainstream with Theocritus and Virgil, renascent in the complimentation and conceit of seventeenth-century verse.[262] This 'magical' efflorescence is taken literally and seriously by the early Church, who view in the renewals of springtime natural response to the Annunciation; and, with Prudentius, imagine the rejoicing paroxysms of landscape at the Nativity itself.

> All the countryside was sprinkled
> with flowers and the desert sands
> became sweetened with the perfume
> of precious nard and sweet nectar.
>
> Child, the world's coarseness felt your birth:
> the grey hardness of granite was
> overcome and all the boulders
> were wrapped in a cushion of grass.
>
> Honey flowed from the earth's fissures
> and the dry branches of the oak
> dripped perfume on the ground; even
> the tamarisk tree gave balsam.[263]

The motif anticipates Milton's 'Nativity Ode', and is in neither case a purely celebrative trope. As in the *Psalms*, land, plant and beast are called to praise:

> The air, moist or dry in turn, the winds, the rains,
> the hail, the rivers likewise, each in their fashion
> proclaim their maker.

262 J. B. Leishman, *The Art of Marvell's Poetry* (1966; rpt. London: 1968), pp. 225–47.
263 Prudentius, *Cathemerinon*, Eleventh Hymn, stanzas 17–19, in *Last Poets*, p. 206.

And we, echoing the harmonious song, say Amen, Alleluia.
The firm earth and its living creatures, those that
are obedient to man and those that the hunter snares,
sing to thee alone and are silent to all others.
And we, echoing the harmonious song, say Amen, Alleluia.[264]

The invocation of nature to mourning, too, passes from classical into Christian verse. At the partition of the Frankish Kingdom, at the death of a margrave, poets summon nature to share their grief: raindrops and the elements, rivers and cities, 'all things' 'including quadrupeds birds and reptiles'. Political compliment is here rendering the theme rhetorical, but, as Curtius points out, 'the adoption of the topos by Christian poetry was expedited by the Evangelists' account of the disturbance of nature at the time of the Redeemer's death. The earth quaked, the rocks were rent [Matthew: 27.51]; a darkness came over the whole land [Mark: 15.33]; the sun lost its light [Luke: 23.45]'.[265]

Equally, scientific interest in nature may command the eye and imagination. The Fathers were quite logically ambivalent as to the value of science. 'What is the use of measuring the earth or knowing the positions of the stars and the course of the sun?' asks Tatian.[266] 'Moses gave no discussion concerning the shape [of the earth] and did not say that its circumference contains 180 thousand stades, nor measured how far its shadow spreads in the air when the sun passes under the earth', remarks Basil primly.[267] Origen feels that physics, having been studied as a preliminary, should thereafter be forsaken for study of what is lasting and eternal; while Theodorus and Cosmas in their Hexaemera, each maintain doggedly a flat-earth theory, the universe being oblong and shaped like the Tabernacle.[268] Nevertheless, as Wallace-Hadrill indicates, we find the Fathers widely incorporating classical scientific ideas into their writings, and investigating natural phenomena often 'in extraordinary detail, not always briefly but sometimes at great length and with doubtful relevance to their professed subject'.[269] Augustine considers 'man's skill in geometry and arithmetic, his intelligence shown in plotting the positions and courses of the stars ... his abundant ... stock of

264 Orientius, *Hymn of Praise*, trans. Frederick Brittain, in *Penguin Book of Latin Verse*, pp. 101–02.
265 Curtius, *European Literature*, pp. 92–93.
266 *Oratio ad Graecos*, 27; Wallace-Hadrill, *Nature*, p. 6.
267 Ibid., 8.3.169–72.
268 See F. E. Robbins, *Hexaemeral*, pp. 59–61.
269 Wallace-Hadrill, *Nature*, p. 8.

knowledge of natural phenomena' to be one of the blessings of the postlapsarian world.[270] For Maximus the Confessor, 'the identity of scriptural with scientific truth was the revelation which the apostles received on the mount of Transfiguration'.[271] It is in this spirit that Gregory of Nyssa attempts exact landscape description in an epistle: his motivation is a meteorological interest in the moisture-cycle:

Suddenly the clouds gathered thick, and there was a change from clear sky to deep gloom. Then a chilly breeze blowing through the clouds brought drizzle with it and made us very damp, threatening such rain as had never been known. To our left there were continuous claps of thunder alternating with vivid flashes of lightning ... and all the mountains in front, behind and to either side were enveloped in cloud.[272]

Something of such scientific and empirical sensibility is brought to bear on the creation in Dracontius:

The third day brought forth the blue water of the sea. The grey-green waters of the deep dissolve into vast waves, and a navigable sea tosses with foaming billows. That same day saw the separation of land and water. The earth is torn up from the mighty deep in which it lay hidden; and, becoming more dense as the globe solidifies, it hangs in space, while the axis makes the heavens rotate, with the waters as foundations. Solid matter – not yet mother earth – which the shapeless waters support, is taken from the fluid mass. Some of it becomes sand, some of it is converted into soil, some swells into stone, and cliffs like mountain-tops appear. Some of it forms river-beds, some stretches out to form a plain, some curves into sea-shores. Some is shaped into mounds, some into bristling rocks. Some stiffens into crags, some is surrounded by a deep valley, and swelling hills raise their lofty peaks. Part becomes fields watered by sweetly flowing streams. Green grass appears, and plants of every kind rise into the air ... The flowering countryside is redolent with perfumes of every kind ...[273]

We note Dracontius' observation of the sea darkening in colour as it deepens, and the imagination influenced by fascination with mechanics and substance-analysis: which contemplates the material earth as a globe slowly condensing under heavens set into rotation, and the differentiation of matter from a single coagulum into the various textures of rock, sand and soil. This is an imagination which, quite

270 *City of God*, 22.24, p. 1073; though contrast his *Confessions*, 5.4.
271 *CHLGEMP*, p. 430: Maximus, 1, *Ambigua*, 6.31.
272 *Epistles*, 3: *Epistle to Ablabius*, trans. Wallace-Hadrill, p. 23.
273 Dracontius, *Carmen de Laudibus Dei*, trans. Brittain, in *Penguin Book of Latin Verse*, pp. 107–08.

unlike *Genesis*, or indeed anything else in the Bible, tries physically to perceive the monistic principle diffused into the manifold, to discern the plastic primary substance swirled and stiffened, curved and compacted into the concrete forms of landscape, from cliffs to river-beds. The tremendous sense of dynamism, of the natural as living, fluid, kinetic – of creation, indeed, as evolution – reminds us of Milton. (Compare, for instance, *Paradise Lost*, III, 708–21.)

At this point we may remark how very much in early Christian nature-sensibility we are to find reproduced in that of John Milton: the vast cosmic canvas; the pervasive scientistic and classical-literary interests; the obsession with light, with fragrance, with insubstantiality as its sweetnesses, as against the antipathy to the textured; and the hungry spiritual energy, seeking out the brightest intensity of divine experience, the aspiring *visio dei*. The attitude to science is precisely Milton's own ambivalence: a compulsive, revelling curiosity tempered by higher priorities.[274]

We turn now to the category of 'analogical' perception: that is, the perception of landscape as received and reflected through the faculty of similitude.

> Streams that wander
> From tall hills
> Down descending
> Often dash
> Against a rock
> Torn from the hill side ... If you desire
> To look on truth
> And follow the path
> With unswerving course,
> Rid yourself
> Of joy and fear ... '[275]

Gregory of Nazianzus testifies to Christianity's priorities in landscape appreciation in his praise of Basil's didactic *Hexaemeron*: 'When I take his *Hexaemeron* in my hand and read it aloud, I am with my Creator, I understand the reasons for creation, and I admire my Creator more than I formerly did when I used sight as my teacher.'[276] More important to perceive in the visible world even than divine order is

274 Milton, *Paradise Lost*, 12.575–79, 8.66–84, 8.159–78.

275 Boethius, *Consolation*, pp. 52–3.

276 Gregory of Nazianzus, *Homilies*, 43, cit. Sister Agnes C. Way, in her introduction to her edition of Basil's *Hexaemeron*, p. vii.

1 Netherworld scene, wall-painting. Tomb of Snedjem, Deir-el-Medina. New Empire.

2 Miniature frieze *Flotilla*, wall-painting. The West House, room 5, Akrotiri, Thera. Circa 1700 BC.

3 Wall-painting. Room Delta 2, Akrotiri, Thera. Circa 1700 BC.

4 *Garden of Livia*, fresco. From the House of Livia, Prima Porta, near Rome. First century AD.

5 *Odysseus in the land of the Laestrygonians*, fresco, from the Odyssey Landscapes. Biblioteca Apostolica Vaticana. First-century AD imitation of Hellenistic original.

6 Central part of the apse mosaic in S. Apollinaire in Classe, Ravenna. Sixth century.

7 *Madonna in a Rose Garden,* Stefano da Zevio. Museo di Castelvecchio, Verona. Early fifteenth century.

8 *August*, the Limbourg brothers, in *Les Très Riches Heures de Jean de Berri*. Musée Condée, Chantilly. 1413–16.

9 *The Country of Good Government*, fresco, Ambrogio Lorenzetti. Palazzo Publico, Siena. 1337–40.

10 *The Madonna of the Chancellor Rollin,* Jan van Eyck. Musée du Louvre, Paris. Circa 1425.

11 *Alpine Landscape,* Albrecht Dürer. Ashmolean Museum, Oxford. Circa 1495.

12 *St Francis in Ecstasy*, Giovanni Bellini. Frick Collection, New York. 1480–85.

13 Frontispiece to John Ogilby's *Britannia,* Wenceslaus Hollar. British Museum. 1675.

14 Frontispiece to Wither's *Emblemes,* William Marshall. Bodleian Library. 1635.

(a)

(b)

15 *By Albury*, Wenceslaus Hollar. British Museum. 1645.

(c)

(d)

divine revelation: landscapes are the pages of the Book of Nature. Its creatures indeed are like letters (*ὥσπερ γραμμασί*),[277] spelling unmistakably the truths of their Creator.

> The shrill voices of the birds perched
> just before dawn beneath the roof
> are a figure prepared for us
> of that Judge who will soon call us.[278]

A natural form is an anagogue (*ἀναγωγή*), giving visible presence to a spiritual reality; and since sensibles participate in intelligibles which themselves participate in the supreme Good, the symbolic forms of created being comprise the lowest rungs of a cosmic ladder. In view of this we ought, perhaps, to conceive the *liber creaturarum* less as the Book than the 'Scroll' of Nature, for it forms a unitary fabric that unfurls upwards into full intelligibility. (The papyrus scroll, indeed, was still in use until the fourth century when superseded by the parchment codex.) Nature 'in voice' is of course a trope frequent in the Old Testament, but 'conversing' with her now is no simple euphonious, choric matter but a more exacting, dialectical affair. In contrast to the call to hosannahs of *Psalms* 66, 96, 100 and 148, or the spontaneous marvelling of *Psalm* 8, it is to a knotting of the brow that the Christian is called. As a storehouse of concepts, a theological manual of ever-changing inscription, landscape spreads before us for conceptual activation and a travelling of thought. The cunning of nature's complex compactions for instance are a meditative marvel.
'How many things produced by nature are combined in one plant! The root of the grapevine, the large thriving branches which hang down from all sides above the earth, the bud, the tendrils, the sour grapes, the bunches of ripe grapes! The vine, intelligently observed by your eyes, is sufficient to remind you of nature.' The tendrils of the vine teach us to cling to our neighbours; their upward growth instructs us to keep our eyes heavenward; and their props remind us of the necessity of our own supports ... the Church, apostles, prophets and teachers.[279] Driving home such admonitions to the pagans of Smyrna, the third-century martyr Pionius felt he need only point to the volcanic landscape of desolate black ash that stretched away on its

277 Athanasius, *Oratio Contra Gentiles*, 34, *PG*, vol. 25, 68B-69A; Glacken, pp. 203–04.

278 Prudentius, *Cathemerinon*, First Hymn, in *Last Poets*, p. 153.

279 Basil, *Hexaemeron*, 5.6, p. 75.

borders. Cindered by God's wrath, he explained, the hot springs and rising steam-clouds of the landscape warned of hell-fires to come, ready and waiting beneath the world.[280]

In some ways, indeed, this new deliberative and interrogative cognition of landscape notwithstanding, Christian insistence upon learning from nature forms part of its *anti*-intellectualist propaganda. Nature is organized as an SPCK (Society for the Promotion of Christian Knowledge bookshop), – 'the invisible things of him from the creation of the world are clearly seen'[281] – and the doctrine of the Book of Nature appears something of an early Christian invention. Peter Brown notes that Christian conversion 'opened a breach in the high wall of classical culture for the average man ... By "revelation" the uneducated might get to the heart of vital issues, without exposing himself to the high costs, to the professional rancours and to the heavy traditionalism of a second-century education in philosophy ... It was as if the inhabitants of an underdeveloped country were to seek to catch up with western technology by claiming to have learnt nuclear physics through dreams and oracles.'[282] Chrysostom and Augustine thus rejoice that God instructs not by written books, which are available only to the literate and wealthy, but by the universal language of creation, open to the poor, the illiterate, to Scythian, Indian, barbarian and Egyptian.[283] Nature's Book is thus a platform of Christian egalitarian populism, a politically suggestive volume, crusading against the jargon and elitist erudition of the pagans on behalf of a 'middlebrow'[284] faith; while for those who wish, a further mode of natural theology can elevate the script of sensibles to a philosophic complexity equal to the pagan, as in the mystical mode of pseudo-Dionysius.

Whilst all nature serves as a field for conceptual extrapolation, it is the imagery of light and the anagogues of resurrection that are

280 Pionius, *Ael. Ar.* 16.11, Fox, *Pagans and Christians*, pp. 474–76.

281 *Romans*, 1.20.

282 Brown, *World*, p. 53.

283 Chrysostom, *The Homilies on the Statues, or to the People of Antioch*, 9.5–9, vol. 9, pp. 162–70; Augustine, *In Psalmum* 45, in *Oeuvres Complètes*, vol. 12, p. 389. Also, *Confessions*, 13.15. References from Glacken, pp. 203–04. E. R. Curtius, *European literature*, pp. 319–26, considers only instances from the Middle Ages, and considers references to a Book of Nature prior to Alan of Lille as mere 'pulpit eloquence': p. 321. I have found reference to an egalitarian and providential Book of Nature also in *Verba Seniorum*, trans. from the Greek by John the Subdeacon, Book 4.16, trans. Helen Waddell, *Desert Fathers*, p. 182.

284 Adjective from Brown, *World*, p. 64.

ubiquitous. The fragility of the blossom reminds Basil and Chrysostom of the brevity of human life; indeed 'There is possibly not a patristic writer who produced a considerable body of work who does not draw attention to the principle of resurrection in the natural world.'[285] But a troubling uncertainty inhabits the business of natural literacy, as Andrew Marvell will note sardonically in a characteristically edged couplet:

> Thrice happy he who, not mistook,
> Hath read in Nature's mystic book.[286]

For Paul, nature was written in neon, and illiteracy here a culpability: 'The invisible things of him ... are *clearly seen*;' but his suggestion elsewhere that we see on earth 'through a glass darkly'[287] implies some cognitive limitation. The doctrines too of nature's post-lapsarian disfigurement and of 'dissimilar' symbols suggest but a partial legibility to natural language. Such shortfall is, however, but the sublime aspect of that mystification of reality at which we earlier looked: though we cannot decide between scientific claims, says Basil, we can 'from the beauty of the visible things ... form an idea of Him who is more than beautiful ... that which in general comes under our observation is so wonderful that even the most acute mind is shown to be at a loss as regards the least of things in the world, either in the ability to explain it worthily or to render due praise to the Creator'.[288] 'Otherness' in nature may be but the unsearchable brilliance of God: 'dark with excessive bright'.[289] As such, this otherness is really man's heartland, and more truly so than humanity fully can grasp. In this perspective, certain aspects of the poetic allure that haunts the ancient countryside of polytheism – the sweet remoteness of Pan's pipes, heard at a distance, the preternatural flowering luxuriance of the primal *locus amoenus*, the indefinable appeal of 'the green life that springs under the shadowy hair of the pathless forest' for Euripides' bacchae – these strange, delicious intimations of mystic vitality and otherness in the natural world may be competitively displaced and eclipsed, by the Christian's contemplative rapture in the 'supreme'

285 Wallace-Hadrill, *Nature*, p. 126; Basil, *Hexaemeron*, 5.2; Chrysostom, *Ad Eutrop.*, 52.393.

286 Marvell, *Upon Appleton House*, stanza 73, lines 583–84, in *Andrew Marvell: The Complete Poems*, ed. Elizabeth Story Donno (Harmondsworth: 1972), p. 93.

287 I *Corinthians*, 13.12.

288 *Hexaemeron*, 1.11.

289 *Paradise Lost*, 3.380.

mysticism of a supernal energy within and beyond all natural sight and sound. 'It is the Lord of the winds that I long for, the master of fire, the maker of the universe, him who lighted up the sun.'[290]

Turning now to technoptic consciousness of landscape – that is, to the perception and description of landscape as influenced by or conceived as art – we find that in this anthropocentric cosmos, nature herself is assimilable to art. Of course, nature as the art of God must not be pushed too far: the analogy is qualified by the fact that God created both form and matter of the cosmos, unlike the artist who actualizes his ideas in pre-existent material. But nature *is* the divine art or τέχνη, and to see nature in terms derived from art is thus not conditioned reflex or fond anthropomorphism but soundness of theology. The beauty of the world, says Augustine, shares the decorative principle of rhetoric: enrichment by antithesis, such as the seasons.[291] Likewise Augustine appreciates the sky's mutability by perceiving it under the aspect of this principle of harmonious variance. 'All ... things which are at variance with one another are in accord with the lower part of creation which we call the earth. The sky, which is cloudy and windy, suits the earth to which it belongs.'[292]

Indeed it is overwhelmingly literary art, rather than pictorial, which focuses nature. In an Exemplarist cosmos, landscape composes Logos; and whilst mere plastic art will disappear with this world, the word is eternal.[293] We have met already with the 'rhetoricized' landscapes of the *locus amoenus*, of neo-classical Eden, of the ubiquitous spring ecphrasis; and we have noted, too, the imagination of Ambrose as drenched in Virgil, and the merriment of Basil over his 'Calypso' retreat. The classical definition of the countryside so conditions Christian imagination of it, in fact, that the Good Shepherd will now lead his sheep to graze in a lovingly composed Greek peritopos, piously installed with Palm trees:

> He will return [writes Prudentius]
> that sheep to its own grazing place where

290 On the real, continuing and enchanting presence of Pan in late antiquity, his cult flourishing even in cities and his image on second- and third-century coins, see Robin Lane Fox, *Pagans and Christians*, pp. 130–32, 673. Euripides quotation adapted from E. R. Dodd's edition of *The Bacchae*, lines 873 ff. (Oxford: 1960). 'Lord of the winds' quotation is of Clement of Alexandria, *Protrepticus*, 6.67.2, trans. Wallace-Hadrill, *Nature*, p. 129.

291 *City of God*, 11.18 and 12.4, pp. 449, 475.

292 *Confessions*, 7.13, p. 149.

293 Basil, *Epistles*, 277.

there are no rough burrs and no thistles
armed with needles. It is a shady
well-watered place.

The grove into which the shepherd takes
his flock is filled with palm trees and grass
and over the running waters bend
branches of bay.[294]

In like bucolic terms was the vision of Paradise of the third-century African martyr, Marian, received shortly before his death: 'Our road lay through a country of lovely meadows, clothed with the lush foliage of green woods, shaded by tall cypresses and pine trees which beat on the very heavens, so that you would think that the place was crowned, amid all its winding perimeter, with green groves. In the middle was a hollow abounding in the teeming veins of a crystal-clear fountain.' 'There is', comments Fox, 'no better literary evocation of the traditional "pleasant spot" in all third-century Latin'.[295]

Censures of plastic art on the other hand are harsh. The authority both of Moses and Plato[296] bring visible images into opprobrium, and the Fathers largely disparage painting as incomplete illusionism, unable accurately to reproduce either outward or spiritual things.[297] Where, occasionally, they evince the painter's concern with optical effects, it is the theologian's passion that is appropriating an established empirical acuity. When we find Clement of Alexandria referring to sunbeams shining through the chink of a window into a darkened corner, or to a spark being kindled by the rays of a sun passing through a vessel full of water, or else Gregory of Nazianzus expatiating upon the strange quivering of light rays that flash upon a wall in a moist atmosphere:[298] we find that Hellenism's fascination for chiaroscuro and light-effects has become piety's hunger for the anagogues of immanence. The tendency of Christian art is otherwise overwhelmingly away from classicism's materialist representation.

Late antique tendencies indeed are generally toward the rejection of naturalism, of solid Latin positivism, under the influence of Neoplatonism, and the tendency of Byzantine and Greco-Eastern art towards abstraction and colour. Figures tend to be flat and discarnate,

294 Prudentius, *Cathemerinon*, Eighth Hymn, trans. Isbell in *Last Poets*, p. 192

295 Robin Lane Fox, *Pagans and Christians*, p. 438.

296 *Republic*, 10,597e.

297 Wallace-Hadrill, *Nature*, pp. 98–99.

298 Clement of Alexandria, *Stromateis*, 7.3.21.7 and 6.17.149.1; Gregory of Nazianzus, *Orations*, 31.31; ref. Wallace-Hadrill, pp. 83, 87.

perspective is eliminated in favour of symmetrical disposition and identical repetitions, landscape is largely foregone. Such purging of landscape definition in favour of abstract colour and frameless light is often apparent in poetry too; we may contrast the Hellenistic dawn description of Apollonius Rhodios that we saw in chapter two, with its lucid light whitening over shores washed clean by the sea, over roads, bedewed plains and hills, with Prudentius' landless dawn in his *Second Hymn*:

> Night and dark and the clouds of night ...
> The murkiness of earth is pierced
> by a stroke of the sun's spear; now
> the colours return to all things
> as the face of the sun rises.
> [So] The darkness in us will be torn ...

and with Boethius' abstract epiphany:

> The sky stands, pelting with cloud and rain,
> The sun goes into hiding.
> Nor yet have ventured out the stars,
> And night is poured from heaven on the earth.
> But come the wind from Thrace,
> The North wind from his cave
> Scourges the dark, unseals the shrouded day.
> And lo, the sudden sun
> Vibrant with light
> Assaults our dazzled eyes.[299]

In graphic art, the forms of the external world are preserved reduced to allusive signs, initially as part of a secret iconographic code in the period prior to the Constantinian settlement, permanently as symbolic forms: the four seasons represent the resurrection, and a series of animals – lambs, doves, fish, peacocks – stand against plain gold backgrounds as *emblemata*. In a remarkable symbolic whole organized upon the apse of Santa Apollinaire in Classe, Ravenna, c. AD 547, the paradise garden, planted with neat rows of flowers, rocks and trees, dotted with birds, is painted quite without recession, to suggest this place beyond time as beyond earthly space; as, symmetrically disposed, twelve brilliant white sheep, representing the disciples, observe St Apollinaris at prayer (plate 6). Above, three sheep

299 Prudentius, *Cathemerinon*, Second Hymn, trans. Isbell, *Last Poets of Imperial Rome*, p. 157; Boethius, *Consolation of Philosophy*, 1.3, trans. Waddell, *More Latin Lyrics*, p. 107.

symbolizing Peter, James and John witness the Transfiguration of Christ, symbolized by a jewelled cross, in a high place above the green world; whilst still higher, quite above the firmament, the twelve sheep emerge from the Heavenly City onto the grass of the Celestial Paradise beneath multi-coloured clouds. Thus, against the fresh green wash of the terrestrial band, the familiar forms of pastoral beauty stand in clarity and plenitude, but the removal of perspective and the organized ascension of the totality clearly project the otherworldly movement and symbolic values of the composition. For further instances of sweeping green vistas that conciliate anagogue and empiric eye we must turn to the High Middle Ages.

Summary

We are on a terrain of ambiguity. Natural reality for late antique Christianity is the divinely structured non-divine. It is richly to be prized and scrupulously observed, for that whose reality makes it worthless as the dust and consigns it irreversibly to oblivion. Deiform, it is disordered through the Fall, yet fallen, it is still a prodigy of intricate utility and beauty. Admiration for its splendour is emphatically deserved, but must be displaced quite elsewhere to the Workman not the work.

Heartfelt appreciation of creation is therefore not to be rendered by the senses, naively captive to merely immediate pleasurings by matter, but to be elevated to the heights of a dissociated contemplation. There, conceptual vigour may track the ascending of sensibles into the intelligible realm of the timeless: and may even, if favoured, be suddenly updrawn into the Godhead itself in the final noesis of an order above form.

Much of the pagan scientific conception of nature as a superbly organized cosmic structure is consequently plagiarized by the Christians and falsely imputed to their own ancestry; yet the cosmology is also radically qualified, since this cosmos is but provisionally determinate, being maintained, most edifyingly, as needy and 'open', forever dependent on the infused sustaining presence of the creator and dissolving submissively before the incursion of miracles and 'local providence'.

To a sceptical modern mind the entire conception may appear as curiously cross-grained to its very foundations by a tension of masochism with filial narcissism. Contemptuous of the flesh, it is insuperably anthropocentric. The universe is provisioned for human use, written in green symbols as humanity's book, subjected to the rule of man as made in God's image, sustained in a harmony of brute life with human, fallen from perfection through appalling human evil, redeemed *in potentia* by a second Adam, restored in parts to paradise by human hermit saints, doomed to flame and ash by humanity's wicked course, and promised regeneration in a further creation for humanity's redeemed.[300] The emotional polarities of one of the theology's great protagonists, Augustine, ranging as they do between bleak insistence on a maximal understanding of original sin to impassioned pantings for the perfumed breath of the Spirit and restorative fusion with Loving 'Mother' Church, exhibit much of this 'Monican' psychology of defeated self-worth and renewing dependence on a radiantly approving Other.

Consequently, one master-principle of Christian natural focus is an instinctive redirection of concern from the solid things of the order of space – wherein man is triumphant master – to those of time – wherein he perceives his crucial dependence. ('The rational creation has been so made that it is to man's advantage to be in subjection to God ... '[301]) The Christian thus looks to meditate the landscape of the seasons in their rhythm of renewal majestically beyond the scale of human intervention; the mortality of nature in time and approaching salvation in starry Eternity; and the active symbolism in landscape signalling mutability and resurrection. Pondering time he meditates the rhythm of the world's first six days, and famous sites that commemorate (in Hebrew fashion) days in time of sacred encounter.

The classical pleasures of landskip and prospect, with their mastering, possessive, materialist eye, their secular confidence in the self-evident value of outward space, cannot survive this climate of renunciation, and its mystic interiority. Though deepening military disorder and the Church's eventual servitude of an imperialistic, undemocratic civilization necessitate a gospel of obedient agricultural energy, the theology of dependence ensures often an 'unseen hands' version of productivity, in contrast to the pictorialism and detailed materiality of perception found in the *Georgics* and the later Middle

300 'Culpat caro, purgat caro; / Regnat deus dei caro.' ('The flesh sins, the flesh atones for sin; / The flesh of God reigns as God.') From the hymn *Aeterne rex altissime*, verse 2, sung on Ascension day.

301 Augustine, *City of God*, 14.12, p. 571.

Ages. Similarly, unlocalized, standardizing accounts of seasonal change supersede concern for individual landscapes and fresh outward observation, while an 'aesthetics of insubstantiality' takes for its pleasures the intangibles of fragrance, taste, light and infinity.

As civil life in the West drifts into commercial decline and economic localism, poets fantasize ideal landscapes of mountain-top retreat, and theologians distance paradise beyond profanation in a rhetorical drenching of the traditional 'negative formula'. As western civilization relapses slowly into the archaic mentality of 'agrarian territorialism', Christian militancy confirms this retreatist imagination, as monastic 'militia' launch assaults against Lucifer in the wild and fiery landscapes of the Ascetic Sublime, desert-rock hagiography replacing civilized periegesis.

In these conditions, ecological perception delights supremely in the spectacle of profuse renewal, the teeming fecundity of vegetable life filling anxious granaries and shooting upward in testimonial new life. Cosmographic focus is concerned for both the *vestigia* of God – described with scientific eye in the world's engineering from the rotation of constellations to the spectacle of the moisture-cycle – and also for the 'mythological' percepts of an echoic, semi-animate nature, blossoming at Easter to commemorate the Annunciation and giving praise through its creatures in varied voice. Everywhere the book (or 'scroll') of nature is expounded by analogical perception, which finds hieroglyphs of resurrection and judgement in falling streams and pre-dawn birdsong, in staked vines, rising steam and recurrent light. Technoptic perception, finally, absorbs the Hellenistic delight in sudden dancing light but baptizes 'aesthetic' appearances with anagogic significance. Saturated in Greco-Roman literature, it perceives creation itself under the aspect of rhetoric, its seasons adorning the world by antithesis; and may conceive the heavenly shepherd as leading us to a shady eschatological *locus amoenus*. Perspective and empiricism, products of mere sense-perception, largely disappear as graphic art places standard *emblemata* on timeless grounds; and poetic depictions likewise spotlight individual natural forms denuded of setting, or evoke dematerialized impressions of abstract colour and frameless light. Only light and Latinity may now shine on as the landscape of the West fades in barbarian darkness.

5

Medieval into Renaissance

In our first chapter we argued that 'landskip', in poetry and painting, emerges only in certain cultures, whose advanced economic and social development have mediated a particular structure of aesthetic attention to nature, composed of five historically evolved attitudes.The development of these attitudes, or primary forms of spatial engagement,we specified and traced in our second chapter, as they accrued in historical evolution through pre-classical into Greco-Roman cultures. This chapter attempts to consolidate the terms of that thesis by indicating the re-emergenceof those architectonic conditions as constructing the medieval and renaissance revival of landscape art. Continuing our historical survey we will begin, however, by examining the emergence, from non-empirical traditions, of 'Gothic' nature-sensibility from the eleventh to thirteenth centuries, and continue into the fourteenth and fifteenth centuries to suggest the generative conditions of pictorial landscape.

Gothic

Pre-empirical traditions

As Jerome in his landscape had a Bible, the critic amid medieval landscapes has Pearsall and Salter. Their *Landscapes and Seasons of the Medieval World* is a miracle of near inerrancy, and to its richly substantiated and authoritative pronouncements I shall necessarily, whilst pursuing lines of fresh argumentation, make frequent and grateful reference.

In order better to appreciate the character of Gothic landscape-consciousness, it will be valuable to glance swiftly at the 'pre-empirical traditions' immediately preceding the High Middle Ages: that is, those historical modes of representing nature in art and verse which either preclude direct sensory perception, or well-nigh exclude the natural world in their narrative economy. The verse, however, of the Irish Celtic and Anglo-Saxon traditions we shall postpone, as being highly empirical.

In the centuries between Augustine and Abelard, 'The ossification of classical landscape in Byzantine, Carolingian and Romanesque painting may be compared... with the formalization of the *locus amoenus* in the Latin poetry of the period.' Each evinces 'a profound distrust of the natural eye'.[1] Instead, a landscape of symbols, hieratic and non-individualistic, articulates a language of concepts with a fixed iconography. Even colours are preordained, as a treatise as late as the twelfth century still specifies:

> Tree-trunks are painted with a mixture of viridian and yellow ochre with the addition of a little black and sap-green. With this colour one also paints the earth and mountains.[2]

Settings are unimportant, gold grounds replace perspectival frames, to emphasize a transcendental reality. In verse, similarly, the formulaic prevails. The established fixed and generalizing archetypes in descriptive writing are conserved by *imitatio*, the compliance with *auctoritas* regarded as proper in medieval literary aesthetics.[3]

These have derived from various streams of classical rhetoric descriptive of nature – the epideictic tradition of praise, the ornamental *demonstratio*, and above all the *descriptio loci* of forensic oratory – whose flow governs medieval rhetoric as both theory and practice. Twittering songbirds, murmuring streams and cooling breezes adorn shady trees heavy with fruit amid fragrantly flowered meadows throughout the Middle Ages. The confectionery of the ideal spring landscape, similarly transmitted, delights an insatiable appetite. The conventional lily and rose bloom in the German *Minnelieder*, though both are exotic to the climate, and abound, with Philomel, meadows flowering anew and gardens growing green again, in the love lyrics of Latin, Provençal, French and German verse.[4] Neither does the pastoral tradition contribute much novelty. Although the *locus amoenus* 'always plays an essential part in creating the wholeness of the pastoral ideal', Helen Cooper considers that 'the modern

1 P&S, pp. 41, 25.

2 *De Diversis Artibus* by Theophilus, trans. C. R. Dodwell (London and Edinburgh: 1961), pp. 15–16; P&S, pp. 25–6.

3 Niels Bugge Hansen, *That Pleasant Place* (Copenhagen: 1973) pp. 26–27.

4 P&S, pp. 49–51.

association of pastoral with the beauty of the natural world is given almost its first expression', one, that is, which 'goes significantly beyond the conventional idyllic landscape with its fountain or its beech-tree shade' only in Shakespeare's *The Winter's Tale*. An exception however is in the 'brilliant iconographic set-pieces' of René of Anjou's fifteenth-century *Regnault et Jehanneton*: with 'the birds catching fish in the *fontaine*, the turtle-doves on the single green branch of a dead stump, the last rays of the sun on the tower of the church which is the narrator-pilgrim's goal'.[5]

In narrative verse, neither saga nor romance incline to detail natural description. Settings in saga are but sparse literalisms of terrain: the terse topography of ridge, grazing-ground, woodland clearing or marsh-land. Though accurate enough to reward literary pilgrims, the economy of such epic naturalism renders 'the Homeric sense of *land* not the Virgilian sense of landscape'.[6] In vernacular romance, natural references, usually to the stock-pieces of dark forest, broad plain and shady, spring-fed pleasance are equally laconic and almost toneless, their 'scenic divestment' a sad lapse from apparently Virgilian models.[7] Where they enter at all, natural features turn out to be the customary literary delicatessen, the *locus amoenus*, encountered in a journey at the heart of forest or wilderness, and resonant with paradisal associations.[8] That religious radiance, rarely far from medieval landscape rhetoric, reminds us of the inescapable symbolicity of natural phenomena in the medieval mind. It is also a tradition at the heart of Gothic nature-sensibility.

Gothic nature-sensibility: the anagogic apology

Omnis mundi creatura
Quasi liber et pictura
Nobis est et speculum.[9]

'As a book, picture and mirror is to us every creature of the world.'

The idea of the Book of Nature as the eloquent notation of the divine mind derives, as we have seen, from the Early Christian period; and may be gauged as the supreme counter-perspective to the post-

5 Helen Cooper, *Pastoral: Medieval into Renaissance* (Ipswich: 1977), pp. 67, 175–76, 70.

6 P&S, pp. 44–46.

7 Theodore M. Andersson, *Early Epic Scenery*, pp. 160–80, quotation from p. 168.

8 Curtius, *European Literature*, pp. 201–02; P&S, pp. 46, 51–52.

9 Alan of Lille, *De Planctu Naturae*, in *PL*, vol. 210, 579A.

lapsarian in the dialectics of the Christian theology of nature. Through the visionary light of the anagogic teaching, the multifarious shapes and sounds of creation may stream into literature, lustrous in symbolicity. Flower gardens had long been organized and enjoyed along symbolic as well as visual lines, as Strabo's praise of his abbot's garden suggests in his ninth-century poem *Hortus*.[10] And Erigena's theophanic emphasis upon the whole creation as a process of divine self-revelation[11] is contemporary. But with the twelfth and thirteenth centuries, 'the conviction of a transcendental meaning in all things', of the world as 'a cathedral of ideas',[12] and a new natural science and naturalistic art, suffuse in religious ardour a vastly extended range of phenomena. Franciscan theologians such as Bartholomew of Bologna seek to combine the metaphysics of divine light with detailed optical treatises such as the *De Luce*, drawing on Arabian science.[13] Roger Bacon insists on detailed geographic study of Biblical sacred locations – their latitude and longitude, height, width, humidity, temperature, colour and conditions of fertility – as the (strikingly pre-Thoreauvian) basis for their spiritual allegorization.[14] Bernard of Clairvaux' famous lines 'Believe me, I have discovered that you will find far more in the forests than in books; trees and stones will teach you what no teacher permits you to hear'[15] might serve as apologia for the autonomous foliage carving of Gothic cathedrals: for though the sculptors 'gazed at every blade of grass with reverence', in their choice of flora 'one does not find a single case of symbolic purpose'.[16] For Bonaventura every object, no matter what, 'betrays the secret presence of its creator' to a cleansed mind, for the Trinity can be read on each page of nature's book.[17] By the fifteenth century, Sebonde is actually proclaiming the Book of Nature superior to the Book of Scripture: 'it cannot be falsified, destroyed or misinterpreted ... heretics cannot misunderstand it'.[18] Though an unorthodox exaggeration, such

10 P&S, p. 77.

11 Gordon Leff, *Medieval Thought, St. Augustine to Ockham* (Harmondsworth: 1962), p. 68.

12 Johan Huizinga, *The Waning of the Middle Ages* (1924; rpt. Harmondsworth: 1976), p. 194.

13 Gilson, pp. 341–42.

14 *Opus Majus*, trans. Robert B. Burke (Philadelphia and Oxford: 1928), vol. 1, pp. 203–07; Glacken, pp. 282–85.

15 Letter to Heinrich Murdach, Glacken, p. 213, who does not further reference this quotation.

16 Emile Mâle, *The Gothic Image* (1913; rpt. New York: 1972), pp. 52–53.

17 Bonaventura, *Itinerarium*, 2.12.

18 Glacken, p. 239.

theophanic rapture was a further testimonial 'of a general confidence in the translucency of a universe in which the least of all beings was a living token of the presence of God'.[19]

What, then, was the cause of such newly emphatic acclaim? The doctrine itself of the book of nature had lain to hand all along, as but one potential emphasis among many in the Christian corpus, a corpus which constituted, as we saw in our patristic chapter, a fluid and multi-accentual ensemble of meditations: to some minds, syncretism more than synthesis. The dynamic that transformed nature-sensibility was the eruptive force of economic resurgence, the expansion of agricultural and revival of commercial productivity made possible from the eleventh century by the new conditions of peace. Here we must make some suggestion of the *mediation* of new structures of feeling for nature from this sphere of fresh productive activity.

Gothic nature-sensibility: social impulses – control, logic, pleasure

In agriculture, 'systematic estate improvement was already common in 1066–86, and long before the twelfth century extensive new settlement was going on all over Western and Northern Europe ... The Red King's colonization of Cumbria, Henry I's settlement of Dyfed and Gower, Strongbow's invasion of Ireland, and the Crusades were all part of this predatory, expansionist phase of Western European endeavour, to which there is no real parallel in the history of the rest of the world.'[20] With new lands being brought under cultivation and with improved diet, dramatic population expansion ensued, its pressure assisting innovation in agricultural productivity. Between 1086 and 1193 the population of England increased by 72 per cent; by 1294 it may have reached five and a half million, 'before the Black Death as great or greater than that of late-Tudor England'.[21] A moderate estimate puts the population increase of Europe between approximately 1,000 and 1,300 at 'at least twofold, and in places much more'.[22] In England, the rise of new urban centres had produced by the

19 Gilson, p. 353. 20 H. E. Hallam, *Rural England 1066–1348*, pp. 3–4.
21 Ibid., p. 246.
22 Maurice Keen, *The Pelican History of Medieval Europe*, p. 84. J. C. Russell, *Late Ancient and Medieval Populations*, thinks the European population increase a rise from twenty million in the tenth century to fifty-four million in the fourteenth century (Philadelphia: 1958, pp. 102–13).

fourteenth century 'hundreds of little market-towns, each serving a radius of three to five miles'.[23]

In this context, the leading themes of traditional Christian nature-writing – nature's symbolicity, order, mutability and ambiguous ideality are rearticulated in terms produced by expansive commercial interests and by an aristocracy living in greater material prosperity and luxury than any enjoyed since Roman times. We may define at least three characteristics of such a culture: the intensified urge to control and exploit the natural world; the application of systematic reasoning in this aspiration; and, with the spectacular achievements in cultivation and human reshaping of the environment, a spirit of optimism and physical enjoyment, particularly among the leisured aristocracy. Let us take these in turn.

'A deep-seated mutation in general attitudes towards nature ... the change from a symbolic-subjective to a naturalistic-objective view of the physical environment' is sketched by Lynn White.[24] Recognizing that 'The new science and its peculiar characteristics arose out of the technology and the related economic interests of the rapidly expanding commercial classes', he quotes from the historian of science James Crowther:

> The medieval bourgeoisie thus accomplished something that had never been done before. It made the properties of materials the chief interest of a ruling class.[25]

Chaucer's tree-catalogue offers, I suggest, one immediately evident projection of these values into literary nature. As a rhetorical device, the tree-catalogue dates back to Roman antiquity, with roots perhaps in Homer;[26] and is reborn in the High Middle Ages in the verse of the *Romance of the Rose*, and Joseph of Exeter's *Iliad*,[27] who share that softness for the sylvan –

23 W. G. Hoskins, *The Making of the English Landscape* (1955; rpt. Harmondsworth: 1979), p. 113.

24 Lynn White, Jr, 'Natural Science and Naturalistic Art in the Middle Ages', *American Historical Review*, 52 (1947), 421–35. Quotation from p. 435.

25 James G. Crowther, *Social Relations of Science* (New York: 1941), p. 239.

26 Ovid, *Metamorphoses*, 10.86–108; Lucan, *Pharsalia*, 3.440–45; Statius, *Thebaid*, 6.91–99; Claudian, *De Raptu Proserpinae*, 2.105–11; Ennius, *Annales*, 187–91; Virgil, *Aeneid*, 6.179–82; cf. also Curtius, pp. 186, 195, on Homer's Garden of Alcinous and Calypso's Grotto as ultimate sources: *Odyssey*, 7.112–16, and 5.63–65.

27 *The Romaunt of the Rose*, 1338–68; *Iliad*, 1.505–13.

Trees ...
Ech in his kynde, of colour fresh and greene
As emeraude, that joye was to seene[28]

which we shall later examine. In Chaucer's catalogue in *The Parlement of Foules*,[29] many of the characterizations are 'trite' and 'commonplace',[30] and Chaucer indeed is usually disappointingly derivative in his natural depiction; but where, in this catalogue, he innovates, the new epithets[31] classify trees, I find, in terms not of their poetic associations or aesthetic appearance but of, in fact, their 'properties' precisely as 'materials'. The 'byldere oak', the 'pilar elm' and the 'shetere ["fit for shooting"] ew' embody a perception of landscape 'natural' to the practical instincts of a wealthy bourgeois, son of a vintner, controller of customs and subsidies of wool, and later indeed appointed sub-forester of Petherton Park. That Chaucer was interjacent between classes, 'moving as easily with wealthy bourgeoisie as with courtiers',[32] his wife the sister of John of Gaunt's wife, is reflected in the simile immediately preceding this utilitarian ledger: the trees bright as emeralds are of courtly, exclusive provenance, a gleam from the *Romaunt of the Rose*, whose conjunction with the builder's yard produces precisely that dissonant pluralism which the poem seeks to construct.

The hunger of the twelfth and thirteenth centuries for practical material understanding of the environment, for 'progress beyond wonderment, simple piety, and commentaries on theology',[33] to an empowering cognition of causation and function, is as clearly seen in the rebirth of natural science as in the inventive achievements of agriculture. William of Conches in twelfth-century Normandy,

28 *Parlement of Foules*, 173–75.

29 Ibid., 176–82. He has also a tree-catalogue in *The Knight's Tale*, 2920–24, which includes a greater number of species but is not epithetized.

30 Robert Kilburn Root, 'Chaucer's Catalogue of Trees' in 'Chaucer's Dares', in *Modern Philology*, 15 (1917), 18–22, employs these adjectives on pp. 21–22. See also Lane Cooper, *Classical Weekly*, 22, 166; and W. B. Sedgwick, *Classical Weekly*, 22, 184.

31 There are only three of these in a catalogue of thirteen species: *pace* Root, and F. N. Robinson, ed., *Complete Works of Chaucer* (1933; rpt. Oxford 1974), pp. 793–94, note to lines 176–82: each of whom claim five original epithets for Chaucer, but whose lists of parallels combined together leave only three that are original. On Medieval uses of trees, cf. Glacken, p. 321.

32 David Aers, *Chaucer* (Sussex: 1986), p. 17.

33 Glacken, p. 245.

irritated by those who ascribe all natural processes with bland piety to the creator's will, replies, 'You poor fools, God can make a cow out of a tree, but has He ever done so? Therefore show some reason why a thing is so, or cease to hold that it is so.'[34] It was the life's work of tramping, peering, verifying Albertus Magnus, prince of mendicant empiricism, to unearth the biological why. 'In the journeys from cloister to cloister, he had walked through Austria, Bavaria, Swabia, Alsace, the Rhine and Moselle valleys to Brabant, to Holland, to Westphalia, Holstein, Saxony, Meissen, Thuringia. Albert was thus well acquainted personally with some of the most dramatically contrasted landscapes of Europe ... He is interested in land classification, in fields first brought into cultivation, in the problem of the roots of felled trees robbing the new crops of their food, of hillside slopes whose soil is carried by the waters to the valleys below.' As such he was well placed to revive the *de natura locorum* tradition of the classical writers and early Christian encyclopaedists like Isidore, discussing systematically and with personal additions both 'gazeteer-like geography' (lists of great rivers, cities, etc.) and ideas of environmental influence.[35] If Albert was able both to comment upon Aristotle and occasionally supplement him, the rational and independent study of nature could actually foreshadow Renaissance achievements in the stance of Roger Bacon in the thirteenth century, under whose pen the name 'experimental science' (*scientia experimentalis*) 'seems to appear for the first time in the history of human thought'.[36] This recommended itself not only as securing certitudes, but as able 'to peer into the secrets of nature, to discover the past, the future and to produce so many marvellous effects that it will secure power to those who possess it'.[37] It is recognizably that same hunger for uncovering in nature appropriable material power which is abroad in the cities where an ambitious nascent bourgeoisie who build, process, travel, buy and sell, and who seek to expand or conserve their gains against feudal overlords and political instability, concern themselves with the environmental understanding of nature: with navigation and geography, hydraulics and mechanics, climatology and astrology.

34 Quoted from Lynn Thorndike, *A History of Magic and Experimental Science during the First Thirteen Centuries of Our Era* (New York: 1923–58), vol. 2, p. 58; as from *De Philosophia Mundi*, in *PL* 90, 1127–78.

35 Glacken, pp. 228–29, 266.

36 Gilson, pp. 309–11.

37 Ibid., p. 311.

Emphasis on concrete fact and material relations is above all spectacularly innovative in nominalism. Where a scientific thinker like Albertus might be content to declare 'It is not sufficient to know in terms of universals; we must seek to know every individual thing according to its own nature',[38] the nominalists 'shook the foundation of high-medieval thought by granting "real" existence only to the outward things directly known to us through sensory perception and to the inward states or acts directly known to us through psychological experience'.[39]

The preference for dropping from high metaphysical definitions of nature into sublunary analysis of her material and efficient causes proved to be theological gelignite. The 'necessitarian' conception of nature as a determinate network of interacting secondary causes, derived from Aristotle and his Arab commentators, could be seen as a radical denial of the liberty and omnipotence of the Christian God, who 'was not only able to create at a single stroke the world with the multiplicity of beings it holds, he still could intervene in it freely at any instant ... without the intervention of secondary causes'.[40] In consequence, the Condemnations of 1277 proscribed such doctrines in alarm.

But the pragmatic spirit underlying Gothic nature-sensibility could not be suppressed. Further evidence was in the rebirth of practical geography. 'The solid anchors of geographical description were the works of the classical geographers – and the inspirations of biblical geography.'[41] We have noted already Albertus' revival of the *de natura locorum* tradition, and Bacon's topographical interests as a basis for spiritual allegorization. But the encyclopaedists of the twelfth and thirteenth centuries, Albertus, Bartholomew of England, Vincent of Beauvais and others contained new emphases in their work.[42] Whereas in the sixth century, Cassiodorus valued cosmography only as enabling recognition of places named in sacred books,[43] Bartholo-

38 Quoted in Nicholas Pevsner, *The Leaves of Southwell* (Harmondsworth: 1945), p. 53, and also P&S, p. 162.

39 Panofsky, *Renaissance and Renascences in Western Art*, p. 120. For contrasts between Augustinian and nominalist emphases, cf. Meyrick H. Carré, *Realists and Nominalists* (Oxford: 1946). For the sociology of Nominalism, cf. Eberhard Conze, 'The Social Origins of Nominalism' in *Marxist Review*, 1 (1937), 115–24.

40 Ibid., p. 407. Cf. also pp. 408–10, 466.

41 Glacken, p. 262.

42 Gilson, pp. 262–64.

43 Cassiodorus Senator, *An Introduction to Divine and Human Readings*, Book 1, ch. 25.

mew, like Albertus, now supplements description of biblical places with empirical accounts based on his own or contemporaries' travel experiences. Roger Bacon, in his plea for geographical knowledge, is gratifyingly explicit. Knowledge of peoples and places is necessary for trade and travel he says, as well as conversion of pagans. 'Men have destroyed themselves and the business interests of Christians because they have passed through places too hot in the hot season, too cold in the cold.'[44]

Such empirical inclination, as we have begun to see, became endemic. 'There is seldom,' says Mâle, 'anything trivial in a thirteenth-century bas-relief, for every detail was the outcome of the artist's direct experience of life and nature. At the very gates of the little walled towns of the Middle Ages lay the country with its ploughed land and meadows and the rhythmical sequence of pastoral toil. The towers of Chartres rose above the fields of La Beauce, the Cathedral of Reims dominated the vineyards of Champagne and the apse of Notre Dame at Paris the surrounding woods and meadows. And so the sculptors drew inspiration from immediate reality for their scenes of rural life.'[45] Jalabert, in her study of the history of the foliated capital, argues that 'from 1140 to 1240 Gothic capitals changed from the barest reminiscence of nature to a naturalism which sacrificed design to exactitude of observation ... floral sculpture became botanizing'.[46]

Yet such empiricizing was companioned by a second novel tendency: the drive to unrelenting systematic reasoning. This derived not only from the rediscovery of the Aristotelian corpus, climacteric as this was, but also from a feature intrinsic to Gothic intellectuality: the combative critical independence nurtured by the Schools, where scholarship could flourish 'without being cramped by the exacting demands made by a regular monastic life'.[47] To inherited dogmatic frameworks, Abelard, Peter Lombard and others opposed speculative reasoning founded upon pure logic. Until 1277, faith and natural philosophy were seen as consonant, commercing in a 'spirit of free and confident collaboration';[48] and thus a basic empirical habit of mind as working within a rational framework, delighting in the measured and

44 Glacken, p. 285, summarizing the arguments of Bacon, *Opus Majus*, vol. 1, pp. 273, 321.

45 Mâle, *Gothic*, p. 67.

46 The words are those of White, p. 427, summarizing D. Jalabert, 'La flore gothique: ses origines, son évolution du XIIe au XVe siècle' in *Bulletin Monumental*, 91 (1932), 181–246.

47 Keen, *medieval Europe*, p. 95.

48 Gilson, p. 408.

systematic, characterizes Gothic nature-sensibility. Examples both abound, and abide: from Aquinas' insistence on the orderly processes of nature, revealed in very leaves, which are so arranged as to protect the fruit of the plant,[49] to the standard encomium of harmonic cosmology echoed two centuries later in Henryson:

> The firmament payntit with sternis cleir,
> From eist to west rolland in cirkill round,
> And everilk planet in his proper spheir,
> In moving makand harmonie and sound;
> The fyre, the air, the watter and the ground –
> That God in all His werkis wittie is.[50]

If such a passage is breezily laconic ('it is aneuch, I wis') because its theme is a millennium and a half old, such passages on wondrous cosmic engineering being to hand in Origen and Basil, Augustine and Boethius as we have seen, we do encounter something distinctively Gothic in Dante. There we find, amongst the sublime digressions on the workings of 'the love which moves the sun and the other stars',[51] that spirit of rigorously logical speculation carried through with superbly sheer coherence in *Inferno* 34. There, 'the two travellers find the shaggy and gigantic Lucifer at the absolute centre of the Earth, embedded up to his waist in ice. The only way they can continue their journey is by climbing down his sides ... But they find that though it is *down* to his waist, it is *up* to his feet. As Virgil tells Dante, they have passed the point towards which all heavy objects move. It is the first "science-fiction effect" in literature,'[52] What we call 'gravitation' was then already common knowledge; what Dante has done is to carry through cosmological speculation in that spirit of fascination for material mechanics and commitment to uncompromised logic, which we have been trying to establish as fresh with Gothic. The spirit of logic could, however, also deaden. Matthew of Vendôme's twelfth century treatment of the *locus amoenus* extends the standard 'charms of landscape' to sixty-two lines by the method of remorseless grammatical permutation (from 'The bird twitters, the brook murmurs,

49 *Summa Contra Gentiles*, Book 3, ch. 3, par. 9.

50 Henryson, 'Morall Fabillis' in *Robert Henryson: Poems*, ed. C. Elliot (Oxford, 1963), lines 1657–63.

51 *Paradiso*, 33, 145 of *The Divine Comedy*, trans. C. H. Sisson (1980; rpt. Lonson, 1981), p. 499.

52 Lewis, *Discarded Image*, pp. 141–42.

the breeze blows warm' to 'The birds give pleasure by their voices, the brook by its murmuring, the breeze by its warmth,' etc.); and by laboriously allocating the charms to their respective senses ('Water pleases the sense of touch, its flavour the sense of taste, the bird is the friend of the ear,' etc.). As Curtius recognizes, 'the logical jargon of dialectics has made its way into the writer's vocabulary'.[53]

We have argued so far for the characterization of Gothic nature-sensibility in terms of a deep-seated drive toward extended power over and use of the natural world: empirically refocused, assisted by systematic logical reasoning, and deriving from the rebirth of commercial production and civil prosperity. One further characteristic was a singing zest for natural beauty, a tra-la-la consciousness of security and affluence.

> The earth lies open-breasted
> In gentleness of spring,
> Who lay so close and frozen
> In winter's blustering,
> The northern winds are quiet,
> The west wind winnowing,
> In all this sweet renewing
> How shall a man not sing?[54]

Contrast with the social conditions of much of Christendom in the ninth and tenth centuries, ravaged by Danish, Viking and Magyar armies, helps explain the new tonality.

> The acts of the synod of Troslé in 909 give us some idea of the despair of the leaders of the Frankish church at the prospect of the universal ruin of Christian society. 'The cities,' they wrote, 'are depopulated, the monasteries ruined and burned, the country reduced to solitude ... As the first men lived without law or fear of God, abandoned to their passions, so now every man does what seems good in his own eyes, despising laws human and divine and the commands of the Church. The strong oppress the weak; the world is full of violence against the poor and of the plunder of ecclesiastical goods ... Men devour one another like the fishes in the sea.'[55]

No wonder then that 'the warfare and stoicism of the Anglo-Saxons gradually gave way to a literature of spring, of joy, of hawthorn

53 Curtius, *European Literature*, p. 198.

54 *Medieval Latin Lyrics*, trans. Helen Waddell (1952; rpt. Harmondsworth: 1962), p. 219.

55 Christopher Dawson, *The Making of Europe* (1932; rpt. New York, 1958), pp. 225–26.

blossoms and nightingales, of cherries and roses, of the greenwood'.[56] Undoubtedly mediated from the realm of agricultural triumphs under the new conditions of peace is the Gothic relish for nature as the principle of replenishment, sumptuously fecund. For Alan of Lille and Bernardus Silvestris, *Natura* is the teeming womb, the *mater generationis,* 'the inexhaustible fecundity from which springs the pullulation of beings'.[57] And we have already seen the religious ardour in which the humblest things of creation could be dipped by fingers turning the anagogic pages of the Book of Nature. The impact of such teachings can be lost on moderns:

In modern, that is, in evolutionary, thought Man stands at the top of a stair whose foot is lost in obscurity; in [medieval], he stands at the bottom of a stair whose top is invisible with light.[58]

We are thus in a countryside haunted by intimations of ideality, as well as by proto-scientists, travellers, and landowners keen for sharper husbandry. Within so inclusive a nature-sensibility, relations with the ideal landscape of literary convention are correspondingly mixed. That the fossil *locus amoenus* continued to flourish in verse is a stolid orthodoxy of every study; but we might also note, I think, the relations between ideal and real in landscape as adjustable in different directions. A more literal consciousness may de-sublimate the ideal, which conversely a more sublime spirit may literalize.

Bi a bonke of a bourne, bryghte was the sone,
Undir a worthiliche wodde by a wale medewe;
Fele floures gan folde ther my fote steppede.
I layde myn hede one ane hill, ane hawthorne besyde,
The throstills full throly they threpen togedire,
Hipped up heghwalles fro heselis tyll othire,
Bernacles with thayre billes one barkes thay roungen,
The jay janglede one heghe, jarmede the foles,
The bourne full bremly rane the bankes bytwene.

56 Margaret Drabble, *A Writer's Britain,* p. 23.
57 Gilson, p. 176. On the medieval career of *Natura* see also Edgar G. Knowlton, 'The Goddess Natura in Early Periods,' *Journal of Early Germanic Philology,* 19 (1920), 224–53; 'Nature in Early German,' *J.E.G.P.,* 24 (1925), 409–12; 'Nature in Early Italian,' *Modern Language Notes,* 36 (1921), 329ff; 'Nature in Middle English,' *J.E.G.P.,* 20 (1921), 186–207. Also 'Some implications of Nature's femininity in medieval poetry' by Winthrop Wetherbee, in *Approaches to Nature in the Middle Ages* ed. L. D. Roberts (Binghampton, New York: 1982), pp. 47–62.
58 Lewis, *Discarded Image,* pp. 74–75.

> So ruyde were the roughe stremys, and raughten so heghe,
> That it was neghande nyghte or I nappe myghte,
> For dyn of the depe watir, and dadillyng of fewllys.[59]

With great originality, the acoustic harmonies and lulling peace of the *locus amoenus* have been inverted into a cacophany, as if a medieval barnyard were to explode around Virgil's recumbent Tityrus. The playful pastiche suggests a sceptical literalism to hand, an inhabitation of very different ways of experiencing nature. The general effect may remind us of Chaucer's sharp-eyed satire in the *Parlement of Foules*; and we may compare too the *drôleries* of the margins of contemporary Psalters and Breviaries, where in the riot of grotesques we see 'an inexhaustible interest in natural appearances, combined with a lively sense of the ridiculous.'[60]

Directly contrary to such satiric distancing from ideal landscape is the achievement of St Francis. C. S. Lewis suggests that *fin amors* was in part the result of too literal a reading of Ovid;[61] and we might almost be tempted to think St Francis, similarly, pitiable victim to the pastoral tradition. For Francis went far beyond the doctrine of cheerful appreciation of created beauty: armed with holiness, he acted out the pathetic fallacy. Just as in pastoral beasts and trees are said to mourn or celebrate the fortunes of individuals, so the flora and fauna of Italy are accredited by Francis with active powers of responsive sympathy: which, according to contemporary tradition, they accordingly display. When he came upon an abundance of flowers, he would preach to them and 'invite them to praise the Lord, just as if they had been gifted with reason. So also cornfields and vineyards, stones, woods, and all the beauties of the field, fountains of waters, all the verdure of gardens, earth and fire, air and wind would he with sincerest purity exhort to the love and willing service of God.'[62] At Cannara, at Francis' command, swallows cease twittering until his sermon is over; and when he preaches a sermon to the birds – 'Therefore, my little bird sisters, be careful not to be ungrateful, but strive always to praise

59 *Winner and Waster*, ed. Sir I. Gollancz (London: 1920), lines 33–44. The poem dates from c. 1353.

60 Derek Pearsall, 'The Visual World of the Middle Ages' in *The New Pelican Guide to English Literature* (1954; expanded 1982), ed. Boris Ford, vol. 1, p. 298.

61 *The Allegory of Love* (1936; rpt. Oxford: 1958), pp. 7–8.

62 Brother Thomas of Celano, *The First Life of St. Francis of Assisi*, trans. A. G. Ferrers Howell in *The Inquiring Pilgrim's Guide to Assisi* (London: 1926), ed. Mary L. Cameron, pp. 80–81.

God'[63] – the birds bow their heads in acknowledgement. The wolf of Gubbio, admonished, extends to the saint a conciliatory paw. It is absurd to see here 'the greatest revolutionary in history', dethroning man from monarchy over the animal kingdom:[64] for valuation of creation as independent of human relations derives from the Old Testament,[65] and the model of saintly reintegration with brute life from patristic theology. The novelty lies rather with the buoyant sense of transformation and newly discovered potential in nature, a reality given supernatural projection. It lies too in the new sense of unity with nature: one so close that it can, at its height, heretically impute moral personality to her objects; so actual as to be the stuff of numberless miracles; and sensed so commonly and so lyrically that folk-hagiography in effect endorses the saccharine fictions of Latin poetic convention. The rejoicing fish, worshipful birds, and responsively blossoming earth of Alan of Lille's 'pastoral hyperbole'[66] may become for contemporaries *more* than literary.

Gothic nature-sensibility: epitome and limitations

The enclosed paradisal garden embodies, I suggest, just that 'structure of feeling' we have been tracing: as a place of ideal felicity it is an ordered and systematic formation; teemingly profuse; and replete with images of sharp naturalistic observation that hold symbolic resonance.

Superlative among these Gardens of Felicity is that of *The Romaunt of the Rose*. Gathering up numerous classical and medieval descriptive traditions, 'No pleasure of the senses is neglected: taste, touch, scent, hearing, sight are indulged.'[67] Just as Gothic painting and manuscript illumination feature 'small over-all patterns (*rinceaux*, diapers, tessellation, and the like)'[68] in an obsessive profusion that will degenerate into a *horror vacui*,[69] so in the *Romaunt* the overcrowding of *millefiore* flowers finds its equivalent in extraordinary super-abundance of vegetation and animal life. The Garden of Mirth is a cornucopia

63 *The Little Flowers of St. Francis* by Ugolino di Monte Santa Maria, trans. Raphael Brown (New York: 1958), p. 75.

64 Lynn White, 'Natural Science', p. 433.

65 *Job*. 38.26–7.

66 Alan of Lille, *De Planctu Naturae*, ed. Thomas Wright, *The Anglo-Latin Satirical Poets of the Twelfth Century* (London: 1872), vol. 2, pp. 445–46; trans. Lewis, *Allegory*, pp. 106–08.

67 P&S, p. 87.

68 Panofsky, *Renaissance and Renascences*, p. 133.

69 Huizinga, *Waning*, pp. 237–38.

containing squirrels and deer, thirty rabbits, thirty-four listed species of tree with an innumerable further quantity the dreamer would find himself 'encombred' to have to name, plus conduits almost numberless and flowers in 'Such plente [as] grew ... never in mede'.[70] Clearly this is a fantasia of private accumulation (Villainy, Poverty and others are explicitly debarred by the enclosing walls): superlatives take the form of limitless provision, indefeasible replenishment, possessed by the few.

This millionaire plenitude subsists within formal measure and order. Its trees are widely spaced and regular; it is even and square in compass.[71] 'The quality to be praised in gardens is that they are "bien ordonnez",'[72] in the *Romaunt*, in the verse of Machaut,[73] and in life. The norm endures long: in *The Flower and the Leaf*, from the latter half of the fifteenth century, the perfect herber is 'well ywrought':

> Wrethen in fere so wel and cunningly
> That every branch and leafe grew by mesure,
> Plain as a bord.[74]

The formula of 'naturalistic detail disposed according to a primarily decorative scheme'[75] holds equally for Gothic book illuminations as even for early landscape frescoes, such as those of the Garde-Robe chamber in the papal palace at Avignon. Stylized clumps of trees (*boquetaux*), terraced rocks, and carpets of flowers suggest a tapestry tradition, rather than a world of space: the impression is still strong in Gozzoli's *Journey of the Magi* (of 1459) when 'the landscape of symbols' had become anachronistic. Only in the margins and *bas-de-pages* is there a move to self-validating naturalism indifferent to symbolism within the Gothic period: in Pucelle's Calendar pictures, for instance, where birds, butterflies and dragonflies embellish the Belleville Breviary.[76] For the most part, symbolic values reconstitute the field of naturalistic depiction; and the whole is enclosed within 'fragile and decorative elegance'.[77]

'Gothic art remained unalterably non-perspective',[78] writes

70 *The Romaunt of the Rose*, in Chaucer's translation, *Complete Works*, lines 1352–1444.
71 Lines 1349–50.
72 Guillaume de Machaut, *Le Joli Mois de May*, P&S, p. 173.
73 P&S, pp. 172–74.
74 *The Flower and the Leaf*, ed. D. A. Pearsall (London: 1962), lines 58–60.
75 P&S, p. 164.
76 Cf. Kenneth Clark, *Landscape into Art*, p. 27; and P&S, pp. 163–65.
77 P&S, p. 164.
78 Panofsky, *Renaissance and Renascences*, p. 133.

Panofsky; pictorial action unfolds across our field of vision rather than advancing and receding in it. Surface rather than a view, inspired by 'the sculptor's way of seeing things'[79] as line rather than volume, nature in the visual arts remains a matter of 'fractional naturalism', an ornamental assemblage of individual forms. Stefano da Zevio's *Madonna in the Rose Garden* (plate 7), 'perhaps the consummation of the Gothic landscape in Europe', though gay with flowers of recognizable species, is 'packed with symbolic detail, but airless, in a void, dematerialized.'[80] In literature, the dream scheme and formulaic ideality preclude localization:

> I com to a launde of whyte and grene;
> So fair oon had I never inne been;
> The ground was grene, y-poudred with daisye,
> The floures and the gras y-lyke hye,
> Al grene and whyte; was nothing elles sene.[81]

Late Medieval and Renaissance

Empiricism and pictorialism

We turn now to the post-Gothic development of 'pictorial' interests in nature. Pictorialism is not the same thing, however, as mere empiricism, whereby a poet may create or enrich his natural description with fresh particulars of his own direct perception. Of this the British Isles had long provided outstanding traditions.

In Anglo-Saxon verse, the poet of *The Ruin* notices among the strewn towers and gaping roofs of the ruined Aquae Sulis walls where grey lichen grows upon red stone, and frost fastens upon the plaster.[82] *The Wanderer* and *The Seafarer*, in which 'we can trace a positive liking for the bleak and desolate, a melancholy and nostalgia that provide a powerful strain in our national feeling for landscape',[83] detail storm-lashed cliffs to whose beatings the icy-winged tern replies, and the seafarer shivering, hung with icicles, hail flying past him in showers,

79 Friedländer, *Landscape, Portrait, Still-Life*, p. 16.

80 A. R. Turner, *The Vision of Landscape in Renaissance Italy* (Princeton, 1966), p. 5; P&S, p. 165.

81 *The Cuckoo and the Nightingale* in *Chaucerian and Other Pieces*, ed. W. W. Skeat (Oxford: 1897), lines 61–65, : late fourteenth century.

82 'The Ruin' in *A Choice of Anglo-Saxon Verse*, ed. Richard Hamer (London: 1970), lines 4 and 10, p. 27.

83 Drabble, *A Writer's Britain*, p. 21.

forging over ice-cold waves.[84] *Beowulf*, according to Andersson, so roundedly maintains the Virgilian tradition of scenic atmosphere that 'Nothing in the Germanic material points to such scenic fullness.'[85] Grendel's Mere has a celebrated power of specificity:

> Mysterious is the region
> they live in – of wolf-fells, wind-picked moors
> and treacherous fen-paths: a torrent of water
> pours down dark cliffs and plunges into the earth,
> an underground flood. It is not far from here,
> in terms of miles, that the Mere lies,
> overcast with dark, crag-rooted trees
> that hang in groves hoary with frost.
> An uncanny sight may be seen at night there
> – the fire in the water! The wit of living men
> is not enough to know its bottom.
> The hart that roams the heath, when hounds have pressed him
> long and hard, may hide in the forest
> his antlered head; but the hart will die there
> sooner than swim and save his life ...
> And the wind can stir up wicked storms there,
> whipping the swirling waters up
> till they climb the clouds and clog the air,
> making the skies weep.[86]

Yet as Pearsall and Salter comment, 'It is impossible to organize the details of this description into a coherent visual "scene", because no such scene was intended.'[87]

In Irish Celtic poetry, even more conspicuously, direct observation of natural phenomena is sharp. Descriptions of winter register bracken turned deep-red and shapeless, reeds withered and lakes swollen to angry seas; winds so strong one hardly can stand and grass frozen so hard a man could stand on a single stalk. The stags become meagre and the eagle miserable as ice penetrates even its beak; trees are bowed in the wind and the blackbird is restless among them, unable to find shelter.[88] The personifications and anthropomorphic tropes (such as

84 Hamer, p. 187, lines 15–24.

85 Andersson, p. 156.

86 *Beowulf*, ed. F. Klaeber (New York: 1922), lines 1357–76; trans. Michael Alexander (Harmondsworth: 1973), p. 94.

87 p. 44. On Anglo-Saxon landscape description, cf. P&S, pp. 41–44, 122–24; also P. L. Henry, *The Early English and Celtic Lyric* (London: 1966).

88 *A Celtic Miscellany*, trans. Kenneth Hurlstone Jackson (Harmondsworth: 1971), pp. 64–66.

'rosy-fingered dawn') of Greco-Roman description are largely absent. Moreover, whereas 'in Homer and Greek lyric, or in *Beowulf* and Anglo-Saxon elegiac poetry, we have adjectives meaning "bright, flashing, glittering, pale, white, dun, dark, gloomy, grey, black" (the adjectives of a colour-blind man), in the Celtic literatures there is a constant use of distinctive colour words, often minor varieties of a colour: "red, rusty-red, blood-red, crimson, purple, sky-blue, blue-grey, green, bright yellow, greyish-brown, auburn", and so on, are frequent'.[89] A stunning example of colour-sensitivity is from *The Exile of the Sons of Uisliu*:

> One day, in winter, Derdriu's foster-father was outside, in the snow, flaying a weaned calf for her. Derdriu saw a raven drinking the blood on the snow, and she said to Lebarcham 'I could love a man with those three colours: hair like a raven, cheeks like blood and body like snow.'[90]

As Kuno Meyer suggests, 'these poems occupy a unique position in the literature of the world. To seek out and watch and love Nature, in its tiniest phenomena as in its grandest, was given to no people so early and so fully as to the Celt.'[91] Yet it is hard to judge to what extent the inspiration of these poems was free of latin influence, and, as claimed, specifically the product of the Irish anchoritic ideal anticipating the spirit of the early Franciscans.[92] Possibly this is a verse allied to a penitential tradition, in expressing the simple lifestyle of the *ailithre* in his solitary natural hermitage close to God.[93] We are in the hands of the translator.[94] What is certain, however, is that 'It is a characteristic of these poems that in none of them do we get an elaborate or sustained description of any scene or scenery.'[95] Celtic verse thus can be seen to be empirical – concerned descriptively more with actuality than authority – but not 'pictorial' or 'phenomenological' in its tendencies. Rather than comprising a body, indeed, of 'nature-poetry', we have genres of elegiac and gnomic poetry in which the natural world serves simply to supply exemplary forms. In Anglo-Saxon verse similarly landscape reference serves to

89 Ibid., p. 169.
90 *Early Irish Myths and Sagas*, trans. Jeffrey Gantz (Harmondsworth: 1981), p. 260.
91 *Ancient Irish Poetry* (London: 1911), Introduction, p. xii.
92 Myles Dillon, *Early Irish Literature* (Chicago: 1948), p. 163.
93 P. L. Henry, *Lyric*, pp. 42–44.
94 P&S, pp. 33–36, are speculatively sceptical as to its autonomy.
95 Meyer, Introduction, p. xiii.

illustrate religious contemplation of earthly life as doomed mortality and vain achieving.

Likewise empirical and likewise lacking in any attempt at arraying multiple images as an ordered field of vision, is the English alliterative verse of the later fourteenth century. Here, as Pearsall and Salter put it, is an 'often indiscriminate accumulation of substantives, an arbitrary concreteness of reference which can break through to a kind of illusory realism', which functions 'on many occasions as a thesaurus of synonyms'.[96] However, in the *tour de force* of the storm at sea from *The Destruction of Troy*, the swamping disorder of nouns proves the perfect realist technique.

> When sodenly the softe aire unsoberly rose;
> The cloudis over cast, claterrit aboute;
> Wyndes full wodely walt up the ythes;
> Wex merke as the mydnighte mystes full thicke;
> Thunret in the thestur throly with all;
> With a launchant laite lightonyd the water;
> And a ropand rayne raiked fro the hevyn.
> The storme was full stithe with mony stout windes,
> His walt up the wilde se uppon wan hilles.[97]

I would agree that these energies are acoustic, and where visual they work by a hail of sudden detail: this is quite the reverse of the measured scopes of pictorialism, and may remind us of the 'grapeshot' technique we found quelling the insurgent *Job*.

Occasionally, however, empiricism in alliterative dream-poetry *can* move into a roomy, spatial framework of declared landscape spectacle, completely at odds with the dry conceptual terms of the schoolman's *locus amoenus* at which we looked earlier through the example of Matthew of Vendôme. In the allegorical dream-poem *Mum and the Sothsegger* (c. 1403–06) for example, I find:

> I tournyd me twyes and totid aboute,
> Beholding heigges and holtz so grene,
> The mansions and medues mowen al newe,
> For suche was þe saison of þe same yere.
> I lifte up my eye-ledes and lokid ferther
> And sawe many swete sightz, so me God helpe,
> The wodes and þe waters and þe welle-springes
> And trees y-traylid fro toppe to þerthe,

96 P&S, p. 177. Cf. also p. 166, 177–79.

97 *Destruction of Troy*, ed. G. Panton and D. Donaldson, Early English Text Society, lines 4625–33.

Coriously y-courid with curtelle of grene,
The flours on feeldes flavrng swete,
The corne on þe croftes y-croppid ful faire,
The rennyng rivyere russhing faste,
Ful of fyssh and of frie of felefold kinde,
The breris with þaire beries bent over þe wayes
As honysoucles hongyng upon eche half,
Chesteynes and chiries þat children desiren
Were loigged under leves ful lusty to seen.

Thereafter, the poet moves 'a-dovne to þe dale' where he hears 'a noise of nestlingz ... among þe heigges'.[98] In all this, the organizational principle is still, as Pearsall and Salter argue in their own excerpts from other alliterative poems, that of the alliterative catalogue; yet, I suggest that in this poem (overlooked by them) the pleasure of high-view prospect and visual acuity are also clear, in details as well as in the explicit framework. Alliterative ordering persists in parts – woods and waters and well-springs seem otherwise random – and the fish in the river, and odour of flowers, lie outside the optical framework. Yet the poet declares, in the first and fifth lines quoted, that it is a *spectacle*, a 360° roving of the eye, that he is enjoying. He has hastened to the summit of 'þe highest hille by halfe alle other';[99] and the draping of the trees in full summer foliage, the briars overhanging paths like drooping honeysuckle, and the 'lodging' of cherries and chestnuts under leafage, are all visual effects. Moreover, this is 'penetrated space', the dreamer's moving from one place to another creating a three-dimensional depth. The flat surface-objects of Gothic are thus left decisively behind, although we have not quite achieved 'landskip' yet: distances, spatial relations, colours, and unusual optical effects have not entered to supply 'pictorial' organization. More than merely empirical, less than pictorial, it is nonetheless, so far as I have been able to discover, the earliest 'prospect' of a landscape in extant English literature.[100]

The fourteenth century is remote enough from consciousness of

98 *Mum and the Sothsegger*, ed. Mabel Day and Robert Steele (London: 1915), p. 53, lines 885–901, 932, 934, 936.

99 Line 884. The landscape passage, which there is not space here to cite in full, extends in fact between lines 884–936, before passing on briefly to a Franklin's garden.

100 Langland's vision of tower, dungeon and 'fair feld, ful of folk' is purely allegoric, and 'owes nothing to the Malvern hills'. *Piers Plowman*, ed. Elizabeth Salter and Derek Pearsall (London: 1969), lines 14–18, and note.

scene in specifically pictorial terms to describe even pictures in a way that unreflectingly admits the data of other senses. The description of the ominous forest surrounding the Temple of Mars in Chaucer's *Knight's Tale* incorporates dire sound-effects, with much the same flushed coenaesthesis as the Homeric 'description' of Hephaestus' shield in the *Iliad* which supplied acoustic and tactile properties to embossed landscapes.[101]

Elsewhere in the fourteenth century we find some hints of the pictorial in verse however. This is not a matter of poet directly imitating painting, even where material may exist in common. Distinctively Nordic conditions such as snowscapes, for instance, are to be found both in Calendar landscape art (the February scene from the Limbourgs' *Très Riches Heures* of c. 1415, and the January fresco at Trento, c. 1410) and in verse: the Gawain-poet describes the Châtelaine:

> Hir brest and hir bryzt þrote bare displayed;
> Schon schyrer þen snawe þat schedez on hillez[102]

but at a slightly earlier date. It may be that the distinctively unstable and damp atmospheric conditions of the British Isles produce heightened awareness of light and hence of optical play. 'Pleasant to me' scribbles a ninth-century Irish Celtic monk on the margin of his manuscript, 'is the glittering of the sun today upon these margins, because it flickers so.'[103] At all events, Gawain registers Bertilak's castle:

> 'Þat holde on þat on syde þe haþel avysed,
> As hit schemered and schon þurz þe schyre okez.'

Of early morning we are told:

> 'Ferly fayre watz þe folde, for þe forst clenged;
> In rede rudede upon rak rises þe sunne,
> And ful clere costez þe clowdes of þe welkyn.'[104]

Here are clear visual effects, the first having a background-foreground structure and the second composing a whole of land, sunrays and sky, where the achievement of structure derives from the impression made

101 'Knight's Tale' in *Complete Works of Geoffrey Chaucer*, p. 36, lines 1975–95; *Iliad*, 18.541–607.

102 *Sir Gawain and the Green Knight*, ed. J. R. R. Tolkien and E. V. Gordon, 2nd edn, Norman Davis (Oxford: 1967), p. 27, lines 955–56.

103 *Celtic Miscellany*, p. 177.

104 *Gawain*, p. 22, lines 771–72, and p. 47, lines 1694–96.

by light. We are entitled to call these 'views', though they have nothing further in common with that concern for perspectival recession and focused composition developed in the 'scientific views' of later painting, and imitated in Renaissance verse. Landscape *appearances* are evidently, however, of an order of interest valuable in themselves: the details of a sharp, clearing morning of frost are otherwise gratuitous; and it is through an optical instability, as filtered and framed by shining oaks, that the castle's miraculousness and allure are constructed.

In Dante too I would argue that a climate of perception approaching pictorial values is clearly emergent. Such is the concrete materiality of his world that even incorporeal evanescence is given visual apprehensibility: spirits vanish from view in Paradise 'as a heavy object does in deep water', and their brightness is discernible within the brilliance of the empyrean 'as in a flame, it is possible to see a spark'.[105] This visual premium is extended beyond sharp particulars, as with Gothic art, into the evocation of space and depth, as in Renaissance. As in the *Odyssey*, we frequently encounter the activity of gazing, and the situating of subjects within enclosing dimensions of space: the farmer gazing from the hillside down into the valley where glow-worms shine in the spot he had worked; the night spent on the high terraces of the mountain of Purgatory under the moving stars watching the colour fade from the horizon; the cosmic vista of the earth a tiny globe at the centre of concentric rings.[106] Above all, the Earthly Paradise of *Purgatorio* 28 embodies what Friedländer refers to in Renaissance painting as 'spatiality, landscape roominess' and 'cubic reality'.[107] Dante's exposition of the garden includes, in Gothic mode, concern with its 'material and efficient causes' in the allusion to its distinctive means of propagating trees (lines 103–20) and its derivation of water directly from the fiat of God rather than from the cyclical condensation of atmospheric vapours (lines 121–26). But the garden is also given 'experiential' naturalism: through definition as a space penetrated by a walker. As he enters the forest, its density tempers the light to his eyes; a breeze strikes on his forehead, that is light yet steady; advancing, he loses sight of his point of entry, but finds

105 *The Divine Comedy*, trans. C. H. Sisson (London: 1981), *Paradiso* 3, lines 122–23, p. 363; 8, line 16, p. 382.

106 Ibid., *Inferno* 26, lines 25–32, p. 155; *Purgatorio* 27, lines 67–92, pp. 317–18; *Paradiso* 22, lines 133–154, p. 449.

107 Friedländer, *Landscape*, pp. 25, 28.

progress blocked by a river; wind undulates branches around him, but not enough to unsettle the birds on them. All this is combined with enchantment: boughs welcome the breeze, swaying to the left like the grasses swayed by the stream, and the rustling of the foliage harmonizes with the birdsong. (One wonders whether Dante was influenced here by the tendency of late thirteenth-century sculptors[108] of foliage capitals to introduce motion into their carved flora?) The 'charms of landscape' of the *locus amoenus* are thus unified, living animation given to antique fustian, in a tonality which merges the magical with sounding naturalism. Above all, this *locus amoenus* is not tapestry but landscape: Dante's experiential order of narration has recorded an extended and organized spatial structure.

Pictorial naturalism will, however, develop through the Middle Ages with no steady chronological regularity. In both art and verse, the coexistence of symbolic and material planes to the reality of the visible world maintains a duality in which either may predominate to the exclusion of the other. For example, 'the landscape of Paradise could be simply drawn in the fourteenth century, sensuously imagined in the ninth. An indefinite number of gradations could be managed in the delicate adjustment of the real to the ideal, the real to the surreal. Historical accident – country of origin, working conditions, availability of materials, pressure of patron or convention – was influential.' Consequently, 'the status of landscape is frequently in doubt, as also its mode of portrayal'.[109] Indeed, I have not found it remarked in literary studies of landscape description that there existed throughout the Middle Ages, re-emerging in the thirteenth century with Roger Bacon, an established framework for the definition of landscape in terms quite foreign to pictorial and sensory concerns: the *De Natura Locorum* tradition described place in terms not only of fertility but also of such 'invisibles' as its humours and airs, the astral influences bearing upon it, and the allegoric import of its geography.[110] Naturalism in art and verse will be subject both to delays in the assimilation of developments – the most celebrated being the obliteration of Giottesque advances in fourteenth century Italy consequent upon the plague[111] – and to formulaic tendencies. 'The tendency to codify and

108 Lynn White, 'Natural Science', p. 427.

109 P&S, pp. 60, 129.

110 Cf. Glacken, pp. 264–70, 283–85.

111 M. Meiss, *Painting in Florence and Siena after the Black Death* (Princeton: 1951), passim.

stabilize was always strong: a formula, once proved successful, would be adopted, time after time. And so the rose garden was often exchanged for a domestic landscape of equally formal components – swan, farmhouse, meadow and orchard sleeping in a June haze as unvarying as the reflected light of Paradise. The flowers of summer may accompany an autumn *Visitation*, while the foliage and colours of spring may serve for the whole sequence of events from Visitation to Crucifixion.'[112]

The perceptual mode of pictorial naturalism has of course no privileged force of truth or finality to it. Our ubiquitous familiarity with it through the photographic image and centuries of landscape painting should not blind us to the fact of its historical contingency and artificiality.[113] The 'naturalism' of fifteenth- and sixteenth-century landscape painting is itself often formulaic. The winding river valleys of Quattrocento Italian art are recurrent because they 'offer the closest approximation in nature to the artificial conditions of one-point perspective. A flat ground plane can be established, banks converge, and objects diminish in orderly fashion.'[114] In Renaissance focused perspective, architectural structures are virtually always set at a foreshortened frontal angle, following the schema of Alberti. Again, sixteenth-century landscapes are not truly 'views' but usually accumulations of generic features, 'conceptual rather than visual'.[115] So conventionalized becomes landscape painting that landscape backgrounds are often left to apprentices.[116] Today's ruling conceptions of natural scenery are likewise so formulaic as to occlude mundane observations encountered with surprise in poets of earlier periods. Since Titian and Tintoretto, evening has entailed the flush of sunset: yet for Henry Vaughan, at evening

> The green wood glittered with the golden sun
> And all the west *like silver shined*.[117]

For Dante, and Milton, dusk is not grey but brown.[118] For St. Francis, Sister Earth is praised for the bright colours not only of flowers but of

112 P&S, p. 157; cf. also pp. 113–14.
113 Cf. ibid., pp. 36, 185.
114 A. R. Turner, *The Vision of Landscape in Renaissance Italy* (Princeton: 1966), p. 7.
115 E. H. Gombrich, *Norm and Form*, p. 116.
116 P&S, p. 191.
117 Vaughan, 'Daphnis: An Elegiac Eclogue', lines 15–16, in *Henry Vaughan: The Complete Poems*, ed. Alan Rudrum (Harmondsworth: 1976), p. 386.
118 *Divine Comedy: Inferno*, 2, line 1. *Il Penseroso*, line 134.

leaves.[119] Such variations remind us that the 'concept of scene', and contemporary perception of the natural manifold, represent only historically specific codes constraining consciousness to conventionalized leading perceptions.

The managerial relation to landscape

A founding condition for the development of landskip is the managerial relation to the natural world: a sensibility in which active, measuring command of and intervention in the natural is a confident practice. We have traced in previous chapters 'the controlling habit of mind, committed Hesiodic surveillance', as well as the tradition in Christian thought of human stewardship of creation.

In the aristocratic *Beowulf* and much Anglo-Saxon verse there is no mention of clearance or farming[120] ('they had no eye for scenery, any more than other hard-working farmers of later centuries' thinks Hoskins). Yet the Old English experience of laboriously clearing smaller trees, bushes and undergrowth by axe, mattock, bill-hook, even by fire, to produce in 'a hand-made world' over twenty generations a land of open-field villages,[121] must have contributed raspingly to 'that sense of human weakness and isolation so prominent in Old English literature generally'.[122] The Anglo-Saxon *Genesis* articulates the predominant attitude:

> How shall you and I now live or endure on this earth
> If the wind constantly blows, from west and east,
> From south and north? The skies darken,
> Hail showers fall ...
> Sometimes the fiery sun beats down from the heavens,
> Scorching us, naked as we stand[123]

It is no accident, I would suggest, that agricultural revolution and the rebirth of pictorial space derive alike from the High Middle Ages. Belief in man's licence to 'make' landscape, faith in art as the agency of nature's authentic realization, is a condition of landscape painting

119 St Francis, *The Canticle of Brother Sun* in *The Little Flowers of St. Francis*, trans. Raphael Brown, p. 317.
120 *Old English Literature* by Michael Alexander (London: 1983), p. 41.
121 Hoskins, *Making*, pp. 55, 57, 79, 45.
122 T. A. Shippey, *Old English Verse* (London: 1972), p. 64.
123 *Genesis*, 805–8, 810–11, in *The Junius Manuscript*, ed. G. P. Krapp (London: 1931), trans. P&S, p. 124.

no less than of agriculture. Of course, human alteration and management of land is a practice common to all cultures that have developed beyond hunter-gatherer stage. But whereas in many cultures agricultural intervention is apologetic, accompanied by propitiatory rites, and the like,[124] Christianity teaches man's pristine appointed stewardship over a non-sacred creation. It is a doctrine that receives especial conviction, moreover, in the medieval experience of radical environmental subjugation.

The eleventh to thirteenth centuries saw a new, resurgent climate of dominative achievement and assurance. The use of the iron plough for tilling, and the three-field system of crop rotation assisted increased agricultural productivity, while the invention of a stiff collar resting on the animal's shoulder allowed the replacement around the tenth century of the ox by the horse as a draft animal, allowing vastly increased efficiency in the work of clearing and transportation of heavy materials. Water-mills and navigable waterways became used on a scale unknown in antiquity, the windmill and the fulling-mill appeared in England towards the end of the twelfth century.[125] Above all, forest, heath, marsh and bog retreated before the environmental offensive. All over Europe lands which had lain waste were brought into productive use, the thirteenth century being in England the period of most intense clearing and draining. 'The reclamation of marsh and fen brought hundreds of square miles of new land into cultivation, and produced a characteristic landscape of willow-lined ditches, rich green pastures that carried thousands of sheep, and scattered farmsteads.'[126] Cistercian monasteries from the early twelfth century onwards[127] engaged in large-scale drainage and the extension of sheep-farming across ranch-like granges,[128] while in a 'fever of borough creation' hundreds of little market-towns came into existence in the twelfth and thirteenth centuries, producing or consolidating the existence of hundreds of bridges and a great number of main roads.[129] The last wolves in England appear to have been exterminated in the thirteenth century.[130] Ecclesiastical building programmes tore up the earth in a

124 Cf. Mircea Eliade, *Patterns in Comparative Religion*, pp. 245–47.

125 Glacken, pp. 319–20; Lynn White, Jr, *Medieval Technology and Social Change* (Oxford: 1962), pp. 80–84. See Glacken's valuable bibliography of works concerning medieval deforestation and environmental change, pp. 288–9.

126 Hoskins, *Making*, p. 100.

127 Keen, *Medieval Europe*, p. 85.

128 Hoskins, *Making*, pp. 101–02.

129 Ibid., pp. 110, 113.

130 Doris Mary Stenton, *English Society in the Early Middle Ages*, p. 104.

giantism of quarrying: 'probably more stone was removed from the earth in this period than in any comparable period in the past. In the three centuries from 1050 to 1350 stone quarried in France built 80 cathedrals, 500 large churches, and tens of thousands of small churches.'[131] In this country 'that very characteristic English view of the church spire rising from the tufted trees or piercing the quiet autumn skies in a wide view'[132] rose before the gaze of men and women from the late twelfth century onwards. Above all, the *âge des grands défrichements* (mid-twelfth to thirteenth century), under the pressure of need for arable land and the establishment of industries requiring wood for fuel and construction, saw a scale of deforestation so large that conservation anxieties arose: in contrast to Carolingian decrees, 'the clearing, not the forest, had to be justified'.[133] We may note that managing and supervising the process of agricultural production was an activity common both to the peasant, free to improve output on his own land-strips during the three days or so per week when not paying labour rent on the seigneurial demesne, and to the nobility below magnate level, whose economic rationality produced far higher productivity on their demesnes than on surrounding peasant plots. Only the higher nobility became economically parasitic to the point of entirely abandoning land management to their reeves and bailiffs.[134] In these conditions, average harvest seed yields between the ninth and thirteenth centuries increased, it has been calculated, at a minimum from 2.5:1 to 4:1, the portion of the harvest at the disposal of the producer effectively doubling.[135]

In consequence, medieval art and thought sanctified labour, alongside contemplation, as enfranchisement. In the sculpture programmes of thirteenth-century cathedral doorways at Amiens and Chartres seasonal labours are pursued;[136] in the stone of Southwell Minster, pigs search among oak leaves for autumnal acorns. Calendar motifs begin, in England, with manuscript painters of the eleventh century,[137] who portray shepherd and flocks, bending reapers,

131 Glacken, p. 350. On English church-building, cf. Hoskins, pp. 106–10.

132 Hoskins, *Making*, p. 82, 108.

133 Glacken, pp. 291, 334–36.

134 Anderson, *Passages, pp.* 184–86.

135 Georges Duby, *Rural Economy and Country Life in the Medieval West* (London: 1968), p. 103.

136 Mâle, *Gothic*, pp. 64–75; figs. 33, 34, 37, 39.

137 British Museum, *Manuscript Cotton Tiberius B.V.*, part one, ff. 3–8v; discussed by P&S, pp. 131–32.

peasants loading waggons and September swine-pasturage; while 'the first Calendar pictures to contain landscape only and the first vernacular poems to contain descriptions of the seasons unconcerned with agricultural labours come from the first half of the fourteenth century'.[138] Both Augustine and Aquinas had considered cultivation to have been the pleasant existence of Adam even in prelapsarian paradise; enjoyable, says Aquinas, 'on account of man's practical knowledge of the powers of nature'.[139]

The Labours of the Months thus provide a framework in which cautious reiteration or expanses of fresh observation figure a symbolically tinged universal pattern. January and February feature indoor scenes of fireside and food, snow or log-piles as domestic exterior. February and March show pruning, pollarding or soil-turning, whilst April and May are for ploughing and sowing, flower-gathering and hare-hunting, tournaments and hawking. June to August centre on mowing meadows, reaping corn, threshing and haymaking, whilst September and October set forth orchards and grape-harvesting, hunting and sowing. The two final months signify swine-pasturage and slaughter, and cutting firewood for the retreat once more to cake-baking, feasting and warming.[140]

> By thys fyre I warm my handys;
> And with my spade I delfe my landys.
> Here I sette my thynge to sprynge;
> And here I here the foulis synge.
> I am as lyght as byrde in bowe;
> And I wede my corne well I-now …
> At Martynesmasse I kylle my swyne;
> And at Cristemasse I drynke redde wyne.[141]

The Gospel of Work with its focus upon 'undying Adam, bent towards the earth'[142] means that 'there is nothing of the somewhat insipid grace of antique frescoes, no cupid masquerading as a grape-gatherer, no winged genii in the role of harvester. Neither are there

138 P&S, p. 140.

139 Augustine, *De opere Monachorum* in *A Select Library of Nicene and Post-Nicene Fathers of the Christian Church*, ed. Philip Schaff (New York: 1886–90), 14 vols., vol. 3, p. 516; Aquinas, *Summa Theologica*, trans. Fathers of the English Dominican Province, 3 vols., vol. 1 (London: 1947), Q. 102, p. 501.

140 Cf. Mâle, *Gothic*, pp. 67–75; P&S, pp. 131–39; Rosamund Tuve, *Seasons and Months: Studies in a Tradition of Middle English Poetry* (Paris: 1933), passim.

141 *Secular Lyrics of the XIVth and XVth Centuries*, ed. R. H. Robbins (Oxford: 1955), p. 62.

142 Mâle, p. 67.

Botticelli's charming goddesses dancing at the festival of the Primavera. It is man alone in his conflict with nature.'[143] Though personifications persist in verse and art – Chaucer's squire for instance 'as fresh as is the month of May'[144] – the contrast between antique calendars where passive personifications bear symbols of their attributes, and medieval months as narratives of realistic intervention in nature, is eloquent.[145] The *summa* of Calendar art is *Les Très Riches Heures du Duc de Berri* of the Limbourg brothers, produced before 1416, which is 'similar to the *Roman de la Rose* for the way in which it gathered up and re-expressed all preceding descriptive material'.[146] Much study has been devoted to this as to the entire Calendar tradition,[147] which it is not to my purpose to recount here. What is supremely significant is that 'it was the Calendar, with its strong attachment to the concept of change, which decisively established the natural world as material both serious and sufficient for artists', and that this was because it afforded 'the reconciliation of moral and aesthetic sensibilities'[148] as observantly illustrating humanity exercising redemptive virtue, restoring as a good steward nature to pristine order and utility. If mutability carried penal significance in autumn and winter, it prefigured eternal joy in spring and summer:[149]

> Now lorde, sende hem somer, and some manere ioye,
> Hevene after her hennes-goynge, that here han
> suche defaute![150]

Contrast with classical antiquity is again sharp, for agriculture there, as we have seen, was in practice stigmatized; it bore in poetry a lingering sentimental apology (as in Virgil's matricidal plough of *Eclogue* 4.31–33), or carried a triumphal swagger, as in villa poetry. Nowhere did it embody, as for the medievals, effortful religious good conscience: even the hymn to the hallowed *vetus colonus* of the *Georgics* bore the wistfulness of elegy, rather than the weight and joy of the actual.

143 Ibid., p. 75.
144 The 'General Prologue' to the *Canterbury Tales*, in *Complete Works*, p. 18, line 92.
145 Cf. James C. Webster, *The Labors of the Months in Antique and Medieval Art to the End of the Twelfth Century* (Evanston: 1938), passim. 146 P&S, p. 156.
147 Cf. P&S, pp. 119–60; also Tuve. For the *Très Riches Heures* in a modern scholarly edition, cf. *Les Très Riches Heures de Duc de Berry*, ed. J. Longnon, R. Cazelles and M. Meiss (London: 1969). 148 P&S, pp. 157, 204.
149 Cf. ibid., pp. 122, 133; and Tuve, *Seasons and Months*, pp. 128–29.
150 *Piers Plowman*, ed. W. W. Skeat (Oxford: 1886), B, XIV, 164–65.

William of Malmesbury, however, is lyrical on the achievement of Thorney Abbey, founded in fenlands, in creating a *paradisi simulacrum*. Trees abound, tall, slim and smooth-barked, struggling towards the stars. There is nothing to stumble on as one hastens through its grassy fields, and its green sea of herbs is level. Not even the smallest part of the land is left untilled, for orchards and vines spread over the ground and rise on trellises into the air. Here, he says, is a rivalry of art and nature, the former creating what the latter had forgotten.[151] Bernard of Clairvaux hymns likewise 'an ideal landscape of the Cistercian order': praising the monastic diversions of the river Aube to run water mills, fill the boiler for the brewer, operate pestles for the fullers, and irrigate the meadows. Writing of this valley at Clairvaux, he finds in the landscape of action the peace of heaven. 'That spot has much charm, it greatly soothes weary minds, relieves anxieties and cares, helps souls who seek the Lord greatly to devotion, and recalls to them the thought of the heavenly sweetness to which they aspire. The smiling countenance of the earth is painted with varying colours, the blooming verdure of spring satisfies the eyes, and its sweet odour salutes the nostrils.'[152]

Landscape art, to conclude, develops as an aspect of man's habitual and self-conscious production of nature, and his confidence that his designing of it is divinely authorized. A pathway is thereby opened which leads toward nature as fresco and botanical illustration, as well as toward valleys of Cistercian clearance and irrigation. This point of departure for landskip had been affirmed by the Fathers, but the historical actuality of measuring mastery in the massive transformation of the European environment in the high medieval period inevitably gave new prominence to the doctrine. The first stage in the re-emergence of landscape art, then, is the belief *not* that physical nature is worthy of art, but, more intimately, that it is only in 'art' – in the broadest sense, as the constructions of man – that nature can find her agency of full realization. Man is rightfully *maker* of landscape.

151 *Willelmi Malmesbiriensis Monachi, De gestis pontificum anglorum libri quinque*, ed. N. E. S. A. Hamilton (London: 1870), Lib. IV, pp. 326–27, this passage discussed by Glacken, p. 313.

152 *Life and Works of St. Bernard, Abbot of Clairvaux*, trans. Samuel J. Eales (London: 1912), vol. 2, pp. 461–65; ref. Glacken, pp. 213–14.

The comparative motive

A second factor in the rise of landskip is the comparative impulse. Concern for individuated and actual landscapes in painting and literature, as against traditional and generic vocabularies of description, perceptibly develop in an era of travel and exploration. In the high Middle Ages, the habit of topographic survey, contrast and classification is exercised not only by noble, reeve and tenant farmer on their estates, but by a nascent merchant class concerned to open up wider markets and map out optimal trade routes. That it also enjoys a broader appeal is suggested by popular interest in exotic places and travellers' tales.

In our first chapter, we suggested the interest in comparative landscape to be a development in nature-sensibility mediated at bottom from the economic transition of civilization from sedentary, defensive cultivation to a commercial productivity involving voyaging, entrepreneurial, cartographic activity: from a culture of 'agrarian territorialism' to an expansionist culture of 'commercial geography'. In the medieval period similarly the rebirth of commerce and comparative landscape are cognate phenomena. In contrast to the land-locked, insular, and economically static civilization of the dark ages, the economy of the high medieval period 'was indissociable from maritime transport and exchange', just as a precondition of classical civilization had been its coastal prosperity. By 1293, for example, 'the maritime taxes of the single port of Genoa yielded $3\frac{1}{2}$ times the entire royal revenues of the French monarchy'.[153] Moreover, thanks to the crusades and to pilgrimages, 'Kings, armies, prelates, diplomats, merchants, and wandering scholars were continually on the move.'[154] In this climate, the development of interest in topography is but one aspect of a hungry comparative interest in the wonders and diversity, social, political and natural, of the kingdoms of the earth.

Only with the Middle Ages did Christian scholarship renew topographic interest. 'The cloistered life of the early Fathers provided few opportunities for the contemplation of the cultural landscape. It was not until men began to travel as they did in the crusading epoch that they began to perceive the varying relationships existing between landscape and life.'[155] We have noted above the fortifying of the *de*

153 Anderson, *Passages*, pp. 193, 20. 154 Lewis, *Discarded Image*, p. 143.
155 George H. T. Kimble, *Geography in the Middle Ages* (London: 1938), p. 176.

natura locorum tradition by contemporary travels. The typical format, as in Bartholomew of England in his encyclopaedia *De Proprietatibus Rerum* (published mid-thirteenth century), is to supply brief characterizations of lands and peoples: whether the land, for instance, bears grains or vines, has marshes, woods, or wild animals. In its empiricism, on many occasions, 'the shopworn wares of Pliny and Isidore are forgotten'.[156] Nonetheless, reports of landscape rarely extend beyond climatology and ethnology to apprehension of scenery purely as an aesthetic phenomenon. '"Fertile" or "infertile" rather than "beautiful" or "depressing" was the first reaction to landscape; humanist, merchant, monk, all had a farmer's eye.'[157]

Sir John Mandeville's 'Travels' (written c. 1356) offer a clear example. Allied to the *de natura locorum* tradition, Mandeville's work furnishes a devotional Baedeker, an itinerary of routes and places in the holy land and far beyond, a medieval reprise of what the Greeks termed περιήγησις. It takes the world to be a field of cultivation, commerce and colonization, and sneers, like Homer in *The Odyssey*, at peoples who have not developed agriculture and technology.[158] Furious though its appetite for natural variety is, and however indulgent its taste for the fabulous – the sea of sand and gravel in Prester John's kingdom for example, ebbing and flowing like the ocean and full of fish[159] – the text nowhere becomes pictorial. The following passage is typical:

From Saidenaya men come through the Vale of Bochar which is a fine fertile valley, producing all kinds of fruit. It is surrounded by hills. There are in it lovely rivers and broad meadows and noble grazing for cattle. Men travel past the mountains of Lebanon, which stretch from Armenia the Greater in the north to Dan.[160]

Sequences of place-names are directionally related, and irregularly enlivened by either anecdote, natural history, or, as here, by a broad adjectivalization centred on fertility values.

Nonetheless, Europe on the move, a taste for landscape reconnoitred, begin to freight literature with circumstantiality, to press description in imaginative writing beyond mythological tropes, the ideal landscape and the *locus amoenus*. In Dante's *Divine Comedy*, an

156 Glacken, p. 273.

157 J. R. Hale, *Renaissance Europe 1480–1520* (London: 1971), p. 42.

158 *The Travels of Sir John Mandeville*, trans. C. W. R. D. Moseley (Harmondsworth: 1983), p. 72. Compare *Odyssey*, 9.105–15, 125–30.

159 *Travels*, p. 169.

160 Ibid., p. 100.

outstanding and early example, the sights and conditions experienced by travellers, the scenery of remoter Christendom, are often the content of metaphor. Of the mount of Purgatory we read that

> Between Lerici and Turbia, the most deserted,
> The most broken-down road, compared to this,
> Is like an open and convenient stairway.

The lake of the ninth circle of Hell is so thickly frozen that

> The Danube, when she flows through Austria,
> Never in winter made so heavy a veil
> For herself, nor the Don under her cold sky.[161]

The loving reproduction of Italian geography, her towns, mountains, rivers and lakes, crowds almost every canto, as simile or in territorial placement of great figures.

> Up there in lovely Italy lies a lake,
> At the foot of the Alps which lock in Germany
> Above the Tyrol ...[162]

The letters of Petrarch show him travelling for curiosity, profiling the faces of Italian landscape beauty;[163] while his *De Vita Solitaria* praises his garden at Vaucluse and the surrounding countryside, his 'transalpine Helicon', in terms partly mythological yet partly empiric.

With the fifteenth century, era of systematic transoceanic exploration, landscape painting's affinity with cartography becomes clearer. Each sought to objectify space: to conceptualize visual images in such a way as to co-ordinate separate forms into a whole of unified extension. The overlap of the two fields is exemplified in the work of Jan van Eyck, whose reach of pioneering genius in landscape art not only established his paintings as 'certainly amongst the most surprising works of art in the world',[164] but also produced a map of the world for Duke Philip of Burgundy, 'on which the town and the countries were painted with marvellous delicacy'.[165] J. R. Hale suggests that 'the habit of conceptualizing space'[166] achieved and

161 *Divine Comedy, Purgatorio*, 3.49–51; *Inferno*, 32.22–27.

162 *Inferno*, 20.61–63. For three stanzas on Italian geography elaborated to serve as simile only for a loud waterfall, cf. *Inferno*, 16.94–105.

163 *Letters from Petrarch*, selected and translated by M. Bishop (London: 1966), pp. 23, 70, 87–89. Cf. also the Proem to his *Griselda*, in *Epistole Rerum Senilium*, xvii, in *Francisci Petrarchae Opera* (Basle: 1554), vol. 2, p. 1311.

164 Clark, *Landscape into Art*, p. 33.

165 Huizinga, *Waning*, p. 236.

166 Hale, *Renaissance Europe*, pp. 51–52.

popularized by landscape art by the fifteenth century indeed fostered a new cartographic credibility, in transforming *mappae mundi* from being 'merely romantic'[167] to becoming 'diagrams of the possible', faith in which encouraged mariners to risk death in search of Terra Incognita existing only in the logic of cartographers.

By the Renaissance, landscape painting has come, like picture postcards today, to supply a market demand for images of overseas, an iconography of travel-adventure. Friedländer writes of Lucas Gassel (c. 1500–60) that 'His one aim is to gratify the curiosity and craving for sensation of travellers and hikers – or rather, to provide a substitute for people who neither travelled nor hiked.'[168] Indeed Edward Norgate, writing in seventeenth-century England, repeats an anecdote declaring the invention of landscape as a pictorial genre to originate in an (unknown) artist's impression of the grandeur of Alpine travel as recounted by a friend: 'what Cities he saw, what beautifull prospects he beheld in a Country of strange scitiation, full of Alpine Rocks, old Castles and extraordinary buildings etc.'[169] Patenier, whose background landscapes were taken as models by contemporary Netherlandish painters, excelled in grotesquely shaped, steep rocks. 'The more sensationally the surroundings differed from the familiar flatness the more natural and suitable they became as the background for sacred adventure ... The lovers and buyers of Patenier's pictures ... sought in them the leisure of a walk full of varied interest or a journey of discovery.'[170] With the sixteenth century and reconnaissance of the New World, the vogue develops for the compositional scheme of mannerism,[171] with its high viewpoint offering vast panoramas bounded only by distant mountains and, tellingly, open oceans.

Where painting and literature alike display travellers' credentials in their landscapes during the later Middle Ages is in the paradisal garden. As early as *Romaunt of the Rose* we find that the fashionable aristocrat – here, Lord Mirth –

167 Lewis, *Discarded Image*, pp. 143–44.

168 Max J. Friedländer, *Landscape, Portrait, Still-Life*, p. 61. See also Arnold Hauser, *Social History of Art*, vol. 1, pp. 240–41 on the late Gothic 'travel landscape' and its affinity with perspective.

169 Norgate, *Miniatura, or the Art of Limning*, ed. Martin Hardie (Oxford, 1919), p. 46.

170 Max J. Friedländer, *From Van Eyck to Brueghel*, vol. 2 (1956; rpt. London: 1969), pp. 80–81, 84.

171 Clark, *Landscape into Art*, pp. 77–78, 95.

fro the land Alexandryn
Made the trees hidre be fet,
That in this gardyn ben yset.[172]

The walled gardens and orchards of the Middle Ages, actual and artistic, appear to have derived from eastern, ultimately Persian, types, encountered during the Crusades and observable also to travellers in Moslem Spain and Sicily.[173] The vogue for oriental paradise gardens[174] – secret walled worlds within whose impenetrable and sequestered space trees stand loaded with blossoms and leaves, sparkling fountains play beside luxuriant turf, and fragrant flowered peace is uninvaded by the burning sun – may have influenced descriptive imagery in Dante and the Pearl-poet via the *Liber Scalae*, which draws on European translations of Moslem accounts of the gardens of paradise visited by Mohammed. Persian garden paintings of princes seated on flower-starred grass within palace walls were probably the inspiration for Christian Madonna-in-a-garden paintings, first developed as a distinct form in Venice: where 'throughout the Middle Ages, European merchants came to buy spices, dyes and textiles, brought from the East by Venetian galleys. The trade routes of the period make out a pattern which could begin to account for the remarkable likenesses between garden pictures from southern Germany, Verona and Herat over the years 1390–1430.'[175] Contacts with the East thus incorporated new landscape motifs into the art and new forms into the garden taste of western Europe, just as Asiatic monsters were carved into the stone of Norman churches in the English countryside, and the portals of French cathedrals.

'Possessive' space

The earliest empirical 'views' flaunt a landscape of display. The great house, in Girouard's term, was a 'power-house'. 'It was the headquarters from which land was administered and power organized. It was a show-case, in which to exhibit and entertain supporters and good connections. In early days it contained a potential fighting-force. It was an image-maker, which projected an aura of glamour, mystery

172 *Romance of the Rose* in Chaucer's translation, lines 602–04, p. 571.
173 H. N. Wethered, *A Short History of Gardens* (London: 1933), pp. 122–23.
174 Cf. Chrétien de Troyes, *Cligés* (written c. 1162), ed. W. W. Comfort, *Arthurian Romances* (London: 1914), p. 174; and P&S, ch. 4.
175 P&S, pp. 78–79.

or success around its owner.'[176] 'After the deeds and exploits of war, which are claims to glory', judged Chastellain in the fifteenth century, 'the household is the first thing that strikes the eye, and that which it is, therefore, most necessary to conduct and arrange well'.[177] Thus the most advanced of medieval Calendar work blazons in triumphal detail the great castles of Jean de Berry soaring over the field, forest and seigneurial park of the *Très Riches Heures* (c. 1416). Likewise, in Deschamps' *Lay de Franchise,* among the descriptions of the ordered scenery and château of Beauté-sur-Marne, we have in:

> Sales y sont; par les fenestres perent
> Les beaux moulins, les froumens et li pré
>
> Great chambers are there; through whose windows appear
> the beautiful mills, granaries and meadows

what may be 'the first conscious "view" in poetry since classical times'.[178] 'The praise of château and estate, for which his profession must have given him a connoisseur's eye, is a favourite theme in Deschamps, and we can perhaps recognize in the topics of his praise the source of the new realism'.[179] Deschamps was in royal service, as '*maître des eaux et forêts*' for the Duc d'Orléans; the Limbourgs were on close terms with the Duc de Berry; Jan van Eyck 'moved constantly in courtly circles'.[180] Yet the link between pioneering empirical prospect and estates painting holds true for republican Italy as for seigneurial France. 'It is no accident that the van Eycks were the contemporaries of the first great generation of the Renaissance painters in Italy ... In the atmosphere of frenetic political competition of Italy in this age of despots and *condottiere,* lavish display and patronage of the arts served, as they did in Burgundy, to give expression to the aspirations of those who sought to live "nobly".'[181] Just as the *Très Riches Heures* of Jean de Berri (plate 8) were painted, defiantly, in the midst of the Hundred Years War that was devastating northern France, so in an Italy become 'a chequerboard of competing city-states, in which the intervening countryside, unlike any other part of Europe, was annexed to the towns',[182] Lorenzetti's civic pride sharpens 'his portrait of Siena and his panorama of the fertile, rolling

176 Mark Girouard, *Life in the English Country House* (1978; rpt. Harmondsworth: 1980), pp. 2–3.

177 Quoted in Huizinga, *Waning,* p. 39.

178 P&S, p. 175; Deschamps, *Lay de Franchise,* lines 241–42, in *Oeuvres,* ed. de Queux de Saint-Hilaire and G. Raynaud, vol. 2, p. 211 (Paris: 1878).

179 P&S, p. 175.

180 Huizinga, *Waning,* p. 248.

181 Keen, *Medieval Europe,* p. 275.

182 Perry Anderson, *Passages,* p. 167.

country nearby' into 'the first postclassical vistas essentially derived from visual experience rather than tradition, memory and imagination'.[183] Adjuration to republican pride and responsibility, these frescoes (plate 9) enclose the chamber of the magistrates in Siena's Palazzo Pubblico; and whilst in the case of the Limbourgs we might say that one kind of 'illusionism' (political) is consoled by another (pictorial), with Lorenzetti the logic of the perspective itself is an objective political congratulation. We may compare Perry Anderson's presentation of the unique 'annexationism of the Italian cities, with their greedy subjection and extortion of provisions and labour from their conquered rural *contado*'[184] with John White's recognition of Lorenzetti's application of a 'lateral perspective' technique to relate Siena to her hinterlands. 'The construction presupposes radiation from a centre ... all the architectural features of the countryside diminish in proportion to their distance from the foreground [city gateway] ... Down and across the landscape foreground the figures steadily grow smaller. The same is true wherever the eye wanders down the roads, or out over the fields, away from the city into the deep countryside.'[185] No less than seigneurial and republican, nationalist pride conduces to vista. The relation between the two in the case of seventeenth-century Dutch art is a supreme and familiar instance; yet in literature the connection is clear as early as the fourteenth century, in Petrarch's taste for view. 'To the west,' he writes of the outlook from a hill at San Colombano, 'we have a wide view over a solitary region, very quiet and pleasant. I don't remember ever seeing from so slight an elevation such a noble spectacle of far-spreading lands. By turning about one can see Pavia, Piacenza, Cremona, and many other famous cities ... To our rear are the Alps separating us from Germany, with their snow-clad peaks, rising into the clouds, into heaven; before us stand the Apennines and innumerable cities ... The Po itself lies at our feet, separating the fat fields in a giant curve.'[186] Petrarch's, write Pearsall and Salter, is 'the first expression of the taste [for view] in post-classical times'.[187]

Comparable instances of early prospect painting as territorial display are van Eyck's *Madonna of the Chancellor Rollin* (c. 1425) and

183 Panofsky, *Renaissance and Renascences*, p. 142.
184 Perry Anderson, *Passages*, p. 192.
185 John White, *The Birth and Rebirth of Pictorial Space*, pp. 93–94.
186 *Letters from Petrarch*, p. 152.
187 P&S, p. 184.

Simone Martini's *Guidorricio da Fogliano* (1328). Van Eyck's celebrated window prospect (plate 10) commemorates Rollin's triumph in engineering the Treaty of Arras, exhibiting the monastery, church, and cross on the bridge at Utrecht whose propitiatory construction by the French the Treaty had secured. Simone's *condottiere* rides between the two fortified towns he had captured for Siena. Simone and Lorenzetti each see 'the Sienese countryside as an object of civic pride, just as Petrach in his metric epistle *Ad Luchinium Vicecomiteur* could look upon his native Italy as a fecund and happy fatherland ... This propagandist function of landscape', notes Turner, 'might be traced right through the Renaissance in a great variety of paintings to find a logical conclusion in the courtyard of the Palazzo Vecchio in Florence, where the frescoes of the possessions of the house of Austria might better be described as aerial maps than as landscapes'.[188] Indeed, with the rise of Italian Renaissance artistic theory, the 'regal' landscape of 'privileged places' becomes formalized by Alberti and Lommazzo, with an eye to Vitruvius, as one of the three styles or degrees of landscape painting.[189]

In another respect, too, landscape art develops as secular, 'possessive' space: as the fashionable picturesque of the urban connoisseur. 'It might be a viable generalization', suggest Pearsall and Salter, 'that all developed landscape art is urban pastoral ... it can hardly escape notice that the two great centres for the growth of landscape painting, Flanders and Northern Italy, were also the two most advanced industrial and urbanized areas in Europe. Cities produced the taste ... they also provided the fashionable demand, and technology (as in the development of oil painting) to satisfy it.'[190] In fifteenth-century Italy clients often demanded elaborated landscape background from their painters simply as comprising conspicuously *costly* virtuosity:[191] landscape served as ostentation now not of property, as with the Duc de Berri, but of urban capital. But as with time the market glutted, the fashion became affordable chic: by 1548 the Italian craze for landscapes, particularly the prestigious work of *oltramontani*, was such that Vasari could sneer 'there is not a cobbler's house without a German landscape'.[192]

188 A. R. Turner, *The Vision of Landscape in Renaissance Italy*, pp. 12, 200.
189 Cf. Gombrich, *Norm and Form*, pp. 111, 119–20.
190 P&S, pp. 26, 161.
191 Michael Baxandall, *Painting and Experience in 15th Century Italy*, pp. 17–18, 23.
192 Gombrich, *Norm and Form*, ed. cit., p. 110.

Further stimulation by fashion lay in Renaissance revival of the classical custom of decorating villa and palace walls with illusionistic landscapes, as in the work of Mantegna in the Gonzago palace at Mantụa, and Peruzzi in the Villa Farnesina. The simulation of real vistas may have driven artists, suggests Gombrich, both to develop a new vocabulary and to study atmospheric effects in deep recession. Paul Bril's change of style from 'syncretic' landscapes of accumulated picturesque details to illusionistic concerns is one instance.[193]

In summary, we have seen, under the headings of 'managerial', 'possessive' and 'comparative' forms of interest in nature, a confidently interventionist, empiricizing, documentative nature-sensibility, from which landscape issues, unsurprisingly, as frequently a husbanded, individuated backdrop to human purpose, a contingent subject realm. This distinctive character is all the clearer in comparison with Chinese landscape art, where 'landscape' defines not a field of vision but a 'world-sense': enveloping human figures within a misty, timeless and autonomous order. In comparison with this, even the uncultivated landscapes of the 'Danube school', though contradicting the mellow amenities of Southern landscape, suggest the essential European tendencies. Their intractable magnitudes (Altdorfer's *Alexander's Battle* and *St. George*) or primitive foreignness (Grunewald's *Isenheim Altarpiece*) nonetheless exemplify, at the level of form, empirical commitment and absorption in topographic difference, whilst at the level of content, they may be seen as ironizing and exploring the limitations of human hegemony: the malediction of *Genesis* 3.17–18.

Landscape and secularization

We have seen that a taste for landskip arises with a triumphantly expansionist society, whose artistic patrons are gratified by 'comparative' and 'possessive' space. What explains the evolution from estates painting to 'pure' landskip, from the Limbourgs to Dürer and Claude, is the unfolding, I would argue, of two further forms of interest in nature: the concern to render 'quotidian space' (everyday, observable scenes, emphasising nature as a medium of expressiveness and pleasure), and to objectify nature as 'rational space', field of 'scientific' analysis.

193 Ibid., p. 119, 152, note 57.

Each of these interests of course was necessary to the production of estates painting: the Limbourgs were clearly concerned to display both an understanding of optical laws and a poetry of seasonal mood. But rational and affective space reflect impulses in landscape development that it is important to extrapolate: for they belong, in their maturity, to a secular scheme of values. Sensuous enjoyment of the world and the prestige of scientific knowledge characterize the emergent secular culture of town and court, as against the asceticism and hieratic codes of clerical culture. We must accordingly pause to say a word about the concept of secularization, and the ambiguity of 'sacred' and 'secular' in medieval and renaissance art. The concept of 'secularization' is notoriously problematic: some sociologists question that it has taken place at all.[194] For our purposes, the term is taken to signify a shift in emphasis from the other-worldly to the this-worldly, the transcendent to the immanent, and from human dependence to comparative human autonomy. Complexity arises from the fact that, in art, a highly realized world of sense may further a thoroughly religious intentionality, given Christianity's traditional ambivalence towards matter.

As we saw in our patristic chapter, Christianity desacralizes the physical world: its landscape descriptions characteristically replace the *genii loci* and anthropomorphic deities of polytheism by an ordered creation, scrutiny of whose detailed materiality becomes a religious duty. We have heard St. Basil detailing every feature of humble plants in an anagogic appropriation of classical science. The monotheistic impetus of Christian nature-sensibility to supplant mythology by reverent natural history, combined with the Gospel of Work, means that Christian 'religious' art can accommodate a scrupulously exact material focus in its landscape art and verse which is absent from the most 'secular' of Greco-Roman art, where the tradition of mythological depiction and the stigma of rural labour normally occlude sustained particularity. A fine early example is the influential Queen Mary's Psalter, which 'naturalizes' zodiac signs: Capricorn acquires a baby goat and a piping goatherd, the Pisces symbol is hauled up a boatside caught in a net, and Taurus is driven lowing, with other cattle, under the stick of herdsmen.[195] From this demythologising materialist imagination will develop precisely that 'rigorous sense of

194 David Martin, *The Religious and the Secular* (London: 1969), part one, pp. 9–57.
195 Cf. P&S, pp. 138–39, 164.

the individual identity of forms'[196] which Clark admires in Bellini's *St Francis in the Wilderness* (plate 12), and which carries into the first properly topographic painting (Conrad Witz' *Miraculous Draught of Fishes*, 1444) an accuracy that makes its site identifiable today.

When, therefore, we write of landscape developing within poetry and painting on secular themes, we have to acknowledge from the outset that this is a secularity which does not run against the grain of the religious; that indeed 'sacred' and 'profane' often occupy the same site, as when the garden setting proves a *hortus conclusus* of erotic love or an Annunciation. Given the conceptions of the religious sphere as comprehending all natural phenomena, and of intellection of the sacred as ascending from contemplation of sensibles; and given that the pictorial documentation of landscape outside the garden establishes an important empirical foundation in Calendar art: it becomes perhaps inevitable that 'secular' themes will not be easily dissociable from religious levels of meaning or traditions of portrayal. Lorenzetti's 'cityscape' of Siena, for instance, at which we glanced earlier (plate 9), is flanked by country scenes of tillage and fowling that expose Calendar lineage; whilst conversely *Flights into Egypt* and *Jeromes in the Wilderness* expand their *parerga*[197] of the diurnal world to the point of eclipsing by panoramas their nominally central figures.[198]

If monotheistic and anagogic doctrines of creation underwrite the piety of luxuriant landscaping, they are necessary but not sufficient conditions for its emergence. Though such metaphysics protected the good conscience of medieval and renaissance artistic naturalism, in earlier cultural climates, as we have seen, they had acquiesced happily in codifying the sensible and preferring the incorporeal. Where not immediately moralized, delight in panorama and natural plenitude is often rebuked, as in Augustine, Petrarch and Langland.[199]

196 *Landscape into Art*, p. 53.

197 A term signifying landscape backgrounds, as used by Italian Renaissance theorists who borrow it from Pliny, *Natural History*, 35.101. E. H. Gombrich, *Norm and Form*, p. 114.

198 Cf. spectacularly, Cornelis Massys' *The Virgin and St. Joseph Arriving at the Inn in Bethlehem* in which a cartload of revelling peasants, mishapen towering trees and a street of rickety houses dwarf the arrival of sainthood.

199 Augustine, *Confessions*, 10.8.15; Petrarch, *The Ascent of Mont Ventoux*, reprinted in *The Renaissance Philosophy of Man*, ed. E. Cassirer, P. O. Kristeller and J. H. Randall, Jr (Chicago: 1948), pp. 36–46; *Piers Plowman*, ed. W. W. Skeat (Oxford: 1886), C XIV.135–8, 174–7, and C XV.169–99.

Quotidian space

It is secular engagement of nature that furthers the development of landscape, and one form of this is the artistic construction of what we earlier termed 'quotidian space'. In brief, this denotes landscapes of the empirical daily world, and the enhanced concern for their sensuous and affective properties. Throughout the fifteenth and sixteenth centuries, portraitists deepen their awareness of the expressiveness of natural forms and colours in supplying landscape *parerga* that further, through sensuous mood as well as iconography, the emotional life of the individual they flank. When, in the nineteenth century the Romantic poets deploy landscape imagery as a language of nuanced subjectivity, they are only drawing into literature resources of perception pioneered in late Medieval and Renaissance painting. Alberti, for instance, in the fifteenth century, treasures landscape for its psychological effect:

Those who suffer from fever are offered much relief by the sight of painted fountains, rivers and running brooks, a fact which anyone can put to the test; for if by chance he lies in bed one night unable to sleep, he need only turn his imagination on limpid waters and fountains which he had seen at one time or another, or perhaps some lake, and his dry feeling will disappear all at once and sleep will come upon him as the sweetest of slumbers.[200]

One area in which secular, affective space develops is the celebration of distinctly temporal recreations – in particular sports, courtly pastimes and sexual *jouissance* – frowned upon by clerical culture.

Let it have no church or convent

writes the courtly Folgore da San Gemignano of settings and pastimes for the month of March. 'Leave the silly priests to their gabble.'[201]

Pre-eminent among secular pursuits whose artistic celebration invites the creating of scenery is hunting. 'Now shall I preve', writes Edward, Duke of York:

how hunters lyven in this world most joyfully of eny other men. For whan the hunter ryseth in the mornyng, he seeth a swete and fayr morow and the clere wedir and bryght, and hereth the songe of the smale fowles, the which

200 Leon Battista Alberti, *Ten Books on Architecture*, Book 9, ch. 4, quoted and Englished from the 1486 edition by Gombrich, *Norm and Form*, p. 111.

201 Folgore da San Gemignano, *Rime*, ed. G. Navone (Bologna: 1880), no. 4, p. 9; trans. R. Aldington, *A Wreath for San Gemignano* (London: 1946), p. 20.

syngen swetely with grete melodye and ful of love, everich in his langage in the best wyse that he may aftir that he lereth of his owyn kynde. And whan the sonne is arise, he shall see the fressh dewe uppon the smale twygges and grasse, and the sunne which by his vertu shal make hem shyne. And that is grete lykeng and joye to the hunters hert.[202]

Given the degree of this aristocratic addiction, it is unsurprising that 'the earliest pictures concerned entirely with natural observation are in manuscripts on sport. The little picture of rabbits in a wood in the *Livre de Chasse* of Gaston Phébus (c. 1400) is done with real love,'[203] whilst other illuminations feature the capture of animals in orchards or enclosed gardens. We may compare this impulse towards naturalism of the narrowed eye of hunting with Greco-Roman paintings of lion-spearing or catching hippos in Nilotics, as well as with Egyptian murals of noblemen fishing and fowling in marshes. As early as 1343, frescoes at the Papal Palace in Avignon create an idyllic setting for elegant sportsmen engaged within leafy glades, amidst fruit, butterflies and birds, upon fishing, ferreting and hawking. Such landscape was probably already well established when the Avignon painter set to work, thinks Kenneth Clark, in the tapestries of Paris and Arras almost all of which now are lost.[204] Renaissance culmination of the landscape of the hunt is of course the masterly *sous-bois* of Uccello (1397–1475), in which breakthrough in the hunt and in linear perspective have become a single exhilaration. There are parallels, too, in innovation in fourteenth- and fifteenth-century music: the composition known as the *caccia* represented the chase complete with blowing horns and baying hounds.[205] Descriptions of boar and deer hunting are common in medieval romances,[206] and their involvement of wild countryside, remote from the pale of cultivation, is suggested in the Gawain poet's presentation of a landscape recalling Grendel's Mere:

> Þen al in a semblé sweyed togeder,
> Bitwene a flosche in þat fryth and a foo cragge;
> In a knot bi a clyffe, at þe kerre syde,

202 Edward, Duke of York, Master of Game in 1406; trans. from the *Livre de Chasse* of Gaston 'Phoebus', Count of Foix and Bearn; in Douglas Gray, *The Oxford Book of Late Medieval Verse and Prose* (Oxford: 1985), pp. 145–46.

203 Clark, *Landscape into Art*, p. 21.

204 Ibid., p. 13.

205 Huizinga, *Waning*, p. 257.

206 Cf. Norman Davis' note, in his edition of *Sir Gawain and the Green Knight* (1967; rpt. Oxford: 1972), to lines 1412 ff., on p. 113.

Þer as þe rogh rocher unrydely watz fallen,
Þey ferden to þe fyndyng, and freketh hem after.[207]

Miscellaneous courtly activities slip easily into country settings with the summer months, and the foreground of the frescoes of the Torre dell' Aquilla (c. 1410), in the castle at Trento in northern Italy, show peasants at their labours whilst their overlords indulge in flower-gathering, maying and courtship: images that frequently reappear on fifteenth-century plates and chests. Similar themes, including seigneurial snowballing,[208] grace the sonnets on patrician rural recreation in the fourteenth-century Italy of Folgore da San Gemignano. Here the verse excludes altogether the landscape of labour:

For June I give you a little mountain covered with the loveliest little trees, with thirty villas and twelve towers, not far from a little town.[209]

Yet this flowery Tuscan countryside remains cousin, as Pearsall and Salter are aware, to the walled gardens of Gothic:

And in its midst, a little fountain with a thousand branches and rivulets, cutting through gardens and little lawns to refresh the little grasses. Oranges, citrons, dates and sweet lemons, and all savoury fruits shall be trained into long pergolas for the walks.[210]

Indeed, in general, aristocratic 'recreative space' as depicting open-landscape pastimes other than the pursuit of animals produces very limited originality in natural perception, save where it blends with the tradition of Calendar landscape. The courtly midsummer picnics of a myriad flowered tapestries, for instance, find their consummation in the Renaissance ideal landscape of Giorgione's *Fête Champêtre*, yet wandering beyond the aristocratic refection remain shepherd and flock; and the construction owes more to contemporary pastoral reverie than to actual patrician experience. The Arcadian verse and drama of earlier sixteenth century Italy, with its flights from court to country in Sannazzaro, Tasso and Guarini, remain, in essence, courtly masquerades immobilised within landscapes of conventional sweetness. 'The setting', feels Helen Cooper, 'is almost reluctantly pastoral';[211] and indeed, Sincero tellingly reflects that 'among these

207 Ibid., lines 1429–33.

208 Torre dell' Aquila, Trento, frescoes, *January*; Folgore da San Gemignano, no. 2, p. 5: also a January scene.

209 *Rime*, no. 7, p. 15; translation p. 23.

210 Ibid; P&S, p. 141.

211 Helen Cooper, p. 104.

Arcadian solitudes ... I can hardly believe that the beasts of the woodland can dwell with any pleasure, to say nothing of young men nurtured in noble cities'.[212]

Accordingly, it is in sixteenth-century popular art, with the genius of Brueghel, 'the first successfully to eliminate the lingering echo of religious devotion',[213] that secular, recreative space finds a new and supreme landscapist. Breughel can move beyond brilliant reworking of the scenes of seasonal labour, into ranges or minutiae of fresh natural observation to gird his peasant revellers. They shin up spring trees, clump in dance by a forested hillside gallows, or sled, skate and play hockey across olive or primrose ice under bare, snow-filmed trees where crows peer and brood.[214] Landscape returns to intense, exploratory naturalism on returning to the peasant commonplace, from which Calendar art had also grown, but which courtly modes, as we shall see, may often disdain. In this land of absorption in concrete, coarse and strenuous work, the invisible realm of religious teaching may easily be occluded; and we may compare the humorous literalism of Brueghel's naturalism with the English Mystery Cycles. Brueghel's comedy of the eclipse of the sublime by indifferent nature in *The Fall of Icarus* and *The Conversion of Saul* may well be paralleled with the perspective of that mordant spokesman of peasant sceptical materialism, the Cain of the Wakefield Pageants, refusing to yield Christianity its tithes.

Abell: 'Caym, leife this vayn carpyng,
For God giffys the all thi lifyng.'

Cayn: 'Yit boroed I never a farthyng
Of hym ...
When I shuld saw, and wantyd seyde,
And of corn had full grete neyde,
Then gaf he me none of his'.[215]

The universe of the palpable rebuffs the hieratic.

212 Sannazzaro, *Arcadia*, seventh prose, trans. Ralph Nash, *Jacopo Sannazaro's Arcadia and Piscatorial Eclogues* (Detroit: 1966), p. 72.

213 Max J. Friedländer, *From Van Eyck to Brueghel*, trans. M. Kay (1956; rpt. London: 1969), p. 142.

214 *Childrens' Games; The Magpie on the Gallows; Winter Landscape*; and *Hunters in the Snow*.

215 *Mactacio Abel* in *The Wakefield Pageants in the Towneley Cycle*, ed. A. C. Cawley (Manchester: 1958), lines 97–100, 124–26, pp. 3, 4.

There is one type of recreative landscape, however, from which the peasant and his dubious familiarity with loam and growth is expelled: the 'pleasaunce' of erotic activity. The association of verdant landscape with sexuality and woman appears to be perennial and 'archetypal'.[216] The *Romaunt of the Rose* notes

> grass, as thicke yset
> And soft as any velvët,
> On which men myght his lemman leye,
> As on a fetherbed, to pleye[217]

and comically urges its leisured courtiers 'Plow, barons, plow', exhorting them to thrust the 'coulter' more deeply in the 'furrow' so as not to waste their 'seed'.[218] Repeatedly in medieval literature, landscape is brought into existence to furnish a natural imagery for love. Romances may embody the hopes of their young lovers in spring landscapes of blossom, sunlit greensward and birdsong among young leaves.[219] 'Woodcuts and engravings produced for a mass audience ... show the country as above all a place for love. From homes where there was no privacy, from mattresses sour with damp and hopping with fleas, the first warm days of spring drew lovers to the fields and woods. Not without reason are the age's two most tranquilly beautiful love scenes, the *Mars and Venus* of Piero di Cosimo and Botticelli, placed in the open air.'[220] Overwhelmingly, however, it is the enclosed garden that is drawn into vision as a setting for love. Latin, vernacular and troubadour poetry of the twelfth and thirteenth centuries set love debates and private passion in paradise gardens or groves dressed from the *hortus conclusus* of *Canticles*.[221] Chaucer's Merchant, characteristically, is basely alert to the convenience of the walled garden:

> And thynges whiche that were nat doon abedde,
> He in the gardyn parfourned hem and spedde[222]

216 Cf. Eliade, *Patterns in Comparative Religion*, pp. 239–64, 332–34, 354–61.
217 Lines 1419–22, Chaucer's translation, p. 578.
218 Ibid., 11.151, 159–60, 117. Paul Piehler, *The Visionary Landscape*, chs. 4 and 6; Aldo Scaglione, *Nature and Love in the Late Middle Ages* (Berkeley: 1963).
219 Cf. Gottfried von Strassburg's *Tristan*, trans. A. T. Hatto (Harmondsworth: 1960), p. 49; P&S, p. 54.
220 J. R. Hale, *Renaissance Europe, pp*. 44–45.
221 P&S, p. 76.
222 *The Merchant's Tale* in *Complete Works*, lines 2051–52, p. 123.

and yet so persistent is the association, that the elevated Lorenzo de' Medici can write

> For 'paradise' ... means nothing more than a most pleasant garden, abundant with all pleasing and delightful things, of trees, apples, flowers, vivid running waters, song of birds, and in effect, all the amenities dreamed of by the heart of man; and by this one can affirm that paradise was where there was a beautiful woman, for here was a copy of every amenity and sweetness that a kind heart might desire.[223]

Medieval paintings of gardens of love could contain religious iconography – fountain, lily, dove – yet remain secular settings. Some fifteenth-century Madonnas in Gardens were almost interchangeable with the ladies in illustrations of Boccaccio's *Decameron*: whose illustrations were so precisely detailed as to become used for garden treatises. Chaucer's gardens in his *Legend of Good Women* and *Troilus and Criseyde* Book II retail the fashionable fourteenth-century design of sanded walks, trellised roses, turfed benches, arbour, and enclosure within the enclosed garden;[224] and by the early sixteenth century, a second rate poet like Stephen Hawes in his 'repetitive and unimaginative description'[225] of garden scenery in *Pastime of Pleasure* will detail at length the complicated flower knots, fantastic topiary and 'resplendysshaunte' highly wrought fountains now in European vogue.[226]

If such outdoor medieval pursuits as sports, summer *divertissements*, and erotic 'aventure' each draw in respective forms of landscape description, the principle outdoor undertaking of the medieval nobility – warfare – was equivocal. Earlier medieval prints and paintings of battle mainly provide, like Homer's *Iliad*, but a 'ghost topography', for combat comprised too intensely social and personal a record of seigneurial fortunes. Fourteenth-century illustrations tend often toward either diagrammatic depictions of armaments and seige technology, or close-ups of equestrian *mêlée* whose interest lies in heraldic identification of glorious blood-letters. In literature likewise, the romance, as we have seen, lacks non-symbolic space, and Malory's Arthuriad lacks place beyond place-names. But at a lower social level, landscape provision becomes integral. Italy and Germany flared into

223 *Opere*, ed. A. Simioni (Bari: 1913), i, 42; trans. in A. R. Turner, *The Vision of Landscape in Renaissance Italy*, p. 39.

224 P&S, pp. 99, 110.

225 Hansen, *Pleasant Place*, p. 55.

226 *The Passetyme of Pleasure*, ed. W. E. Mead (London: 1927), line 2021; cf. Hansen, pp. 54–55.

decades of war at the height of their artistic renaissances, so that battle-and-landscape scenes fed a sustained complex of appetites. Fifteenth century interest in delineating occupational types placed soldiers (who belonged to no ordained social category) in a variety of civic or natural settings: soldiers became 'the most interesting of wayfarers',[227] *habitués* of wild woods or outsiders to farm and lakes. Sieges indulged artists' architectural fascination in townscapes, battles evoked skilled panorama. The simple early conventions of birds-eye view woodcuts, with infantry clashes before background town or fortress, were surpassed from the 1490s by the intricate draughtsmanship of manuscript illustration, paintings and tapestries, as noble patronage made the military genre profitable. Charles VIII took artists with him to war; Wilhelm of Bavaria commissioned a cycle of inspirational martial paintings that produced Altdorfer's masterpiece *Alexander's Battle*. Illustrated chronicles of the sixteenth century trained 'pictorial journalists' to mix accounts of battle with cartographic work presenting labelled cities – the tradition from which Altdorfer emerged. Giulio Romano's famed *Battle of Constantine* (1523) with its massed heroic physiques upon an airy, mountain-backed plain became, as Vasari noted, 'a guiding light' for Italian artists of the genre.[228] Netherlandish manuscript ateliers standardized a scheme of foreground scattered victims, mid-ground clash (often with 'forest of pikes'), and backgrounds of landscape perspective. The scenery of militarism is transferred too into religious art, where seashores of smashed walls and flaming houses, bivouacs among improvised gallows and fleeing populations, horizons of rolling smoke and burning cities, enter medieval fantasias of hell or apocalypse, which climax in Bosch and Brueghel.

In summary of 'possessive' and 'recreative' space as creators of landscape in late medieval art, we may note a persistent class-correlation to naturalism, conditioned in part by respective relations to manual labour. Whilst naturalism, and therefore landscape development, have flourished as meted to the portrayal of the peasant's world from the burgeoning of Calendar art in the twelfth century to Brueghel in the sixteenth, the representation of aristocratic life has taken, in respect of naturalism, sharply contradictory lines. Whilst noble sensibility views landownership, animals and sports with a

227 J. R. Hale, *Artists and Warfare in the Renaissance* (New Haven: 1990), pp. 54, 109–11. 228 Ibid., pp. 252, 192–93, 182–84, 167.

factual relish that commissions naturalism, when it comes to figures and costume or gardens, elegant, even hieratic, transcendence of the diurnal world stipulates enchantment and stylization. Brute material power, over man and animals, must be displayed, yet aristocratic interests dictate also 'ideal forms, gilded by chivalrous romanticism ... a dream of beauty in the forms of social life'[229] to conserve hereditary exclusiveness in the face of dissolving fiefdom and an emulous bourgeoisie. Thus the seasonal landscapes of Folgore's patrician sonnets banish the enabling world of labour as consistently as will the country house verse of early seventeenth-century England. Fifteenth-century costume boasts its 'opulent parasitism' in 'pinched-in waists and dangling pointed sleeves guaranteed to prevent any useful physical activity on the part of the wearer';[230] and the 'International Style of about 1400' in which these are painted reveal, as Panofsky notes, 'unresolvable conflict' with naturalism in its 'Manneristic' style: 'a preference for calligraphical and decorative stylization at the expense of pictorial verisimilitude'.[231] In contrast, 'the naturalistic mode of expression, almost amounting to a class distinction, was reserved for the "lower orders", animals and inanimate objects'.[232] We may remember the precisely painted upturned buttocks and exposed underwear of the peasants toiling on the Duc de Berri's estate in the Limbourgs' *September*, realism as comic, peasant mode 150 years prior to Brueghel; and we may remember the same class correlation of naturalism in the frescoes of ancient Egypt. Thus it is that nobility-riding-in-a-landscape paintings may detail sophisticated costume, yet place the wearers amid carefully formulaic settings of Gothic International rocks and *millefiore* carpeting, in the Trento frescoes and the North Italian *Adoration of the Magi* (1410): a discrepant empiricism, preserved in Gozzoli's late fifteenth-century *Journey of the Magi*. The nobleman is to be elevated above workaday nature just as his serf is forever bound to it. More spectacularly, the contradictory directions of these impulses to celebrate possession of the diurnal material world, yet also its transcendence, may generate flatly different modes within the same pictorial cycle. Of the seasonal frescoes adorning the hall of the dukes of Ferrara (1470), whilst the

229 Huizinga, *Waning*, p. 38.
230 Margaret Schlauch, *English Medieval Literature and its Social Foundations* (1956; rpt. New York: 1971), p. 204. 231 *Renaissance and Renascences*, p. 160.
232 Ibid., p. 161.

March scene depicts, with detailed realism, labourers vine-pruning 'in real northern Italian countryside',[233] the following month drops graceful courtiers onto an idealized river-bank where a swan-drawn barge, passing between grotesque rock-formations where rabbits nudge and Graces dance, displays the Triumph of Venus. Landscape, then, is detailed in the ostentation of economic power, stylized in the celebration of cultural exclusiveness.

In the same way, the garden may unfold in terms of horticultural realism, or as a privileged timeless world of refined pleasure in which emancipation from labour and material reality is evident not only in the literal exclusion of the peasant – 'com nevere shepherde theryn'[234] – but in the 'aristocratizing' of the descriptive language itself. The walled garden early comprised a private noble retreat from the commotion and vulgarity of hall and household, and correspondingly in medieval verse these garden landscapes are transformed from the textures of organic nature into courtly refinement or costly synthetics. In the garden of the *Romaunt of the Rose*

> than bycometh the ground so proud
> That it wole have a newe shroud,
> And makith so queynt his robe and faire
> That it hath hewes an hundred payre
> Of gras and flouris, ynde and pers,
> And many hewes ful dyvers.[235]

Birds here sing 'As angels don espirituel', or like 'sereyns' of 'layes of love'.[236] In Lydgate's *Complaint of the Black Knight* the 'parke' furnishes grass 'softe as velvet', its soil

> smothe and wonder softe
> Al overspred wyth tapites that Nature
> Hath made herselfe,

and its river reveals 'gravel gold, the water pure as glas'.[237] This courtly vision becomes widely fashionable in the fifteenth century, usurping outer nature in the 'decorated Gothic'[238] extravaganza of Dunbar's *Goldyn Targe*:

233 P&S, p. 131.
234 *Romance of the Rose*, Chaucer's translation, line 482, p. 570.
235 Chaucer's translation, p. 566, lines 63–68.
236 Ibid., pp. 571–72, lines 672, 684, 715.
237 In *John Lydgate: Poems*, ed. J. Norton-Smith (Oxford: 1966), pp. 48–49, lines 80, 50–52, 78.
238 P&S, p. 194.

The cristall air, the sapher firmament,
The ruby skyes of the orient,
Kest beriall bemes on emerant bewis grene;
The rosy garth depaynt and redolent
With purpur, azure, gold, and goulis gent,
Arayed was by dame Flora the quene.[239]

Heightening the privileged, precious apartness of the aristocratic garden was, as we have seen, the religious silhouette of the *hortus conclusus*; and the two forms of description – nature as a sparkling outdoor palace, and the unearthly tones of sacred love – converge in the motif of bejewelled waters. The motif is to become obsessive in medieval literature, and is very much a characteristic creation of the courtly Middle Ages in its hard, unnatural brilliance,[240] and its blend of secular opulence with religious aura. It is precisely the type of landscape which Lucretius' scientific materialism had ridiculed (despising 'fairy tales' of the Golden Age wherein rivers of gold supposedly flowed over the earth and trees bore jewels for flowers[241]), yet its literary ancestry includes, so far as I have been able to uncover it, classical as well as biblical lineage. From the Bible (and also from Plato)[242] derive the association of precious stones with paradise, and from the classical *locus amoenus* (Theocritus, Ovid, Claudian)[243] the delight in clear, pure waters whose bright depths glitter with light. Late antique rhetorical landscape, with its preference for 'richness of décor'[244] introduces bejewelled motifs (Claudian's colours of nature that exceed kingly gems and Tyrian cloth, Tiberianus' radiant pebbles, crystal streams and flowers like jewelled coronets),[245] which the *Romance of the Rose* heaps and strews across subsequent verse. In Narcissus' well, 'Two cristall stonys craftely / In thilke freshe and faire welle' flash out with 'an hundrid hewis / Blew, yelow, and red, that

239 'The Golden Targe' in *Poems*, ed. J. Kinsley (Oxford: 1958), lines 37–42.

240 On medieval enthralment by brilliant colours and flashing light, cf. Huizinga, *Waning*, pp. 257–58.

241 *De Rerum Natura*, 5.910–12.

242 *Genesis*, 2.11–12; *Ezekiel*, 28.13–14; *Revelation*, 21.19–21; Plato, *Phaedo*, 110 d.

243 Theocritus, *Idylls*, 22.40–41; Ovid, *Metamorphoses*, 5.587–89; Claudian, *De Raptu Proserpinae*, 2.119–20.

244 Curtius, *European Literature*, p. 195. For the enrichment of the classical *locus amoenus* by other sources in Medieval Latin verse, cf. E. Faral, *Recherches sur les sources Latines des Contes et Romans Courtois du Moyen Age* (Paris: 1913), pp. 202, 239, 328–35, 369–72.

245 *De Raptu Proserpinae*, 2.92–100; Tiberianus, 'Amnis ibat inter arva', in *Oxford Book of Latin Verse* ed. H. W. Garrod (Oxford: 1912), p. 372.

fresh and newe is' when struck by sunlight, and hold in their refulgence reflections of all that is in the garden, 'peyntid in the cristall there'.[246] In Lydgate's crystal well:

> Þe gravel and þe brizte stoon
> As any gold ageyn þe sonne schon.[247]

More imaginatively, the pool of the *Pearl* contains banks of pure beryl, on which stones of emerald and sapphire blaze:

> As glente þurz glas þat glowed and glyzt,
> As stremande sternez, quen stroþe-men slepe,
> Staren in welkyn in wynter nyzt.[248]

The association of gemlight and starlight illustrates again the fusion of courtly and sacred in this sensibility: the light in this pool is spiritual, and the Earthly Paradise itself is very close. This 'religio-lapidary' infatuation that converts Greek pebbles into a numinous jewellery (we may compare the precious gems and gold filigree of medieval sacred artefacts such as reliquaries) persists, with much else of the tradition of *diamanté* meads and enamelled walks, into the seventeenth century, in the 'cistern full / Of divers stones' that dance in Vaughan's allegoric *Regeneration* for instance. Its medieval culmination, however, is the avaricious bathos of that Midas milieu, Mandeville's land of Prester John: where the great river direct from Paradise rolls its waves all of precious stones, with no drop of water, for three days a week, considerately allowing locals, on remaining days, to wade in and pluck what diamond takes their fancy.[249]

In conclusion then, the naturalism of noble 'possessive' and 'quotidian' space sharply contrasts with bejewelled bowers in court poems of the high style, descended from the *Rose*. The Gothic International style is intrinsically hierarchic, preserving its noble protagonist above the daily world, the peasant's realm of labour, pain and famine, within decorous scenery consonant with his refinement, an exquisite art-world meet for his piety and chivalry. The same decorum, by which nature is the exteriorization of courtly being, had been observed in the *Roman de Thèbes*, where nature was rarely described save when – and then as an entire landscape of mountains, plains and forest – she was embroidered on the garments or pavilion-

246 Chaucer's translation, lines 1567–1600, p. 580; cf. also lines 125–31, p. 566.
247 Lydgate, *Troy-Book*, ed. H. Bergen (London: 1906), lines 2459–60.
248 *Pearl*, ed. E. V. Gordon (Oxford: 1953), lines 114–16.
249 *The Travels of Sir John Mandeville*, section 30, p. 169.

flaps of the noble.[250] That fourteenth-century England could relish both Chaucer's translation of the *Rose*, and the Gawain-poet's barbarous winter wildernesses; that a nobleman should be expected to enjoy madrigals among the trellised roses of his secluded garden, and expertly to hack off the limbs and scrape out the stomach and bowels of slain deer,[251] exactly corresponds to this extraordinary dualism of ideality and naturalism in medieval aristocratic nature-sensibility.

Rational space

A final form of interest in nature conducing to formulation of the sensible world as pictorial landscape was the desire to construct 'rational space': the desire, that is, to regain and display a 'scientific', rational understanding of the material world, independent of theological constraint, and reviving if not surpassing classical achievement.

'Proto-scientific' studies of the thirteenth century had produced drawings of natural reality so accurate that Franco-Flemish Calendar painters of the fourteenth and fifteenth centuries learned to study the meticulous illustrations of flora and fauna in Italian zoological textbooks, herbals and *Tables of Health* or *Tacuina*.[252] Empirical study of natural forms reached a climax with the minute, obsessive studies of Leonardo and Dürer. 'No man has ever described natural objects, flowers and grasses and animals, more minutely' writes Kenneth Clark of Dürer,[253] whose watercolour of grasses has a flawless photographic verisimilitude. Leonardo's studies of geological strata and Alpine ranges feed directly into the landscape backgrounds of his *Virgin of the Rocks* and *Virgin and Child with St. Anne*. 'If Petrarch was the first man to climb a mountain, Leonardo was the first to make a close scientific study of one.'[254]

The intellectual status of a meticulous science of material appearances that could enlist the energies of such geniuses as Leonardo and Dürer suggests the gains inevitably accruing to landscape art in the post-Scholastic, partially secular ferment of thought aspiring to triumphs of independent Reason. Michelangelo's contemptuous relegation of landscape painting to pleasing trifles fit for monks and

250 *Roman de Thèbes*, ed. L. Constans, 2 vols. (Paris: 1890), lines 2923–62.

251 *Gawain and the Green Knight*, note to line 1325, p. 111.

252 O. Pächt, 'Early Italian Nature Studies and the Early Calendar Landscape', *Journal of the Warburg and Courtauld Institute*, 13 (1950), 13–47.

253 *Civilisation* (London: 1969), p. 151.

254 Clark, *Landscape into Art*, p. 90.

women is well known.[255] But through its appropriation as a site of intellectual endeavour by the new 'scientific' aspirations of artists in Quattrocento Italy landscape became elevated above such strictures, achieving recognition as an independent genre, and a new bravado of technique.

Gombrich has shown how Italian neo-classical art theory assisted that elevation to genre: conferring dignity upon landscape as a vogue of the ancients; supplying it with a definitional inventory drawn from Pliny and Vitruvius; and above all commending it as a field in which moderns might surpass antique achievement.[256] If Northern landscape paintings were thereby translated from frippery to genre, Italian landscape practice was challenged to achieve a *dimostratione*: the feat of ingenuity by which artistic problems of a traditional subject are solved.[257] This was precisely the transforming achievement of geometric perspective.

The ancients, too, had produced illusionistic perspective, yet in it 'space and things do not coalesce into a unified whole nor does the space seem to extend beyond our range of vision'.[258] The perspective of Flemish art had been intuitively constructed, and 'aerial' – effecting recession by colour graduation – rather than geometric. The Renaissance achievement, pioneered by Brunelleschi and theorized by Alberti, was to place optical truth to life on a scientific basis through constructing focused recession with a vanishing point within a frame of mathematically calculated co-ordinates. The breakthrough constituted 'a lever with which to ease the humble craft of painting into the lordly circle of the liberal arts. With this ascent the formerly humble, but now scientific, painter was to move into the sphere of the princely patrons and attendant men of letters.'[259] Moreover, we can see from this that landscape art, as argued in our study of landscape in antiquity, becomes increasingly realized as a secular mode of reality. Panofsky, it is true, has suggested affinities of Brunelleschian space not only with the 'sensualistic' premises of Nominalism, but with the homogenous, infinitely extended universe of Cusanus and Descartes.[260] Complete externality to a religious framework of thought is perhaps impossible. Yet, as in classical antiquity, we can see that the mastery of spatial

255 A remark to Francisco da Hollanda: Clark, *Landscape into Art*, p. 54.
256 *Norm and Form*, pp. 107–21.
257 Ibid., pp. 7–10.
258 Panofsky, *Renaissance and Renascences*, p. 121.
259 White, *Birth and Rebirth of Pictorial Space*, p. 126.
260 *Renaissance and Renascences*, p. 123.

illusionism derived its impetus from a body and climate of thought independent, in any direct way, of religious revelation, aspiration or perception. The emotion with which a naturalistic landscape is painted may well be devotional, as with Bellini's *St. Francis in Ecstasy* (plate 12); but the perceptual mode, the epistemological foundation of the technique, is secular and materialist. In Bellini's painting, 'A spiritual experience ... is understood in wholly natural terms.'[261]

The studies of Dürer and Leonardo, and that 'systematization of optical observations into exact perspectival construction'[262] which is geometric perspective, arguably share that same classifying, mathematizing impulse towards 'rational space' that developed over time from the interest in 'material and efficient causes' separated out by the Schoolmen, to the 'verification' of mechanist cosmologies by Galileo and Newton.[263] Indeed, John White demonstrates the indebtedness of Renaissance artificial perspective to medieval thought, as the application of medieval optical theory to the solution of certain new representational problems in humanist art.[264] Hauser summarises that 'the Renaissance deepens the influence of ... medieval development with its striving towards the capitalist economic and social system ... in so far as it confirms the rationalism which now dominates the whole intellectual and material life of the time ... The unification of space and the unified standards of proportions ... express the same dislike for the incalculable and uncontrollable as the economy of the same period with its emphasis on planning, expediency and calculability; they are creations of the same spirit which makes its way in the organization of labour, in trading methods, the credit system and double-entry book-keeping, in methods of government, diplomacy and warfare. The whole development of art becomes part of the total process of rationalization.'[265]

Probably the most crucial aspect of this process of secular rationalization for landscape, though I have not found the point suggested elsewhere, is the overwhelming transfer of interest from time to space: a process, of course, precisely the reverse of that effected by the Fathers. It is widely recognized that the impulse

261 A. R. Turner, *The Vision of Landscape in Renaissance Italy*, p. 65.

262 Panofsky, *Renaissance and Renascences*, p. 130.

263 Cf. Collingwood, *Idea of Nature*, pp. 103–05, 106–10.

264 White, *Birth and Rebirth*, pp. 126–30.

265 Arnold Hauser, *Social History* (1951; rpt. in 4 vols., London: 1962), vol. 2, pp. 11–12.

subjecting space to geometry, subjects time to the clock; space and time are each converted into a regulated, uniform continuum. But more than this, the proceedings of science come increasingly to conceive reality in terms primarily not of time but of space: no longer the teleological phenomenon, the narrative of divine creativity and eschatological scheme, but the phenomenon of matter in motion. When Descartes comes to define the reality beyond that of spirit or mind, he terms it 'extension'. Teleology, gibed Bacon, like a virgin consecrated to God, produces no offspring.[266]

In space, man recognizes his agency and acquisitions; in time, man feels his dependency. Landscape painting emphatically endorses secular priorities in progressively dethroning time: redefining its attentions from mortality and recurrence, the imperatives of the seasons, to the medium of mastery, prospects of the object. The decline of interest in zodiacal detail we have glimpsed already in the naturalization of astrological symbols, and the withdrawal of their arc from above the fields of Calendar task. By the late fifteenth century, in Italy, landscape content is defined in terms of inventories of objects: landscape's essence as a pictorial genre is conceived in terms of groves, rivers, rocks, shrines, shepherds, cattle.[267]

Robert Campin's *St Joseph*, from the Mérode Altar, (mid-fifteenth century) precisely conveys the new ground of interest. St. Joseph sits at a 'windowscape' that gives onto an urban square, with merchant houses, busy pedestrians and distant spires: but the absence of all vegetation makes the season of the year unguessable, irrelevant. This is space that has decisively outgrown time.

As artistic definition of the natural world breaks gradually free from the grip of prescribed religious perception, with its dualism of sensory versus anagogic levels to form, the new naturalist mode will instead come to divide the sensory world itself, along a subjective/objective axis. Historically, the drive of 'rational space' towards an objectifying, even geometricizing naturalistic draughtsmanship becomes increasingly distinct from, and antipathetic to, certain impulses arising in our category of 'quotidian space' which move towards a highly expressive rendition of space, towards landscape as a nuanced language of mood.

266 *De Dignitate et Augmentis Scientiarum* 3.5.
267 Cf. the characterizations of 'landscape' by Paulo Giovio, Paulo Lomazzo and Edward Norgate, cited by Gombrich, *Norm and Form*, pp. 113, 120, 116.

If the divergence of emphases between the 'scientific' and the 'poetic' is already observable in Brunelleschi as against El Greco, in Poussin as against Claude, it will later fissure into the outright cosmological antagonism of mechanistic materialism and Idealist thought, and the artistic alternation of Classical and Romantic.

In the Renaissance, however, no absolute contradiction is felt to exist between aspiration to a 'Cartesian', objective and impersonally verifiable truth of nature – *certezze* rather than *opinioni*[268] – and Neoplatonism's commendation of a personal, visionary contemplation of nature by which to stimulate imagination of ideal beauty. Animistic and mathematical models likewise coexist in Renaissance cosmology until the ascendency of Galileo and Newton.[269] Neoplatonism takes the mind as a *speculum vivens*, whose *simulacra* surpass the *naturalia* of sense-perception. In Sidney's terms:

> Nature never set forth the earth in so rich tapestry as divers poets have done; neither with pleasant rivers, fruitful trees, sweet-smelling flowers, nor whatsoever else may make the too much loved earth more lovely. Her world is brazen, the poets only deliver a golden.[270]

Moreover, the *Idea* or 'fore-conceit' may well be stimulated by a certain suggestible, imaginative openness to the emotive language of sensible form. 'I have seen shapes in clouds and on patchy walls which have roused me to beautiful inventions of various things'[271] declares Leonardo.

> If you have to invent some setting you will be able to see in these the likeness of divine landscapes, adorned with mountains, ruins, rocks, woods, great plains, hills and valleys in great variety.[272]

As such, the 'rational space' of this philosophy opens a pathway to the appreciation of landscape as mood, as a tonal lexis liberated from the limits of the old iconographic dictionary. It personalizes the meaning of the visual image, and commends engagement of natural forms on an affective level.

268 Luca Pacioli, Clark, *Landscape into Art*, p. 43.

269 Collingwood, *Idea of Nature*, pp. 95–96, 103–04.

270 Philip Sidney, *An Apology for Poetry*, ed. Geoffrey Shepherd (Manchester: 1973), p. 100.

271 *Treatise on Painting, Codex Urbinas Latinus 1270*, ed. A. P. McMahon (Princeton: 1956), vol. 2, fols. 62r; Englished by Gombrich, p. 60. Vasari records that Piero di Cosimo would discover, on walls upon which sick people spat, fantastic cities and extraordinary landscapes: Giorgio Vasari, *The Lives of the Painters, Sculptors and Architects*, trans. A. B. Hinds (London: 1963), vol. 2, p. 177.

272 Ibid., fol. 35v; Englished by Clark, *Landscape into Art*, p. 90.

For Leonardo accordingly there must be 'an interplay of the conscious and unconscious mind ... a union of science and fantasy'.[273] Artistic sensitisation to the expressive charge of sensibles must be matched by meticulous study of their material form. 'See to it', he directs, 'that you first know all the parts of the things you want to represent, be it those of animals, of landscapes, of rocks, plants or others'.[274] In Leonardo, the objectification of space and the phenomenological responsiveness to images converge to one end; and in certain seventeenth-century verse likewise, we shall see that intuitive or inspirational responsiveness is not yet extruded from the proceedings of a rational understanding of nature, as it will be with the triumph of experimental science, proceeding by inductive logic.

Section 3: The territorial imagination: wilderness, countryside and paradise

Response to natural scenery, we have argued, will be conditioned, among other things, by the location of the place or features within a structure of territorial understanding. It is an impulse perhaps natural, and certainly developed by the conditions of sedentary civilization, to divide the environment in a fundamental way into known and unknown, homeland and outlands, into the centre and orbit of cultural belonging as against the fearful alien realms beyond its frontiers. In early and Classical civilizations this duality carries, as we have seen, a religious dimension, being conceived in terms of the domain of divine order and protection as against unholy places assimilated to chaos and populated by monsters or evil spirits. This archetypal imagination persists, despite the metaphysic of monotheistic universal suzerainty, in the attitudes accompanying monastic clearance in the Dark and Middle Ages.

> The cloister is a 'true paradise', and the surrounding countryside shares in its dignity. Nature 'in the raw', unembellished by work or art, inspires the learned man with a sort of horror: the abysses and peaks which we like to gaze at, are to him an occasion of fear. A wild spot, not hallowed by prayer and asceticism and which is not the scene of any spiritual life is, as it were, in

273 Clark, *Landscape into Art*, pp. 90 and 87.
274 *Treatise on Painting*, fol. 35v; Gombrich, p. 62.

the state of original sin. But once it has become fertile and purposeful, it takes on the utmost significance ... a 'Beaulieu' is a place which has been made fertile.[275]

I wish to argue that medieval and Renaissance attitudes towards landscape and countryside, particularly towards the 'wilder' landscape of mountain, moor, forest and sea, can only be fully understood with reference to changes within contemporary imagination of territorial relationality; changes which follow upon that economic and social transformation we have earlier defined as the supersedure of a defensive culture of 'agrarian territoriality' by an expansionist one of 'commercial geography'.

In the English landscape of the eleventh century, writes Hoskins, 'vast areas remained in their natural state, awaiting the sound of a human voice'. The Midlands were an ocean of primaeval forest, whilst 'inland, especially in the far west and north, there still remained millions of acres of stony moorland haunted only by the cries of the animal creation, where the eagle and the raven circled undisturbed'.

Around nearly every village stretched its open fields ... each covering a few hundred acres, but hardly anywhere had these fields reached the frontiers of the village territory. If one walked half a mile, a mile at the most, out from the village, one came to the edge of the wild, to a wide stretch of moory or boggy ground that formed a temporary barrier, or the massed tree-trunks of the primeval woods still awaiting the axe. Every village had its own frontiers ... [276]

Even to the scholar of the eleventh century, beyond the periphery of Europe (Constantinople and Jerusalem at the farthest) lay lands known only from the territory of ancient books.

The succeeding centuries witnessed, however, as we have seen, domination of the natural environment by deforestation, drainage, extended cultivation, urban development and road networks, as well as the politico-military expansion of Christian Europe culminating in the Crusades. These developments created a newly unitary and confident 'Christendom', wherein localism was diminished yet further by the international communities of European universities, knightly orders, mendicant friars and new scholarship.[277]

275 Jean Leclercq, *The Love of Learning and the Desire for God*, trans. Catharine Misrahi (1961; rpt. New York: 1982), p. 130.

276 Hoskins, *Making*, pp. 76–77, 82.

277 Southern, *The Making of the Middle Ages*, pp. 209–44.

The totality of these changes revolutionized the territorial sense: the romance takes Europe as a whole for its field, and the world of threatening alterity, no longer the virgin forest encircling the village community, is thrust far away to lie beyond the frontiers of Christendom. In Chrétien de Troyes 'we move effortlessly from Winchester to Regensburg or Constantinople'; the thousands of 'Mary-stories' of the thirteenth century have 'a wide sweep which takes in Pisa and Chartres (and in [some] stories Germany, England and Spain) all within a few pages'.[278] The Crusades, the thirteenth-century journeys of Franciscan missionaries and the Polos across Asia, and the Mongol invasions all helped open mens' minds to the vastness of the unconverted world: a revelation to Europe of comparable impact with the later discovery of the Americas. Perhaps these developments underlay Cusanus' radical cosmology of non-geocentric, centreless infinity, and they must certainly have stimulated the new appetite for panorama in the landscape painting of the van Eycks and the Mannerist tradition. Archetypal demonization of regions outlying the Christian pale is clear in the *Owl and the Nightingale*, in the latter's mockery of the Owl's missionary work in the Norselands.

> þat lond nys god, ne hit nys este,
> Ac wildernesse hit is and weste;
> Knarres and cludes houenetinge,
> Snov and hawel hom is genge.
> Þat lond is grislich and vnuele,
> Þe men beoþ wilde and vnsele ...
> ac libbeþ also wilde dor:
> hi goþ bi-tizt mid ruze uelle,
> rizt suich hi comen ut of helle.[279]

Yet developing consciousness of cultural 'otherness' beyond the boundaries of an integrated Christendom modifies in turn, I would argue, the way in which wilder landscape *within* Europe is conceived. Its fearful mystique, its polarized opposition to Christian culture, is thereby moderated: local crags and forests are less alien, no longer unassimilable, in contrast with reports of the fantastic kingdoms of the Moslems, Mongols, Chinese, 'the cauldron of unreason beyond the curtain of Christendom'.[280] The margin of fear is relocated.

278 Ibid., pp. 233, 237.

279 *The Owl and the Nightingale*, ed. John Wells (Boston & London: 1909), lines 999–1004, 1012–14, trans. Brian Stone, *The Owl and the Nightingale* (Harmondsworth: 1971), p, 216.

280 Southern, *Middle Ages*, p. 233.

In landscape description, the abatement of an absolute and religious opposition between 'culture' and 'wilds' is evident, I think, in Gavin Douglas, the fifteenth-century Scottish diplomat, bishop and poet, in whose brilliant Prologues to his translation of the *Aeneid* is established 'the independence of landscape description as a literary form for the first time'.[281]

> The lyght begouth to quynchyng owt and faill,
> The day to dyrkyn, declyne and devaill;
> The gummys rysis, doun fallis the donk rym,
> Baith heir and thar scuggis and schaddois dym.
> Upgois the bak with hir pelit ledderyn flycht,
> The lark discendis from the skyis hycht,
> Syngand hir complyng sang, efter hir gys,
> To tak hir rest, at matyn hour to rys.
> Owt our the swyre swymmys the soppis of myst,
> The nycht furthspred hir cloke with sabill lyst,
> That all the bewte of the fructuus feld
> Was with the erthis umbrage cleyn our held;
> Baith man and beste, fyrth, flude and woddis wild
> Involvyt in tha schaddois warryn syld ...
> And schortlie, every thing that doith repar
> In firth or feild, flude, forest, erth or ayr,
> Or in the scroggis, or the buskis ronk,
> Lakis, marrasis, or thir pulys donk,
> Astabillit lyggis still to slepe, and restis ...
> Als weill the wild as the taym bestiall.[282]

In these extraordinary lines the poet evokes a unitary 'world-sense' not in the standardized features of orthodox seasonal headpieces but in fresh empiricisms (the leathery flight of the bat, mists swimming up from the valleys). Moreover, in its calm ecumenicism cultivated landscape and wilds become as one substance: 'the bewte of the fructuus feld' and the ecclesiastical imagery of the lark's compline and matin are at one with 'fyrth, flude and woddis wild' – 'Als weill the wild as the taym bestiall'. Such harmony and universal benediction would have been inconceivable in the defensive territorial conditions of manorial localism.

281 P&S, p. 200.

282 *Virgil's Aeneid, Translated into Scottish Verse by Gavin Douglas*, ed. D. F. C. Coldwell (Edinburgh: 1960), Prologue to Book 13, lines 29–42, 51–55, 59, vol. 4, pp. 141–46.

If the expansionism of Christendom and its agricultural environmental offensive moderate the sense of wilderness as an absolute and threatening alterity, they also animate a transformed spirit of crusading challenge towards unknown lands and landscape. With the Romance culture of the twelfth and thirteenth centuries 'men think of themselves less as stationary objects of attack by spiritual foes, and more as pilgrims and seekers',[283] and the imagery of journeying preoccupies secular as well as religious literature. Even the medieval peasant population was far more mobile than was once supposed, and in fourteenth-century England few families stayed in the same village for even three generations.[284] In pastoral verse one reflex of these conditions is a new celebration of the shepherd as the fixed point in a roaming world:

> Je suys la a les regarder
> Passer; les uns, en chavauchant,
> Vont chantant, les aultres preschant,
> En contant de leurs aventures,
> Et je repose a mes patures,
> En l'ombre d'un beau bisonnet

I stay there watching them go by; some go singing as they ride, others preaching and telling stories about themselves, and I rest in the meadow in the pleasant shade of a bush

declares the Berger of *Mestier et Marchandise* (1440).[285] For Dante's Ulysses, no moral power could check the craving to experience the outlying world and put his boat out on the open sea, a *frisson* metaphorically re-echoed by Dante himself, who, rising to the Heaven of the Moon, marvells

> The water I venture upon has never been sailed.[286]

We must not of course make the mistake of assuming that all forest and mountain under manorialism were impenetrable realms of terror. When the Bishop of Mainz in the tenth century was told that Hell was encircled by dense forest, he joked 'I would like to send my swineherd there with my lean pigs to pasture'.[287] Forest usage and transhumance

283 Southern, *Middle Ages*, p. 212.
284 H. E. Hallam, *Rural England 1066–1348*, pp. 253–54.
285 *Mestier et Marchandise*, in Edouard Fournier (ed.), *Le Théâtre Français avant la Renaissance* (Paris: 1889), p. 46; ref. and trans. Helen Cooper, pp. 61–62.
286 *Inferno*, 26.94–102; *Paradiso*, 2.7: trans. C. H. Sisson, p. 355.
287 Helen Waddell, *Medieval Latin Lyrics* (Harmondsworth: 1962), p. 161.

throughout the Middle Ages entailed overlapping the perilous frontiers of 'cultural space' and virgin wilderness. Nevertheless, the Anglo-Saxon poet of the *Phoenix*, composing a landscape beautiful, emphatically expels the rugged:

> No hills or mountains stand there
> steeply, nor do stone cliffs arise
> aloft, as here with us; nor are there
> valleys or dales, or hill caves,
> mounds or rising ground; nor are
> there any rough slopes there at all.[288]

In the fourth century by contrast the 'otherness' of crag and forest may compose a landscape of spiritual enchantment, the shock of the primitive figure the imminently marvellous. The soul of the *Pearl*-poet, speeding 'In aventure þer mervaylez meven', finds:

> I ne wyste in þis worlde quere þat hit wace,
> Bot I knew me keste þer klyfez cleven;
> Towarde a foreste I bere þe face,
> Where rych rokkez wer to dyscreven.[289]

Though flashing with unearthly brightness, it is rock, cliff and forest rather than the flowered plains and blossoming groves of the Anglo-Saxon *locus felix*, that denote the realm of spiritual breakthrough and entrancement.

In *Gawain* supremely, primitive wilderness has evolved and expanded from being the demonic other of culture, a shunned likeness of hell, into a challenging haunt of adventure, empirically focused.

> Bi a mounte on þe morne meryly he rydes
> Into a forest ful dep, þat ferly watz wylde,
> Hize hillez on uche a halve, and holtwodez under
> Of hore okez ful hoge a hundreth togeder;
> þe hasel and þe haz þorne were harled al samen,
> With roze raged mosse rayled aywhere,
> With mony bryddez unblyþe upon bare twyges.[290]

'Who, before this', ask Pearsall and Salter, 'had noticed the thick rough moss growing in virgin forest, or the twisted thickets of hazel

288 'The Phoenix', lines 21–26, in *Anglo-Saxon Poetry*, trans. R. K. Gordon (1926; rpt. London: 1954), p. 240; from *Anglo-Saxon Poetic Records* (Columbia: 1936), vol. 3, p. 96.

289 *Pearl*, ed. E. V. Gordon (Oxford: 1953), lines 64–68, p. 3.

290 *Sir Gawain and the Green Knight*, ed. cit., lines 740–46, p. 21.

and hawthorn?'[291] The trailing festoons of moss recur in Grunewald's *Isenheim Altarpiece* of 1513, but in the case of a fourteenth-century poet constitute empirical genius: we note that moss is not even an alliterative necessity in its line. One context of this eye, however, is surely philosophy. From Aristotle to Chalcidius and Bernardus Silvestris, the word 'hyle' or 'silva' had denoted not only 'forest' but also, in opposition to 'mind', the raw matter of pristine Chaos, and by association the wilderness of man's darker instincts.[292] As such, perception of forests would be naturally directed to what in them seemed ancient, tangled, disorderly.

> Mony klyf he overclambe in contrayez straunge,
> Fer floten fro his frendez fremedly he rydez:[293]

Here the traditional terror of territorial otherness is insisted upon ('fremedly' from 'fremede' meaning 'alien'), and these wilds are replete with wild men, wolves and ogres; but these conventions are telescoped into five lines (718–23) and dismissed – 'Hit were to tore for to telle of þe tenþe dole' – and supplanted by the reality of bitter natural conditions and scenic experience, lovingly elaborated. On occasion, the context of Crusader adventurism, of military sortie, perceptibly shapes authorial imagination of Gawain's engagement of raw nature:

> ... *werre wrathed hym not so much* þat wynter nas wors,
> When þe colde cler water fro þe cloudez schadde,
> And fres er hit falle myzt to þe fale erþe;
> *Ner slayn* wyth þe slete he *sleped in his yrnes*
> Mo nyztez þen innoghe in naked rokkez,
> þer as *claterande fro þe crest* þe colde borne rennez.[294]
>
> (My italics.)

Similarly locus of invaded mystery and challenged alien vitality are the dense medieval forests. Still partly within the 'hyle' tradition, Filippo Lippi's allegoric *Madonna Adoring a Child in a Wood* places the infant saviour in the flowered clearing of a steep wood that symbolizes the postlapsarian condition. But light breaks through the soft greenness of these trees: the forest, terrain of expiation, exile and

291 P&S, p. 149.

292 For the concept of 'hyle' from Plato to Chalcidius, cf. J. C. M. van Winden's *Calcidius on Matter: His Doctrine and Sources* (Leiden: 1959).

293 *Sir Gawain and the Green Knight*, lines 713–14, p. 20.

294 Ibid., lines 726–31, p. 21.

testing in early medieval romances,[295] the *selva oscura* through which Dante approaches Hell, the territory of transgression, whether by bandit or outlawed lovers, no longer bulks hideously alien. Significantly, Lippi's woodland is thinned by logging: the process whose consequences, across medieval Europe, 'a civilization of wood',[296] help transform traditional attitudes to forest, so that the sombre 'wild wood' cedes to the youth and freedom of the greenwood. Forests originally covered about 95 per cent of central and western Europe, but by 1300 this had been reduced to about 20 per cent.[297] In England the provisions of the Forest Charter (1215) together with local disafforestation transactions all over the country had considerably reduced the area of forest by the fourteenth century,[298] and the growth of the Robin Hood stories in this century reflect the altered symbolic significance:

> And mony ane sings o'grass, o'grass,
> And mony ane sings o' corn,
> And mony ane sings o' Robin Hood,
> Kens little whare he was born.
> It wasna in the ha', the ha'
> Nor in the painted bower,
> But it was in the gude green-wood,
> Among the lily-flower.[299]

The forest kingdom holds in its remoteness a spell of primal vitality. This may be a matter of an unspoiled realm of sequestered prettiness, 'faire under fete, / And litel used'[300] whose teeming animal life does not jar a basic paradoxical orderliness: Chaucer sets his self-exiled, mourning 'man in black' in a delicate, lucid woodland, stolen from the enclosed parkland of the *Rose* and naturalized, of tall, evenly spaced trees, clean boles soaring high overhead without protruding lower branches and interleaving a shady canopy.[301] Its abounding fauna form a frame of natural health and liveliness to combat the corroding melancholia of the widower. The same combination of secluded peace, luxurious verdure and rich animal life as oriented around a consolatory, religious centre composes Pisanello's woodland *Vision of St Eustace*. These Gothic woods curiously coexist in Chaucer with the *Gawain*-

295 Cf. W. Calin, *The Epic Quest* (Baltimore: 1966). 296 Glacken, p. 318.
297 Ponting, *Green History*, p. 121. 298 Stenton, p. 113.
299 *The Birth of Robin Hood*, Drabble, p. 23.
300 Chaucer, *The Book of the Duchess* in *Complete Works*, lines 400–01, p. 271.
301 Ibid., lines 414–44.

like depths of awesome forest, landscapes of adversarial challenge, whose dense, engulfing greenery swallow up Altdorfer's dwarfed paladin *St George*, and also his *Dead Landsknecht*. The vegetative ogres of *Gawain* and Grunewald, enemies of Gothic symmetry and light, tower in the gloom of Chaucer's *locus vilis* in 'The Knight's Tale', gnarled, irregular and darksome.

> First on the wal was peynted a forest,
> In which ther dwelleth neither man ne best,
> With knotty, knarry, bareyne trees olde,
> Of stubbes sharpe and hidouse to biholde,
> In which ther ran a rumbel in a swough,
> As though a storm sholde bresten every bough.
> And downward from an hille, under a bente,
> Ther stood the temple of Mars armypotente.[302]

Again we notice the military connection of the inhuman outlands, as in Gawain's rocky bivouac, and the *horror sylvanum* of Brueghel's *Suicide of Saul*. Yet it is not brutality but vitality that primarily characterises nearly all medieval forests. Not even Argus, declares the dreamer in the *Book of the Duchess*, could number the squirrels, deer and other creatures roaming his dream-forest, 'The wondres me mette in my sweven.'[303] Indeed, these medieval woodlands in their sequestered, private enchantment have the same strange intentness and obsessiveness as the dream-framework of medieval verse. The dreamer of *Pearl* walks among 'holtewodez' where birds of all colours beat iridescent wings, where rustling leaves flash like silver, and tree-boles seem blue as dyed silk.[304] In classical literature, forests had not borne similar tones: the great mantled trees and humming life, vibrant with bird trills and bright colours, and teeming with animals. Perhaps owing to the virtual deforestation of the Mediterranean effected by the first millennium, in Greek and Roman poetry one cannot step into deep forests experienced, as in the *sous-bois* of Pisanello, Uccello, Altdorfer, the verse of *Pearl*, *Gawain* and Chaucer, as places where life is quietly *abounding*: dim depths whose stillnesses are rich and thick in half-seen life. The starring of an initial dimness by areas of gem-like, brilliant colour possibly owes something to the experience of medieval church and cathedral: and may thus have abetted Quattrocento speculation that the pointed arch of Gothic architecture derived from the arching

302 'The Knight's Tale', in ibid., lines 1975–82, p. 36.
303 *Book of the Duchess*, in ibid., line 442, p. 271.
304 *Pearl*, lines 75–80, 89–90, pp. 3–4.

tree-roofs of the forest.[305] Certainly, the woodlands of antiquity, when not the sites of violence and dementia, or routine sacred groves, offer only secluded tranquillity: most notably in the 'Tempe' motif, or Ovid's cool sylvan pools.[306] Only the fresco of the villa of Livia at Prima Porta (plate 4), studded with gleaming fruits, flowers and birds, seems comparable. 'Magically impenetrable' Berenson called it;[307] the essential appeal of the high medieval forest is precisely that it *is* magically penetrable.

We have seen that one revolution in the medieval territorial imagination produced an adventurist attitude to wilds, a thrill in ranging through the unknown world, which reclaims mountain, moor and forest from the condition of demonized and evaded alterity. A related revolution is the birth of the mellow, innocent 'countryside', constructed as the 'other' of the new urban centres and their distinct culture. Indeed the word 'country' is from Middle English, and derives, according to the *OED*, from the Medieval Latin 'contrata' signifying the 'contra-terra' or land lying opposite or facing one. Territorial relations are thus no longer the polarization of cultural space and an infernal Beyond, but increasingly the overlapping, interpenetrating divergence of urban and rural: with the latter as hinterlands subdivided into cultivated and uncultivated landscape.

The townsman's 'countryside' as we encounter it at the close of the Middle Ages is usually the pleasant locus of refined patrician retreat, contemplative, tranquil, exempt from the incessant contingencies of city and court. In fifteenth- and sixteenth-century Europe the castle was softening into the country house, whilst in fifteenth-century Italy the country villa had come to constitute a sound financial investment in an economy of alarming commercial recessions, as well as a retreat from crowds and plague. 'The villa permitted a demilitarised feudal life, still further removed from class suspicion by its classical associations.'[308] Back in the twelfth century the wave of 'proto-humanist' *litterati* had momentarily resumed the Virgilian-Horatian celebration of rural retreat –

> My uncle has a farm out in the woods,
> Where I withdraw, having cast off the squalor
> Of all the worries that torment mankind.

305 Cf. Panofsky, *Renaissance and Renascences*, pp. 23–24.
306 Geikie, *The Love of Nature among the Romans*, ch. 7, pp. 141–60.
307 Bernard Berenson, *The Passionate Sightseer* (London: 1960), p. 32.
308 Hale, *Renaissance Europe*, p. 44.

Its verdant grass, the silent woods, the gentle
And playful breezes, and the spring, vivacious
Amidst the herbs, refresh the weary mind –
Restore my self to me and make me rest
Within me ...[309]

– but with the fifteenth century the theme returns as vogue. Alberti's dialogue *Della Famiglia* and Politian's *Rusticus*, following Petrarch's *De Vita Solitaria* make country life triumph entirely over civic in this ancient topic of rhetorical debate.[310] In painting, that earlier expression of a select, secluded landscape, the enclosed garden, weakens during the fifteenth century, trellis and hedge becoming merely decorative frames themselves backgrounded by a beautiful outer world, as the enclosure motif declines into an artistic 'bouquet' for any theme.[311] A south German miniature of 1500 actually places the Virgin *outside* her *hortus conclusus*, her back turned upon it.[312] We may remember that the patron saint of contemplative integration into nature, St Francis, had been the son of a merchant, reared in a thriving town, and that 'He and his followers worked primarily with the urban population, and for a century at least enjoyed their favour.'[313]

It is important here to note the unprecedented heterogeneity of the medieval town. 'The feudal mode of production ... was the first to permit it an *autonomous development* within a natural-agrarian economy. The fact that the largest medieval towns never rivalled in scale those of either Antiquity or Asian Empires has often obscured the truth that their function within the social formation was a much more advanced one ... The paradigmatic medieval towns of Europe which practised trade and manufactures were self-governing communes, enjoying corporate political and military autonomy from the nobility and the Church.'[314] Consequently, 'modern history is the urbanization of the countryside, not, as among the ancients, the ruralization of the city'.[315] Arguably, it is precisely due to the new disengagement of bourgeoisie and nobility from the traditional productive and social relations of feudal agrarianism – in the former case through distinct urban culture,

309 Marbod of Rennes (died 1123) in *PL*, 171 col. 1665; quoted and trans. by Panofsky, *Renaissance and Renascences*, pp. 74–75.
310 Wilkinson, *The Georgics of Virgil*, pp. 296–97.
311 P&S, pp. 110–15.
312 *The Grimani Breviary*, P&S, p. 113.
313 Lynn White, '*Natural Science*', pp. 434–35.
314 Perry Anderson, *Passages*, p. 150.
315 Karl Marx, *Pre-Capitalist Economic Formations* (London: 1964), p. 78.

in the latter through the dissolution of fiefdom, recompensed by building the centralized State machine and juridical order of political absolutism[316] – that the 'countryside' became a sphere sufficiently remote and discrete to turn frequently the object, during the fifteenth to seventeenth centuries, of a nostalgic and sentimentalizing artistic reconstruction. It was developing, in short, the externality of playground and supply-factory, in a long and uneven evolution of estrangement that was to culminate, centuries later, in Romantic sublimation of the marginalised green world. In the later fourteenth century, Philippe de Vitry created the contented, humble woodcutter Franc Gontier to embody 'the supreme value of the simple life', in a re-emergent poetry of 'idyllic pastoral' whose landscape resumed connotations of the Golden Age shared by Christine de Pisan's fifteenth-century shepherdess. René of Anjou turned his court into a kind of mock-pastoral in its poetry and pageantry, and indeed staged, as the Elizabethans were to do, a pastoral tournament, in 1449.[317] Above all, fifteenth-century courtly and urban back-to-nature found its 'soft primitivism'[318] poeticized in Sannazzaro's Arcadia, whose 'sweet, lingering plaintiveness' centralized a vein of elegiac feeling peripheral in Virgil's Arcady.[319] A distanced and neo-classically inflected urban and courtly culture could frequently thereby completely mythicize rural reality; and the contrast in available emphases between the busy feudal landscapes of the Limbourgs and the greenswards of idyllic pastoral, between the working pastures of *Piers Plowman* and the golden countryside of Gontier and Sannazzaro, is some measure of the urban alienation in process.

Additional to wilderness and countryside, a third domain reconceived in high medieval territorial imagination was that of the otherworld: comprising the realms of Eden, Heaven, Hell and Purgatory. Regarding paradise, the medievals, like the Fathers, construed the classical poets' Golden Age as an impaired reminiscence of Eden.[320] By consequence, the ideal landscapes of classical verse, unmistakeably mediterranean as exquisite refuges from fierce sunshine

316 Cf. Perry Anderson, *Lineages of the Absolutist State* (London: 1974), pp. 15–42.
317 Helen Cooper, pp. 67, 49, 68.
318 For 'hard' and 'soft' primitivism defined and distinguished, cf. Arthur O. Lovejoy and George Boas, *Primitivism and Related Ideas in Antiquity*, vol. 1 (Baltimore: 1935), pp. 9–11.
319 Erwin Panofsky, *Meaning in the Visual Arts* (1955; rpt. Harmondsworth: 1970), pp. 349–50.
320 Cf. Dante, *Purgatorio*, 28.139–44.

in shadowy groves and breeze, are paraded once more; and it is easy to lose sight of significant distinction amidst the endless, monotonous recycling of the *locus amoenus* by late antique and high medieval Christian poets alike.[321] As Giammati dejectedly confesses, 'Toward the height of the Middle Ages, the descriptions of the earthly paradise become more numerous and more conventional. In the twelfth century Bernardus Silvestris, in *De Mundi Universitate*, and Godfrey of Viterbo, in *Pantheon*, and Alexander Neckham, a century later in *De Laudibus Divinae Sapientiae*, all present us with traditional portraits of the earthly paradise.'[322]

Yet inevitably historical difference makes entry; and the distinction, I would argue, between paradises medieval and early Christian lies less in the central properties of verse description than in the general conception of the relations between the temporal world and the otherworld. In sum, the otherworld becomes less other. Its reality, like that of Cathay, remains marvellous yet becomes more concretely predicable; conceived more as the fruition of conditions in the familiar world than as a realm utterly heterogenous, sublimely incommensurable.

The terrestrial paradise, of course, was a place actually located on the globe, established by the twelfth century as lying in the East but cut off from the world by a mountain-top location or ocean barrier or barrier of fire.[323] As such, where early Christians had been content to hymn it, intrepid travellers now hoped to find it: the legend of Alexander's *Iter ad Paradisum* was entirely retold in Latin in the twelfth century; Mandeville sketched directions, though warning of nigh-impossible hardships; and when Columbus discovered the New World he thought himself close to the Garden of Eden.[324] In art and verse the 'spiritualization' of Eden was achieved not by detracting from the material concreteness of the Greco-Roman model, but through supervening details from *Canticles* and *Genesis*.[325] One novelty is that in several thirteenth-century depictions we find, additional to the four rivers and eastern location, the inhabitation of

321 Cf. Duncan, *Milton's Earthly Paradise*, and Howard Patch, *The Otherworld according to Descriptions in Medieval Literature* (Cambridge, Mass.: 1950) for catalogues of the surface recurrence of formal properties under the name of diverse poets.

322 Giammati, *Earthly Paradise*, p. 79.

323 Cf. Patch, *Otherworld*, pp. 176–82, 148–58.

324 S. E. Morison, *Admiral of the Ocean Sea, A Life of Christopher Columbus* (Boston: 1942), vol. 2, p. 282.

325 P&S, pp. 64–65.

the garden by wild animals. Though these may have some basis in *Genesis*' lurking serpent, Giammati suggests that these unprecedented creatures import 'a general mood of wonder and despair'.[326] Quite the contrary may be suggested, however, in the light of our foregoing study of 'wilderness': their presence may perhaps inject that authenticating sense of adventurist breakthrough into new territory, which we found in medieval forests: in Uccello's *sous-bois* of fabulous penetration, or the *Pearl*'s numinous primaevalism, or the discovery, in medieval romances, of a *paradisi simulacrum* in the form of a *locus amoenus* in the heart of forest depths.[327] As such the animals would comprise a projection into the classical parfumerie of a new realism: the primal vitality, other yet close, felt in the lushness of the natural world.

The patristic allegorization of Eden, as the Church, the virtuous soul, or the prefiguration of the celestial paradise, of course persists, the literal and spiritual levels of truth holding simultaneously. Yet in even the celestial paradise, we find again, despite the ultimate inapprehensibility of beatitude to souls on earth,[328] suggestions of a less otherworldly, more tenaciously material conception. In paintings of the *hortus conclusus*, for example, typologically foreshadowing the paradise to come, 'the descent of the Virgin and Child from the high austere thrones of the twelfth century onto the flowered meadows or into the walled gardens of the fourteenth and fifteenth century' adumbrates heaven in a language which, though 'figural', so teems with the sensuously delicious as to seem to evince the conviction that earthly 'tree and flower ... might contribute uniquely to statements of religious truth'.[329] To appreciate the truth of this, we may again contrast the approach of the first Christian centuries.

The Fathers, we saw, sought to effect a secure, perfecting distancing from the sensible realm, concussed by barbarian crises, of the paradise of eternal stasis. Both epistemological thought and artistic orientation consolidated that polarization of heaven and the processes of spiritual life from the material order. In Augustine's Idealism, all knowledge, including apparently optical 'vision', is of the substance of the mind, rather than deriving from sense-experience: sense-experience comprises in truth the concurrence of the two processes, bodily perception

326 Giammati, *Earthly Paradise*, pp. 81–83.
327 Curtius, *European Literature*, pp. 201–02; P&S, pp. 53–54.
328 1 *Corinthians*, 2.9; 1 *Corinthians*, 13.12.
329 P&S, p. 57.

being connected with though not the cause of that of the soul.[330] The third heaven enrapturing St Paul is understood as the climax of this autonomous interior life, identified as the highest hierarchic level of 'sight': the 'vision' of the divine by the faculty not of 'corporeal' nor 'spiritual' but 'intellectual' sight.[331] In heaven, we shall be able directly to 'see' the invisible realities of the divine pervading all things; and 'the faith, by which we believe, will have a greater reality for us than the appearance of material things which we see with material eyes'.[332] Similarly Origen, in his commentary on *Canticles* (*In Canticum Canticorum*) explains that 'I sleep, but my heart waketh' (*Canticles* 5.2) refers to our condition in paradise where each of our physical senses will be reconditioned for a higher mode of purely spiritual perception. Correspondingly, contemporary paradisal and natural description observed, as we saw, 'an aesthetics of insubstantiality', refining materiality away into fragrance, odour and taste. In contrast to this patristic craving for spiritual disengagement from the bonds of the material is the medieval feeling for the utility and expressiveness of matter, for matter as the vehicle of spirit. For Aquinas and Dante, as for Aristotle, cognition *is* based on sensory experience: all our knowledge originates from sense.[333] With this cognitive model goes an aesthetics of 'accommodation', a readiness to realize eternal events in images of terrestrial reality, as Beatrice explains to Dante.[334] The medieval is thus a crystallizing habit of mind, a materially 'realising imagination',[335] translating idea into object in allegory, as readily as nature into supernature in theophany and portent. In Chaucer, perhaps parodically, the very words of men ascend to the 'Hous of Fame' bodied in the likeness of their speaker.[336] In a climate of developing interest in optics and the limitations of human perception, this habitual concern for the material correspondence of spiritual being expounds illumination and beatitude in terms not of the shedding but the extraordinary improvement of physical vision. In his twelfth-century *Vita Sancti Anselmi*, Eadmer tells how the saint, lying awake in his bed meditating on the scriptures, was able suddenly to gaze clear through the masonry of the dormitory and

330 *De Genesi ad Litteram*; discussed *CHLGEMP*, pp. 374–79.
331 2 *Corinthians*, 12.2–4; *De Genesi ad Litteram*, ch. 12.
332 *City of God*, 22.29, p. 1086.
333 Aquinas, *Summa Theologica* 1, q. 1, ad. 9.
334 *Paradiso*, 4.40–48.
335 Lewis, *Discarded Image*, pp. 206–07.
336 *Hous of Fame* in *Complete Works*, lines 1074–83, p. 292.

chapel to observe the monks preparing candles for matins.[337] The *Pearl* dreamer finds his vision able to pierce the shining city walls and dwellings of the heavenly Jerusalem.[338] Fifteenth-century Italian treatises *On the Sensible Delights of Heaven* by both Bartholomew Rimbertinus and Celso Maffei affirm that vision in paradise will be so keen as to discern the slightest graduations of colour and variations in form, and also to pierce solid bodies, seeing the front of an object from the back and the face through the back of the head.[339] The blessed, then, will be optical supermen, savouring like great painters the finest nuances of material loveliness and encompassing, like the artist's perspectival construction, all planes of a solid in a single visual field. This conception of beatitude as elevation to a corrected and mathematically objective material perception would, one feels, have outraged Augustine and Origen as sensory debasement.

Yet it expresses clearly that medieval approximation of the otherworld to the terrestrial developed to its radical sharpest in Dante, in the 'figural realism' of whose *Inferno* and *Purgatorio* 'the beyond is eternal yet phenomenal'. There, writes Auerbach, 'the waves of history do reach the shores of the world beyond'.[340] In the sensory precisions of the narrative, the material character of the *contrapassi* (punishments) and the enchantment of Eden, as well as the retention of memory of mortal past and concern for earthly future on the part of the dead, Dante's eternity becomes, in effect, a setting to magnify the essence of the historically ripened individual, framed in concretised sensualist landscapes. The nine circles of Hell and nine terraces of the mount of Purgatory are rendered in the most solid immediacy through a thousand inductions of temporal experience. On the burning sands where the violent are punished, the raining flakes of fire strike the ground without disintegration, like snow falling on windless heights. Dante makes a bed on a shelf of the Purgatorial mountain like a ruminating goat between two rocks, which impede his view yet still permit him to perceive stars larger and brighter than usual. The dazzling of his eyes by an approaching angel persists even after he has raised a shielding hand, for the brightness is refracted upward at an

337 *Vita Sancti Anselmi*, ed. and trans. R. W. Southern (London: 1962), pp. 12–13.

338 *Pearl*, lines 1049–50.

339 Bartholomeus Rimbertinus, *De Deliciis Sensibilibus Paradisi* (Venice: 1498), pp. 15 v. – 26 r.; Celsus Maffeus, *De Sensibilibus Paradisi* (Verona: 1504), pp. A viii v. – B ii r.; Baxandall, *Painting and Experience*, pp. 103–04.

340 Auerbach, *Mimesis*, pp. 197–98.

angle from the ground before him as light may strike upwards from a mirror or water.[341] Never before had this realism been carried so far. 'In the very heart of the other world, he created a world of earthly beings and passions so powerful that it breaks bonds and proclaims its independence'.[342] In becoming at home in the world the Middle Ages are becoming at home in the otherworld, their 'mythic space' itself achieving materiality, optical special conditions, landscapes.

Summary

We have seen that 'landskip' is different in kind from either the serial empiric particulars of Anglo-Saxon and Irish traditions, acute yet unco-ordinated into a view, or the depthless organization of Gothic art. Resurgent economic expansionism and the emergence of the middle classes promoted the social impulses we found constructing Gothic landscape-consciousness: the search for command over nature; commitment to the method of systematic logical reasoning upon observed material form; and the exuberant sense of nature as a resource of affluence and well-being, as luxurious fecundity. Early medieval landscape-writing is thus marked both by a nascent bourgeois 'scientific' and instrumental reason, and by rhapsodic intimations of ideality: the two often united through the legacy of the early church that material reality is a wondrous cathedral of living anagogues of divine truth. Symbolic thought and rigorous material observation may thus proceed hand in hand: just as we find it in manuscript illumination and cathedral foliage capitals, in Bonaventura and in *The Romance of the Rose*.

Gothic art remains, however, distinctively non-perspectival. The slow and uneven evolution of the post-Gothic art of landskip from the fourteenth to the sixteenth centuries arises with the return of that nexus of interests in space which we traced behind landskip development in the ancient world, and which, I have argued, are of a preponderantly secular mentality. The '*managerial space*' of venerable seasonal landscape acquires pictorial depth when allied with the impulse to display of '*possessive space*': Lorenzetti's industrious Siena, the Duc de Berri's soaring chateaux (plates 9 and 8) seek, unlike piety's timeless *genera* of reaped field and piled waggon, proudly specific definition in worldly time and space. These works are

341 *Inferno*, 14.28–33; *Purgatorio*, 27.67–92; *Purgatorio*, 15.7–30.

342 *Mimesis*, pp. 199, 200.

inventories of possession and manpower, assigned through the ultra-naturalism of perspective a local habitation and a name. Indeed the vaunt of the possessive eye establishes, as we saw, the very logic of the 'lateral perspective' technique in Lorenzetti, rhythmically diminishing figures and hinterland in relation to their distance from Siena's lofty gateway.

Such taste for topographic and ethnographic definition is also, we suggested, the 'domestic' aspect of the enthusiasm for '*comparative space*', for the delineation and contrast of varied lands and peoples, that arose with the excitement of a new geography. European expansion, the crusades and inter-continental trade and exploration all inevitably contribute to this comparativist appetite for the world's appearances. Travel scenery imprints its fascination in the realist metaphors of Dante and the fabulous accounts of Mandeville, promotes Mannerist panoramas and the Renaissance tradition of travelogue views. Oriental encounters stimulate enthusiasm for Persian-style paradise gardens, in vogue in romances and an active influence on the development in Venice of Christian Madonna-in-a-garden paintings (plate 7).

Both the aristocratic ethos of privileged display and the bourgeois experience of a diverse and fluctuating urban environment promote the artistic creation of '*quotidian space*': an order of representation, perhaps intrinsically secular, that profiles common scenes and daily experience rather than the mythological and hieratic, and becomes inevitably highly sensitive to the affective and expressive properties of sense-objects. Close artistic concentration on natural form and tone in the depiction of sports and picnics, tillage and hunting, of urban bustle and sexual *jouissance*, helps encourage in poetry a direct, sensuous relation to the material and natural world that is the contrary of the patristic legacy of 'closed' descriptive rhetorics and symbolic orientation.

The status of landskip as '*rational space*', finally, implementing through the scientific achievement of geometric perspective an intellectual achievement to equal those of classical antiquity, consolidates the emergence and popularity of landskip as a reliable, 'objective' representation of space.

We may clearly see that landskip, conceived both in theory and practice in terms primarily of space rather than of time, as 'prospects of the object', is a fundamentally secular product at the level of form, content nothwithstanding. It is the construction of reality as material extension; computed in accordance with optical laws formulated in a science without direct dependence on divine revelation; and frequently constituting as its field of interest the realm of terrestrial geography, everyday experience, economic ownership and political power. Even where its objects are religious figures and events, these are themselves 'made real' through their implication in the observed world of material and working life (plates 10 and 12). Italian walled towns and seigneurial fortresses topped by watchtowers, cultivated fields and grazing flocks, wide bridges and radiating roads are the regular pictorial adornment of late medieval and Renaissance crucifixions, martyrdoms and wilderness-saints.

Transformations of Christendom's territorial imagination also bear witness to the medieval revolution of its economic base. Agricultural expansionism and the rise of bourgeois city-culture shatter the old, fearful world-dualism of cultural space and demonized outlands. The realm of 'wilderness' is confidently subjected to elating penetration, and the great medieval forests become joyous greenwoods or places of enchanting sanctity. The idea of 'the countryside' is born, as the urban 'contra-terra' is constructed as a realm of urban and courtly recreation and idealization. Finally, the 'otherworld' of Eden and paradise is itself subjected to a more materialist conception, as the blessed are credited with optical superpowers and otherworldly landscapes are defined in a more concrete sensory mode than has existed since Greco-Roman antiquity.

6

Seventeenth-century English poetry

The landscapes of seventeenth-century English poetry recapitulate almost the entire history of western descriptive sensibility: a garden in which exquisite forms of diverse origin are ornamentally reassembled, like the statuary of the Earl of Arundel. Christian hieroglyph and three-dimensional pictorialism, Biblical 'declarative' landscape and Greco-Roman personifications are all shipped into a new literary climate of unprecedented descriptive versatility.

The briefest conspectus of the field in terms of our methodological concern with categories of perception makes evident this extended choice among ways of seeing and presenting for poets of the time. In the 'ecological' category consciousness of laborious agriculture lingers, though the rise of a self-occupied metropolitan culture renews a marginalizing, idyllic vision akin to the imperial Roman: the merchant's fanciful reverie of Horace's Alfius.[1] In the 'cosmographic' category, the ferment of scientific and religious ideas excites the eye to fertile empiricism, while the impact of telescope and microscope[2] revolutionizes the sense of dimension. The 'analogical' habit of mind exercises itself eagerly in nature, meditating anagogues in the manner of the emblem books,[3] choreographing flowers and trees in courtly appropriations of the pastoral hyperbole,[4] and re-creating a poetics of delicate sensuous simile. Above all, 'technoptic' perception sets poets emulating the painters' feat of 'landskip'. 'Upon Appleton House' exemplifies all four categories: as Marvell wanders the Fairfax estate, he engages landscape as ecological space (agricultural labour and the

1 Horace, *Epode*, 2.

2 Marjorie Nicolson, 'Milton and the Telescope', in *English Literary History*, 2, 1935, 1–32; also her *Science and Imagination* (Ithaca: 1956). For 'microscopic' poetics see also Kitty Scoular, pp. 84–6.

3 Rosemary Freeman, *English Emblem Books* (London: 1948).

4 See J. B. Leishman's discussion of this as 'Clevelandish wit' in *Art of Marvell's Poetry*, pp. 221–46.

grove's 'refuge values'), as analogical ('nature's mystic book'), as art (revolving 'scenery') and as a field of scientific curiosity (riddling optics and the intrigue of organic metamorphosis).

In many of its aspects, the period's nature-sensibility has received abundant scholarly documentation. Seventeenth-century science and technology,[5] cosmological controversy and mystical traditions,[6] travel literature and the cult of rural retreat,[7] pictorial landscaping and 'georgic' description,[8] all have received a coverage it would be pointless to reduplicate here. As such, there is no need with this chapter to initiate a characterization of the fundamentals of this well-mapped nature-sensibility; its basic lines of determination may be brought out with more originality in consideration of landscape-consciousness. This chapter is devoted therefore to a study more closely literary-critical than hitherto: one properly responsive to the fact that the period's conditions of perception and its range of descriptive resources stimulate in certain writers, above all in Milton, Marvell and Henry Vaughan, landscape writing that is extraordinary and novel not only in visual and tactile acuity, but in a new quality of experiential 'authenticity'. By the mid-century, descriptive poetry has so developed in expressive sophistication and artistic prominence that it may articulate in microcosm the most delicate textures and tensions of authorial subjectivity: landscape in poetry is now a record and medium of finely personal affectivity. With a view, then, to an original

5 Among many titles, see in particular *A History of Technology*, vol. 3, eds. Charles Singer, E. J. Holmyard, A. R. Hall and Trevor I. Williams (London: 1956); Charles Webster, *The Great Instauration* (London: 1975); R. F. Jones, *Ancients and Moderns* (1936; 2nd edn1961); John Prest, *The Garden of Eden: The Botanic Garden and the Recreation of Paradise* (London: 1981).

6 Francis Yates, *Giordano Bruno and the Hermetic Tradition* (London: 1964); Kitty Scoular, *Natural Magic*; Keith Thomas, *Man and the Natural World* (London: 1983); Stanley Stewart, *The Enclosed Garden* (London: 1966); Victor Harris, *All Coherence Gone* (Chicago: 1949).

7 J. W. Stoye, *English Travellers Abroad: 1604–1667* (London: 1952); Ruth Pitman, *Landscape in Poetry from Spenser to Milton*, B. Litt. thesis: University of Oxford: 1964; M. C. Bradbrook, 'Marvell and the Poetry of Rural Solitude', *R.E.S.* 17, 1941, 37–46; Marie-Sofen Røstvig, *The Happy Man*, vol. 1 (Oslo and Oxford: 1954); Janette Dillon, *Shakespeare and the Solitary Man* (London: 1981).

8 James G. Turner, *Topographia and the Topographical Poem in English: 1640–1660*, D.Phil. thesis, University of Oxford: 1976; also his *The Politics of Landscape* (Oxford: 1979); Anthony Low, *The Georgic Revolution* (Princeton: 1985); H. V. S. and Margaret Ogden, *English Taste in Landscape in the Seventeenth Century* (Michigan: 1955); H. M. Richmond, *Renaissance Landscapes* (The Hague and Paris: 1973).

and a more literary study, this chapter will focus three central tendencies in seventeenth-century verse landscape: the idealizing tonality, the development of empirical and 'phenomenological' description, and the evocation of landscapes of animistic energy and of struggle.

The paradisal tonality

'If Eden be on earth at all, / Tis that, which we the *country* call'.[9] Country air in the mid-seventeenth century is redolent with the spices of paradise. We may identify, I think, at least four causes responsible for suffusing English meadows with the apparency of unearthly loveliness. Millenarian beliefs fountained anticipations of reawakening paradise; whilst idealizations of the countryside that drew with new urgency on components of the traditional conception of paradise were virtually compelled by three social and political developments. Urban separation from the field labour whose harvests it appropriated fostered the mirage of self-producing nature; radical disturbances of landownership produced passionate nostalgias of 'true' possession and settled rural security; courtly propaganda and the cavalier self-image promoted 'luxury' landscapes of costliness, ease and merriment.

The millenarian dawn

By the middle of the seventeenth century jeremiads on the decay and senescence of nature, her harvests ever thinner, her aged sun paling, her swarms of insects and disease multiplying yearly,[10] had been shouldered aside by powerful millenarian optimism. There had been apocalyptic overtones in the poetry of Spenser and the older 'Spenserian' poets such as Greville, the Fletchers and Samuel Daniel, descending with this tradition to William Browne and George Wither.[11] The scientific optimism of Bacon and early experimental scientists had carried a millenarian charge. But with the 1640s and 1650s, the absence of the normal restraints allowed millenarian

9 Henry Vaughan, 'Retirement' (III), lines 27–28, in *Henry Vaughan: The Complete Poems*, ed. Alan Rudrum (Harmondsworth: 1976).

10 R. F. Jones, *Ancients and Moderns*, pp. 22–24.

11 David Norbrook, *Poetry and Politics in the English Renaissance* (London: 1984), chs. 3, 5–9.

rhetoric to race at all levels of society.[12] That Christ was soon to establish his new Earthly Paradise, and that the chosen site of the new Eden was England, accounts for much of the 'fascination with gardens, paradises and a restored state of innocence in the poetry of the first half of the seventeenth century'.[13] The landscape of Eden could be designer-built by new learning. Walter Blyth, the agricultural reformer, thought that England 'might be made the Paradise of the world, if we can bring ingenuity into fashion'.[14] Oxford's Botanic Garden, founded in 1621 and completed in 1640, was conceived as a restoration of Paradise as the ordered recreation of nature's totality. In this thinking, the discovery of new flora in America at last permitted complete knowledge of nature; possession of all the world's herbs facilitated remedy of all disease; while shading walls and planted evergreens re-achieved the *ver perpetuum.*[15] Evelyn's *Kalendarium* recommended that our gardens be made 'as near as we can contrive them' to resemble Eden;[16] and, influenced by the Botanic Gardens of Padua, Pisa and Paris, he commended a miniature version of their features for incorporation into great noble gardens.[17] Moreover, the earth of herself was now perhaps re-evolving her pristine perfection. Hakewill, foremost demolitionist of deteriorationist thought, in his *Apology* of 1627, was anticipating a massive increase in the earth's abundance, while the Biblical commentator John Stoughton prophesied that the land would become more fruitful, mountains regenerate precious stones, and Eden be once more revealed.[18]

Particularly striking within the logic of this climate is its expansionist, centrifugal sensibility, its enthusiasm for paradisal holiness as overflowing beyond enclosed precincts, in sharp contrast with the *hortus conclusus* tradition and the Catholic reverence of sacred ground. Samuel Hartlib and John Evelyn urged the planting of apple, pear, quince and walnut trees over every piece of waste ground across

12 Christopher Hill, *Milton and the English Revolution* (1977; new edn London: 1979), ch. 22.

13 Graham Parry, *Seventeenth Century Poetry: the Social Context* (London: 1985), pp. 13, 118.

14 Webster, *Great Instauration*, p. 86.

15 John Prest, *Garden of Eden*, pp. 42–86.

16 John Evelyn, *Kalendarium* (London: 1664), Introduction.

17 Prest, pp. 47–48.

18 George Hakewill, *An Apologie, or Declaration of the Power and Providence of God in the Government of the World* (Oxford: 1627). See Ronald W. Hepburn, 'George Hakewill: The Virility of Nature' in *Journal of the History of Ideas*, 16 (1955), 135–50; Webster, *Great Instauration*, p. 17.

the breadth of England, a paradisal reclamation of wilderness for delight and communal plenty on the grandest scale.[19] Milton's contempt for veneration of consecrated ground was common enough among Protestants defending their purchase of former church lands,[20] but he extended this 'levelling' of all land to an equal sacramental fitness into the poetry of *Paradise Lost*, and devalues even Eden to the status only of a 'capital seat' in a militant understanding of divine omnipresence.[21] Vaughan and Marvell each counterpose the sacramentality of open natural landscape to the sterility of conventional enclosure. 'No mercy-seat of gold', insists Vaughan, 'no dead and dusty *Cherub*, nor carved stone, / But his own living works did my Lord hold / And lodge alone; where *trees* and *herbs* did watch and peep',[22] while Marvell's Mower laments of formal gardens:

'Tis all enforced, the fountain and the grot,
While the sweet fields do lie forgot:
Where willing nature does to all dispense
A wild and fragrant innocence.[23]

The endemic enthusiasm of the mid-century for emblem books[24] exemplifies the same inspiration, in which all nature may appear deiform. 'The moral lessons and spiritual types that previously were shut up within literary confines were now to be sought not only in books but in the stuff of life itself.'[25] The very word 'landscape' is invested in the seventeenth century with optimistic connotations, signifying the fair view of countryside as gliding from darkness into sunlight.[26]

Inevitably, the millenarian momentum stimulating 'the general instinct of holy and devout men' and revealing 'all concurrence of

19 Prest, *Garden of Eden*, p. 92.

20 Keith Thomas, *Religion and the Decline of Magic*, pp. 58–59, 65–67, 114–21.

21 *Paradise Lost*: 11.286–354. See Chris Fitter, 'Native Soil': The Rhetoric of Exile Lament and Exile Consolation in 'Paradise Lost' in *Milton Studies*, 20 (1984), 147–162.

22 'The Night' in *The Complete Poems of Henry Vaughan*, ed. Alan Rudrum (Harmondsworth: 1976), lines 19–23.

23 'The Mower Against Gardens' in *Andrew Marvell: The Complete Poems*, ed. Elizabeth Story Donno (Harmondsworth: 1972), lines 31–34.

24 Freeman, *English Emblem*, ch. one.

25 Scoular, *Natural Magic*, p. 14.

26 Turner, *Politics*, pp. 21–24; compare Richard Blome in *The Gentleman's Recreation* (London: 1686), p. 226, drawing on Peacham's *Graphice* (London: 1612): a 'landskip is the expressing the perfect vision of the Earth.' Ref. John Dixon Hunt, *The Figure in the Landscape* (London: 1976), p. 39. Cf. also Ogden and Ogden, *English Taste*, pp. 49–50.

signs'[27] to God's Englishmen touched common natural sights with visionary enchantment and promise. Traherne writes that his religious appetite 'did incessantly a Paradice / Unknown suggest, and som thing undescried / Discern',[28] and he finds the childhood faculty of surcharged vision, 'A *Seeming* somewhat more than View / That doth instruct the mind', so revitalised that mere reflections of sky and feet in puddles are urgent with suggestion of a spiritual 'new Antipodes'.[29] To Lucretius the phenomenon had merely exemplified the waywardness of optics.[30] 'Surely light is so broke out that it will cover the earth' cries Winstanley:[31] and the expectation of Time's great new dawn may well have heightened appreciation of dawn's return. 'How fresh, O Lord, how sweet and clean / Are thy returns!' breathes Herbert.[32] Celebration of early rising,[33] a standard schoolboy theme, is perhaps refreshed by the 'noble and puissant nation rousing herself like a strong man after sleep'[34]: Herrick advises Corinna 'tis sin / Nay, profanation to keep in'.[35] Vaughan repeatedly hymns the 'early, fragrant hours', 'the only time / That with thy glory doth best chime, / All now are stirring, every field / Full hymns doth yield',[36] while Winstanley writes:

> The windows of heaven are opening, and the light of the son of righteousness sends forth of himself delightful beams and sweet discoveries of truth ... The warm sun will thaw the frost and make the sap to bud out of every tender plant that hath been hid within ... Now the tender grass will cover the earth, the Spirit will cover all places with the abundance of fruit.[37]

27 Milton, *Areopagitica* in *Complete Prose Works* (Yale), vol. 2, p. 553.
28 'Desire' in *Centuries, Poems and Thanksgivings*, ed. H. M. Margoliouth (Oxford: 1958), vol. 2, lines 10–12.
29 'Shadows in Water', in ibid., lines 4–5, 38.
30 *De Rerum Natura*, 4.414–19.
31 'The Law of Freedom in a Platform' in *Winstanley: The Law of Freedom and Other Writings*, ed. Christopher Hill (Harmondsworth: 1973), p. 354.
32 'The Flower' in *The Works of George Herbert*, ed. F. E. Hutchinson (Oxford: 1941), lines 1–2.
33 For example, Spenser, 'Epithalamium', stanza 5; Milton, 'Carmina Elegiaca'.
34 Milton, *Areopagitica*, p. 558.
35 'Corinna's Going A-Maying' in *The Poetical Works of Robert Herrick*, ed. L. C. Martin (Oxford: 1956), lines 11–12.
36 'The Dawning' in *Complete Poems*, lines 9, 13–16; compare 'The Day-Spring', 'The Morning-Watch', and 'Rules and Lessons' stanzas 1–5.
37 In *The Writings of Gerrard Winstanley*, ed. G. H. Sabine (Cornell: 1941), p. 207.

Urban distance

Independently of millenarian stimulus, idealizing tendencies in landscape-consciousness flow from a sociological development of the highest importance, the growth in London of a rapidly expanding commercial metropolis. London's population grew from about 60,000 in 1500 to about 450,000 in 1640;[38] by the end of the seventeenth century perhaps one-sixth of England's total population spent at least part of their lives there, 'many of them returning to their rural communities with newly acquired urban habits of living'.[39] Urging foundation of agricultural colleges, Cowley frankly concedes of agriculture that 'the Utility of it (I mean plainly the Lucre of it) is not so great now in our Nation as arises from Merchandise and the trading of the City'.[40] Moreover, the continuing sprawl of the city's suburbs was such that one had by the early seventeenth century to walk as far as Islington even to hear a cuckoo.[41] The overwhelming majority of mid-seventeenth-century poets accordingly write within cultures of metropolitan or courtly orientation, whose material interests and social experience are decisively distinct from the older world of primary, unremitting struggle against nature. That artistic construction of the rural as the 'other' of the city which we have traced in the late Middle Ages now dominates bourgeois as well as noble perspectives. The terms 'countryman' and 'country-seat' derive from the late sixteenth century, and 'countryfied', 'bumpkin' and 'country bumpkin' from the mid-seventeenth. 'Urbane' and 'rustic' acquire their modern social implications in the same period.[42]

The formerly 'aristocratic' engagement of the countryside as a field of seasonal pleasure, the recreative golden world of Folgore da San Gemignano, is consolidated and disseminated in seventeenth-century England by the final dissolution of the fief system. The monetarization of labour relations tended to see hereditary local magnates either displaced by profiteering landowners unrestrained by paternalist traditions, or absconding to the capital for the developing London 'season'. Repeatedly and fruitlessly, royal proclamations are issued

38 Lawrence Stone, *Causes of the English Revolution: 1529–1642* (London: 1972), p. 70.
39 Thomas, *Religion and the Decline*, p. 4.
40 Abraham Cowley, 'Of Agriculture' in Abraham Cowley, *Essays, Plays and Sundry Verses*, ed. A. R. Waller (Cambridge: 1906), p. 401.
41 M. St Clare Byrne, *Elizabethan Life in Town and Country* (1925; 7th edn, London: 1961), p. 83.
42 Williams, *The Country and the City*, p. 369.

commanding the gentry to turn to their estates: in 1603, 1622–24, 1626–27, 1630, 1632, 1639 and 1640. Wealth made in court or commerce thus fêtes itself in a countryside that is often more a displaycase and play-world than a practical soil of community and grind. 'The explosion of architectural construction – the biggest boom in country-house building in English history'[43] threw up between the mid-sixteenth and mid-seventeenth centuries 'piles' of 'envious show / Of touch, or marble ... polished pillars, or a roof of gold',[44] in whose gardens banqueting houses were confected, whilst lodges penetrated sites of delicious 'romancey' seclusion.[45] In royal progresses, the pastoral hyperbole was realized in a literal transfiguration of the landscape before the royal feet, undulations of land being levelled and whole lakes dug. Visiting Lord Hertford in the autumn of 1591, Elizabeth was met by Hours and Graces who sprinkled flowers in her path as they sang of the spring that her presence rekindled.[46]

The natural world is perhaps most evidently conceived as a realm of pacified, recreative otherness in noble gardens. European gardens, often 'veritable compendia of idea and image',[47] become, as it were, 'inter-territorial', incorporating idealized images of wild nature. John Evelyn, visiting the Palace of Negros at Genoa in 1644, declares his favourite discovery the 'hilly Garden' where grey stone statues of shepherd, sheep and wild beasts stand among the rough-work of rocks and trees, so that 'casting your eyes one way, you would imagine your selfe in a Wildernesse and silent Country, side-ways in the heart of a great Citty, and backwarde in the middst of the Sea; and that which is most admirable, all this within one Aker of ground, and I thinke the most stupendious and delightfull in the whole World ... '[48] The ideal, found in Pliny, of a vantage-point scanning open fields beyond the garden is echoed in Bacon's 'Of Gardens', in Spenser and Milton, and its implementation in Bramante's Belvedere garden

43 Stone, *Causes*, p. 73.

44 Jonson, 'To Penshurst' in *Ben Jonson: The Complete Poems*, ed. George Parfitt (1975; rev. edn Harmondsworth: 1988), lines 5, 1–3.

45 Girouard, *Life*, pp. 106, 108. For 'romancey' scenery, cf. Leishman, *Art of Marvell's Poetry*, pp. 263–66.

46 Roy Strong, *The Renaissance Garden in England* (London: 1979), p. 48; Bruce R. Smith, 'Landscape with Figures: the Three Realms of Queen Elizabeth's Country House Revels' in *Renaissance Drama*, New Series 8 (1977), 57–115.

47 Hunt, *Marvell*, p. 91.

48 *Extracts from John Evelyn's Diary*, printed in Hunt and Willis, *Genius of Place*, pp. 60–61.

influences such English gardens as those at Hatfield, Moor Park and Hadham Hall.[49] The Roman tradition of a 'wilderness' is widely imitated in English gardens, with their thickets, grottos and mountains,[50] just as Stuart masques commonly feature wild nature tamed by art or the royal person. Salomon de Caus projected for Prince Henry at Richmond a bristling mountain eighty-four feet square by fifty-five feet high, to be topped by the speaking statue of a giant.[51] At Longleat, 'walks among woods and the wilderness with its summer-house upon the hillside could be read as a significant exercise in a "natural" taste compared with the canal, basins, squared gardens and fountains round the house'. Violent cataracts and 'theatres of water' representing storms and sea-monsters likewise ornamented European and Stuart gardens;[52] whilst landscape paintings of wild scenery decked their terrace walls and summerhouses.[53] Treatises on landscape painting desiderated scenic encyclopaedias of pastoral, urban, mountains and far sea.[54] In all this, the countryside, both the tended and the untamed, forms the complementary contents of a single framing box where sweets compacted lie. In sharpest contrast to the worlds of *Gilgamesh, Beowulf* and *Gawain* where the explorer-hero dares beyond a menaced cultural pale, the primitive is assimilated as a quaint alterity, a courtly lady's dangerless *frisson*. We are reminded of Bottom's most solicitous lion, and recognize in what we might christen the seventeenth-century *hortus inclusus* not only the incipient 'pleasing horror' of Salvator Rosa and Burke's 'Sublime', but the precursors of today's English 'safari' parks. Antique Roman gardens,

49 Spenser, *Faerie Queene*, 10.24.5 (the paradise of Venus' Temple); Milton, *Paradise Lost*, 4.144–45; Bacon, *Of Gardens*, printed in *Genius*, p. 55; Strong, *Renaissance Garden*, pp. 17–19, 181.

50 Strong, *Renaissance Garden*, pp. 14–15, 102, 138–41; Hunt and Willis, *Genius of Place*, pp. 8, 55, 98. Cf. the parallelism of pastoral drama and gardenist dramas of *boschetti* and marvels in Italy: James J. Yoch, 'Renaissance Gardening and Pastoral Scenery in England and Italy' in *Research Opportunities in Renaissance Drama*, 20 (1977), 35–43.

51 Strong, *Renaissance Garden*, ed. cit., pp. 101–2.

52 Hunt and Willis, *Genius*, p. 8, 64, 86; compare William Temple's praise of *Sharawadgi* or the Chinese aesthetic of naturalistic controlled irregularity, pp. 98–99.

53 Hunt, *The Figure in the Landscape*, p. 36. For the *frisson* of the primitive, including wilderness and saint, and ruin pieces, cf. Ogden and Ogden, *English Taste in Landscape*, pp. 52–53.

54 Cf. H. V. S. and M. S. Ogden, 'Principles of Variety and Contrast in the Seventeenth Century and the Poetry of Milton' in *Journal of the History of Ideas*, 10 (1949), 159–82.

with their caged animals and 'mannerist' marvels, and Nero's Golden House with its alternating woods, ploughland and formal order, had offered a similarly cosmopolitan splay of landscape types: a 'wine-tasting' relation intrinsic to cultures of 'commercial geography' and technological confidence. Hapsburg princes collected Brueghels[55] just as the luxurious courts of the Ptolemies enjoyed Theocritus' poetically shaggy Lycidas.

That most 'country' verse is actually *urbs in rure* has been well documented. The countryside, in Sidney's 'Sweet Woods', Marlowe's 'Passionate Shepherd', the Duke's opening speech in *As You Like It* and throughout most seventeenth-century verse is a greened town, site of banquets and choirs, philosophers and counsellors, amours and jewellery, 'painted' lodgings and softest beds.[56] Not only is 'the whole agenda urban':[57] the perfect retirement spots are close to the city. Hollar's prints celebrate the outskirts of London, as do Shirley's 'Hyde Park', Revett's 'Barn-Elms' and Sheppard's 'Journey to Totnam Court'.[58] The tone is caught perfectly in Jonson's epistle to Wroth at Durrants, urging the good fortune that

> Abed canst hear the loud stag speak.[59]

Even by night, nature's close otherness is fear-free, luxurious: one music of quilted living.

But country experience was now the epicureanism too of the London citizen. From the Elizabethan period the humanist cult of the individual encouraged temporary withdrawal from society as pleasurable,[60] whilst Protestantism traditionally counselled periodic solitude as spiritual wisdom. London's pollution heightened the sense of rural retirements as 'Retreat from the world, as it is man's; into the world, as it is God's', and Cowley writes in strikingly Dickensian terms of 'the monster London'.[61] Likewise Evelyn's *Fumifugium* of 1661,

55 Friedländer, *Van Eyck to Brueghel*, vol. 2, p. 139.

56 Compare the burlesque of such taste in *Appleton House*, stanza 88, where a complete drawing room rises upon the meadows.

57 Turner, *Topographia*, p. 280.

58 Ibid., pp. 280–84.

59 'To Sir Robert Wroth' in *Jonson: The Complete Poems*, line 22. Compare Sir Thomas Wortley who, Girouard records, built a lodge on a remote crag in 1510 'for his pleasure to hear the hart's bell'. Girouard, *Life*, p. 78.

60 Janette Dillon, *Shakespeare and the Solitary Man*, pp. 3–31.

61 Cowley, *Essays, Plays and Sundry Verses*, pp. 401, 396.

protesting against the city's air pollution, writes of its 'sooty jaws' resembling 'the suburbs of hell'.[62] Such a climate made almost inevitable Milton's comparison of Satan's escape from hell into Eden with a Londoner's excursion:

> As one who long in populous city pent,
> Where houses thick and sewers annoy the air,
> Forth issuing on a summer's morn to breathe
> Among the pleasant villages and farms
> Adjoined, from each thing met conceives delight,
> The smell of grain, or tedded grass, or kine,
> Or dairy, each rural sight, each rural sound.[63]

Anne Kemp praises Bassets-down Hill that 'Here are no smoaking streets, nor howling cryes ... No noysome smells t'infect, and choake the aire',[64] and Cowley asks 'Who, that has Reason and his Smell, / Would not among Roses and Jasmin dwell, / Rather than all his spirits Choak / With Exhalations of Durt and Smoak?', imagining that for country retreats the gods themselves quit their 'metropolis above'.[65]

Cotton's 'Lord! would men let me alone' in his praise of retirement[66] highlights the appeal of the countryside as escape from urban crowds and claustrophobia. Spenser's 'Bower of Bliss' had offered 'The dales for shade, the hilles for breathing space.'[67] Habington admits 'I hate the Countries durt and manners, yet / I love the silence,' enjoying the capital only during the summer vacation when 'We beginne / To live in silence'.[68] Gardenists like Evelyn seek intimacy in their arrangements, building 'solitudes and retirements,' an impulse overwhelming with the outbreak of the civil wars.[69] Throughout the first half of the century, however, the absence of monasticism may have reinforced the impulse to devotional retreat in gardens: 'For the Protestant the summer house replaced the cloister in which one might seek solitude and dwell on *contemptus mundi* and in which the trees and plants

62 John Evelyn, *Fumifugium* (1661; 1772 edn rpt. Oxford: 1930), p. 19.

63 *Paradise Lost*, 9.445–451.

64 Anne Kemp, 'Contemplation on Bassets-down-Hill', (1658), lines 25–27; a unique single leaf in Antony Wood's collection. Turner, *Topographia*, pp. 1–2.

65 Cowley, *Essays*, pp. 424, 395.

66 Charles Cotton, 'The Retirement' in *Poems of Charles Cotton*, ed. John Buxton (London: 1958), stanza 10.

67 *The Faerie Queene*, 2.12.58.6.

68 'To My Noblest Friend, I. C. Esquire', lines 1–2, and 'To My Worthy Cousin, Mr. E. C. In Praise of the City Life', lines 24–25, in *The Poems of William Habington*, ed. Kenneth Allott (Liverpool: 1948), pp. 95, 77.

69 Hunt, *Figure in the Landscape*, pp. 30–31.

become ladders of contemplative ascent.'[70] The cult of the solitary melancholy man encouraged in seventeenth-century portraits and gardens the impulse towards naturalistic space: the convention of greenwood tree, shade and brook, recurring in *Il Penseroso*.[71] The century's voluminous retirement poetry accordingly moves in a variety of directions, Neoplatonic, neo-stoic and neo-epicurean, producing 'innocent epicureans' and 'hortulan saints',[72] just as *L'Allegro* and *Il Penseroso* each mingle their tones between the contemplative and the recreative.[73]

Landscape verse can thus appear as the epitome of the frivolous poetic vogue: 'Is it no verse, except enchanted groves / And sudden arbours shadow course-spunne lines?' demands Herbert, echoed by Vaughan's lament that the Cotswolds' shades and groves are 'idolised' to the exclusion of the Mount of Olives. Marvell hastily bundles away his quills and angles, 'toys' and 'pleasures slight' at the appearance of the high-minded Maria; and the period ambivalence over prettinesses footling parallels imperial Roman strictures on landscape purple passages in the *Ars Poetica*.[74] Yet to an urban-raised devotionalism, the countryside's beyondness may prove truly numinous. 'The [city] gates were at first the end of the world. The green trees when I saw them first through one of the gates transported and ravished me' recalls Traherne. Evoking childhood excitement within Hereford, he writes:

> The streets like Lanes did seem,
> Not pav'd with Stones, but green

precisely the contrary of Herrick's merely fashionable invitation to the country:

70 Strong, *Renaissance Garden*, p. 211.

71 *Il Penseroso*, lines 133–39; Strong, *Renaissance Garden*, 215–19.

72 Phrases from Marie-Sofen Røstvig, *Happy Man*, pp. 227, 119. For categories of retreat poetry, see M. C. Bradbrook, 'Marvell and the Poetry of Rural Solitude', *Review of English Studies*, 17 (1941), 37–46; for further studies of the motif of rural solitude see Dillon, chs. 1 and 2; Turner, *Politics*, ch. 5; Leishman, *Art of Marvell's Poetry*, ch. 6; Ruth Wallerstein, *Seventeenth Century Poetic* (Madison, Wisconsin: 1950), pp. 264–77; and H. M. Richmond's survey of Petrarch and Ronsard in this regard, *Renaissance Landscapes*, pp. 38–76.

73 *L'Allegro*, lines 129–30 as against 69–70; *Il Penseroso*, lines 131–54 as contrasting lines 49–50.

74 Herbert, 'Jordan' (1.), lines 6–7; Vaughan, 'Mount of Olives' (1.), lines 1–16; Marvell, *Appleton House*, stanza 82; Horace, *Ars Poetica*, 15–17.

Come, my Corinna come; and coming, mark
How each field turns a street, each street a park.[75]

Another strain of distinctively urban idealization of nature is the 'consumerist' perspective of pleasured consumption. James Turner has noted the mercantile language entering landscape description in the seventeenth century: 'Flowers and plants combine' like early capitalists

That in those sweet Exchecquers they
May that stock of spices lay,
Which (like Easterne winds) thy breath
Does to'th perfum'd ayre bequeath.[76]

More prominent, however, is an identification of nature with an almost sycophantic servitude and wealth, a culmination of that form of feeling we located as arising in the High Middle Ages with the development of bourgeois hunger for material agency and noble fantasies of gardens of plenitude. Herrick's joy in returning to London as 'everlasting plenty'[77] exposes the enabling metropolitan appropriationism enjoyed by those classes who write comfortably of 'Nature's endless treasure', and 'the great Treasury of Nature's Womb'.[78] Vaughan marvels over 'all the vast *expense* / In the Creation shed,' thanks God that he 'fills the world's unemptied granaries', and thrills to 'The unthrift Sun' that can shoot 'vital gold. A thousand pieces'.[79] Revett conceives corn as 'the rich-bowel'd earth burst out':[80] gold in natural combustion. Similarly Herbert is sure that 'More servants wait on Man, / Than he'l take notice of', thanking God for nature as 'our cupboard of *food*, / Or cabinet of *pleasure*': 'Thy cupboard serves the

75 Thomas Traherne, *Centuries*, 3.3; and 'Christendom', lines 81–2; in *Centuries, Poems and Thanksgivings*; Herrick, 'Corinna's Going A-Maying', lines 29–30 in *Poetical Works*.

76 Thomas Philipott, *Poems*, ed. L. C. Martin (London: 1946), p. 32; Turner, *Politics*, p. 138.

77 'His Return to London' in *Poetical Works*, line 8.

78 Cowley, 'The Royal Society' in *Abraham Cowley: Poems*, ed. A. R. Waller (Cambridge: 1905), line 27; anonymous late seventeenth-century poem, 'How beautiful the World at first was made', in *The Oxford Book of Seventeenth Century Verse*, ed. H. J. C. Grierson and G. Bullough (Oxford: 1934), p. 954.

79 *The Tempest*, line 18 (my italics), 'Rules and Lessons', line 100, and 'Regeneration', lines 41–42, in *The Complete Poems*.

80 'Summer' in *Eldred Revett: Selected Poems Humane and Divine*, ed. Donald M. Friedman (Liverpool: 1966), line 8.

world.'[81] Habington cannot doubt nature's unstinting providence that 'apparels lilies in their white' and 'affords A feather'd garment fit for every bird.'[82] Taking a hint perhaps from Spenser's denial that nature is 'niggard',[83] Milton is assured of nature as 'good cateress', agreeing with Comus that she 'pour(s) her bounties forth' with 'a full and unwithdrawing hand, / Covering the earth with odours, fruits, and flocks, / Thronging the seas with spawn innumerable.' In *Paradise Lost* 'Nature boon / Poured forth profuse on hill and dale and plain' flowers worthy of paradise, and 'spread her store' across irriguous valleys.[84] Country House poetry carries this 'unseen hands' view of natural fertility as spontaneous, sybaritic providence to an extreme. Nature as pleasuring, freely producing agency, as actively servicing mankind, laying on all things for languid human tippling, crushing the grape onto the mouth as in a Poussin 'Bacchus', emerges in the sumptuous, child-reached fruit of 'Penshurst', the pheasants and partridges 'willing to be killed', the self-sacrificing flocks of Saxham.[85] If such motifs represent 'the familiar hyperboles of the aristocracy and its attendants', concealing 'the brief and aching lives of the permanently cheated' who actually drudge all lifetime to coerce nature into plenty,[86] it is nonetheless a poetics of consumption whose tonality is shared by those middle-class writers and London citizens who likewise enjoy a labour-free relation to natural fertility. For Herbert providence means 'The beasts say, Eat me', whilst Marvell's delirious 'Ripe apples drop about my head'[87] is in part, we can see, a parody of this line of feeling. This myth of self-producing nature deliberately re-activates, of course, the *sponte sua* motif of the classical Golden Age,[88] yet without comprising a blatant falsehood for those who write it. Biblical praise, we have seen, reinforces it, though the

81 *Man*, lines 43–44, 29–30, and *Providence*, line 49, in *The English Poems of George Herbert*, ed. C. A. Patrides (London: 1974).

82 *To Castara*, lines 6, 3–4, in *Poems*.

83 *The Faerie Queene*, 2.12.50.7.

84 *Comus*, lines 764, 710–13, *Paradise Lost*, 4.242–43, 255, in *Poems*.

85 Ben Jonson, 'To Penshurst', lines 39–44, 28–30, in *Complete Poems*; 'To Saxham', lines 21–28, in *Poems of Thomas Carew with his Masque Coelum Britannicum*, ed. Rhodes Dunlap (Oxford: 1949).

86 Williams, *Country and the City*, pp. 46, 70.

87 'Providence', line 21, in *English Poems*; Marvell, 'The Garden', stanza 5, in *Complete Poems*.

88 Hesiod, *Works and Days*, lines 117–18; Virgil, *Eclogues*, 4.18–45; *Georgics*, 1.125–54; Ovid, *Metamorphoses*, 1.90–112; Lucretius, *De Rerum Natura*, 2.1158–59.

nervous, propitiatory acclamation underlying *Psalms* is very different in aim from the refined orgiastics, the proprietary Pomona, of the seventeenth century; and the vision of nature as effortless, prodigal largesse was much stimulated by its apparent authentication in the New World, 'Where nature hath in store, / Fowle, venison and fish, / And the fruitfull'st soyle, / Without your toyle.'[89]

The urban and courtly disengagement from an antagonistic relation to nature is reflected in a pained ambivalence toward animal slaughter. In contrast to the embellished blood-lust of the feudal *Livre de Chasse*, the hunting scenes and pig-sticking of Calendar art, and the seigneurial expertise in disembowelling in *Gawain*, Izaak Walton commands as the most fitting recreation in natural landscape 'the irreprovable employment of fishing'.[90] Hunting, he notes, was forbidden by the Fathers as 'turbulent, toilsome, perplexing'.[91] But the queasiness is urban. During the later Middle Ages civic authorities had tried to drive shambles outside town walls as offensive; in More's *Utopia* freemen were not allowed to witness animal slaughter. With the seventeenth-century arguments for vegetarianism are becoming disseminated (by Evelyn among others), and thinkers from Matthew Hale to Isaac Newton confess to feeling unease over the killing of animals.[92] Jaques' compassion for Arden's gored deer, 'native burghers of this desert city',[93] is thus an early aporia in this new structure of paradisal feeling – this idyllic world, this natural cupboard, is blood-stained – just as James I's passion for hunting, and his favourite trick of plunging his legs into the stag's bowels, accorded ill with the Stuart accent on the arts of peace: 'The manners made me devise', Harrington remarked of James' hunt, 'the beasts were pursuing the sober creation'.[94] 'E'en beasts must be with justice slain' cries Marvell's Complaining Nymph; and a poetry of lament over lost pets, taking hints from the classics, is revived in the seventeenth century by Marvell, Drummond, Herrick and Cartwright.[95]

89 Michael Drayton, 'To the Virginian Voyage', lines 25–28, in *The Works of Michael Drayton*, ed. J. William Hebel, 5 vols. (Oxford: 1961), vol. 2. Cf. Marvell's 'Bermudas' and Waller's 'Battle of the Summer Islands'; and see Leishman, *Art*, pp. 278–82; Harry Levin, *The Myth of the Golden Age*, ch. 3.

90 *The Compleat Angler* (Everyman edn, London: 1906), p. 37.

91 Ibid., p. 39. 92 Keith Thomas, *Man and the Natural World*, pp. 292–94.

93 *As You Like It*, 2.1.23.

94 J. P. Kenyon, *The Stuarts* (1958; rpt. London: 1970), pp. 41–42.

95 'The Nymph Complaining for the Death of her Fawn', in *The Complete Poems*, line 16; for the lost pet poetry, cf. Scoular, *Natural Magic*, p. 99.

Andrew Marvell's feeling for nature grows from precisely this series of urban sentiments and contradictions. There is little in it of the medieval awareness of agriculture as a penal condition of intensive labour: even the Mower feels beloved by nature and integrated ('On me the morn her dew distills / Before her dainty daffodils'),[96] and his work, like that of Milton's Adam and Eve, is the struggle not to create but only to control and appropriate natural fertility. Marvell's agricultural metaphors likewise suggest effortless fecundity. (The 'fertile storm' that 'to the thirsty land did plenty bring', for instance, and 'the large vale [that] lay subject to [the] will', in 'The First Anniversary'.[97]) Though the verse employs such ancient descriptive structures as *chronographia* ('time-painting' through scenic activity) and the Catalogue of Delights,[98] the world portrayed is the early capitalist one of global trade, luxury products and deranging exchange-values. The Mower inveighs against the fetish of rarity flowers whose 'painted cheeks' are sought across the New World, against bulbs sold for a meadow, against sybaritic gardens of display.[99] (We may compare the poet Brian Fairfax's lament that oaks and acres are sold to purchase fans and satin beds, reducing country estates to a handful of landscape paintings and tapestries.[100]) Marvell's conceit of the cave in 'Clorinda and Damon' as a 'tinkling' 'concave shell' suggests an ornamental conch: the kind of thing that General Fairfax will have had in the cabinet of curiosities we know he kept at Nun Appleton. Nun Appleton, however, resists exchange-values, being a world where 'everything does answer use'.[101] Above all, Marvell registers the urban distance that is both exploitative and elegiac: a brutally functional hegemony coupled with a sorrowing sense of nature domineered and betrayed. The mower figure supersedes the shepherd in the pastorals precisely because he embodies a murderous relation to his fields, 'Depopulating all the ground.' In gardens, likewise, ''tis all *enforced*': a rueful perspective upon human ordering of

96 'Damon the Mower', stanza 6.

97 'The First Anniversary of the Government under His Highness the Lord Protector, 1655', lines 236–37, 285–88.

98 *Chronographia*: 'Damon the Mower', stanza 2; cf. Virgil, *Eclogues*, 2.8–13; Catalogue of Delights: 'Damon the Mower', stanza 7.

99 'Mower Against Gardens', lines 11–18.

100 Brian Fairfax, 'The Vocal Oak', British Library MS. Eg. 2146, f.3; Turner, *Politics*, p. 137.

101 *Appleton House*, line 62; 'Clorinda and Damon', lines 13–14.

growth in marked contrast to the Calendar tradition. Architects, alas, 'do square and hew / Green trees that in the forest grew', levelling whole forests to pastures, tyrannizing 'wild ... innocence'.[102] Such dissociated urban wistfulness, remote from the unsentimental imperatives of a subsistence-economy, prompts antipathy to deforestation elsewhere: in Drayton's *Polyolbion* (Song 17) and in *Il Penseroso*'s repugnance for the 'rude axe with heaved stroke'.[103]

The sense of alienation from nature, perennial to civilized societies, receives here, in Marvell, its fresh and distinctively metropolitan structure. Whilst to the medieval mind the marker of that alienation had been the harshness and violence of nature, the postlapsarian *maledicta in terra*, its form is now the harshness and the violence of civilization. The guilt of 'luxurious man', violating and corrupting, develops from 'The Mower Against Gardens' to Jean-Jacques Rousseau. The same shift of alienation from hardship to guilt had been made in the ancient world, the barren 'iron age' of Hesiod succeeded by the matricidal plough of Virgil. The same conditioning transition, from agrarian economy to instrumentalizing commercial metropolis, underlay both histories.

Paradise as settled ownership

'Hail, old Patrician Trees, so great and good! / Hail, ye Plebeian underwood!' With the seventeenth century, metaphors of settled social order frequently structure landscape perception, above all the metaphor of tenancy:

> Oh Fields! Oh Woods! When, when shall I be made
> The happy Tenant of your shade?[104]

Revett notes the winter departure of 'The tenant-birds' that 'paid a Rent to every tree / From their melodious treasurie'. Herbert wishes

102 'Damon the Mower', line 74; 'The Mower Against Gardens', line 31; 'A Dialogue between the Soul and Body', lines 43–44; *Appleton House*, line 4; 'Mower Against Gardens', line 34.

103 *Il Penseroso*, line 136. There were hard prosaic reasons for antipathy to felling: Evelyn's *Sylva* (1664) complained that glass- and iron-works, the spread of tillage and selfish greed for timber were devastating the forests, and in this popular work that went rapidly through four editions urged systematic planting. Glacken, pp. 484–89; Thomas, *Man and the Natural World*, pp. 198–99.

104 Cowley, 'Of Solitude', stanza 1, in *Essays, Plays and Sundry Verses*, p. 395; and 'The Wish', stanza 3, in *Poems*, p. 88.

himself, in his affliction, a tree: in which condition 'at least some bird would trust / Her household to me, and I should be just'.[105] Property relations in nature, we note, are fair: poets project onto landscape the paradisal absence of those inequities and instabilities they see in the social order foundering about them.

Through the seventeenth century both the precariousness of the hold on land by those in possession and the incidence of homelessness – the ultimate form of landlessness – escalate. The decades to 1660 see an ever vaster turnover in the land. As early as 1616, a Jonson character remarks:

> We see those changes daily: the fair lands
> That were the client's, are the lawyer's now;
> And those rich manors there of goodman Taylor's
> Had once more wood upon them, than the yard
> By which they were measured out for the last purchase.[106]

'It was agrarian plunder', remarks Tawney, 'which principally stirred the cupidity of the age, and agrarian grievances which were the most important ground of social agitation'.[107]

Subsequent to the devolution of tenurial relations onto a purely monetary basis, and the huge transfer of lands at the Dissolution, 'Rack-renting, evictions, and the conversion of arable to pasture were the natural result, for surveyors wrote up values at each transfer, and, unless the last purchaser squeezed his tenants, the transaction would not pay ... The psychology of landowning had been revolutionized, and for two generations the sharp landlord ... had been hunting for flaws in titles, screwing up admission fines, twisting manorial customs, and, when he dared, turning copyholds into leases.'[108] By 1660 the extirpation of the yeomen – the copyholders and small proprietors – was confirmed, the interregnum parliament of 1656 and Restoration parliaments proving equally adamant in their refusal to intervene.[109] But the most flagrant form of the new agrarian economics, swelling the pauper, vagabond and squatter population was enclosure. Sidney's

105 Revett, 'Winter', lines 19–22, in *Selected Poems*; Herbert, 'Affliction' (1), lines 59–60 in *English Poems*.

106 *The Devil Is An Ass*, 2.4.33–37.

107 R. H. Tawney, *Religion and the Rise of Capitalism* (1926; rpt. Harmondsworth: 1980), p. 143.

108 Ibid., pp. 145, 152.

109 Christopher Hill, *The Century of Revolution* (1961; 2nd edn, Wokingham, Berkshire: 1980), p. 127.

'Arcadia' had been written in a park created by evicting and levelling an entire village.[110] Things had not improved. Between 1640 and 1644 alone there were enclosure riots in twenty-six counties.[111] 'The rich', observed Henry Vaughan, 'eat the poor like bread'.[112] The parliament of 1656 rejected the bill that, for the last time, sought to check enclosures. As Christopher Hill so aptly puts it: 'The rich inherited the earth.'[113]

Yet even for the rich landlessness could strike. Between 1640–60 the lands of more than 700 Royalists were confiscated and sold, for over £1,250,000: 'It was an upheaval comparable with the dissolution of the monasteries.'[114] Lower down the scale, tenants of confiscated lands unable to produce written evidence of their titles were liable to eviction. At the bottom of the scale, the Digger movement, whose leader Winstanley saw his little colony on Cobham Heath finally routed in April 1650 after two years of brutal persecution, 'can plausibly be seen as the culmination of a century of unauthorized encroachment upon the forests and wastes by squatters and local commoners, pushed on by land shortage and pressure of population'.[115] Yet Winstanley saw the problem with absolute clarity: 'Do not all strive to enjoy the land? The gentry strive for land, the clergy strive for land, the common people strive for land; and buying and selling is an art whereby people endeavour to cheat one another of the land.'[116] If we add to all this the appalling conditions of the rural poor fortunate enough to be granted work – their wages officially fixed below the cost of subsistence,[117] their legal condition as propertyless excluding them from all constitutional power, condemned to the same legal status as foreigners or conquered peoples, suffering between 1620–50 years of hardship described as the most terrible in English history,[118] with acute food-shortages aggravated by forced billeting of troops – we can see how the sovereign dream of the age, reverie of

110 Tawney, p. 145. On enclosures in seventeenth-century verse, cf. Turner, *Politics*, pp. 122–25, 158–59, 163.

111 J. S. Morrill, *The Revolt in the Provinces* (London: 1960), p. 34.

112 'The Bee', line 10, in *Complete Poems*.

113 *Century of Revolution*, p. 129.

114 Ibid., p. 125.

115 K. V. Thomas, 'Another Digger Broadside' in *Past and Present*, 42, 58; ref. Hill, *Law of Freedom*, pp. 21–22.

116 *Law of Freedom*, p. 185.

117 Christopher Hill, *Change and Continuity in Seventeenth Century England* (London: 1974), p. 220.

118 P. J. Bowden, *The Agrarian History of England*, vol. 4, *1500–1640*, ed. J. Thirsk (Cambridge: 1967), p. 621; ref. Hill, *Law of Freedom*, p. 21.

rich and poor, is the dream of an undisturbed and settled security on a sufficiency of God's good land.

Winstanley perfectly expresses this truth from the angle of the poor. 'True religion and undefiled is to let everyone quietly have earth to manure.'[119] Panegyrics to power envy the same repletion that goes with landownership and its economic autonomy.

> [Thou] canst, at home, in thy securer rest
> Live, with un-bought provision blessed.[120]

A poetry of place comes into being with the Country House verse of the seventeenth century, precisely because land, always power, is a power now 'seen to be transferable and alienable'.[121] Penshurst and Saxham, praised by Jonson and Carew as timelessly settled estates, are themselves products of agrarian disturbance and courtly engrossment;[122] and the former house was extended in traditional Gothic style precisely to legitimize the Sidneys recent possession.[123]

One response to this phenomenon of landlessness and fear of landlessness was the revival of the paradisal motif of nature as commonality: held in common possession, or agent of common beneficence. The doctrine of the egalitarian state of nature, originally Stoic, passing into Virgil, Ovid, Seneca and Lucian[124] and subsequently into patristic theology, re-emerging with Wycliff and the Great Society,[125] was a poetic element of Golden Age fantasias, 'acorn-eating commonage',[126] which could yet become 'a revolutionary myth as soon as it was presented to the turbulent poor and fused with

119 *The Writings of Gerrard Winstanley*, ed. G. H. Sabine (Cornell: 1941), p. 428.
120 Jonson, 'To Sir Robert Wroth', lines 13–14, in *Complete Poems.*
121 George Parfitt, *English Poetry of the Seventeenth Century* (Harlow, Essex: 1985), p. 5; cf. also pp. 59–60. On Country House poetry as a genre, see William Alexander McClung, *The Country House in English Renaissance Poetry* (Berkeley: 1977); G. R. Hibbard, 'The Country-House Poem of the 17th Century', *Journal Warburg and Courtauld Institute*, 19 (1956); Paul Cubeta, 'A Jonsonian Ideal: 'To Penshurst', *Philological Quarterly* 42: 1 (1963); Alastair Fowler, 'Country House Poetry: The Politics of a Genre', in *The 17th Century*, 1: 1 (January 1986), 1–14; Williams, *Country and the City*, pp. 38–47; 54–56; 64; 72–77.
122 Williams, *Country and the City*, pp. 54–55.
123 J. C. A. Rathmell, 'Jonson, Lord Lisle, and Penshurst', in *English Literary Renaissance*, 1 (1971).
124 Virgil, *Georgics*, 1.125–54; Ovid, *Metamorphoses*, 1.135–36; Seneca, Epistle 90; Lucian, *Saturnalian Letters*, 1.
125 Norman Cohn, *The Pursuit of the Millennium* (1957; rpt. St Albans: 1970), pp. 187–97.
126 Levin, *Myth of the Golden Age*, p. 71; cf. also pp. 28–29, 87–92.

the phantasies of popular eschatology'.[127] At the explicitly revolutionary level, Winstanley movingly pleads that 'the earth be made a common treasury of livelihood to whole mankind, without respect of persons'.[128] The dream of a society where naught is 'cald mine or thine',[129] recurrent in Tudor literature from *Utopia* to Spenser and Chapman,[130] becomes urgent enough in the mid-seventeenth century for the propertied to encourage the muses to apostasy, confessing the landscapes of the Golden Age to have been in fact primaeval chaos: before 'division of the parts did breed / The publique harmony ...'

> Woods yet unto the Mountaines did not passe,
> Nor Heards beneath in grassy Meadowes feed,
> Nor Corne inrich the Middle Grounds; but Grasse,
> And woods, and stifled Corne, were shuffled in one Masse.[131]

But the dream lingered: persisting, when not a revolutionary politics, as a structure of feeling, an affective reflex, frequently summoned as a lyrical resource in landscaping. If Milton is conscious of political allegiances in declaring marriage to be 'sole propriety / In Paradise of all things common else', Marvell is not so in his juxtaposition to 'enforced' gardens of the sweet fields

> Where willing nature *does to all* dispense
> A wild and fragrant innocence.[132]

Denham likewise, praising the Thames, adds that its bounty is 'free and common'; whilst the delicious 'anatomical landscape' of Carew's mistress in 'The Rapture' is a 'common' 'enclosed' by 'greedy men'.[133] The motif's wide provenance reflects, it would seem, a revulsion, autonomous of political alignment, for the new ruthlessly individualistic conception of ownership: the post-feudal unconditional power of landowners to dispense at whim however immorally with 'their own', a new latitude including settlement of property entirely at pleasure in wills, and refusal of any economic independence to copyholders, left evictable at will.[134] The course of Country House

127 Cohn, *Pursuit*, p. 197.

128 *Law of Freedom*, p. 127.

129 Spenser, 'Mother Hubbard's Tale', line 149, in *Poetical Works*.

130 See Levin, *Myth*, pp. 87–92; Williams, *Country and City*, pp. 57–60.

131 Richard Fanshawe, *Shorter Poems and Translations*, ed. N. W. Bawcutt (London: 1964), p. 20.

132 *Paradise Lost*, 4.751–52; 'Mower Against Gardens', lines 31–34. (My italics.)

133 'Coopers Hill', line 180, in *The Poetical Works of Sir John Denham*, ed. Theodore Howard Banks (New Haven: 1969); 'The Rapture', line 19, in *Poems*.

134 Hill, *Century of Revolution*, p. 127.

poetry, at best able to praise only anomalous 'islands of charity in an otherwise harsh economy',[135] as it passes from Jonson's 'Penshurst' (1612) through Carew's 'Saxham' (c. 1620) to Lovelace's 'Amyntor's Grove' (mid-1630s), exhibits this derelinquishing individualism: declining from a celebration of communal co-operation and public responsibility to one of retreat into a private, epicurean ataraxia.[136]

The most striking instance of an urgent yet apolitical insistence upon the commonality of nature, a 'radical idea defused of its revolutionary content',[137] lies I think, in Traherne. As with Winstanley, the abjection of landlessness and poverty breed, in contemplation of landscape, a sense of rapturous potential fertility, the tantalized ecstasy of the dispossessed; but the reappropriation of land is by spiritual sublimation.

> The corn was orient and immortal wheat, which never should be reaped, nor was ever sown ... The skies were mine, and so were the sun and moon and stars, and all the World was mine ... I knew no churlish proprieties, nor bounds, nor divisions: but all proprieties and divisions were mine: all treasures and the possessors of them.

As an adult, he is able to believe of the phenomena of nature that 'They serve us all; serv wholy ev'ry One / As if they served him alone' because as a child he had perceived landscapes in such uncorrupted 'natural' terms:

> Cursed and devised proprieties,
> With envy, avarice
> And fraud, those fiends that spoil even Paradise,
> Flew from the splendour of mine eyes,
> And so did hedges, ditches, limits, bounds,
> I dreamed not aught of those,
> But wandered over all men's grounds,
> And found repose.[138]

This visionary love of nature, then, is mediated from deep-seated social agitation over property-relations that have become so inhuman

135 Williams, *Country and City*, p. 41.

136 Mary Ann McGuire, 'The Cavalier Country-House Poem: Mutations on a Jonsonian Tradition', in *Studies in English Literature*, 19 (1979), 93–108.

137 Christopher Hill, *The World Turned Upside Down* (1972; rpt. Harmondsworth: 1975), p. 413.

138 Thomas Traherne, *Centuries*, 3.3; 'Poverty', lines 73–74, 'Wonder', stanza 7: in *Centuries, Poems and Thanksgivings*, ed. H. M. Margoliouth, 2 vols. (Oxford: 1958).

as to popularly establish 'nature' as their impassioning contradiction. Landscapes are registered as part of an enrapturing counter-order of loving providence and abundant common inheritance, the ground of an ecstatic de-reification of identity. Traherne's consciousness of poverty, he explains, was an agony relieved when he remembered his personal importance as a beneficiary of providence and her riches in nature – an insight 'To enrich the Poor, cheer the forlorn'.[139] If nature as bounty derives from property as theft, reparation is made, for Traherne, purely on the level of a quietistic, compensatory aesthetics. Had Traherne's perspectives prevailed, a kind of nature-mysticism would have been the opium of the masses.

As it is, during the middle decades of the century consolatory aesthetic 'ownership' is often an opiate of the Cavaliers. Land litigation throughout the century is fierce – even the gentle mystic Henry Vaughan is often immersed in it[140] – and climaxes with the Interregnum in widespread parliamentary expropriations and desperate compounding to regain estates. Randolph, praising the chase in his invitation to country pleasures, notes:

> Our pleasures must from their own warrants be,
> For to my Muse, if not to me,
> I'm sure all game is free;
> Heaven, earth, are all but parts of her great royalty.[141]

We note the discomfited sense of proprietorial exclusion, and the *retaliatory* pleasure of imagination. The poet, says Randolph, is richer than the millionaire, for he owns Elysium, Hesperides, Tagus and Pactolus: 'Mine, mine is all: / Thus am I rich in wealth poeticall.' Robert Heath similarly consoles a fellow-poet who had failed to inherit land 'we have fields to walk in' on Parnassus.[142] Contemning 'dirty ore' and enslaving riches, Henry Vaughan promenades instead through his 'speculations', where

> I may be
> Lord of all Nature, and not slave to thee.

139 'Poverty', line 41.

140 F. E. Hutchinson, *Henry Vaughan: A Life and Interpretation* (Oxford: 1947), pp. 11–12, 224–37.

141 'An Ode to Mr. Anthony Stafford to Hasten Him into the Country', lines 69–72, in *The Poems of Thomas Randolph*, ed. G. Thorn-Drury (London: 1929).

142 Randolph, *Poems*, p. 28; Robert Heath, *Clarastella*, (London: 1650), f. G6; ref. Turner, *Topographia*, p. 395.

The world's my palace. I'll contemplate there,
And make my progress into every sphere.
The chambers of the *air* are mine; those three
Well furnished *stories* my possession be.
I hold them all *in capite*, and stand
Propped by my fancy there. I scorn your land.[143]

Enjoying a deep prospect, Henry Wotton revels that the '*Lordship* of the Feet' or proprietorial possession is offset by a '*Lordship* likewise of the *Eye*' whose '*Usurping sense*, can indure no narrow *Circumscription*.'[144]

I can enjoy what's yours much more than you,

claims John Norris to the owner of the landscape he is contemplating.

Your meadow's beauty I survey
Which you prize only for its hay ...
What to you care does to me pleasure bring;
You own the cage, I in it sit and sing.[145]

The imagination of common belonging, the unjust artifice of the new, absolutist ownership, are thus far from merely a poor man's topos. Izaak Walton, townsman angler, perfectly elides the motif of 'happier possession' with the classic sentiments of Virgil's 'O Fortunatos' passage.[146] In a memorable scene, the angler seats himself to admire a midsummer view – fish leaping at coloured flies on a silver stream, woods and groves spotting far hills, meadows at hand of lilies and lady-smocks – and ends in 'pitying this poor rich man that owned this and many other pleasant groves and meadows about me'. Quiet-spirited men, he concludes, 'enjoy what the others possess' without distraction by 'restless thoughts, which corrode the sweets of life'.[147] Secure himself on an urban commercial income, and writing during the seismic early years of the cavalier defeat,[148] it is even possible that he meant it. Landscape could be innocent pleasure as landownership could not.

143 Vaughan, 'The Importunate Fortune', lines 33, 35–42.
144 Henry Wotton, *Reliquiae Wottoniae*, p. 204.
145 'My Estate', in L. Birkett Marshall, ed., *Rare Poems of the 17th Century* (London: 1936), pp. 162–63.
146 *Georgics*, 2.458–74.
147 *The Compleat Angler*, p. 176.
148 First published in 1653, substantially revised and extended in a new edition of 1655.

The Cavalier self-image

The medieval and Renaissance aristocracy customarily enjoyed, authenticated and justified their social ascendency by imaging themselves as the bearers of an ideal form of life, a dream of grace that bordered enchantment. We have seen how the medieval fictions of courtly love and chivalry, the world of Froissart and Chastellain, produced in the International Style of 1400 a dualism that ordained naturalism for the lower orders whilst enveloping the nobility in stylized immaculacy. With the seventeenth century, the ostentation of privileged exclusiveness embroidered with its fine aesthetic textures no longer militarism and a cult of sexual devotion, but a leisured elegance among choice pleasures and costly *objets d'art*. In a Country House poem like Jonson's 'To Penshurst' we perhaps detect a dualism kin to the medieval: material security is precisely catalogued – the fat estate, whose lower lands bending to the river graze sheep, bullocks and calves whilst ponds stock carp, nearby woods pheasants, and orchards and espaliers supply varieties of fruit[149] – whilst the hyperboles of magical order gild the picture with a requisite higher perfection.

That the poetry of rural retreat is substantially a courtly fiction, its worldly renunciations an exercise in urbanity, its idyllicism furthering the purpose of royal proclamations, has been widely demonstrated.[150] But 'The Cavalier's *need* of sensuous beauty in all his surroundings',[151] the indispensability of soft refinements to his self-image, is real enough. He is allergic to roughness and prolonged exertion. Just as the Duke of Newcastle, though gallant on the field during the Civil War, instantly retired at the end of each battle 'to his delightful company, music, or his softer pleasures' refusing interruption for several days by even the King,[152] so Carew rejoices over his delivery from the 'bleak mountains' and 'sterile fern, thistles and brambles' of the Tweed in the expedition against the Scots in 1639, whence he can psychically convalesce in Wrest, 'steeped in balmy dew,' where:

149 'To Penshurst', in *Complete Poems*, lines 22–44.

150 Williams, *Country and City*, pp. 39–47, 54–55; Turner, *Politics*, pp. 4, 92, 123, 158; Norbrook, *Poetry and Politics*, pp. 188, 190–92, 201, 209, 242.

151 W. Lamont and S. Oldfield, ed., *Politics, Religion and Literature in the Seventeenth Century* (London: 1975), p. 83; cf. also pp. 92–94.

152 Edward Hyde, Earl of Clarendon, in *Selections from Clarendon*, ed. G. Huehns (Oxford: 1955), pp. 255–58.

the pregnant earth
Sends from her teeming womb a flow'ry birth,
And cherished with the warm sun's quick'ning heat,
Her porous bosom doth rich odors sweat
Whose perfumes through the ambient air diffuse
Such native aromatics as we use

and where nature's 'genuine sweets refresh the sense'.[153] The voluptuous sexualization of the landscape here, seductive as a mistress and fertile as an exemplary wife, represents a characteristic appetitive projection. The converse metamorphosis, in Suckling's satire, makes clear the interchangeability of woman and landscape as a site of pleasure. Lady Carlisle, whilst activating the garden she meanders, herself exudes 'rare perfumes' such as 'bean-blossoms newly out / Or chafed spices give'.[154] Tastefully lascivious, this is the ideal landscape characterised, in the Reverend Herrick's contented phrase, by 'cleanly wantonness'.[155] The Mistress, indeed, like Waller's Sacharissa, subjects landscapes to the same elevating transformation as the Cavalier's poetic imagination:

Her presence has such more than human grace,
That it can civilize the rudest place.[156]

Living deliciously – 'we eat and drink and rise up to play and this is to live like a gentleman, for what is a gentleman but his pleasures?'[157] – the landscape of the Cavalier's verse must be stress-free, work-free, blight-free: an exquisite *otium* silently contrasting with the georgic world of calloused hands, insects and mud. Further, I'd suggest, its naturally dazzling graces comprise a kind of topographic *sprezzatura*, just as the descriptive ecstatics of pricelessness project the ethos of conspicuous consumption[158] and display.

Charles I was a committed collector of landscape paintings: the total royal collection sold by the Commonwealth reveals a percentage

153 'To my Friend G.N., from Wrest', in *Poems*, lines 4, 8, 9–14, 18.
154 'Upon My Lady Carlisle's Walking in Hampton Court Garden Dialogue', lines 7–9, in *Works*.
155 'The Argument', to *The Hesperides*, line 6, in *Poetical Works*.
156 Edmund Waller, 'At Penshurst' (1), lines 7–8, in *Poems 1645 together with Poems from Bodleian MS Don 55* (Facs., Menston, Yorkshire: 1971).
157 Viscount Conway, cit. M. Walzer, *The Revolution of the Saints* (Cambridge, Mass.: 1965), p. 252; ref. Turner, *Politics*, p. 155.
158 For aristocratic conspicuous consumption, see Lawrence Stone, *The Crisis of the Aristocracy 1558–1641* (1965; abridged edn Oxford: 1967), pp. 249–67.

of landscapes higher than in any other known collection save that of the Countess of Arundel. For her part, an inventory of 1641 reveals that of 119 pictures hanging in her house at St. James' Park, 30 are called landscapes.[159] Inigo Jones was a great admirer of landscape, and travelled to Italy specifically in order to study it.[160] In court masques landscape is always prominent, the kinds of scenery being essentially the same as in landscape painting; and these masques frequently close in the representation of peace as rural views.[161] In verse, however, aristocratic taste is not for prospect: the countryside is contracted into miniature exquisites, tiny and close enough to the person to be 'private' pleasures, brilliant enough to be worthy of noble enjoyment: a glittering experience of landscape as ornaments, the rarities of flower and petal, raindrop and dew.

In his anthem to the Cavalier code, 'To live merrily, and to trust to good verses', Herrick opens with the concomitant natural splendour: 'For with the flow'ry earth / The golden pomp is come'. Trees here wear 'rich beads of amber', just as in Corinna's maying the dew 'bespangles' herb and tree, leaves shower 'gems', and dawn throws 'Fresh-quilted colours through the air'.[162] Herrick, once apprenticed as a goldsmith, takes a jeweller's delight in delicate miniatures; and the elfin goblet

> A pure seed-pearl of infant dew,
> Brought and besweetened in a blue
> And pregnant violet[163]

shows how smoothly the countryside as a field of exquisites is imbricated with a fairy topos reminiscent of Shakespeare. 'I sing of dews, of rains and piece by piece / Of balm, of oil, of spice and ambergris ... I write of groves, of twilights, and I sing / The court of Mab, and of the fairy King' runs 'The Argument' to 'the Hesperides'.[164] Perfumes and rich spices are thus integral to this epicurean tonality: 'sweets for the smell, sweets for the palate here'

159 Ogden and Ogden, *English Taste*, pp. 17–18. 160 Ibid., pp. 21–22.

161 John Norris, *The King's Arcadia. Inigo Jones and the Stuart Court* (London: 1973), pp. 159–84; Ogden and Ogden, *English Taste*, pp. 22–23.

162 'To Live Merrily, and to Trust to Good Verses', lines 3–4, 8; 'Corinna's Going A-Maying', lines 6, 19–20, 4: in Herrick, *Poetical Works*.

163 'Oberon's Feast', lines 21–23.

164 'The Argument' to *The Hesperides*, lines 7–8, 11–12.

sighs Carew of Wrest's estate, whilst Habington compares his mistress' breath with 'Th'Arabian wind, whose breathing gently blows / Purple to th'Violet, blushes to the Rose'.[165]

But the bejewelled landscape is sovereign. So inescapable is it that a few examples may suffice. Habington's dew that 'hangs a jewell on each corne' and 'liquid Pearle ... on every grass'[166] is the cliché given a twist by Wotton:

> Go, let the diving Negro seek
> For Gemmes hid in some forlorne creeke:
> We all Pearles scorne,
> Save what the dewy morne
> Congeals upon each little spire of grass;
> Which careless shepeards beat down as they pass;
> And gold ne're here appears,
> Save what the yellow Ceres beares ...[167]

Revett presents winter, with its 'Diamond-Ice' as a nobleman's retinue and banquet, with 'glittering cloth of silver frost' that 'strutting plate and stones uphold'.[168]

Cowley competitively appropriates such courtly opulence for the chaste pleasure of the garden. 'The prize of Bravery / Was by the Garden from the Palace won; / And every Rose and Lilly there did stand / Better attired by Nature's hand'. In the choice garden, the 'true Epicure' finds 'cheap and virtuous Luxurie'.[169] Strikingly, though a keen horticulturist, pioneer advocate of agricultural colleges, and one of the first men to be nominated for the Royal Society, Cowley will not break free from this decorative, essentially 'pastoral' description into 'georgic': no fresh perceptions enlarge the repertoire of the leisured genteel mode. Although at one level he 'moved meditative verse out into a garden of real things',[170] his horticultural endeavours are still given in mythological rather than descriptive style, and as products rather than process. Of his breakthroughs in grafting, for

165 Carew, 'To His Friend G.N., from Wrest', line 96, in *Poems*; Habington, 'To Castara, Upon a Trembling Kisse at Departure', lines 1–2, in *Poems*.

166 'To the Dew', lines 3, 16–17, in *Poems*.

167 Henry Wotton, *Reliquiae Wottoniae* (London: 1651), pp. '232'–'333', i.e. 532–33; Turner, *Politics*, pp. 135–36.

168 'Winter', lines 8, 10–11, in *Selected Poems*. For further instances of bejewelled description see Turner, *Politics*, pp. 137–40.

169 'The Garden', stanza 7 and stanza 6, in *Essays, Plays and Sundry Verses*.

170 Hunt, *Figure in the Landscape*, p. 14.

instance, we read that Daphne now 'blushes in her fruit' as bearing cherry, and the crab apple bears 'golden fruit, that worthy is / Of Galatea's purple kiss'.[171] Cowley frankly admits that what he has 'to say of the Country Life, shall be borrowed from the Poets, who were alwayes the most faithful and affectionate friends to it'.[172] As such, though his *Several Discourses by Way of Essays* (1688) includes the century's fullest collection of verse translations from Virgil and Horace on husbandry and country life, these merely 'bring together in a crowning summary the fruits of a century-long practice of extracting happy-husbandman poems from the classics without offending the English taste for gentlemanly leisure', and they effectively transpose georgic into pastoral, as a poetics of luxury and repose.[173]

'Where do we finer strokes and colours see' asks Cowley, than in natural vegetation.[174] The refining hint of decorative art is ubiquitous. Jonson's elegant landscaping of Wroth's path 'Alongst the curléd woods, and painted meads, / Through which a serpent river leads / To some cool, courteous shade, which he calls his'[175] (note the possessive touch again), textureless, manicured, deferential, a masque-like tableau of tranquillity, promotes the 'curléd' motif: such ringlets subsequently adorning the trees of Browne, Drayton and Milton.[176] For Cotton, the 'curléd brows' of the groves at Chatsworth are 'far above ... [the] Painter's baffled Art'.[177]

Perfume and spices, jewellery and coiffure usually preclude visual fidelity, yet occasionally confect an inspired touch. Strode's line on snow – 'the feather'd rayne came softly down'[178] – may possibly derive from pleasure in the sartorial article, but certainly evokes beautifully the texture, the weightless delicacy of snowfall. Again, the pre-existing language of jewelled opulence can supervene upon natural appearances to emancipate colour from form: Revett on a landscape of 'vegetable shine' which does 'Irradiate a Noon of Corn

171 'The Garden', in *Essays, Plays and Sundry Verses*, stanza 10.
172 'Of Agriculture', in ibid., p. 405.
173 Low, *The Georgic Revolution*, pp. 126–7; also pp. 17–18, 13.
174 'The Garden', in *Essays, Plays and Sundry Verses*, stanza 9.
175 'To Sir Robert Wroth', lines 17–19, in *Complete Poems*.
176 Leishman, *Art*, pp. 273–74, who traces the origin of the phrase to Sylvester's translation of Du Bartas.
177 Charles Cotton, 'The Wonders of the Peake', lines 1301, 1303, in *Poems of Charles Cotton*, ed. John Buxton (London: 1958).
178 William Strode, 'On Chloris Walking in the Snow', line 2, in *Poetical Works*, ed. Bertram Dobell (London: 1907).

... burnish'd to the Sun, / Dazzled in Repercussion'[179] transforms it from concrete detail or scale into a distant echo of the senses, an isolated and intense abstraction, sparkling in the immaculacy of an essential indeterminacy.

Prominent among these gleaming meads of streaming gems and damascene fragrance is a repeated aesthetic impulse towards boxed riches, a framed and secure concentrate of delight or luxury. One example is the garden, the 'hortus inclusus' as we described it, sealed from the world by the new and ornate gateway of separation introduced by Inigo Jones in around 1615.[180] The garden, writes Hawkins in *Partheneia Sacra*, is 'A monopolie of all the pleasures and delights that are on Earth, amassed together, to make a dearth thereof els-where'.[181] The landscape painting is itself another instance. Just as Denham enjoys from Cooper's Hill the power of the eye that 'swift as thought contracts the space'[182] between remote objects, Norgate admires of the 'cozening' of the prospect painting that 'many tymes in a table of not a spanne long a manns imaginacion may be quite carried out of the country over seas and citties'.[183] Moreover, the optimal view must 'neither suddenly debarre the prospect, nor suffer the sight to bee too much dispersed through the emptie aire'.[184] The viewer desiderates for himself a range of clear and distinct beauties, encased in a vista of lucid display. Moreover, the pictures themselves become 'portable property' as oil paintings, substantial and palpable. 'What distinguishes oil painting from any other form of painting is its special ability to render the tangibility, the texture, the lustre, the solidity of what it depicts. It defines the real as that which you can put your hands on.'[185]

Most explicit, however, is the simile of the cabinet. During the early seventeenth century, the aristocracy's 'accepted forms of symbolic justification' changed profoundly: 'less money was spent on huge

179 'Summer', lines 22, 20, 11–12, in *Selected Poems*.

180 See Strong, *Renaissance Garden in England*, pp. 171–74, 185.

181 Henry Hawkins, *Partheneia Sacra* (Rouen: 1633), p. 6; cit. Scoular, *Natural Magic*, p. 164.

182 'Cooper's Hill', line 13, in *Poetical Works*.

183 Edward Norgate, *Miniatura* (1649 version), ed. M. Hardie (Oxford: 1919), Ogden and Ogden, *English Taste*, p. 172.

184 John Barclay, *Icon Animorum* (1614), tr. Thomas May as *The Mirrour of Mindes* (London: 1631), p. 37; cit. Turner, *Topographia*, p. 9. Compare the identical condemnation by Wotton of 'indefinite views which drown all apprehension of the uttermost *Objects*' in *Reliquiae*, p. 204.

185 Berger, *Ways of Seeing*, pp. 87–88; cf. also 93, 109.

houses, servants, horses, and food, and more on books, pictures, sculpture, furniture and gardens'. The new cultural ideal of the 'virtuoso' emerged: the man whose concern is with aesthetic appreciation, antiquarian research and the establishment of collections of natural or artificial curiosities.[186] The 'cabinet' as display case, or a private chamber where intimates may be shown one's most exquisite and costly jewels, is an influential seventeenth-century development.[187] A painting by Georg Hinz, *The Cabinet of Curiosities* (1666) shows one such case, exhibiting jewellery, intricate ornaments and a variety of sea-shells.[188] Herbert's extraordinary description of spring as 'A box where sweets compacted lie' clearly derives from this form of familiarity with nature, for elsewhere he writes of nature as our 'cabinet of *pleasure*', and describes night as 'thy Ebony box' in which man by God is 'inclosed'.[189] For Traherne, nature's 'spaces fill'd were like a cabinet / Of joys before me most distinctly set', and his *Centuries* refer to rifling 'curious cabinets' for natural secrets. It is perhaps a cabinet that Vaughan has in mind when he strews 'questions intricate and rare' upon the flower whose 'curious store' has been 'ruffled all' by winter.[190] Cotton's 'Invitation to Phillis' promises her that a 'rustick jewell of the Rock' shall 'Queene's Casketts mock'.[191] Queen Elizabeth indeed had possessed cabinets studded with curios from all over the world, and her so-called 'Paradise Cabinet' was described by dazed ambassadors as dazzling like the sun among stars with diamonds and rubies, its walls glittering with gold and silver.[192] Charles I filled his 'Cabinet Room' at Whitehall with his favourite landscape paintings:[193] and thus we have both cabinets in landscapes and landscapes in cabinets.

The sweetness of compressed riches motif draws also on a favourite contemporary paradox. If Herbert is explicit in his cabinet metaphor for landscape, he also enjoys the idea, in 'The Pulley', that 'the world's

186 Stone, *Crisis*, pp. 263, 266; on the virtuoso, see pp. 325–29.

187 Girouard, *Life in the English Country House*, pp. 128–35.

188 Reproduced by John Dixon Hunt, *Andrew Marvell: His Life and Writings* (London: 1978), plate 16, p. 45, who notes that General Fairfax possessed at Nun Appleton such a cabinet, ibid., p. 88.

189 'Vertue', line 10; 'Man', line 30; 'Even-Song', lines 21–22.

190 Herbert, 'Nature', lines 75–76, in *Centuries, Poems and Thanksgivings*; and *Centuries*, 3.25; Vaughan, 'I Walked the Other Day', lines 22, 6, 5 in *Complete Poems*.

191 Lines 15–16, in *Poems*.

192 Byrne, *Elizabethan Life in Town and Country*, pp. 34, 36.

193 Ogden and Ogden, *English Taste*, p. 18.

riches, which dispersed lie, / Contract into a span' in the creation of man. If Marvell's drop of dew 'frames' and 'incloses' its native element in 'its little globe's extent', he also imagines 'composing' discrepant pictures into the 'one gallery' of his soul, and conceives Celia as a 'treasure made / Of all [nature's] choicest store'.[194] If Habington rates cowslips in a garden 'sweeter then ith' open field', he sees man's soul as the 'Exchecquer' where nature chooses to 'hoord her wealth, / And lodge all her rich secrets'.[195] If Satan examines Eden from his tree – 'in narrow room nature's whole wealth' – as a Caroline nobleman inspects his cabinet or prospect painting, Milton also writes of Christ's tomb as 'the casket of heav'ns richest store'.[196] The recurring motif here which is cognate is the paradox of 'infinite riches in a little room',[197] that haunts landscape consciousness just as it does love poetry and elegy.[198] There are certainly traditional literary influences here: not only the commanding *hortus conclusus* tradition,[199] but the Catholic incarnational paradox of Christ as infinitude, as *omnis plenitudo* compressed within Mary's womb: 'in little roome / Immensity cloystered in thy deare wombe' as Donne formulates it.[200] Christ is often compared with gems, gold and coinage in this tradition, and Herbert's line on the Virgin as 'the cabinet where the jewell lay'[201] highlights the overlap, in a seventeenth-century mind, with the new connoisseurship and landscape applications.[202]

There are also, however, urgent determinants in contemporary and material experience. The sentiment proverbially applied to ointment boxes and treasure chests – 'Great worth is often found in things of

194 Herbert, 'Pulley', lines 4–5; Marvell, 'Drop of Dew', lines 6–8, 'The Gallery', lines 3–4, 'The Match', lines 1–2.

195 'To Roses in the Bosome of Castara', lines 7–8; 'To the Honourable Mr. Wm. E.', lines 19–20, in *Poems.*

196 *Paradise Lost*, 4.207; 'The Passion', line 44, in *Poems.*

197 Christopher Marlowe, *The Jew of Malta*, 1.1.37.

198 John Donne, 'The Good-Morrow', lines 10–11; Habington, 'Elegie Three', lines 12–13: 'The wealthy empyre of that happie chest / which harbours thy rich dust', in *Poems.* See also the much-in-little theme as examined by Scoular, which commends brevity as a stylistic ideal, and poetry on nature's wondrous minutiae: a theme Scoular connects with the advent of the microscope: *Natural Magic*, pp. 81–115.

199 See Stewart, *The Enclosed Garden*, passim.

200 John Donne, 'Annunciation', lines 13–14, in *Poems.*

201 'To All Angels and Saints', line 14, in *The English Poems.*

202 On the patristic lineage of the incarnational paradox see G. K. Hunter, 'The Theology of Marlowe's *Jew of Malta*', in *Journal Warburg and Courtauld Institute*, 27 (1964), 221–25.

small appearance / in little boxes'[203] – inflames with a new cupidity in relation to land enclosures: boxes whose sweets, compacted, lucratively multiply.[204] Further, it is difficult to avoid recognizing in the motif a reflex of the drive toward capital accumulation, at just the period when, with the formation of joint-stock companies in the 1580s and 1590s and concomitant boom in foreign commerce, with the development of deposit banking and with the reduction between 1620–50 of interest rates to 5 per cent, capital was newly freed and fluid, and in abundant circulation.[205] The ubiquitous motif of plenitude delectably contracted into narrow bounds and privately owned is thus a structure of feeling much fed by the appetite for liquid capital and enclosing fields. The very terminology of our instances above – 'monopolie' and 'exchecquer' – confirm this. Indeed, in Berger's apt dictum, the European oil painting 'is not so much a framed window on to the world as a safe let into the wall, a safe in which the visible has been deposited'.[206] In sum, the seventeenth-century gentleman will pride himself on a tasteful possessive corralling of nature in his house and grounds: on his walls as landscape paintings, in his cabinet as choice curiosities, and in his garden as a concentration of delights. Landscape thus beheld resembles a bourgeois acquisitive individualist version of the medieval park of plenty that we have studied elsewhere.

A final item one must note decorating the Cavalier landscape is the 'cabinet' in another of its seventeenth-century senses: as well as the virtuoso's display-case, it may denote a rustic cottage, summerhouse or bower, and appears to carry the familiar connotations of a higher luxuriousness. Spenser's Colin conceives the abode of 'soveraigne Pan' to be a 'greene cabinet', and Spenser draws the line in question from Marot's eclogue with its 'vert cabinet'.[207] The divine creature in

203 M. P. Tilley, *A Dictionary of the Proverbs in England in the Sixteenth and Seventeenth Century* (Michigan: 1950), W 921; cf. also the analogous quotations given by N. W. Bawcutt in his edition of Marlowe's *Jew of Malta* (Manchester: 1978) to 1.1.37, p. 69.

204 For the greater fertility of enclosed ground as a metaphor common in seventeenth-century verse, see Turner, *Politics*, p. 128; and compare Bacon's epistemological commendation of 'the inclosures of particularity' as against the sterile 'spacious liberty' of 'a champion region' in *The Advancement of Learning*, ed. G. W. Kitchin (London: 1915), 8.1, p. 99.

205 Stone, *Causes*, pp. 68–70; *Crisis of the Aristocracy*, pp. 233–48.

206 Berger, *Ways of Seeing*, p. 109.

207 *Shepheardes Calender*: 'December', lines 7, 14; Clement Marot, *Eclogue* 3, line 13, in *Oeuvres Lyriques*, ed. C. A. Mayer (London: 1964), p. 343.

the cabinet is usually, however, female: the most ogled trophy in the Cavalier's cabinet is actually his mistress. Lovelace's 'metaphysical' poem on his mistress' glove terms it her 'snowy Farme' or 'pretty *Ermin* Cabinet', and awaits the return of its 'Alabaster Lady'.[208] The cabinet may escalate into a kind of rural temple or palace: Cotton offers Phillis a bower-palace, hidden in a grove of ageing oaks, with walls of polished marble, porphyry pilasters, crystal windows and carpets of woven flowers, where she is apparently to sate her epicurean appetite upon apples, and 'Water in a grot hard by'.[209] Court masques frequently place Henrietta-Maria in such structures amid paradisal landscapes. In 1635 she dwells, in a closing scene, in a 'Temple of Love', whilst in Montague's 'Shepherd's Paradise' of 1633 she is displayed in 'Love's Cabinet': a wooded scene featuring a small, open, hexagonal temple, supported by caryatides and topped by a cupola, ornamented by climbing plants.[210] It was for his attack on the alleged prurience of this masque that Prynne's ears were sliced off, and he was condemned to life-imprisonment.[211] It is hard to believe the assocation with erotic licence unfounded however. The 'palace' in the woodland derived, I'd suggest, from the hunting lodges and banqueting houses of the late sixteenth and seventeenth centuries, which had evolved from the self-contained 'super-towers' of fifteenth-century castles, 'geared toward luxury and magnificence rather than security', their architecture in the seventeenth century 'often fanciful'.[212] These so-called 'secret houses', often remote, and offering escape from the noble household, were known as places of accommodation for mistresses.[213] In this tradition of paradise landscape, then, the shade in which the Cavalier sports with Amaryllis is that of a secluded cabinet: a Caroline nobleman's Bower of Bliss.

208 'Elinda's Glove', lines 1, 6–7, in *Poems*, p. 58.

209 'The Entertainment to Phillis', lines 12–50, in *Poems*, pp. 43–44. Cf. Chamberlayne, *Pharonnida*, first pagination, pp. 149–50.

210 Cf. Harris, *The King's Arcadia*, pp. 177 and 163; for 'Love's Cabinet' see fig. 302, p. 163.

211 Prynne's attack was in *Histrio-Mastix* (1633): cf. Harris.

212 Girouard, *Life in the English Country House*, pp. 74, 108. For this evolution, see ibid., pp. 73–78, 106–09.

213 Ibid., pp. 76, 78.

Advances in descriptive particularity

Empirical

In 1644 Wenceslaus Hollar, the most important topographer of seventeenth-century England, engraved the Royal Exchange, bustling with Dutchmen and Italians, with turbaned Turks and fur-capped Muscovites. Two years later, 'science entered Oxford behind the Parliamentary armies',[214] where the nucleus of the Royal Society was established. Between them, the Royal Exchange and the Royal Society, or the expansive spirits of commerce and of science, exerted powerful impulses in the seventeenth century towards a more detailed knowledge of the material world.

In the 1620s John Tradescant assembled the first major natural history collection in England, supplied by trading companies with carefully catalogued animal skulls, reptiles and shining stones.[215] Treatises on the 'new husbandry' or advances in agricultural science proliferated from the mid-century, discussing the floating of water-meadows, marling and liming fields, and the introduction of new crops on a large scale.[216] John Evelyn established in his Deptford garden not only axial avenues but a scientific 'elaboratorye' for chemistry, a transparent beehive, an aviary and a garden of rare specimen flowers. Here, 'We are witnessing the shedding of the old hieroglyphic and analogic reading of the garden in favour of empirical study.'[217] The same subjection of space and time to uniform quantification that we saw promoting pictorialism in the Italian Renaissance is active in the Puritan mind, with its anti-miraculism and deep sense of the rationality of the universe. The Puritans 'cleanse' the calendar of its medieval 'evil days',[218] regulating and desacralizing time into an even continuum, cleared of supernatural obstacles to comprise an order of human utility. Hollar's engraving for Ogilby's 'Britannia' (plate 13) marvellously depicts an England becoming likewise mathematized into 'rational space', coursed by cosmographers and cartographers with every variety of measuring instrument. Indeed, the word 'survey'

214 Hill, *God's Englishman*, p. 250.
215 Stone, *Crisis*, p. 326; Thomas, *Man and the Natural World*, p. 227.
216 Low, *Georgic Revolution*, pp. 146–51.
217 Strong, *Renaissance Garden in England*, p. 221.
218 Thomas, *Religion and the Decline*, pp. 735–45.

– twice used in Marvell's poetry – is first used as a noun to denote topographical computation in 1610.[219]

Commercial and political interests foster 'comparative space' or geographic and topographic familiarization with Europe. Burghley's Theobalds possessed landscape paintings of all the most important cities in Europe,[220] a gallery of seats of power such as befitted a cosmopolitan and keenly informed European statesman; and he recommended his ward the Earl of Rutland on his foreign travels to note in a diary the fortifications and garrisons of the towns he visited, as well as curious natural phenomena he might encounter.[221] Milton's 'Of Education' similarly commends studying from horseback 'all places of strength, all commodities of building and of soil for towns and tillage, harbours, and ports for trade'.[222] The Grand Tour dates from the early seventeenth century; and as for travel literature, Samuel Purchas' *Hakluytus Posthumus or Purchas his Pilgrims* (1625) comprised the largest English work yet printed in England.[223]

The late sixteenth and seventeenth centuries – 'the age of lenses' as Clark calls it, mindful of the achievements of Leuwenhoek, Boerhaave and Galileo[224] – witness a vogue for prospect. Country Houses build prospect chambers on upper levels, adapt their long galleries to prospect functions, and place banqueting houses on rooftops for the same purpose.[225] Landscapes were painted across tavern walls and ceilings: Vaughan composes 'A Rhapsody' on one such, adorning the Globe in Fleet Street. Caroline noble gardens are designed to break from allegoric items viewed by a seated, static spectator to the creation of constantly changing vistas to surprise the stroller, and they borrow new optical principles from the court masque.[226] In this climate, unsurprisingly, 'landskip'[227] or consciously pictorial definition of space is introduced into English verse, imitating the painter's art of

219 Marvell, *Upon Appleton House*, line 81; 'Mower's Song', line 1; *OED*, 'Survey', sb., 5.

220 Byrne, *Elizabethan Life*, p. 45.

221 Stone, *Crisis*, p. 314.

222 *Of Education*, in *Complete Prose Works*, vol. 2, p. 413.

223 Douglas Bush, *English Literature in the Earlier Seventeenth Century* (1945; 2nd edn, Oxford: 1962), p. 189.

224 *Landscape into Art*, p. 60.

225 Girouard, *Life*, pp. 78, 102, 106; John Buxton, *Elizabethan Taste* (London: 1963), p. 52.

226 Strong, *Renaissance Garden*, pp. 200, 203.

227 This term, signifying a landscape painting, derives from 1598, and is used by Marvell in *Appleton House*, line 458. 'Lantskip', 'landscope' and 'launce-skippe' are also employed from the 1590s; and perhaps derive from the Dutch words 'landschap', pronounced 'land-skap', or 'lantschap', the latter of which may refer

perspectival recession, balanced land-masses and *chiaroscuro*, in contrast with the old medieval carelessness about prospect which allowed Dante to perceive, from beyond the sphere of the Fixed Stars, landscapes from Cadiz to Asia, and Chaucer to pick out, from the altitude of a soaring point beneath the moon, mountains, plains, cities and even 'grete trees' in a single perspective.[228] Whereas the traditional techniques of Spenser, Browne and Drayton present as landscape the balancing pairs of shady ground and open, rough and smooth, hill and vale,[229] or employ such ancient devices as the flower catalogue,[230] seventeenth-century poets come to see nature as a landscape painting:

> Straight mine eye hath caught new pleasures
> Whilst the landscape round it measures ...
> Mountains on whose barren breast
> The labouring clouds do often rest:
> Meadows trim with daisies pied,
> Shallow brooks and rivers wide.
> Towers, and battlements it sees
> Bosomed high in tufted trees.[231]

Chamberlayne in *Pharonnidda* (1659) is conscious both of wide visibility and the hindered eye:

> Here lovely landskips, where thou mightst behold,
> When first the Infant Morning did unfold
> The Dayes bright Curtains, in a spatious Green,
> Which Natures curious Art had spread between
> Two bushy Thickets, that on either hand
> Did like the Fringe of the fair Mantle stand,
> A timerous herd of grasing Deer, and by
> Them in a shady Grove, through which the eye
> Could hardly pierce, a wel-built Lodge, from whence
> The watchful keepers careful diligence

to a 'drollery' painting of rustic clowns. See Turner, *Topographia*, pp. 14, 377–80; *Politics*, pp. 22–23.

228 Dante, *Paradiso*, 27.81–3; Chaucer, *Hous of Fame*, 2.896–903. I take the 'carelessness' point from Lewis, *Discarded Image*, pp. 100–02.

229 Cf. Turner, *Topographia*, 33–34, 182–84; *Politics*, 13–14, 26.

230 Homeric *Hymn to Demeter*, 5–10; Virgil, *Eclogues*, 2.45–55; Shakespeare, *Midsummer Night's Dream*, 2.1.249–52, *The Winter's Tale*, 4.4.116–27; Spenser, *Muiopotmos*, 187–200, *April* Eclogue, 136–44; Jonson, *Pan's Anniversary*, 11–38; Milton, *Lycidas*, 141–52.

231 *L'Allegro*, 69–70, 73–78.

Secures their private walks; from hence to look
On a deep Valley, where a silver Brook,
Doth in a soft and busie murmure slide
Betwixt two Hils, whose shadows strove to hide
The liquid wealth they were made fruitful by
From ful discoveries of the distant eye ...[232]

With the virtuoso exception of the vertiginous Dover Cliff in *King Lear* (4.6.11–24), such pictoriality is fresh in England with seventeenth-century poetry.

The new pictorialism has been brilliantly documented by James Turner[233] and I shall therefore not multiply examples; but I think we may supplement his point by remarking certain new poetic forms and terms generated by this more particularizing, pictorially influenced landscape-consciousness. Vaughan, Marvell and Milton refer, predictably, to 'scenes'; Milton and Cotton specify a 'plat' of land; whilst Vaughan writes of 'paisage' (sixteenth-century Italians referred to landscape painting as '*paesetto*',[234] and the French by the mid-sixteenth century adapted '*paysage*' to refer to paintings).[235] 'Loco-descriptive' or 'topographical-reflective' verse appears to have roots in medieval travel-poems and perhaps the 'hodoeporicon' or travel-verse of Renaissance Latin literature[236]; certainly Drayton's *Polyolbion* and Browne's *Britannia's Pastorals* have sixteenth-century precedents in Thomas Churchyard's *Descriptio Angliae* (mid-sixteenth century) and *Worthines of Wales* (1587): the latter a 'shambling, haphazard survey' of towns, scenes, churches and castles.[237] But the seventeenth century not only sees the proliferation of regional and patriotic poetry: it witnesses an outreach beyond place-name and myth towards a material particularity such that genre boundaries become blurred. If Cotton's 'Wonders of the Peake' is a 'regional' poem, its visual relish and acuity link it with Denham's consciously pictorial study, *Cooper's Hill*, and with much of the artistic acumen of *L'Allegro* and *Il Penseroso*.

232 1659 edition, first pagination, pp. 144–45; Turner, *Politics*, p. 25.

233 See *Politics*, pp. 8–35 on pictorial verse, and *Topographia*, pp. 10–13 on the general prospect craze.

234 'Scene': Vaughan, 'Rules and Lessons', line 92, Marvell, *Appleton House*, line 441, Milton, 'The Passion', line 22; 'plat': Milton, *Il Penseroso*, line 73, and *Paradise Lost*, 9.456, Cotton, 'Wonders of the Peake', line 1419; 'paisage': Vaughan, 'Mount of Olives' (II), line 17; 'paesetto': Gombrich, *Norm and Form*, p. 109.

235 Turner, *Topographia*, p. 378.

236 Cf. Robert Arnold Aubin, *Topographical Poetry in Eighteenth Century England* (New York: 1936), pp. 9–11, 260.

237 Ibid., p. 17.

Neither travel-poems, pastoral nor retirement verse, these works 'break fresh ground' in genre as they do in content. Likewise, on precisely what *Upon Appleton House* comprises no-one seems able to agree. For Alastair Fowler it is 'georgic', for H. M. Richmond it is 'subjective epic' (a term he leaves open to the imagination), for Roy Strong it is accounted for at the level of content as patterned on the surprise marvels of a Mannerist garden, whilst for James Turner it is a panegyric on the fortunes of the Fairfax family.[238] Røstvig confesses that indeed *beatus ille* poetry and 'genre pictures from rural life' are often conflated in this period.[239] The common factor here is the novelty of an extended scenic concentration effectively establishing itself at the poetry's core: the impulse we have defined in painting as toward 'quotidian space' is here creating the earliest distinct 'loco-descriptive' verse.

A closer descriptive realism peppers seventeenth-century verse. Where Spenser enthuses over clear rivers as free from mud, Vaughan praises the Isca as unmixed with nitrous clay. Where Spenser on nature's heavenly aspiration notes simply 'everything doth upward tend', Vaughan elaborates that '*waters* that fall / Chide, and fly up; *mists* of corruptest foam / Quit their first beds and mount'.[240] Strode remarks the seemingly 'wave-swolne earth' of Westwell Down's 'landskipp' below him.[241] Cotton's 'Wonders of the Peake' is minutely documentary –

> Plashing through water, and through slabby Sand
> Till a vast Sand-hill once more bids us stand –

noting how stones dropped to fathom holes sound 'nearer flat, sharper when more remote', and enjoying the way that a cave waterfall sprays droplets 'sparkling quite round the place'. Only on confronting Chatsworth House, the final Wonder, does he wad his senses in the heavy fabric of panegyric convention: hymning muses, warbling

238 Alastair Fowler, 'Country House Poetry: The Politics of a Genre', in *The Seventeenth Century*, 1:1 (January 1986), 1–14; Richmond, *Renaissance Landscapes*, p. 117; Strong, *Renaissance Garden*, p. 214; Turner, *Topographia*, p. 389, *Politics*, pp. 61–84. For most critics, e.g. Harold Toliver, *Marvell's Ironic Vision* (Yale: 1965), p. 114, the lack of definite structure is crucial.

239 Røstvig, *Happy Man*, pp. 9, 44–45, 313.

240 Spenser, *Faerie Queene*, 6.10.7.3, and Vaughan, 'To the River Isca', lines 56–57; Spenser, 'An Hymne of Heavenly Beautie', line 44, and Vaughan, 'The Tempest', lines 25–27.

241 'On Westwell Downs', lines 6, 3, in *Poetical Works*, p. 20.

'people of the air,' and groves of curled brows.[242] Herbert's 'Sweet day, so cool, so calm, so bright' is distinctively British in its heat-free light, just as Vaughan's enjoyment of the grove pierced by 'unthrift sun' is emphatically un-mediterranean.[243]

The contrast of such anglicised and empirical writing with Elizabethan rural verse is sharp. For the Elizabethans, the local and individual nature in experience is rhetoricized into melodious generality. 'It is the formal rehearsal of past artificiality that is most striking', note modern editors of English Renaissance pastoral.[244] Often simply allegorical ('My sheep are thoughts'),[245] Elizabethan pastoral is concerned at bottom with the idea of settlement, not nature, and retails a mythicized social order in which nature is but a glimpsed, formulaic setting. Where empiric, it focuses animals and people in the rhythms of season and weather rather than landscapes: as with Shakespeare's birds sitting brooding in the snow, and coughing, raw-nosed servants 'when icicles hang by the wall', or Cuddie's 'ragged rontes' shivering in February winds.[246] Browne's empiricisms brilliantly extend this tradition in the seventeenth century in his celebrated morning description, with its glittering wainscot snail-trails, its fly-stung stonehorse lashing its tail, and fields of milk-white gossamer untouched by chewing cattle.[247] 'Shakespeare lived in a world of time, Milton lived in a world of space.'[248] Such 'topocosmic' writing binding man, beast and landscape bears us back not only to Brueghel but to Calypso's grotto, to a form of interrelationship with nature pre-urban, pre-scientific, close to oral and working tradition: a multi-sensory and organic *stimmung*, in contrast with whose roundedness the technically developed 'landskip', separating, calculative, objectifying, may seem a coldly dissociated artifice. Most Elizabethan landscapes, however, in their resolute Arcadianism, are descriptively inferior to the lyrics and seasonal headpieces of the Middle Ages, let alone the masterpieces of Gavin Douglas and the Gawain-poet; and

242 'Wonders', lines 985–86, 537–38, 1064; Chatsworth: 1282–1312.

243 Herbert, 'Vertue', line 1; Vaughan, 'Regeneration', line 41.

244 John Barrell and John Bull, *The Penguin Book of English Pastoral Verse* (London: 1974), p. 141.

245 Sir Philip Sidney, *The Countess of Pembroke's Arcadia*, ed. Maurice Evans (Harmondsworth: 1977), p. 232.

246 'When Icicles Hang By the Wall', song in *Love's Labour's Lost*, 5.2.900; Spenser, *Shepheardes Calender*, 'February', lines 1–8.

247 *Britannia's Pastorals* (1616; rpt. Menston, England: 1969), 2.1–18.

248 Nicolson, *Mountain Gloom*, p. 381.

there is some truth in C. S. Lewis' remark that Sir John Davies' *Orchestra*, a didactic fantasia on the cosmic dance, 'was as truly "nature-poetry" for the Elizabethans as Wordsworth was for the Romantics'.[249]

Marked as seventeenth-century advances in literary pictorialism and empiric acumen are, their limitations must also be emphasised. Patriotic and regional concern for English scenery in *Polyolbion* and *Britannia's Pastorals* is overwhelmingly confined to the supply of anecdotalized place-names: we may compare the entirely non-visual listing and hymning of great English rivers in Cotton's 'Retirement' (stanza 7) and Walton's *Compleat Angler*.[250] The earliest topographical paintings of England, which are by Dutchmen, are largely restricted to 'possessive space', featuring royal palaces in glorious valleys or such great buildings as at Windsor, Richmond, Ham House, Putney and Westminster. Evelyn desiderates that engravers 'extreamely gratify the curious, and virtuosi generally, that they would endeavour to publish such excellent things as both his Majesty and divers of the noblesse of the nation have in their possession... and render our nation famous abroad'.[251] Occasionally topographical paintings outstrip the patrician pale, as with Hollar's quiet scenes of lakeside walks around Albury (plate 15). Yet even these are designed as consolation to the Earl of Arundel, exiled in Antwerp, as views close to his seat in Surrey. And elsewhere non-aristocratic landscape space, where not purely 'ideal', tends to remain within determinate generic frames as furnishing 'drollery' or rustic clown scenes (an alternative meaning of the Dutch word 'lantschap'), as when Joris Hoefnagel paints views both of Windsor and Nonsuch, and also a carnivalesque 'Marriage at Bermondsey'.[252] Concomitant of a far more developed empirical natural science, poetic landscape will not advance to 'an intricate working of particularity, as opposed to the more characteristic attribution of single identifying qualities in most earlier writing'[253] until the late eighteenth century. So limited indeed is seventeenth-century landscape depiction that I know of no description, in verse or

249 *English Literature in the 16th Century, Excluding Drama* (Oxford: 1954), p. 526.

250 pp. 194–7.

251 John Evelyn, *Sculptura, or The History of Chalcography* (London: 1662), ch. 4; Graham Parry, *Hollar's England: A mid-Seventeenth-century view* (Salisbury, Wiltshire: 1980), p. 16.

252 Cf. Turner, *Topographia*, pp. 17–24; *Politics*, p. 9; Ogden and Ogden, *English Taste*, pp. 3, 57.

253 Williams, *The Country and the City*, p. 166.

painting, of the major transformation of the land's appearance from the vast tracts of thin-stripped fields of 'champion' into the compact holdings of 'several' or hedged enclosures.[254]

The Compleat Angler, I suggest, epitomizes the ambiguity of the period's empirical advance. Izaac Walton is perhaps the nearest thing we have in seventeenth-century literature to the modern 'nature-lover'. The *Angler* focuses nature as secular, not hieroglyphic and mystical; as disengaged from a displayed social formation in contrast to the pastoral sociality of feast, amour and *débat* and the 'house-keeping' of Country House verse (the Angler's social encounters have an 'urban' unrootedness as chance bonhomie with strangers in alehouses); and as a field of close observation. As a prosperous draper's son, married into pious ecclesiastical circles, he writes no 'bejewelled' or 'perfumed' landscape, nor does his royalist quietism – 'study to be quiet'[255] – allow of millenarian intimation. His is a dirty-fingered, textured nature of grubs, rain and tenaciously detailed natural history. ('If you be nice to foul your fingers, which good anglers seldom are, then take this bait ...')[256] Yet even Walton's cherished verses are whistling reversions to Elizabethan Arcadianism ('old-fashioned poetry, but choicely good'),[257] nostalgic excerpts whose descriptive quality is crushingly banal. His own prose descriptions are clearly derivative from formulaic verse. 'And pray let's now rest ourselves in this sweet shady arbour, which nature herself has woven with her own fine fingers; 'tis such a contexture of woodbines, sweetbriar, jasmine, and myrtle; and so interwoven, as will secure us both from the sun's violent heat, and from the approaching shower.'[258] The structure here combines the classical 'peritopos' and flower-list with the mildest Anglicized touch: the bower shelters from rain as well as the conventional (mediterranean) heat. The word 'contexture' itself, dated by the *OED* from 1649 as signifying an interwoven fabric, derives from Latin (*contextura*). The work thus represents the paradox of a 'holiday realism', its bulk of dense natural observation leavened by an idyllic escapism of bookish patterning.

There are stringent limitations also to seventeenth-century pictorialism. First, it was not thoroughly absorbed. Not only was ideal

254 For a twentieth-century reconstruction of such scenic contrast, cf. Byrne, pp. 131–34. 255 *Compleat Angler*, p. 215. 256 Ibid., p. 184.
257 Ibid., p. 68. 258 Ibid., p. 210.

landscape painting far more sought after than topographical landscape in earlier seventeenth-century England;[259] the response of a spectator to masque scenery in Oxford in 1636 – that he saw only a series of 'partitions ... resembling the desks or studies in a library' – shows that the mass of the population had, as Roy Strong points out, not yet learnt the new perspectival principles constructing pictorial depth.[260] Spatial depth is often absent or bungled even in poets who refer specifically to the new word 'landskip' or 'landschap'. Cotton, for all the acuities of his 'Wonders of the Peake', fails, when recounting his terror of the stranded mountain-climber on Mamtor who 'downward cast his woful eyes', to evoke any perspectival impression or swaying view – the example of Dover Cliff in *King Lear* notwithstanding.[261] Milton, despite several landscapes of skilfully organized vastness, has Raphael see from the gate of Heaven, a point 'outside the whole sidereal universe', not only Eden but cedar trees.[262] Revett, though ahead of his time in alertness to autumn tints ('discovered' widely only with the eighteenth century), nonetheless manages in 'The Landschap between two hills', a poem specifically imitating the effects of painted scenery, only a single optical effect:

> Here the grass rowls, and hills between
> Stud it with little tufts of green.[263]

Moreover, technically skilled pictorial description was not for the most felt to be self-validating in poetry. The precept '*ut pictura poesis*', though widely subscribed to, seems to have enjoined only subordinate illustrative or expressive particulars to further the poet's theme, not a parade of details for their own sake.[264] The poet undoubtedly vies with 'the Painter's Art',[265] yet his primary aim is not, *pace* Turner, to 'emulate landscape in its accuracy of colour and texture'.[266] The aim, even in the ordering of nature into clarified spatial relations, is not the better exhibition of nature but the activation of the mind's own

259 Ogden and Ogden, *English Taste*, p. 61.

260 Stephen Orgel and Roy Strong, *Inigo Jones. The Theatre of the Stuart Court* (Berkeley: 1972), chs. 1 and 2; quotation from Strong, *Renaissance Garden*, p. 203.

261 'Wonders', lines 740–52.

262 *Paradise Lost*, 5.257–61; ref. Lewis, *Discarded Image*, p. 101.

263 'Autumne', lines 17–18; 'Land-schap', lines 41–42, in *Selected Poems*.

264 Rosemund Tuve, *Elizabethan and Metaphysical Imagery* (1947; rpt. London: 1972), pp. 50–60.

265 Revett, 'Land-schap', line 5.

266 James Turner, *Politics*, p. 19.

powers, its 'fancie' or interpretive profundity. Marvell and Denham continue '*paysage moralisé*', prising out innate structures of meaning from landscape in the hieroglyphic tradition:

> O could I flow like thee and make thy stream
> My great example, as it is my theme:
> Though deep yet clear, though gentle yet not dull,
> Strong without rage, without o'erflowing full.[267]

Denham's 'More boundless in my fancie than my eye' echoes the classic Augustinian inturning.[268] Painter and poet each are concerned to promote not a sharper material definition of a contingent space so much as a triumph of the human mind in its artistic construction. The painter compresses a thousand acres within three feet of canvas in a bravura act of control and possession; and the poet, in a competitive parallelism, reclaims the mastery of these expanses for literature through the mercurial actions of 'sprightly fancie ... / Inliv'ning by transcription', which seeks to 'Teach the dumb Rhetorick [of painting] Eloquence'.[269] It is notable that in Revett's attempt in 'The Land-Schap', the poetic input accompanying the imitation of optical detail is not one that returns pigments to sense-data, redescribing the land in experiential terms: there are no odours, bodily sensations or temperature, and little sound. Rather, the colours of fancy are thrown over form in a mastery by wit and ideation: the 'Age-bow'd oak' is humbly prostrating itself, the river winds as if drunk, just as distant objects are but weakly perceptible to eyes 'Quite tippled with varietie'.[270] We can see this principle, of observation introduced only as conceit, in seventeenth-century attention to the oddity of the swirl of bark on trees. The 'writhèd bark' of the oak at Penshurst commemorating Sir Philip Sidney's birth is remarked only through association with the pastoral motif of lovers carving their names on trees.[271] The 'twisted curls' of Strode's ancient tree enclose what seem to be a hall, parlour and chambers within its hollow trunk.[272] The 'thousand winding curls' of trees in Carew's *Rapture* suggest 'artful

267 Sir John Denham, 'Cooper's Hill', in *Poetical Works*, lines 189–92.

268 'Cooper's Hill', line 12; Augustine, *Confessions*, 10.8.

269 Revett, *Land-schap*, in lines 3–6.

270 'Land-schap', lines 27–28, 45–46, 40.

271 Ben Jonson, 'To Penshurst', line 15: compare Virgil, *Eclogue*, 10.53–54; *As You Like It*, 3.2.5–10; Habington, 'To My Honoured Friend Mr. E.P.', lines 15–17 and 'Cogitabo pro peccato meo', lines 3–4, in *Poems*.

272 William Strode, 'On a Great Hollow Tree', lines 27–30, in *Poetical Works*.

postures' of copulation carved by local lovers.[273] Observed minutiae and pictorial space in verse are thus validated by sprightly exposition: eagerly inducted as a vogue performance to be mastered by conceit.

Phenomenological

Companion to these empiric attentions to outward nature is an inward or 'phenomenological' writing, articulating nature-in-sensation. The impulse here is toward engaging subtler textures of sense-experience and the emotive properties of the sensate. The seventeenth, after all, is the century of both Newtonian physics and the Cartesian 'cogito', of both objectified mechanism and of the new philosophic subjectivism.

Many seventeenth-century lyrics seek the feathering of poetic intelligence in finely discriminated textures of sensation: as when Strode compares music with snow falling on wool, or Jonson, predicating Charis, asks 'Ha' you mark'd but the fall o' the snow / Before the soyle hath smutch'd it? / Ha' you felt the wooll of Bever? / Or Swan's Downe ever? / Or have smelt o' the bud o' the Brier? / Or the Nard in the fire?'[274] Such display of a hypersensuous apperception may appear somewhat precious beside the naturalness of Herbert: who is no less remarkable in his sharply impressionable directness of involvement in *sensa*. His spring rose, for example, 'whose hue angrie and brave / Bids the rash gazer wipe his eye'; or, quite unforgettably,

> I once more smell the dew and rain,
> And relish versing.[275]

Inevitably, landscape description in poetry comes to exercise such phenomenological interests. St-Amant's 'La Solitude'[276] is perhaps the clearest example of an elaboration of the tonal vocabulary, the rarefied mood-music of the Jonsonian lyric above; and as such it moves towards Romanticism's appropriation of the natural as a delicate interior notation. Aside from the direct influence of this poem, four factors, I'd suggest, underlay interest in landscape as a play of affective

273 'Rapture', lines 120–25, in *Poems.*

274 Strode, 'The Commendation of Music', line 21, in Jonson, 'A Celebration of Charis', lines 23–28 in *Complete Poems.*

275 'Vertue', lines 5–6, and 'The Flower' lines 38–39, in *English Poems.*

276 Cf. Leishman, *Art,* pp. 263–67, 294, 315–17.

stimulus. Urban culture disengaged poetics from the ancestral agricultural eye, encouraging as we have seen a 'consumerist' perception of the countryside as a realm of pleasure and recreation. Scientific questionings encouraged a material focus on nature independent of hieroglyphic imagination, and the proliferation of warring theories promoted intense observation. The tradition of religious contemplation and Protestant favour of sessions of solitude helped secure regular periods of studied attention. Finally, landscape painting and new gardening ideas sought expertise in mood manipulation. Gardening experiments in mood control had, as Hunt has remarked, obvious affinities with the epistemological speculations of Locke's Associationist philosophy.[277] Landscape painting, however, long had deployed a double vocabulary of iconographic images and expressive colouring and form, evolving 'recognizable moods, strains of sentiment which could be touched on at will', as Gombrich puts it[278]; and we may compare Alberti's praise of landscape for its calmative effects on the spirit (quoted in the previous chapter) with the horticulturist John Woolridge's valuing of gardens for the 'influence they have upon the passions of the mind, reducing a discomposed fancy to a more sedate temper',[279] and with Vaughan's perception of landscape as replenishing, affective experience:

> So have I known some beauteous *paisage* rise
> In sudden flowers and arbours to my eyes,
> And in the depth and dead of winter bring
> To my cold thoughts a lively sense of spring.[280]

In Milton's poetry, it seems to me, this new and direct affective engagement of sense-experience is evident as conditioning the deployment of solidity and insubstantiality in his descriptions. Milton's aspiration to a condition of being 'more refined, more spiritous and pure' frequently catapults his imagination into ecstatic heavenly upsoarings, in a widely-remarked 'earth-escaping drive'.[281] Concomitant is the association of beatitude or purity with weightless-

277 Hunt, *Figure in the Landscape*, pp. 25, 36, 45, 47.

278 Gombrich, *Norm and Form*, p. 121.

279 Woolridge, *Systema Horti-Culturae* (London: 1677), cit. Hunt, *Genius*, p. 88.

280 Vaughan, 'Mount of Olives' (II), lines 17–20.

281 *Paradise Lost* 5.475; John Carey, *Milton* (London: 1969), p. 54. Cf. 'Vacation Exercise', 33–44; 'Elegy V', 10–18; *Il Penseroso* 52, 165–66; 'Death of the Bishop of Ely' 46–64; 'On the Gunpowder Plot' 5–8; *Paradise Lost* 5.78–81; *Lycidas* 172–81.

ness: Adam at creation levitates at the touch of his hand to glide into Eden 'over fields and waters, as in air / Smooth sliding without step.' Christ's 'dear might ... that walked the waves' is matched by the apotheosis enabling Sabrina to set her 'printless feet / O'er the cowslip's velvet head / That bends not as I tread'.[282] Associated with the feeling for 'bright aerial spirits' soaring 'swift as the sparkle of a glancing star'[283] over the earth's surface is a delight in unimpeding and open landscape: the 'meadows trim with daisies pied' of *L'Allegro*, the 'trim' gardens of *Il Penseroso*, the 'smooth enamelled green' of 'Arcades' 'where no print of step hath been', and 'lawns or level downs' of Eden.[284] Everywhere Milton is attracted to the 'spiritously' intangible, and his comely spaces are an openness of fragrance, light and fluvial motion. His favourite words – 'orient', 'beam', 'amber', 'gloom', 'odour', 'fragrant', 'sweet' – are themselves 'discarnate' in sound, with their long, gliding vowels and soft consonants. This 'angelicizing' imagination links him with the bent for etherealizing the sense-world which we remarked in the Fathers and early Christian verse, particularly since, conversely, mortal clay can gather creatively baleful connotations. The unhallowed is associated with tangle, obstruction, overgrowth: the 'tangled thickets' of the *Nativity Ode*, 'the gadding vine o'ergrown' of *Lycidas*, the fear of nature 'strangled with her waste fertility' in *Comus*.[285] (The exception, the desire to be hid in a close covert in *Il Penseroso*, is a standard item of the Renaissance melancholy landscape.)[286] Texture, temperature, solidity clog, weigh down with terrestrial bodiliness, and are often used to evoke repulsion or menace: the lady in *Comus*, for instance, is lost in 'the chill dew, amongst rude burs and thistles ... Perhaps some cold bank is her bolster now, / Or gainst the rugged bark of some broad elm / Leans her unpillowed head'.[287] Just as Satan grows 'squat like a toad', so Hell is frozen into metrical monoliths,

> Rocks, caves, lakes, fens, bogs, dens and shades of death,
> A universe of death[288]

whose ponderous sterility contrasts with the roving energies of Eden (which we shall examine later), where the very syntax is irriguous,

282 *Paradise Lost* 8.300–02; *Lycidas* 173; *Comus* 877–79. 283 *Comus* 3, 80.
284 *L'Allegro* 75; *Il Penseroso* 50; 'Arcades' 84–85; *Paradise Lost* 4.252.
285 *Nativity Ode* 188; *Lycidas* 40; *Comus* 729.
286 *Il Penseroso* 139–40; Strong, *Renaissance Garden*, p. 216.
287 *Comus* 352–55. 288 *Paradise Lost* 4.800; 2.621–22.

serpentine: a single flowing and dispersing sentence traverses the entire landscape.[289]

Contrary to the Fathers', however, Milton's sensory imagination is also monistic and evolutionary. Raphael's exposition of the hierarchy of the elements and species 'by gradual scale sublimed' from grossness of weight to airy purity, is standard theology, with Platonic and New Testament authority.[290] It influences *Comus*' aspiration that the body turn 'by degrees to the soul's essence', and its fear lest the soul 'grows clotted by contagion, / Imbodies and inbrutes'.[291] Milton's insistence, however, on 'one first matter all, / Endued with various forms, various degrees of substance' is heresy, although one current among radicals of the period.[292] Milton's descriptions of creation are deeply sensitized to the paradoxes of this universal materiality, within which scheme it follows that *all* being, 'spiritual' as well as brute, is apprehensible to the senses, exists as a disclosure of sensation. Milton's consciousness, where dualistic at all, exchanges, one might say, an ontological for a sensualist dualism. Just as he engaged in daily physical exercise 'to render lightsome, clear and not lumpish' his physique, just as Adam and Eve are promised that their bodies in Eden 'may at last turn all to spirit ... and winged ascend / Ethereal',[293] so the spiritous potential and nisus of 'matter' is always quick upon his senses. In Eden heavier substances issue finer: from the 'shaggy' mountain leaps a fountain, trees exude 'odorous gums and balm', leaves are tremblingly 'attuned' by 'vernal airs', rills are happily 'fuming', and running waters spread into 'a liquid plain ... Pure as th' expanse of heav'n'.[294] At creation, within one sentence, the egg 'bursting with kindly rupture' discloses the young who 'feathered soon ... summed their pens ... soaring th'air sublime'.[295] In

> So from the root
> Springs lighter the green stalk, from thence the leaves
> More aery, last the bright consummate flow'r
> Spirits odorous breathes

289 4.223–63; Turner, *Politics*, p. 33.
290 *Paradise Lost* 5.469–85; Plato, *Phaedrus* 81–82; 1 *Corinthians* 15.42.
291 *Comus* 462–69.
292 *Paradise Lost* 5.472–74; Hill, *Milton and the English Revolution*, ch. 26, pp. 324–33.
293 *Complete Prose Works*, vol. 1, p. 886; *Paradise Lost* 5.497–99.
294 *Paradise Lost* 4.224–30, 248, 264–66; 5.6; 4.455–56.
295 Ibid., 7.419–21.

we have, as John Carey brilliantly perceives, a 'weight-picture'. 'The bulky 'consummate', balanced on the flower, seems too heavy, but 'spirits' and 'breathes' keep it fuming into the air, and we recognize that Milton is getting across the contrast between the precarious size of the petals relative to the stalk, and their filmy lightness.'[296]

Above all, from his materialist heresy of consubstantial nature follow not only Milton's 'etherealizing' of the physical but its converse: an insistence on the substantiality of the intangible. So pure an entity as the sun has material properties, tangibly pressing upon objects: sunbeams 'impress' themselves upon cloud, fruit and rainbow, just as God's glory is 'impressed' and 'transfused' upon the Son, as though palpable, densely luminous.[297] The sun leaves prints in the sky, and angels slide along sunrays. Sun and 'moon / Globose' are said to 'drink liquid light', and the air itself is some degree tangible and solid: Satan's wings are 'incumbent on it' and it supports 'unusual weight'.[298] From such a universe it follows that the hypallage discussed by Christopher Ricks entails more than a poetically enhancing 'flicker of hesitation'. When Milton writes that Eve 'strews the ground / With Rose and Odours from the shrub unfum'd', or of Eve 'Veil'd in a Cloud of Fragrance' and the arbour 'deck't' with 'fragrant smells'; when he recounts groves of 'flouring Odours', and by consequence the ensuing 'spicy forest' suggests the forest as actually a massiness of fragrance:[299] the substantiality of these scents represents less a trope than a theological literality; or rather, the immediacy of the theologian's ontology upon the senses and imagination of the blind poet. The materialist heresy here, and its realization through the delicately attentive sensory imagination developing variously in different seventeenth-century poets, is, I suggest, a far more pressing influence on the scented fields, the 'pure now purer air'[300] of Milton's Eden than the laborious putative parallels sought with Renaissance dictionaries.[301]

296 Ibid., 5.479–82; Carey, *Milton*, p. 118.

297 *Paradise Lost* 4.150–51; 3.386–89. Compare 4.558, where vapours 'impress' the air.

298 *Nativity Ode* 20; *Paradise Lost* 4.556; 7.356–57, 361–62, compare 7.264; 1.226–27.

299 Ricks, *Milton's Grand Style* (Oxford: 1963) pp. 94–96; *Paradise Lost* 5.384–89; 9.425; 5.379; 5.293, 298.

300 *Paradise Lost* 4.153.

301 Duncan, *Milton's Earthly Paradise*, pp. 32–35; also D. T. Starnes and E. W. Talbert, *Classical Myth and Legend in Renaissance Dictionaries* (North Carolina: 1955), pp. 308–16.

In wide landscape views, the force and materiality of the intangible is repeatedly sensed in its power to transform the substantial world, as the sudden touch of heaven's breath, the dramatic emergence of sunshine or moonlight through cloud-mass, or the reviving caress of returning light:

> As when from mountain tops the dusky clouds
> Ascending, while the north wind sleeps, o'erspread
> Heaven's cheerful face, the louring element
> Scouts o'er the darkened landscape snow, or shower;
> If chance the radiant sun with farewell sweet
> Extend his evening beam, the fields revive,
> The birds their notes renew, and bleating herds
> Attest their joy, that hill and valley rings.[302]

Beelzebub hopes he may 'Dwell not unvisited of heaven's fair light / Secure, and at the brightening orient beam / Purge off this gloom; the soft delicious air, / To heal the scar of these corrosive fires / Shall breathe her balm.'[303] Frequently fragrance at morning or after rain 'From th' earth's great altar' rises as 'silent praise / To the Creator'[304] in a reciprocity of loving and refining process, just as passages of air always bear spiritual sweetness: 'But here I feel amends, / The breath of heaven fresh blowing, pure and sweet, / With day-spring born.'[305] The light of sun and moon, themselves in one sense 'bright effluence of bright essence increate'[306] are repeatedly portrayed in dazzling breakings of cloud,[307] whilst first light heartens birds as Satan:

> And now the sun with more effectual beams
> Had cheered the face of earth, and dried the wet
> From drooping plant, or dropping tree; the birds
> Who all things now behold more fresh and green,
> After a night of storm so ruinous,
> Cleared up their choicest notes in bush and spray
> To gratulate the sweet return of morn.[308]

To the 'transfiguring aerial' of air, breath and light, potent agencies of transforming purity, we may add the very 'elements' of Eden, whose

302 *Paradise Lost* 2.488–95. 303 Ibid., 2.398–402.
304 Ibid., 9.195–96. 305 *Samson Agonistes* 9.11. Cf. *Paradise Lost* 4.645–66.
306 *Paradise Lost* 3.6.
307 Ibid., 3.378–82; 1.593–600; 2.488–95; 4.150–52, 605–09; *Comus* 221–25, 331–35; *Il Penseroso* 71–72.
308 *Paradise Regained* 4.432–38. Cf. *Paradise Lost* 2.1034–42; 3.427–30.

fineness purge off gross objects and sinful humanity;[309] and the 'stellar virtue' of the 'arch-chemic sun' which, 'With gentle penetration, though unseen, / Shoots invisible virtue even to the deep'.[310]

A curious coda to such concerns is Milton's delighted immersion in the riddlings of Chaos. Satan's 'shoaling' through a wholly new dimension of space carries a science-fiction fascination, as he wallows and plummets through silted semi-vacuum and deranged gravitation.[311] The 'stunning sounds' that are 'Borne through the hollow dark'[312] suggests a blind man's fineness for acoustic weight, its sudden blows of dense sound packing vacancy (compare the sensitivity to stillness at 2.308–09). More than this, however, the detailed realization of this non-Biblical episode can be argued as a logical outcome or inevitability of the Miltonic imagination. Chaos arrays the intriguing plurality of the forms of physical substance, luxuriously juxtaposing their violent antipathies yet refusing them constitutive determinacy: a realm of foundering substance and dissolving natural boundaries. The riddles of this non-world, densely fluvial,[313] a 'windy sea of land', a 'palpable obscure',[314] clearly spring from the imaginative concern with the antinomies of weight and substance, the fibrous air and blossoming matter, whose architecture is the created world. Moreover, the abrupt mutations and mutual interruption of elements – the gusts, waves, resistances, meltings – can be seen to reproduce in negative version what we might call the ontological restlessness, the dynamic interflow and evolution, of Creation. Deprived of ordering nisus, its energies are randomized, conflictual. Milton's Chaos, then, is no quaint adjunct, but deeply integral, to his cosmological sensibility.

Marvell's *Upon Appleton House* develops a poetics of sensuous affective particularity to a degree of acuity unprecedented in the English language. Whilst it has been amply demonstrated that the poem 'remodels topography in forms suggested by didactic emblems, theatrical scene-building, perspective distortions and architecture',[315] to describe it as 'a typical locodescriptive poem of the post-war years'[316] is to entomb Marvell alive beneath a ponderous cairn of

309 *Paradise Lost* 2.139–42, 11.50–53.
310 *Paradise Lost* 3.585–86, 606–12; 4.642–45.
311 2.890–1046; cf. 10.285–88.
312 Ibid., 2.952–53.
313 Cf. Satan's reaching 'emptier waste, resembling air' at 2.1045.
314 Ibid., 3.440; 2.406.
315 Turner, *Politics*, p. 49.
316 Ibid., p. 62.

contemporary parallels. Whilst this is regularly Marvell's fate,[317] this is murder by bland homogenizing, much like summing up *Paradise Lost* on the basis of its Pauline and Augustinian moments as a typical Christian poem. Whilst one nods as Ruth Wallerstein speaks of the 'intense sensuous realization' of *Appleton House*, declaring 'Nothing in the range of English Literature ... more fresh with observation',[318] her disappointing belief in the poem's safe syncopations of beauty and meaning within neo-platonic tradition serve to scuttle the poem in tepid tides of homogeneity. Marvell is better appreciated, I would argue, in the spirit of the ideas of Machiavelli and Arminius than the letter of those of Aquinas and Bonaventura: a thought-world of precarious self-determination, of blocked teleology and vigilance amidst novelty, distinguishes his sensibility, his riddling keenness to the affective nuances of sense-experience.

The nature-sensibility within which Marvell's landscape-consciousness moves is conditioned by an idiosyncratic understanding of the Fall. A lost consonance with nature, a fugitive quest of stasis, haunts the pastorals as well as *Appleton House*. The Mower's mind that 'was once the true survey / Of all these meadows fresh and gay,' the fauns and fairies who 'the meadows till / More by their presence than their skill'[319] bespeak the pristine communion, the completing mutuality, briefly regained in the process of ecstatic self-transcendence in 'The Garden'. Paradoxically, however, the Fall in Marvell means empowerment: a sophisticated ease won through brutal subjugation by 'Man that sovereign thing and proud'.[320] We have written already on Marvell as poet of urban instrumentation and pathos, and we may take the celebrated garden of Tivoli's Villa D'Este (which he probably visited) for emblem of this post-medieval relation to nature: its leisured vista of command across imposed and ruthless order, the despotic mathematics of its amenities (the squared gardens, *parterres de*

317 As, for example, in Leishman's reduction of Marvell's poetics to typicality in *The Art of Marvell's Poetry*; Ruth Wallerstein on Marvell's 'neo-platonism', in *Seventeenth Century Poetic*; Donald M. Friedman on Marvell as belonging with the Cambridge Platonists: *Marvell's Pastoral Art* (London: 1970); Rosalie L. Colie, who claims of Marvell that he 'ends a great tradition ... looks back at it, studies it, criticises it, but neither questions its absoluteness, nor offers radically different expressive alternatives ... he turns back into his tradition': *My Ecchoing Song* (Princeton: 1970), p. 4.

318 *Seventeenth Century Poetic*, pp. 185 and 300.

319 'The Mower's Song' lines 1–2; 'The Mower Against Gardens' lines 35–36.

320 'Mower Against Gardens' line 20.

broderie and regular fountains) contrasting sharply with the feudal relation of precarious subsistence, war upon hinterlands, and calendar toil. The fruit of sin is power, resting on force – the 'forced power' of parliamentary victory, or of the seventeenth-century garden where 'tis all enforced, the fountain and the grot, / While the sweet fields do lie forgot'.[321]

The cost of such sin is the intense anxiety of a world of genuine novelty. The historical pragmatics of the 'notable English Italo-Machiavellian'[322] – 'Though justice against fate complain, / And plead the ancient rights in vain: / But those do hold or break / As men are strong or weak'[323] – here assume rather pre-Kierkegaardian connotations of total possibility. The world's order has passed from the harmonic integrity of man and nature under the divine scheme, into a condition of contingency and hazard. 'And for the last effect / Still keep thy sword erect.'[324] Since the divine telos – 'the stars' – require man's executive co-operation, the refusal of 'man unruled' may mean 'the ill delaying what the elected hastes'.[325] Whilst providence may redeem us where human will compounds with divine (as in Cromwell who 'urged his active star', where 'High grace should meet in one with highest power', 'Doubling that knot which destiny had tied', just as the Fairfaxes 'make their destiny their choice'[326]) in a world where such 'doubling' is refused, 'the gods themselves with us do dwell.'[327] Human postlapsarian identity exercises a tense, problematic governance of a world of precarious mutation.

In this realm of dislocated freedom, of apostate relations with Creation, where man has 'dealt between the bark and tree / Forbidden mixtures there to see', nature herself founders into incalculability, 'uncertain and adulterate'.[328] It is this relocation of history's mutating openness in the experience of landscape, his reading within the book of nature itself the postlapsarian perversion into inestimability and

321 'An Horatian Ode upon Cromwell's Return from Ireland', line 66; 'Mower Against Gardens' lines 31–32.

322 A phrase used of Marvell during his travels in France in 1656: see *Poems and Letters of Andrew Marvell*, ed. H. M. Margoliouth, 3rd edn, rev. Pierre Legouis and E. E. Duncan-Jones, vol. 2 (Oxford: 1971), p. 378.

323 'An Horatian Ode' lines 37–40.

324 'Horatian Ode' line 116.

325 *Upon Appleton House* line 9; 'The First Anniversary of the Government under His Highness the Lord Protector, 1655' line 156.

326 'Horatian Ode' line 12; 'First Anniversary' line 132; 'A Poem upon the Death of His Late Highness the Lord Protector' line 44; *Upon Appleton House* line 744.

327 'Mower Against Gardens' line 40.

328 Ibid., lines 21–22, 25.

flux, that generates the uniqueness of Marvell's landscape description. Not only is the empiricism anxiously acute; this is frequently a poetry of truth to the senses aimed at exhibiting the falsehood of the senses. The self-subverting sensualist poetics, its keen particularities distended in a parodic, hyperbolical mode, articulates the rediscovery in meadow, wood and garden of man's unlodged insecurity of perspective, a non-finality both of being and knowledge.

The most obvious instance of this agnosticism is Marvell's much-remarked sleight-of-perspective. Paradoxes of perspectival diminution tease even a dutiful public elegy, in the 'felled tree' of the Lord Protector: 'The eye / Detracts from objects than itself more high ... The tree erewhile foreshortened to our view / When fall'n shows taller yet than as it grew.'[329] Fuller treatment unfolds in the private contemplative vision of *Appleton House*, with the giant grasshoppers amid the 'precipices tall / Of the green spires' of the meadow-grass, and the virtuoso oscillations of magnitude as grazing cattle shrink to facial spots, abruptly magnify as fleas beneath microscope, then splay into an astronomy of slow-travelling constellations.[330] Reference to quick-change 'scenes' doubtless was influenced by the practice of setting masques in gardens,[331] the grasshoppers may echo those of *Numbers* 13.33, and Marvell may well have seen contemporary looking-glasses literally adorned with landscapes on their surface.[332] But the emphasis in stanzas 47 and 58 upon jumping, disarranged vision, upon swallowing ambiguities of scale, seeks to enact an epistemological disorientation, and not merely a light play of conceits. The hyperbolical distortions of the grasshopper passage, alarmed hallucinations immediate from the physical sensations of sinking into deeps of 'unfathomable grass',[333] are in a sense confirmed by the scientific laws of optical relativism structuring stanza 58.

For Marvell, simply to wade into deep grass is to re-encounter on the flesh the lost footings of contemporary knowledge. The 'bold tube' of the astronomers[334] has revealed the duplicities or limits of human vision, and the revolutions of microscope and telescope – stimulating theories of heliocentricity and a plurality of worlds – seem

329 'Death of the Lord Protector' lines 273–74, 269–70.
330 *Upon Appleton House* lines 375–76, 457–64.
331 Ibid., lines 385, 441, 465: Hunt, *Andrew Marvell*, pp. 20–24.
332 Turner, *Topographia*, Additional Note 2.
333 *Upon Appleton House* line 370.
334 'The Last Instructions to a Painter' line 949.

to prove man's mind, or natural optics, no 'true survey'[335] of a world now immeasurably vaster and tinier about him. Unlike Milton and Chamberlayne, Marvell's art will not, may not, adduce panoramic prospect, calculably subject: one was available at Bilborough hill (which still commands a fine vista today, though the hill has lost its steepness since the seventeenth century), and he ignored it. His landscape instead subverts the 'lordship of the eye'[336] into a spinning visual vassalage.

Sceptically alert to our cozening boundaries of perception, he notes how the wood, whose mass appears impenetrable at a distance, opens in fact 'passable and thin'; recognizes that music, as a 'mosaic of the air', can invisibly 'wreathe / ... fetters of the very air / I breathe'; and conceives in the brilliance of summer flowers the blazing of inaudible shots.[337] Eruptive violence indicates the lack of settlement of a nature of shaken foundations: the meadow quilted with slain and pillaged grass, the cattle 'astonished' by sudden cataract and flood, the fledgeling heron insouciantly dropped by a parent to its death, and the rail, helpless to fly, hacked and bloodied in the grass[338] report a realm where 'lowness is unsafe as height, / And chance o'ertakes what 'scapeth spite'.[339] Disturbance invades meaning as well as order: scenic incongruities obtrude themselves upon Marvell's consciousness – the obscurely perturbing 'hatching throstle's shining eye', the oranges as 'golden lamps in a green night', the caterpillars crawling

335 'The Mower's Song' line 1. The influence of contemporary painting upon Marvell – who probably had access to Maria Fairfax' copy of Norgate's *Miniatura* (Colie, p. 194) – is often acknowledged, but Marvell's sceptical emphasis on optical relativism and fraudulence understated. Colie, for instance, notes of Marvell's emblems that he 'alters his traditional sources in favour of problematics', and that his 'pictorialism' admits the 'distortive' tradition of catoptric and anamorphic landscape: yet her often perceptive study still sees *Upon Appleton House* as displaying 'a coherent series of pictorial descriptions', and refers to Marvell on occasion as presenting 'nature plain and pure' – a serene positivism which his project in problematizing had sought to disable. (pp. 200–01, 210, 195–96, 211.)

336 Henry Wotton's term, as he revels in the intellectual masterfulness of prospect painting: *Reliquiae Wottoniae*, p. 204.

337 *Upon Appleton House* lines 497–506; 'Music's Empire' line 17 and 'The Fair Singer' lines 11–12; *Upon Appleton House* lines 305–8.

338 *Upon Appleton House* lines 420–24, 465–80, 533–36, 395–98.

339 Ibid., line 411.

between the oak leaves of the contemplative's 'cope'[340] – and in this instinct for the bizarre, the unaccommodated, Marvell's is a poetry rather of cosmographic crisis, of anagogic aporiai, than of mastering hieroglyph. It is hard on occasion not to feel a certain hysteria as quelled and ordered by the disciplined couplets and crisp octosyllables:

> Then as I careless on the bed
> Of gelid strawberries do tread,
> And through the hazels thick espy
> The hatching throstle's shining eye,
> The heron from the ash's top,
> The eldest of its young lets drop,
> As if it stork-like did pretend
> That tribute to its Lord to send.[341]

There is an almost manic note here: a smooth glide into a senseless violence beneath an unchanged suavity of surface. The closing simile suggests a nervous 'recuperation' of the grotesque for pattern or norm, just as Marvell elsewhere recovers hieroglyphic securities of meaning by willed returns of *paysage moralisé*, of coping normativity – as in the suddenly banal 'traitor-worm' of sin in stanza 70[342] – which themselves reissue violence: the worm torn from the tree and devoured by the hewel's young, the crashing oak 'content' to know its destruction shared. Marvell's poetic style, its fastidious precision creating the sense of enigma, of the reaching for an unavailable synthesis, has clear affinities with contemporary scientific investigation and philosophic thought, ateleological, clinically dispassionate, scanning from a *tabula rasa*, just as his grotesques and amphibii belong with contemporary concern for a fantastical nature of marvels, riddles and freaks.[343] Rosemary Freeman notes that in English emblem books of the seventeenth century the emblems are far less naturalistic than in earlier periods, their particulars of significance now laboured and elaborate: with the 'Disintegration of a unified allegorical conception of the world', such correspondences 'are not taken for granted.'[344]

Further to this world of total possibility, of stabilities in dissolution, is the haunting of Marvell's eye by mutations of substance. 'Uncertain and adulterate', a nature of bastardized biology, the earth's firm fibres

340 *Upon Appleton House* line 532; 'Bermudas' lines 17–18; *Upon Appleton House* lines 587–88.

341 *Upon Appleton House* lines 529–36.

342 Cf. the standard complimentation of Maria, the 'pastoral hyperbole', of stanzas 87–88.

343 Cf. Scoular, *Natural Magic*, passim.

344 Freeman, *English Emblem Books*, pp. 20–23.

seep. Solids run aqueous, coagulate, congeal. The soil itself, like the fish in Appleton's brook, may be 'stupefied', and 'putrid earth exhale'.[345] The oncoming of evening intrigues as a fluvial treachery of being. The air grows 'viscous' (673), 'the jellying stream compacts' (675), creeping mist silently 'charms' or mesmerizes onlookers. Only Maria's presence can 'vitrify' (688) the scene, reimposing a fixity and clarity as of glass. Elsewhere manna is 'congealed and chill', strawberries form a 'gelid ... bed', and oxygen, trapped, may solidify into 'A dead and standing pool of air'.[346] In this alchemical indeterminacy, where 'the nutriment doth change the kind', the undifferentiated bulk of the wood suggests some foreign biological mutation, eerily 'thrusting up' some 'fifth element'.[347]

Marvell, then, has no truck with 'landskip': that process of pressing nature out and away from the person by means of measure and optical law into outspread planes of externality and depth, the process comparable with objectifying the engulfing experience of a symphony by unfolding before the eyes the printed pages of its score. Rather, he displaces 'landskip' by tactile landscaping, by a language of texture and metamorphosis that expresses the instability of creation and the subjectivism of human understanding.

Another important point is here. 'And for the last effect / Still keep thy sword erect.' Marvell, however, repeatedly lays down his arms, has nature infiltrate his body-space. Persistently, his tactile landscaping haunts thresholds of fusion, derelicts the ordering, observing, meditative human self for a guilty sensuous deliquescence. His encounters, in their textural impressionability, renounce the cerebral, mastering drive for a pleasuring bodily subjectivism, a knowledge of the pores and tongue,[348] a trespass of the senses. There is at a deep level in Marvell's imagination an homology between the worms' invasion of the body of the Coy Mistress and the caterpillars that crawl on the flesh beneath the nature – 'lover's' antic cope: nature, like death, may become a 'consuming' of the self, a condition of self-loss, where bliss and annihilation merge.

For, inescapably dualistic within a Christian imagination, nature

345 *Upon Appleton House* line 677 and 'Mower Against Gardens' line 8; *Upon Appleton House* line 686.

346 'On a Drop of Dew' line 38; *Upon Appleton House* line 530, compare 'Damon the Mower' line 28; 'Mower Against Gardens' line 6.

347 'Mower Against Gardens' line 10; *Upon Appleton House* line 502.

348 Pores: *Upon Appleton House* line 596; tongue: lines 635, 590.

inevitably holds opposing aspects for Marvell, albeit characteristically idiosyncratic. Measure of postlapsarian instability and menace (flux and violence, oddity and distortion), of fallen humanity's imperative vigilance, simultaneously she offers refuge from such tensions of dominion: in the amnesia of sensual glut, and intimations of transcendence. Marvell's engagement of nature moves repeatedly between these principles, between surveillance and self-loss, coercion and consonance, psychomachia and abandon, just as his style is the imbrication of the dialectical and the sensuous, the monitoring, interrogative mind and the tantalized, tasting body.

The urge to self-loss, to release from identity as alienated command, is evident in the motif of the immuring, contracting circle (the fairy ring around the mower, the 'garlands of repose' of trees and flowers of 'The Garden', the encircling woodbines and vines of the Appleton estate).[349] Possibly unconscious, the quest for a merging and forgetfulness is also a structuring principle of the narrative movement from meadow to wood and the appearance of Maria. Entering the 'unfathomable grass', he experiences in the 'green sea' the ambiguity of underwater movement: 'none does know / Whether he fall through it or go'.[350] Phenomenologically acute, the perception derives, like the garden's 'pool of standing air', from the underflowing concern for opposition between self-determination and self-loss: does one here 'fall or go': surrendering to gravity or retaining independent movement? The appearance of the mowers with their carnage extirpates any possibility of absorption into nature, just as the wood unpromisingly appears to debar man. Yet it admits him, and an extreme of integration, physical and psychic, ensues within its seething closure. 'And little now to make me wants / Or of the fowls, or of the plants.'[351] The 'inverted tree' conceit (lines 567–68), fascinatingly, is a universal of world mythology;[352] but 'No leaf does tremble in the wind / Which I, returning, cannot find'[353] is the ecstatic boast of a tenderest discrimination, a superlatively intimate affective bonding with material particulars, that is unthinkable, absurd, in preceding Christian traditions. That this is a wood not a grove is again provocative novelty: the wood has long been synonymous with the

349 'Damon the Mower' line 64; 'The Garden' line 7; *Upon Appleton House* lines 609–12.

350 *Upon Appleton House* lines 370, 390, 379–80.

351 Ibid., lines 563–64.

352 Eliade, *Patterns*, pp. 274–76.

353 *Appleton House* lines 575–76.

ὕλε or chaos which is its Greek name. From this fantasia of self-loss, however, Maria – the public, historical world, of duty, 'judicious eyes'[354] – recalls him.

The escapist motif continues, however, in the language of natural capture. Marvell has already importuned nature's 'silken bondage', her vines to curl him about, has enjoyed the voluptuously 'familiar' ivy that 'Me licks, and clasps, and curls, and hales', and projected this salacious innocence onto the meadow with its 'wanton harmless folds'.[355] With Maria's arrival the poet, correctly disengaged from his thrilling couplings, conceives in the evening a now ominous process of entrapment. Creeping shadows emerge to close shutters upon 'the river as it flows'. 'Admiring' the halcyon, nature gives pursuit to 'suck' her dye. The stream compacts as if to 'fix' her shadow (in retaliation perhaps for itself being enclosed by shades), even as it 'stupefies' its fish, captured as are flies in crystal. Embraces in nature are become 'an horror [or paralysis] calm and numb'.[356]

The poem's express solicitations of seduction, the language of flagrant erotic inflammation – the imagery of sliding foot, of 'abandoned' body sinking luxuriously onto its 'lazy side', 'languishing with ease' and 'treading' (Renaissance slang for sexual intercourse) upon delicious 'beds'[357] – these all provoke a deliberate ambivalence, activate explicitly ethical reflexes. The fervours of self-loss they articulate are not the wise distantiations from war and city familiar from pastoral. 'The Garden' knows such innocent diversion – 'Society is all but rude, / To this delicious solitude' – but there the physical transcendence is total: 'Annihilating all that's made / To a green thought in a green shade.'[358] On the Nun Appleton estate the 'body's vest' is not 'cast aside' but retained, fondled, impurely inflamed. For the narrator's flight is neither celestial, nor, simplistically, from social chaos: it is from human identity itself. Seduced by a Circe-like nature, he is abdicating that vigilant relation of command which is the essence of human being. The eroticizing of the language perfectly re-enacts the transgressive, furtive excitement: the guilt of a *self-denaturing* communion. ('And little now to make me wants / Or of the fowls, or of the plants.') At Maria's arrival the poet steps out blushing from the coils of his antic cope: a dubious figure, an ontological transvestite.

354 Ibid., line 653.
355 Lines 609–16, 589–90, 633.
356 Stanzas 84–85.
357 Lines 643–45, 593, 529–30.
358 'The Garden' lines 15–16, 47–48.

In summary, then, Marvell's 'phenomenological' landscaping derives from both mistrust and desertions of controlling human reason. The former produces a feverish versatility of perception, a fantasia of epistemological pluralism, whose mercurial conceits are no more 'uncertain and adulterate' than their mutating physical objects. The latter flaunts an apperception of mood and its sensory stimuli, unmanning enticements from sobriety and duty. This astonishing poetry derives, ultimately, not only from the obvious determinants: the long Christian tradition of natural contemplation; the seventeenth-century emphasis on solitary introspection and the regulation of the affections; the 'cosmographic' crisis, theological and scientific, heightening a delirium of undigested acuities. It is also a product of Marvell's class position. As a middle-class urban professional he has a 'role-free' relation to landscape (as most Romantics are to have): his is neither the agrarian calendar nor the seigneurial recreative eye. As a Puritan he favours neither the Cavalier landscape of *amours* nor the royalist attempt to recuperate and extol 'country games.' In contrast with these, he is an 'easy philosopher',[359] free for a purely cognitive-aesthetic relation. Again, his position in Fairfax's household as a tutor designated him part-servant, part-gentleman: an ambiguity which must have helped heighten his vision of man's conditional authority: the strain of and reaction against an insecure ascendance.

Sprezzatura vs. *Asprezza*: The landscape of the active life

In contrast to contemporary Dutch landscapes, with their busy ferries, canals and windmills, their fields of neatly staked vegetables and hard-won corn, landscape paintings of England in the seventeenth century largely feature work-free idylls: lakeside walks and ancient mansions, panegyrics to unobtrusive lordly rule (plate 15). In seventeenth-century verse similarly, 'Like a new colony, the land is cleared of its troublesome natives and planted with a new and more loyal population – hilarious bumpkins, contented morons, fauns, fairies and demigods ... There is virtually no mention of land-clearance, tree-felling, pruning, chopping, digging, hoeing, weeding.'[360] Fanshawe writes rather of the 'everlasting rest' of White Peace in England: 'one blest isle: / Which in a sea of plenty swamme / And turtles sang on

359 *Upon Appleton House* line 561.

360 Turner, *Politics*, pp. 185, 165.

ev'ry bowgh, / A safe retreat to all that came / As ours is now.'[361] There are elements, however, of a counter-tradition to the hankering for *otium* of panegyric, pastoral tradition and paradisal imagination. The Puritan spirituality of trial, and the spirit of commitment to political or religious reform, favour in poetry landscapes of vigour, struggle and hazard, and contribute both to impressions of exhilarating energy in nature herself, and to a corresponding distaste for the 'decadent', stagnant luxury of garden and bower. The landscape of struggle as concomitant of a politically endeavouring vision and sensibility has affinities with the turbulent, 'disturbed' pastoral of Petrarch and his imitators, darkened by war and hardships; but in the English Renaissance it may be identified with the tradition of reforming 'prophetic radicalism' descending from Spenser to Milton.[362]

Antony Low has endeavoured to unearth a 'Georgic Revolution' in the seventeenth century: its foundations in the medieval ploughman tradition and in Spenser, and its stimulus in bourgeois values of practical industry, particularly the 'new husbandry' of the century. Yet though Spenser praises 'use' (4.10.8.8), on occasion associates his knights with commendable rural labour (1.10.66; 6.9.37), and dispraises brigands who cannot 'live by plough nor spade'[363] (6.9.39.4), this 'fundamental revision of aristocratic ideals, away from preoccupation with leisure, grace, and *sprezzatura*'[364] does not, I would argue, produce a new 'eye' for landscape in *The Faerie Queene*: in which calendar scenery is quite absent, and whose *loci amoeni* and *viles* remain largely typicalities of the tradition of medieval romance. In Milton likewise, though the prose writings are dense with references to and metaphors from the dignity of labour and husbandry, the poetry knows little georgic. *Comus* acknowledges a 'laboured ox' and 'swinked hedger', *Paradise Lost* notes the pleasing 'smell of grain, or tedded grass, or kine, / Or dairy', and *Paradise Regained* includes an agrarian prospect of 'Fair champaign' and 'fertile glebe'[365]: but these are not dissimilar to the smiling, backgrounded labour of Country

361 'Ode upon Occasion of His Majesty's Proclamation in the year 1630. Commanding the Gentry to reside upon their estates in the Countrey' in *The Oxford Book of Seventeenth Century Verse* ed. H. J. C. Grierson and G. Bullough (Oxford: 1934), p. 448.

362 Cf. Norbrook, *Poetry and Politics*, passim.

363 Note the same derogation in *Odyssey* 9.134ff, echoed as we have seen by Mandeville.

364 Low, *Georgic Revolution*, pp. 42–43.

365 *Comus* lines 290–92; *Paradise Lost* 9.450–51: compare the wheatfield metaphor at 4.980–85; *Paradise Regained* 3.253–60.

House verse. Had the corn been reaped rather than smelled, the glebe been harrowed rather than purviewed, we would have been in the realm of georgic. Only in his fellow parliamentarian Wither do we encounter a landscape of vigorous action:

> Before the *Plowman* hopefull can be made,
> His untill'd earth good Hay or Corne will yeeld,
> He breakes the hillocks downe, with *Plough* or *Spade*;
> And harrowes over all the cloddie Field …
> Our craggie *Nature* must be tilled, thus,
> Before it will, for *Herbes of Grace*, be fit …[366]

A liberal Arminian, like Milton, Wither focuses on labour in no less than fourteen plates in his *Collection of Emblemes* (1635).[367] Emblems of accompanying poems detail the freeing of furrows from weeds, worms and moles, depict fence-mending, seed-sowing, ploughed lands and gathered ears of corn (emblems to pp. 50, 106, 144). This is highly original. As Low confesses, the temper of the Church of England and the dominant sects was unfavourable to such landscape-consciousness: 'the ascendency of Calvinist doctrine in the earlier seventeenth century made it rare for anyone to do much more than reiterate the customary injunctions against idleness'.[368] Indeed Christian other-worldliness could slight husbandry, as when Vaughan dispraises man that he 'Adores dead dust, sets heart on corn and grass / But seldom doth make heaven his glass', or Herbert writes: 'We talk of harvests; there are no such things, / But when we leave our corn and hay: / There is no fruitfull yeare, but that which brings / The last and lov'd, though dreadfull day.'[369]

What runs counter to lyrical *otium* in seventeenth-century landscape poetry, then, is not, I would argue, a georgic revolution, a landscape of manual exertion: it is rather a landscape of venture.

Spenser is the important foundation. Emphasis in *The Faerie Queene* is not on resolution but on constant quest and the dangers of complacency:[370]

> Where ease abounds, yt's eath to do amis:
> But who his limbs with labours, and his mind
> Behaves with cares, cannot so easie mis.
> Abroad in armes, at home in studious kind

366 *A Collection of Emblemes* (London: 1635), Book 3, Illus. x, p. 144.
367 Low, *Georgic Revolution*, pp. 203–212. 368 Ibid., p. 214.
369 'The Constellation' lines 19–20 in *Complete Poems*: Herbert, 'Home', lines 55–8.
370 Norbrook, Poetry and Politics, pp. 15, 110–111.

> Who seekes with painfull toile, shall honor soonest find.
>
> In woods, in waves, in warres she wonts to dwell,
> And will be found with perill and with paine.[371]

Aware 'dayly how through hardy enterprize, / Many great Regions are discovered' (2 Proem 2.3–4), Spenser's landscapes subsist as the medium of the active life and self-achievement, and their character is often influenced by the landscapes of the New World – 'fraught with fabulous dangers and trials ... a world of riches and menace'.[372] Given the internationalism of Spenser's vision in another regard – his support of armed aid to the continental reformed churches and his personal involvement in the ruthless war of attrition in Ireland – it is natural that his imagination inhabits 'open' landscapes, wide and fraught, as against the quietistic, protected enclaves of paradise garden and faraway pastoral playworld, the 'closed' space of stasis and private hedonism. Even his 'paradises' seem 'open' in emphasis rather than charmed circles: vast in extent and sites of vigour, inviting of roving exploration. The landscape of Venus' temple for instance is said to offer greater 'ioyance free' than the Elysian Fields, and supplements the *Roman de la Rose*-style cornucopia of all trees and flowers by 'High reared mounts, the lands about to vew; / Low looking dales, disloigned from common gaze ... False Labyrinthes, fond runners eyes to daze' as well as 'walkes and alleyes' and seats to 'rest the walkers wearie shankes.'[373] The hilltop paradise of Mount Acidale scans 'the lowly vale' and offers an entire 'spacious plaine' (6.10.8). While we may link such preference with that 'expansionist' paradisal sensibility we remarked below in seventeenth-century poetry under 'the millenarian dawn' as overflowing the boundaries of the enclosed garden, Spenser's aim is the destabilization of paradisal security rather than its extension, as he subjects it to disappearance and invasion. On Acidale, Calidore, 'rapt with pleasaunce',[374] suddenly is robbed of the vision of the Graces, who 'being gone, none can them bring in place'; gathering strawberries in the greenwood, Pastorella is attacked by a tiger; her gentle pastoral village is razed by brigands, her friends robbed and killed (6.10.34, 39, 40). An order of genuine moral seriousness emerges with these dangerous ambiguous landscapes of fairness and evil, whose tensions elevate them above the enamelled

371 *Faerie Queene* 2.3.40.5–9, 41.1–2.

372 Stephen Greenblatt, *Renaissance Self-Fashioning* (Chicago: 1980), p. 180.

373 *Faerie Queene* 4.10.23.9; 24.5–6, 8; 25.1, 4–5.

374 Ibid., 6.10.17.4; 20.4.

world of so much Renaissance pastoral and affiliate them to the landscapes of Homer and Virgil, of the New Testament and politicized medieval pastoral. Behind them is also the pressure of experience: Spenser's castle in Ireland, Kilcolman, was surprised and burned to the ground, and Spenser in Ireland was himself involved as agent and apologist in 'massacre, the burning of mean hovels and of crops ... the forced relocation of peoples'.[375] The Irish landscape itself harboured brigands in its forests, and Spenser witnessed there an old woman drink the blood of an executed 'traitor'.[376] *The Faerie Queene* thus unsurprisingly unfolds landscapes of hazard, of alien energies in need of subjugation, sites of climactic struggle.

Correlative with the endeavouring, reforming, self-determining spirit producing Spenser's 'open' landscape is a contempt for the retreatism and sybaritic fantasy of 'closed' landscape, such as informed much contemporary pastoral (the tonality of Marlowe's 'Passionate Shepherd to his Love') and was to structure so much Cavalier lyric. His *loci amoeni* – Mount Acidale, Arlo Hill, the Garden of Adonis – are strikingly free of 'bejewelled' writing, featuring only 'crystal' streams. The amenities and retirements of such landscapes – the bowers and arbours, mounts and labyrinths – are insisted upon as natural formations, not the softening seductions of art.[377] Supreme instance of reviled 'closed' landscape is the Bower of Bliss, the overwrought 'art-landscape' whose *voluptas* is gratuitous, insulting the sufficiency of nature. Its 'lavish affluence' does 'too lavishly adorne' nature, 'as halfe in scorne / Of niggard Nature'. Here, where it seems that 'Art at nature did repine', where golden fruit are 'so made by art, to beautifie the rest', nature's branches are bowed down, 'over-burdened ... with so rich load opprest'.[378] Otiose and over-rich, a snub to nature's own beauties and oppressor of natural energy and force, this 'effeminating'[379] landscape stupefies the will as it bends the branches, its corruptly idle indulgence threatening to paralyse the purposive, self-

375 Greenblatt, *Renaissance Self-Fashioning*, p. 186.
376 Norbrook, *Poetry and Politics*, pp. 144–5.
377 *Faerie Queene* 3.6.44.2–3; 4.10.24.1–9; 6.10.6–8.
378 Ibid., 2.12 stanzas 42.9; 50.8, 6–7; 59.4; 55.2, 5–6.
379 Greenblatt, p. 181, cites the use of this word by Peter Martyr, who fears the adverse effects of voluptuous New World landscape upon 'good behaviour': *The Decades of the New World*, trans. M. Lok, in *A Selection of Curious, Rare, and Early Voyages and Histories of Interesting Discoveries chiefly published by Hakluyt* (London: 1812), p. 530.

fashioning will, to disable appetency for the rugged condition of venture and endurance, the ambiguous openness of the world of 'nature'. Unseduced from his forward-tensed spirituality ('lookd still forward right, / Bridling his will'),[380] Guyon razes 'all those pleasant bowres and Pallace brave', enemies of vigilance and strenuous virtue: 'Their arbers spoyle, their Cabinets suppresse, / Their banket houses burne, their building race.'[381] What fall here are precisely the exquisite emblems of so much Cavalier landscape of the seventeenth century: the cabinets and banqueting houses of so many actual noble estates, the delicately lascivious hypnosis of *carpe diem* and the charming cup.[382] The landscape of *sprezzatura* (spontaneous, effortless grace), the 'cult of the too-easy', must cede to the virtue of *asprezza* (roughness, hard going), just as the art of *The Faerie Queene* itself, unlike the self-concealing art of Acrasia, foregrounds difficulty of meaning and progress, 'announces its status as art-object at every turn'.[383]

Spenser similarly is wary of country sports and festivals. He attacks May games in the May eclogue, and presents 'a reformed spring ritual, directed to the service of a godly ruler' in 'April'.[384] Puritanism long campaigned to replace the traditional seasonal ceremonial and feasts, which it regarded as relics of paganism, by a culture based on literacy, and Milton's *Comus* echoes sage and serious Spenser when it contemns the 'riot' and 'wanton dance' of the 'loose, unlettered hinds' who thereby 'thank the gods amiss' for their 'teeming flocks, and granges full'.[385] But the same anxious political conservatism that feared popular literacy strove to maintain an imaging of the English countryside as a realm of ease and feast: James I strongly encouraged rural festivities as keeping the populace loyal to the established church through its ancient agrarian calendar, and as defusing in its sanctioned revelries political discontent. In consequence, Cavaliers such as Jonson in 'To Penshurst' and Herrick in 'The Hock-Cart' celebrate a country feasting that consolidates traditional order, whilst Spenserian poets such as Drayton and Browne come to praise the countryside as nurturing unluxurious moral hardihood, and, as pressure mounts to support continental Protestantism, as nourishing martial virtue. Part

380 *Faerie Queene* 2.12.53.4–5.
381 Ibid., 2.12.83.1, 7–8.
382 Charming cup: 2.12.56.1.
383 Greenblatt, *Renaissance Self-Fashioning*, p. 190; compare Norbrook, *Poetry and Politics*, p. 112. On the influence of the Yucatan as a landscape of enchanting idleness and sexual profanity, see Greenblatt, pp. 180–84.
384 Norbrook, pp. 71–72, 85.
385 *Comus* lines 171–76.

one of *Polyolbion* (1612) recalls in its rovings of English scenery not only courts and cities, but past military glories, and portrays its dedicatee, Prince Henry, in full armour on its title-page; whilst part two (1622) praises great English victories. Likewise *Britannia's Pastorals* iii (1624) hymns the triumphs of the English navy under Drake and Greville – though censorship ensured that the volume remained unpublished.[386]

If these Spenserians take the countryside as *site* for crusading energy and mighty struggle, Milton's sensibility relocates these qualities within the landscape itself. Milton's deep 'animistic' feeling for the natural world led him twice to translate Psalm 114, whose exuberance in the dancing of crags and skipping of mountains cancels the didactic limits of traditional cosmology: 'Only the earth does stand forever still'[387] is a bloodless pedantry beside Milton's poem, just as *Orchestra*'s cosmic dance as measured, stately motion feels constrained and courtly alongside the primitive and sacred animation of Milton and his Psalmist. Something of this unsophisticated energy appears in the 'wavering morris' danced by the finny drove of *Comus* as the stars circle and fairies trip, and in the teeming Nature who 'pour[s] her bounties forth, / With such a full and unwithdrawing hand, / Covering the earth with odours, fruits, and flocks, / Thronging the seas with spawn innumerable'.[388] His habitual sense of the inwardly driven object made Milton the first, it appears, to use the word 'instinct' to signify the internal propulsion of an object (in this case, God's chariot 'instinct with spirit').[389] Though doubtless encouraged by the Hebraic tradition of festal animation, the classical motif of the pastoral hyperbole, and Paul's conviction of creation yearning in travail (*Romans* 8.22), Milton's landscaping is distinctive, I feel, in taking the dynamism of vast animate energies in nature as the norm. His early poem against deterioration in nature establishes the contradiction, in tone at least, of a perfect perpetuity of primal violence: lightning bolts forever strike and shatter cliffs, winds buffet clouds and waves pound mountain-bases, as huge whales scud the waters echoing to Ocean's trumpet.[390] Such scenes of elemental

386 For these rival constructions of the countryside, see Norbrook, pp. 188–89, 208–09, 219–21, 242, 254.

387 Sir John Davies, *Orchestra* line 351, in *Silver Poets of the Sixteenth Century* ed. Gerald Bullett (London: 1947), p. 328.

388 *Comus* lines 116, 710–13.

389 *Paradise Lost* 6.752; the *OED* lists Milton's as the earliest usage in this sense.

390 'Naturam Non Pati Senium' lines 51–65.

combat clearly derive from Milton's own contending, endeavouring personality – 'he was born for whatever is arduous,' conceded Johnson[391] – and from the spirit of heroic religious belligerence of seventeenth-century puritanism, so well captured in Cromwell's remark 'Truly, I think he that prays best will fight best'.[392] The spirituality convinced that it 'May trace huge forests, and unharboured heaths, / Infamous hills, and sandy perilous wilds ... Yea there, where very desolation dwells' to win victory[393] may well remind us of the topography of oppugnancy of the desert fathers warring against the devil amid crags and molten wilderness. Antagonism is built into the law of the universe: 'Elemental and mixed things ... cannot suffer any change of one kind or quality into another, without the struggle of contrarieties ... No marble statue can be politely carved, no fair edifice built, without almost as much rubbish and sweeping.'[394] Militarist imagery mingles in his landscapes with peaceful daily process: *L'Allegro*'s dawn features the lark in his 'watch-tow'r in the skies' that 'startles' the night, and the cock that 'scatters the rear of darkness thin' (lines 43, 50). The *genius loci* of 'Arcades' patrols among his plants to 'save' them from 'blasting vapours', thunder and the 'smitings' of the 'dire-looking planet'; he 'numbers [their] ranks', and inspires their morale ('visit every sprout / With puissant words and murmurs made to bless': lines 48–52, 59–60). Given that a 'nature' thus emerges which closely recalls that which we encountered in the New Testament, (a scheme of menace and sudden death,) guardian spirits are unsurprisingly recurrent in the poetry: Sabrina 'Visits the herds along the twilight meadows, / Helping all urchin blasts', Lycidas becomes 'the Genius of the shore', and even in Eden 'bands' patrol on 'nightly watch', while plants need Eve at dusk and dawn to rear and water them.[395]

Just as he spurns idyllic landscape for a realm of powerful combats and sentinel spirits, so Milton Agonistes transforms the pastoral mode in *Lycidas*. Clay Hunt has shown how Milton elevates the smooth flowery ease of pastoral to the 'rugged going' of the heroic style: its roughly energetic movement, harsh textures, unpredictable stops,

391 Life of *John Milton* in *Lives of the English Poets*, ed. George Birkbeck Hill, 3 vols., vol. 1 (Oxford: 1905), p. 194. 392 Hill, *God's Englishman*, p. 75.

393 *Comus* lines 423–24, 428.

394 *Complete Prose Works*, ed. D. M. Wolfe (Yale: 1953), vol. 1, pp. 795–96.

395 *Comus* lines 844–45; *Lycidas* lines 183; *Paradise Lost* 4.684–85; 11. 275–79.

sudden starts, frequent copulas and speeding enjambments implement Tasso's ideal of *asprezza* – the effect of one stumbling in rough paths, in imitation of the labours of epic heroes.[396] This 'invigorated arduousness'[397] in Milton designedly disrupts the closed couplet that is the favourite form of Jonson and the Cavaliers, just as Spenser had always rejected facile harmonies for an emphasis on difficulty and struggle.[398] The pastoralism here is thus not Arcadian but, as David Norbrook notes, Spenserian-didactic: Milton pointedly repeals the exquisite flower catalogue of lines 133–51 as the 'dallying' of 'frail thoughts' (153), suggesting a renunciation of the escapism in this tradition. He hints at political apocalypse not far off (the 'two-handed engine'), and replaces the customary nightfall close of Eclogue by the unwearied accent of his 'uncouth' shepherd on future activity: 'Tomorrow to fresh woods, and pastures new'.[399]

We have seen that Spenser in *The Faerie Queene* eschews serene and closed landscapes, immune to the incursions of challenging reality, and sets his knights among 'open' landscapes whose want of security is underlined. In the seventeenth century, under the pressure of civil unrest and war, the 'closed' landscape grew ever more dear to, ever more emblematic of, the high Anglican and royalist. The *hortus conclusus* enters countless emblem books and meditative poems[400] just as the Jonesian ceremonial gateway dominated fashionable noble gardens, ornamenting exclusion and retreat. 'Anglican' and ('harmless') 'Angler' become almost identical terms by mid-century comments Douglas Bush,[401] whilst in the interregnum 'The writing of poetry in praise of a peaceful rural retirement must ... have been practically tantamount to a confession of loyalty to the Crown. This is true to such an extent that one is tempted to view the classical figure of the Happy Man as a conscious counterpart to the Puritan concept of the Christian pilgrim or warrior.'[402] '*Bene qui latuit, bene vixit*' sums up Cowley, in *Of Obscurity*. ('He lives well who lives retired.')[403]

396 Clay Hunt, *Lycidas and the Italian Critics* (New Haven and London: 1979), pp. 105–08.
397 Ibid., p. 106.
398 Norbrook, *Poetry and Politics*, pp. 272, 110–111.
399 Norbrook, pp. 272, 283–84; *Lycidas* lines 130, 186, 193.
400 Stanley Stewart, *Enclosed Garden*, passim.
401 *English Literature in the Earlier 17th Century* (1945; 2nd edn Oxford: 1962), p. 239.
402 Røstvig, p. 48. Christopher Hill suggests this somewhat over-simplified, adducing poetry unexamined by Røstvig, in *Puritanism and Revolution* (1958; rpt. Harmondsworth: 1986), p. 336, n. 1.
403 *Of Obscurity* in *Essays, Plays and Sunday Verses*, p. 398.

Against this sensibility Milton, who had praised in *Areopagitica* 'the true wayfaring Christian' who sallies out to see his adversary,[404] when he returns to poetry in 1658, paints, like Spenser, 'open' landscapes: imaginative concomitants of a bracing condition of liberty as exposure and trial, a challenging openness to all possibility. Like Spenser's, his paradise paradoxically evokes not enclosure but panorama, vast wandered tracts and deep prospects, an amplitude of champaign, hill and forest. The protected, retreatist tonality of the *hortus conclusus* and of idyll is spurned, even in Eden, for a more rugged condition. Not only are the defensive tree-walls of 'Insuperable highth' (4.138) overleaped effortlessly within forty-five lines. This Eden is presented only as Satan enters, its immunity shattered from the outset, a paradise truly 'exposed' in Milton's telling word (4.206). Transformed from the 'closed' landscape of haven to the 'open' landscape of venture and struggle, Eden is an arena of perfective trial. Milton will not praise a fugitive and cloistered landscape; for, in Eve's words:

> If this be our condition, thus to dwell
> In narrow circuit straitened by a foe,
> ... we not endued
> Single with like defence wherever met,
> How are we happy, still in fear of harm?
>
> (9.322–26.)

Though penned at the Restoration, these lines suggest something of what must have been the Spenserian perspective in the earlier decades of the century upon the induration of the Stuart nobility: retreated within adorned gardens for anxious masques apotropaically asserting a Golden Age Restored. Eve's words, moreover, are aptly ironic: it is precisely within her 'sweet recess' that Eve is tempted and falls (9.546).

Eden is 'open' landscape indeed as a functioning instance of the ideal active life. In general impression (4.223–66), this naturalistic landscape of flowing motion, a moulded, coherent effluence, contrasts sharply with the usual disconnected, 'itemized' landscapes of poetry, mere series of objects. It may remind us of Dürer's extraordinary *Alpine Landscape* (plate 11), where the same principle of broad, simple lines traversing vast tracts in easy, rhythmic undulation, a balanced rise and fall of inner flow, suggests large and calm animistic feeling. In

404 *Areopagitica* in *Complete Prose Works*, vol. 2, p. 515. (Some editors, incorrectly in my view, prefer 'warfaring'.)

each, landscape detail is subordinated to the fluid totality: in Milton, through the flowing issue of the description in a single encompassing sentence, in Dürer through the crafted blurring of particulars in thickened impressionistic strokes. Yet Milton's Eden is everywhere dynamic in its detail too: a field of distinct forms in self-directing, explorative motion, entirely exemplifying, in Helen Gardner's fine phrase, 'a universe of independent energies and wills'.[405] Hints of the old martial nature persist, in the 'smiting' sun and 'unpierced' bower (244–5), but calmly fluid motion is the keynote: in Nature who 'pour[s] forth profuse', the 'irriguous valley' that 'spreads her store', and the vine that 'Lays forth her purple grape, and gently creeps / Luxuriant' (4.243, 255, 260–61). Dominating this landscape of active free will is the insistent, animistic drive of the river, which 'Southward went ... nor changed his course', then 'runs diverse', 'wandering', 'visiting' and 'feeding', to 'murmur', 'fall' and 'disperse' (223–24, 234, 240, 260–61). 'Fall' and 'disperse' recall the destiny of Adam and Eve, as do the river's 'mazie error' and later 'liquid lapse' (4.239, 8.263): a parallel furthered by the facts that, like them, it enters Eden from an origin without, continues out of Eden, and is said to 'wander' – as does the human couple in the epic's closing lines. 'Wandering many a famous realm / And country whereof here needs no account' (4.234–35) could as easily designate humanity in the poem's final moments.[406] As ever in Milton, true beauty means freedom, whose price is hazard: via the current of this great restless, roving river, Satan enters Eden (9.74–75).

It is similarly a landscape of action in that its teeming fecundity engages Adam and Eve in daily struggle: to quell plenitude with order. Despite a long medieval tradition of toil before the Fall,[407] no other poet actually presents labour in Eden.[408] Lopping and pruning, training up and trellising nature's over-abundance, such gardening is, as Hill suggests, a form of dialectic, an interplay of primitive energy and disciplining process: another facet of that antipathy to induration and stasis that marks Milton's conception of paradise.[409]

405 Helen Gardner, *A Reading of Paradise Lost* (Oxford: 1965), p. 35.

406 John Carey notes 'wander' as a verb usually applied to fallen characters in the epic: *Milton*, p. 95.

407 K. V. Thomas, 'Work and Leisure in Pre-Industrial Society' in *Past and Present*, 29 (1964), 50–67.

408 Duncan, *Milton's Earthly Paradise*, p. 161.

409 See Evans, *Paradise Lost and the Genesis Tradition*, ch. 10; and Hill, *Milton and the English Revolution*, pp. 259–61, 395–96.

Spenser in the Bower of Bliss and Milton in Eden are alike hostile to the 'art-garden': insofar at least as art, in each case, embodies the antithesis to the active life, a place where vigour is bound in sybaritic bonds, 'nice art' and 'curious knots' (4.241–42). Such a locus, as with Spenser's cabinets and banqueting houses, is deeply aristocratic in connotation. Milton's Eden, an antinomian landscape, 'wild above rule or art', its bliss 'e/normous' (5.297), thus is warring fiercely with the high geometric formality of the seventeenth-century 'great garden', its severe regimentation the expression of the autocratic spirit, its symbolic designs long encoding royal and noble power and prerogative.[410] It is no accident that after the execution of Charles I in 1649 the royal gardens of Whitehall, Hampton Court and Nonsuch, as well as those at Theobalds, Somerset House, Richmond and Greenwich, were stripped of their ornament and auctioned off by parliament.[411] 'One cannot wish to dominate and remain a Christian', felt Milton.[412] The formal garden seems to represent to him the alliance of authoritarianism with triviality. The 'curious knots' he contemns, recalling the 'curious taste' rejected by the Lady in *Comus* (713), suggest a foppish delicacy of artifice, pallid beside the elemental of 'nature boon'. (It was the fallen Adam, we recall, who conceived Eve in the choice, aesthetic terms of the connoisseur: 'I see thou art exact of taste, / And elegant' (9.1017–18)). Herbert had likewise contrasted rugged virtue with vanity as natural growth and artificial garden: 'We are the trees, whom shaking fastens more, / While blustring windes destroy the wanton bowres, / And ruffle all their curious knots and store.'[413]

Though Milton's Eden has been received as the *locus classicus* of the naturalistic landscape garden, the *jardin anglais*, it was not entirely novel. Painting had already seen naturalistic Edens by Jan Brueghel and Roelandt Savery, the melancholy cult had long entailed naturalistic garden settings, and, contemporaneously, John Rea[414] explicitly preferred 'pure' nature to formal gardens. Milton's Eden nonetheless merits its eminence for having contradicted dominant contemporary gardening impulses, to privileged enclosure and externally ordered

410 Strong, *Renaissance Garden*, pp. 10, 43, 48, 161–64.
411 Ibid., p. 197.
412 *Complete Prose Works*, vol. 4, p. 534.
413 'Affliction' V, lines 20–22. Compare Bacon, who in his 1625 *Of Gardens* wrote of knots that 'they be but Toyes: You may see as good Sights, many times, in Tarts.' Reproduced in Hunt and Willis, *Genius of the Place*, p. 53.
414 Rea, *Flora: seu, De florum cultura. Or, a Complete Florilege* (London: 1665), p. 1.

landscape, by an 'unrepressed' landscape of spontaneous, independent energies, whose freedom from the 'tyranny' of regimentation and likeness to the state of nature outside the garden appear disordered by Stuart standards. His landscape of free will is one of exposed, open spaces and free-flowing life-forms, wandering at will like the eye of *Areopagitica*'s citizen exposed to all and any influence, freed from the 'nice art' of the censor to 'mazy error'. Yet on closer inspection, many of these autonomous primal forms in this 'wilderness of sweets' (5.294) turn out I suggest to compose 'naturalizations' of the amenities of contemporary formal gardens. As in this Eden, water was the major organizing principle in many English gardens, introduced from Italy by the De Caus brothers.[415] Brilliant engineering feats, emphasised as crucial to seventeenth-century gardening development by Roy Strong,[416] are accredited to God, whose hydraulics within the mountain – itself a standard item – are admired at lines 225–30. The bowers unpierceable by sun and walls of 'pillared shade / High overarched' are likewise ubiquitous: Bacon, for example, desiderates 'a Covert Alley' to protect from 'great Heat of the Yeare, or Day'.[417] The Caroline principle of perspectival gratification is fulfilled in the 'happy rural seat of various view' (4.247), and the 'darksome passage' of line 232 from which the river issues suggests a natural grot. The 'prospect large' into nether regions 'neighbouring round' (4.144–45) was a Roman ideal introduced into English gardens from the sixteenth century, whilst the device of coloured earths, derogated by Bacon, perhaps lies behind the 'orient pearl and sands of gold' of line 238. The memory of mazes is explicit in the windings of the river at line 239, whilst the arbours, rose-trellis, paths and bowers created by the human couple (9.215–19, 244) are felt not to transgress against the character of the surrounding landscape. That Spenser's paradise around Venus' Temple (*Faerie Queene* 4.10.24) was similarly adorned with naturally realized standard garden features is not entirely the point: which is rather that no dream of nature can entirely transcend contemporary norms. Milton's garden unfolds not things-in-themselves, but an important variant on a received formula or model: just as one had long been constituted by the *locus amoenus*, and much as the

415 Strong, *Renaissance Garden*, p. 10; compare Evelyn's description of the Aldobrandini garden near Rome, Hunt and Willis, *Genius*, p. 64.
416 *Renaissance Garden*, p. 75.
417 *Paradise Lost* 4.245–46; 9.1106–07. 'Of Gardens' repr. in *Genius*, p. 53.

'Ideal' landscape of the eighteenth century was to be so deeply imitative of Claude's paradigm.[418]

Firmly amid the rugged paths of the Spenserian tradition of the active landscape, a minor figure but four-square, stands George Wither. His *Emblemes*' concern for the details of husbandry, noted earlier, is matched by his reworking of the *Song of Songs*, supreme *locus* of the closed landscape in the seventeenth century. Normally the polarization of walled garden from open field is underlined, the latter conceived in terms of seasonal mutability and the rigours of weather, the former offering the sweet and restful shade of the apple tree, under which the fatigued soul's passivity yields to the active power of Grace.[419] Wither quite reverses the longing to escape 'all taint of labour',[420] proudly expositing the 'blackness' of the Bride not as the discolouration of sin but the sunburn of sturdy vineyard labour, and replacing the passive receipt of Grace in the garden by another emphasis: 'Begin but Thou to draw me on, / And then wee after Thee will runne ...'[421]

The frontispiece to his *Emblemes* (plate 14), which I have not found discussed elsewhere, seem to me to fascinatingly reassemble many of the 'Spenserian' landscape motifs we have been examining. The crowded verticality of the plate depicts the progress of souls to a point of choice between paths leading respectively to the heavenly city and the fires of hell. Though details remain obscure (Wither's *Preposition to the Frontispiece* suggests that only a 'second Oedipus' could unriddle them all), a basic contrast of landscape-types is clear. Flanked by a church, and accessible only through the spirit of *asprezza* of the man who struggles amid harsh ways through crags, lie the open meadows of the virtuous life. It is something of a georgic landscape, featuring a sower at work, and is also an 'agonistic' landscape: the pilgrim, with staff, must continue upward through its uncertain windings past figures of temptation. Relaxing self-discipline, the (Platonic) chariot of the soul will career off a mountain-side to disaster. Contrasting 'perfective trials' amid natural abundance in the fields of the righteous life is a bleak mountain track plagued by violent death. At its entrance, however, smile the familiar features of the Cavalier 'luxury' landscape.

418 On the influence of the Claude paradigm, see John Barrell, *The Idea of Landscape and the Sense of Place* (Cambridge: 1972), ch. 1.

419 Stewart, *The Enclosed Garden*, pp. 60–67, 86–96.

420 Ibid., p. 96.

421 Wither, *Song of Songs* in *The Hymnes and Songs of the Church* (London: 1881), Song 9, p. 37. Cf. Biblical *Song of Songs* 1.4.

A palace or cabinet of erotic bliss (fronted by a female nude) beckons from a woodland retirement. Close beneath a tree, an enticing female flourishes above a leaning gentleman a 'charming cup', clearly pirated from Acrasia or Comus. The languour of posture and arboreal ease compose a scene of *otium*, conflicting pointedly with the counter-posing sharp, unshaded cliffs. Above all, the pathway to sin is a pleasant, level perspective through an ordered avenue of trees: again aristocratic in connotation. 'By the early seventeenth century the avenue of lime, elm or horse chestnut had become a recognized aristocratic symbol' writes Keith Thomas, referring to the widely imitated estates of Theobalds and Buckingham's New Hall, Essex.[422] The parliamentarians, indeed, felled and sold for timber the avenues of trees in royal gardens at the interregnum.[423] It's not, I suggest, entirely therefore by coincidence that it is 'stately walks' of trees which Satan traverses to locate and undo Eve in her garden 'recess' (9.435, 456). Wither's combination of seductive charming cup, ordered woodland and brave palace also recur elsewhere in the *Emblemes*[424] to illustrate destructive intemperance of lifestyle.

It would be Procrustean to conclude from all this that the opposition between the open, Spenserian landscape of the active life and the Cavalier landscapes of pleasured withdrawal and sybaritism is an opposition whose terms are either entirely mutually distinct, or of close political alignment. Wither's plate may recall Spenser's 'easie is the way, and passage plaine / To pleasure's pallace',[425] as well as much in his Bower of Bliss, but it also suggests Virgil's '*facilis descensus Averno*';[426] and a number of Bowers of Bliss[427] are destroyed in seventeenth-century verse – not all of them by Spenserian poets. Moreover, Puritans were by no means either consistently or wholly hostile to the secluded pleasures of the garden: Prynne, for example, enjoys them as surrogate Bibles, whose natural symbols replace papist icons.[428] Marvell, characteristically supple, recognizes the garden as

422 Thomas, *Man and the Natural World*, p. 207.

423 Strong, *Renaissance Garden*, p. 197.

424 Book 2, plate 6, p. 68.

425 *Faerie Queene* 2.3.41.7–8.

426 *Aeneid* 6.126.

427 Giles Fletcher, *Christ's Victorie and Triumph* in *Poetical Works*, ed. F. S. Boas, 1 (London: 1908), p. 49; Ralph Knevet, *A Gallery to the Temple*, ed. G. Pellegrini (Pisa: 1954), pp. 101–02; Joseph Beaumont, *Psyche* (London: 1648), pp. 14–22; Samuel Sheppard, *The Fairie King* (Bodleian M. S. Rawl. poet 28), f. 42v. Ref. Turner, *Topographia*, pp. 129–31.

428 William Prynne, *A Christian Paradise* in *Mount-Orgueil* (London: 1641), p. 126.

locus of epicurean retreatism (a 'green seraglio'; or, in Hill's phrase, a seventeenth century 'equivalent of the ivory tower'[429]), yet also of authentic sacramentality: a place where 'heroic activism is sidetracked or abandoned as well as recuperated'.[430] Cromwell junior 'Beats on the rugged track', yet his father in his 'private gardens' had managed to live both 'reserved and austere'.[431] As ever, the aesthetic should not be conflated with the political: the seventeenth-century articulation of these orders is particularly complex. Walton, for instance, with his royalist leanings and friendship with Donne, Cotton and Waller, quotes no pastoral songs from Spenser; yet he does quote from the puritan favourite, Du Bartas, and is a friend too of the 'Spenserian' Drayton, whom he also cites. Again, the Circean charming cup was in the mid-seventeenth century variously symbolic: associated by occasion with political servitude, the papal Antichrist and atheism.[432] Further, Wither's frontispiece was not of his own composition: initially disliking its complexity, he kept it on recognizing that its engraver 'by meere *Chance* had hit'[433] on figures whose veiled allusions delighted him. Clearly these landscape types and figures offer a flexible symbolic notation, 'structures of feeling' accessible to an engraver's instincts precisely because they float free of monopoly by a single political or religious purpose. The woodland palace or cabinet itself reappears, baptized, among the *Emblemes*, gay with pennants, obelisks and statuary, as the mansion of Eternity amid the things of time.[434]

But if we cannot plot clear symmetries of political and aesthetic in the period, the 'idealist' criticism which smartly uncouples them with pained, averted face leaves dimensions of impulse and mediation unviewed. The poetry of Henry Vaughan is a remarkable case in point. Its determinants and language have overwhelmingly been construed as literary and metaphysical: glosses and discussions revolve around Hermetical borrowings, Biblical allusion, Herbert's canon, the *Vita Paulini* or Protestant prayer. The disjunction or revulsion from political actualities seems endorsed by a deeply unempiric landscaping, a

429 'Mower Against Gardens' line 27; Hill, *Puritanism and Revolution*, p. 336.

430 Hunt, *Marvell*, p. 188.

431 'A Poem upon the Death of His Late Highness the Lord Protector', line 306; 'An Horatian Ode upon Cromwell's Return from Ireland', line 30.

432 Hill, *Milton and the English Revolution*, p. 45.

433 *A Preposition to this Frontispiece* line 19.

434 Book 3, plate 23, p. 157: perhaps modelled on *Ezekiel* 28.13.

transcendental imprecision: the 'shadows of eternity' and 'bright shoots of everlastingness'[435] that stand in for the features of scrutinized flower and cloud capture this blurring of fact into radiance.

Nature in these poems is clearly animistic, and a number of literary and very general influences can conventionally be arrayed: the classical 'pastoral hyperbole'; the festal animation of *Psalms* and the Pauline creation 'exerto capito observantes';[436] Neoplatonic concern with a pervasive, invisible spirituality; the tradition of cosmic dance; intimations of millenarian awakening, as discussed above; the need in the protestant mind, bereft of Catholic saints, for 'secondary' spiritual presences;[437] and the abolition of traditional forms of devotional experience in the Anglican service under the commonwealth, which in turn heightens the sacramentality of natural contemplation.[438] Vaughan's 'animistic nature', however, is both dynamic and static; its animation is characteristically perfected and accommodated within a larger stillness: the crash of the water-fall into the pool, for example, whose 'streaming rings restagnates all'; the rising, falling and hurling of the spring morning within 'hymning circulations' and 'sacred hymns, and order'; the 'true beauty' of the 'Mount of Olives' (II) 'active as light, and calm without all noise'.[439] It is as if nature offers an immaculate activism: intimations of driving spontaneity, releases of force, which are enviably undisruptive. 'The age, the present times are not / To snudge in, and embrace a cot / Action and blood now get the game' writes Vaughan in 'Misery': 'I'd loose those knots thy hands did tie, / Then would go travel, fight or die.'[440] This is the restless self-accusation of Vaughan the non-combatant in the late 1640s; whose brother, William, dies, probably of war-wounds, in July 1648; whose elegy for his friend 'Mr. R. Hall, Slain at Pontefract, 1648' praises one 'In [his] own blood a *Soldier* and a *Saint*';[441] and who, meditating a storm, knows his own blood has 'boiling streams that rave / With the same curling force, and hiss, / As doth the mountained wave'.[442] Vaughan had seen action in 1645, but never

435 'The Retreat' line 20.

436 Vaughan gives as prefatory note to 'And do they so?' the Latin version of *Romans* 8.19 by Beza, in which the craning necks occur, notes editor Alan Rudrum, *Complete Poems*, p. 557.

437 Parry, *17th Century Poetry*, p. 170.

438 Ibid., pp. 102, 117–18.

439 'Water-Fall' line 34; 'Morning-Watch' lines 10–13, 16–18; 'Mount of Olives' II lines 1–2.

440 'Misery' lines 65–67, 73–74.

441 Line 74.

442 'The Storm' lines 6–8.

took up arms again after the end of the first Civil War – even when, during 1647–48, all Wales was smouldering, and Colonel Horton made Brecon his headquarters for dealing with Welsh royalist gentry, bringing troops to deal with 'divers gentlemen of the county' in early 1648.[443] It is during these last years of the 1640s that *Silex* I is composed, being published in 1650. It is scarcely surprising to find then, what is not discernible from the *Corpus Hermeticum* or *Vita Paulini*, that Vaughan's vocabulary for nature is also often that for war.

Not only do we find stars of 'swordlike gleam', 'calm and well-trained' constellations whose every star has 'glory' without 'war', retainers going fearfully to their deaths in 'The Water-Fall', a perpetual obsession with 'blood', always synonymized with ardent authenticity, and a 'constant war' with clouds he beseeches God to 'bow' and 'rend'.[444] The exuberant adjectives of such a 'nature-piece' as 'The Morning-Watch' – words like 'hurled', 'glory', 'blood' and 'shoot' – are precisely the language of military action in his elegies: where we likewise encounter rising and falling, and a 'Morning-Watch' – like movement from bright rapidity to the grave and hiddenness.[445] The very title, 'Morning-Watch', allows military connotation. In the religious meditations 'Peace' and 'The Relapse' we encounter a 'sentry', 'files', a 'fortress', a 'challenge' and 'stabs'. Even the 'bright shoots of everlastingness' (and 'shoot' is a favourite word, recurring in 'shoots of glory' in the 'Watch') suggests a process of military sublimation, since the word can in this period refer to the discharge of muskets: 'R.W.' 'So near to lightning moved' that 'like shot his active hand / Drew blood'; and the metaphor is transferred onto nature in 'Unprofitableness', where 'Each snarling blast shot through me'.[446] In sum, the 'emanations / Quick vibrations / And bright stirs', the 'Active brightness'[447] of Vaughan's skies and landscapes, the

443 F. E. Hutchinson, *Henry Vaughan: A Life and Interpretation* (Oxford: 1947), pp. 55–71.

444 'Joy of My Life!' line 29; 'The Constellation' lines 30–32; 'Water-Fall' lines 5–10; 'Love-Sick' lines 8–10.

445 'Morning-Watch' lines 2–16; 'Elegy on the Death of Mr. R.W.' lines 22, 54–64, 70; 'Elegy on the Death of Mr. R. Hall' lines 39–40, 60: note the many similarities between 'R.W.' lines 54–77 and 'The Morning-Watch'. Note also God's preservation of Vaughan in battle as 'thy bright arm, which was my light / And leader through thick death and night': 'Abel's Blood' lines 31–32.

446 'Shoots' and 'shot': 'The Retreat' line 20; 'Morning-Watch' line 2; 'Elegy on the Death of Mr. R.W.' line 59; 'Unprofitableness' line 4.

447 'Midnight' lines 11–13, 28.

suddenness, rapidities, ardour and gleamings, suggest a nature of victorious energies at once struck from and contrasting the historical world of heroic animation and darting Cavaliers: a realm where, poignantly, velocity and vigour are undestructive, the 'hurling' of energies within ordered calm.[448]

A dialectic of royalist 'quietistic' with Puritan 'active' landscape thus helps structure Vaughan's apprehension of nature: embodying the zest and assiduity of active service, couched often in martial imagery as a field of spiritual virtue or joy, its peace is yet so unalterable that Vaughan can envy the indefectible 'staidness' of the rhythms that are removed from history: 'no new business breaks their peace'.[449]

Nature's ideality has a further facet: in the exuberant autonomy of history, triumphs of energy are often linked with those of voice. 'Hills and valleys into singing break ... While active winds and streams both run and speak',[450] writes Vaughan, who wishes to model himself on 'this restless, vocal *spring*' that 'All day, and night doth run, and sing'.[451] 'The Morning-Watch' knows 'hymning circulations', nature 'hurled / In sacred hymns'. In 'The Dawning', 'All now are stirring, every field / Full hymns doth yield.'[452] At Judgement Day, stones and hedges will 'into loud discoveries break, / As loud as blood', sand and dust 'With one attesting voice detect' mens' secret crimes.[453] Behind the imagination of beloved landscapes as full-voiced congregations and prosecution witnesses lie the facts of suppressed services, ejected rectors and closed churches[454] across Wales from the late 1640s into the 1650s: precisely the period of composition of *Silex Scintillans*' two volumes. Vaughan's old tutor, Matthew Herbert, Rector of Llangattock was sequestered in 1646; friends Thomas Powell, Rector of

448 Cf. the reference to Christ, 'whose blood peace brings' ('Abel's Blood' line 39), and 'The Constellation' line 60: 'Where God is, all agree'. Note how to be 'restless' in man is folly ('Man' line 17) but in springs and stars is pure and joyous ('Dawning' line 33; 'Star' line 17). Nature and soldiering are linked by the word 'active' ('Elegy on R.W.' lines 20, 59; 'Midnight' line 28 and 'Mount of Olives' II line 2) and contrasted in their 'commissions': 'Constellation' line 37, 'Star' line 10.

449 'Man' lines 9, 11.

450 'The Bird' lines 13, 15.

451 'The Dawning' lines 33–34.

452 'Morning-Watch' lines 10, 16–17; 'The Dawning' lines 15–16.

453 'The Stone' lines 23–24, 40.

454 Note how the stones and dust of natural landscape may become the stones and dust of the church building, which 'Jointly agree / To cry to thee': 'Church-Service' lines 18–19.

Cantref, and Thomas Lewes, rector of Llangfigan, as well as Thomas Vaughan, the poet's brother, were ejected in 1650.[455] The Act for the Propagation of the Gospel in Wales (February 1650) expedited so vigorous a purgation of royalist clergy that many unserved churches were forced to close.[456] When Colonel Freeman, Attorney-General for South Wales, petitioned the House of Commons in 1652 for a supply of ministers in lieu of those who had been ejected, he was placed in custody and eventually relieved of his post. A local roundhead commander, one Captain Jenkin Jones, engaged in threatening correspondence with evicted clergymen, including Thomas Vaughan, over illegal preaching: seizing and gaoling certain of them in the spring of 1653, and threatening local gentry and ejected rectors with a troop of mounted, pistol-carrying soldiers in 1654.[457] It is beyond these dead chapels and silenced churchmen that surging landscapes lift up their voice.

Within this climate of legal harassment and sudden arrest, devotional experience in Vaughan's poetic imagination is pervaded by imagery of secret relations and juridical inquisition. God, within Vaughan's poetry, is the heart of the clandestine numinous. 'Silence, and stealth of days', for instance, moves from the imagery of lost battle ('fled', 'retreat', 'defeat thy power': lines 13–16) to inquisition and torture ('I search, and rack my soul'; 'souls must / Track one the other': 17, 25–26), whilst *Silex* II (composed 1650–55) refers to 'secret rooms, / Silent as tombs' and the 'secret searches' and hidden paths[458] that lead to God. The frustrated nature-contemplation of 'I walked the other day' is framed in just these terms. The poet seeks to 'track' God's 'steps', and reach him by 'hid ascents'. The buried flower, a 'warm recluse', lies 'unseen' and 'alone', like a recusant or hidden Cavalier in 'the secret rooms' of 'The Stone'. Indeed, he gains in Cavalier association as being 'gallant', connected with a 'bower' now 'ruffled', destined soon to come forth and 'repair' his 'losses', and having 'clothes' hastily thrown 'quite o'er his head' by the poet 'stung with fear'.[459]

'The Dawning' is one of many poems associating religious meditation of nature with the experience of surprise, capture and

455 Hutchinson, p. 109.

456 Ibid., pp. 93, 111–15.

457 Ibid., pp. 116–20.

458 'The Stone' lines 6–7; 'The Hidden Treasure' lines 11–12.

459 'I Walked the Other Day' lines 49, 52, 19, 21, 4, 5, 25–26, 29–30.

judgement by authority: just as local preachers and gentry were subject to sudden arrest or searches of property, and indeed as seems to have befallen Vaughan's father: arrested in July 1648 and again, this time to be carried off by foot-soldiers, in 1656 (though on neither occasion for religious offences). Matthew Herbert was twice imprisoned under the Puritan regime, on dates unknown. Vaughan had himself been secretary to Judge Sir Marmaduke Lloyd, back in 1642–45,[460] and may as such have initiated or abetted such visitations himself. At all events, 'Or will thy all-surprising light / Break at midnight?' is Vaughan's perspective on the Parousia. 'Or will' perhaps the early hours 'Unlock thy bowers?' Clouds will militaristically 'disband and scatter', the morning star 'triumph', Angels, like supporting troops, arrive 'in the *van*', and Christ 'Descend to judge poor careless man' in his 'corrupt security'.[461]

At 'Midnight', Vaughan imagines, the stars in their 'watches' are God's 'host of spies' noting whom sleep 'catches'. Similarly, the sacred solitudes of 'The Night' know 'God's silent, searching flight', his 'knocking time', when 'Spirits their fair kindred catch' during the soul's 'watch.' The poet can only wish that his 'loud, evil days' were 'unhaunted' save likewise by 'some *Angel's* wing or voice'.[462]

Tensely secretive, bleakly vigilant, yearning alternately for relieving dam-bursts of hymning, righteous upsurge and for a retreat of perfected concealment ('where I in him / Might live invisible and dim'[463]), the spirituality of these poems and landscapes, consciously or subconsciously, is moulded from the bones and blood of war and military occupation.[464]

Summary

In this concluding chapter of period-survey, we sought to demonstrate how, with English verse of the seventeenth century, poetic landscape description came finally of age. Versatile heir of multiple traditions of representation, and popular alike within middle-class and courtly culture, poetic landscape became a substantial component of many genres, achieved new levels of descriptive realism, and created what

460 See Hutchinson, pp. 96, 116–20, 199–202, 49–50.

461 'The Dawning' lines 5–6, 10, 21, 23–24, 27–28, 30.

462 'Midnight' lines 2–4; 'The Night' lines 31, 35–39.

463 'The Night' lines 53–54.

464 For fuller treatment of these ideas see Chris Fitter, 'Henry Vaughan's Landscapes of Military Occupation', *Essays in Criticism*, 42: 2 (1992) 123–47.

posterity would term early instances of the genre of 'loco-descriptive' verse. We saw, above all, that the concept of 'landskip' and the related concern for a 'phenomenological' order of perception, whose emergence and decline we traced in the ancient world, were firmly established once more with seventeenth-century poetry.

Landskip, we saw, is eagerly imitated from the painters as vogue performance, evocations of deep prospect featuring in Denham and Milton, Chamberlayne and Revett, even as the earliest authentic paintings and engravings of English topography are being made by Dutch experts. Perspective, however, is an art still new enough in verse for a poet even such as Milton to err in it; and poets feel challenged not just to reproduce the new technique but to outgo it in the terms of their own medium through a draughtsmanship of 'conceits', masterful as the eye's motion, acutely perceived as the painter's foreshortenings.

The period's mature conditions of description encouraged our exceptionally close analysis of Milton and Marvell's verse, in each of whom we found a delicate, individual sensory attention structuring natural description. The yield of a direct, sensuous engagement of landscape is not only deployed by each poet as a fluent and subtle language of philosophic vision, but becomes 'a record and medium of finely personal affectivity', a highly expressive notation of interiority. Such writing we classified as phenomenological description: an order of natural evocation we had identified in the ancient world in Theocritus and in 'The Song of Songs', and one that was made possible again in the legacy of that medieval concern for 'quotidian space' which focused the sights and tones of common experience. Milton's extraordinarily sensitive landscape description thus embodies minutely the very paradoxes of his materialist ontology: it articulates his sense both of the 'spiritous' drive of matter and the residual materiality of the spiritual and aerial. The textural impressionability of Marvell's verse, its eye for mutating substance and incongruous sensory juxtapositions, for sudden violence and erotic intoxication, form likewise a language of acute empiricism and mood-response that articulates a personal philosophy: in his case, a vision of alienated human sovereignty and incalculable historical fluctuation. Such is the ambiguity of this vision that Marvell passes over the putative objectivism of landskip or prospect: landscape means for him an agnostic terrain, a subjective realm of the intrigue of flux and of riddling perceptual mendacity.

The economic and political conditions which structure the period's nature-sensibility dispose it to a near obsession with gardens, natural innocence, and the re-creation or recreation of paradisal landscape. In part this derives from a millenarian excitement, escalating during the century's earlier decades among certain of 'God's Englishmen' who anticipate the imminent paradisal transfiguration of creation; and many of whom are busy with transformational schemes of their own to extirpate barrenness through national campaigns of fruit-tree planting or to reconstruct Eden in perfected botanical gardens. In part, the paradisal tonality is also the further development of that urban idealization of the countryside we saw emerging in the Middle Ages. This rural world has long been a 'greened town', an 'urbane' construction of the 'countryfied', but Marvell's poetry can now consciously 'register the urban distance that is both exploitative and elegiac'. What also is new is the profoundly informing impact of bourgeois autonomy of agrarian productive relations. Not only is nature unfailingly an easy, smiling 'good cateress', an overflowing barn apparently filled *sponte sua*; landscape paintings now project the private, asocial understanding of natural space mediated from the new quiritary property relations, wherein land-ownership has shed hereditary social and moral obligations to community. Where once the medieval landscapes of the Duc de Berri (plate 8), in their synergy of field and local population, depicted in the land the ground of community, a primary commonality of endeavour and dependence, in Hollar's seventeenth-century engravings of lakeside walks at Albury (plate 15), the depopulated scenery of the private stroll, we find projected the sequestered pleasures of atomistic private consciousness. These views are icons of a triumphant landscape reflex of bourgeois and genteel autonomous individualism.

The elegant celebration of Cavalier lifestyle and values is another feeding stream of the paradisal imagination. Fantasias of bejewelled landscape turn common fields into diamanté spectacles, choice realms of raindrop-gems and pearl-dew, perfumed breeze and golden fruit; while noble banqueting and 'secret' houses stimulate lyric creation of exquisite palaces or 'cabinets' that befit queenly mistresses found deep in forest or grot. The lucrative practice of field enclosures and the new availability of capital in a nascent banking system heighten the poetic motif of the luxury of compressed riches. This ideal of beauty as a framed and rich distillation, an opulent essence, is clearly a possessive aesthetic, a formula realized alike in the gentleman's landscape paintings, his private gardens and his connoisseur cabinet, each of them boxes where sweets compacted lie.

Just as in this century Cavalier confronts Puritan, and all manner of transformers varieties of conservative, so the 'closed' landscapes of idyll, *otium* and *sprezzatura*, the Bower of Bliss, gardens of serenity and dappled meadows of naive *jouissance*, find confronting topographies of oppositional ideals. The Spenserian tradition favours 'open' landscapes of hazard, endeavour and sudden struggle, sites of transformative challenge and 'rugged going'. In Spenser and Milton the paradises themselves take on epical dimensions, the retreatist haunts of stasis and ease being disallowed 'the true wayfaring Christian'. Sir Guyon's razing of the cabinets and arbours of the Bower of Bliss, and Wither's frontispiece with its emblematic opposition of the perditious luxury landscape and the steep and testing fields of righteousness, highlight the establishment and availability of these landscape types for the articulation of clashing ideals in contemporary religion, politics and culture. We may perceive this opposition, finally, as structural to the landscape-consciousness of Henry Vaughan, operating as the deeply internalized dialectic of the 'royalist' landscape – of the sweetness of peace, withdrawal and immunity – with the 'oppositional' active landscape of sublimated military energy. The tensions, stealth, sudden discoveries and vigorous uprisings of his landscape intimations make of Vaughan an undiscovered poet of military occupation.

Landscape consciousness, here as ever, spontaneous or erudite, in epiphany or in fashion, is a field of political and economic determination.

CHESTER COLLEGE LIBRARY

Select bibliography

Clark, Kenneth. *Landscape into Art* 1949; rev. edn London: 1979.

Giammati, F. Bartlett. *The Earthly Paradise and the Renaissance Epic* Princeton: 1966.

Glacken, Clarence. *Traces on the Rhodian Shore* Los Angeles: 1967.

Groenewegen-Frankfort, H. A. *Arrest and Movement: Space and Time in the Art of the Ancient Near East* 1951; rpt. Cambridge, Mass.: 1987.

Kemal, Salim, and Gaskell, Ivor. *Landscape, Natural Beauty and the Arts* Cambridge: 1993.

Leach, Eleanor Winsor. *The Rhetoric of Space* Princeton: 1988.

Nicolson, Marjorie. *Mountain Gloom and Mountain Glory* Cornell: 1963.

Passmore, John. *Man's Responsibility for Nature* 1974; rpt. London: 1980.

Pearsall, Derek and Salter, Elizabeth. *Landscapes and Seasons of the Medieval World* London: 1973.

Thomas, Keith. *Man and the Natural World* 1983.

Turner, James G. *The Politics of Landscape* Oxford: 1979.

Wallace-Hadrill, D. S. *The Greek Patristic View of Nature* Manchester: 1968.

Williams, Raymond. *The Country and the City* 1973; rpt. St Albans: 1975.

Index

Index